Advance praise for

Religion, Politics and Cults in East Africa

"Emmanuel Twesigye's book chronicles the different religious traditions and practices in East Africa. It synthesizes the broader topics of religions, politics, and health in the overall experience of the Black community. Not since works by Mbiti has much been written about religious cults in Africa. This book is at the cutting edge of the best scholarship on the subject. It is recommended for those interested in appreciating the religious and cultural experiences of Africans."

Randolph Quaye, Ph.D., Associate Professor and Director of the
Black World Studies Department, Ohio Wesleyan University

Religion,
Politics and Cults
in East Africa

Bible & Theology in Africa

Knut Holter
General Editor

Vol. 11

PETER LANG
New York • Washington, D.C./Baltimore • Bern
Frankfurt • Berlin • Brussels • Vienna • Oxford

Emmanuel K. Twesigye

Religion, Politics and Cults in East Africa

God's Warriors and Mary's Saints

PETER LANG
New York • Washington, D.C./Baltimore • Bern
Frankfurt • Berlin • Brussels • Vienna • Oxford

Library of Congress Cataloging-in-Publication Data

Twesigye, Emmanuel K.
Religion, politics and cults in East Africa: God's warriors
and Mary's saints / Emmanuel K. Twesigye.
p. cm. — (Bible and theology in Africa; v. 11)
Includes bibliographical references and index.
1. Africa, East—Religion. 2. Religion and politics—Africa, East.
3. Christianity and politics—Africa, East. 4. Religion and state—Africa,
East. 5. Church and state—Africa, East. 6. Cults—Africa, East. I. Title.
BL2464.T84   201'.7209676—dc22   2010009688
ISBN 978-1-4331-0995-9 (hardcover)
ISBN 978-1-4331-1112-9 (paperback)
ISSN 1525-9846

Bibliographic information published by **Die Deutsche Nationalbibliothek**.
Die Deutsche Nationalbibliothek lists this publication in the "Deutsche
Nationalbibliografie"; detailed bibliographic data is available
on the Internet at http://dnb.d-nb.de/.

The paper in this book meets the guidelines for permanence and durability
of the Committee on Production Guidelines for Book Longevity
of the Council of Library Resources.

In Celebration
Of
All the Martyrs of God
In East Africa
&
All Saints & Holy Servants
Of God
Everywhere and in Every
Religious Tradition

TABLE OF CONTENTS

ACKNOWLEDGEMENTS

I am especially indebted to Bishop John Baptist Kakubi, the retired Bishop of Mbarara Catholic Diocese and the Archbishop Paul Bakyenga of Mbarara Catholic Archdiocese and Western Province, for granting me audience and answering my intrusive questions concerning their roles in the ecclesiastical alienation of the new apocalyptic and moral reformist Marian Movement leaders and their followers. They provided valuable information and important pastoral letter, which they had written to the Marian Movement leaders, denouncing the errant doomsday prophecies.

My Uganda research assistants include: Ms. Margarite Tibayungwa, who provided me with newspaper articles and valuable contacts; Chief John Karooro, the Dean of Kinkizi University College, Provia Atuhaire, Caroline Ayebare and Oliver Nankunda made it possible to carry out the research with some reasonable ease and comfort. Without their valuable input, the research in Uganda would have been impossible. Some of my relatives and friends, especially the Rev. Gershom Kalenzi Tumuhairwe, Dr. William and Mrs. Vicky Muhairwe generously supported the project and provided the essential necessities of housing and transportation. Other relatives and friends provided security, food, information, contacts, advice and moral support. Their support was invaluable and indispensable. I am truly indebted to them.

I am also grateful to a great number of people whom I interviewed for this book. Only a selected few are mentioned here. I am truly grateful to Mrs. Theresa Kibwetere, who was the first 12 Apostles of the Marian Movement, which Joseph Kibwetere and Keledonia Mwerinde, co-founded in her home in Kabumba, Ntungamo in1989. Mrs. Kibwetere was gracious enough to provide the secret insider's core information concerning the Marian Movement. I am also grateful to Mrs. Theresa Tibayungwa for her commentary and insight on the Kibweteres' lives before and the founding of the Marian Movement. She also provided information on Mrs. Seforoza Bamurumba, her long time neighbor in Kakoba, Mbarara, who died in the Movement.

I am truly indebted to the students, who contributed ideas for improvements and served as research assistants and editors, especially Jerry Newell, Asegedech Shimellis, Sam Chesser, Matthew Mackenzie and Ashley Kniola. Matthew and Ashley did excellent work, as senior assistant editors.

Ultimately, I am truly grateful to Ohio Wesleyan University Provost David Robbins and Prof. Richard Fusch, the former Academic Dean, for the generous institutional and administrative support for this scholarly project. The University provided some generous travel and research funds. In addition, the University granted me, a scholarly leave to write this book. The University purchased for me the necessary computer hardware and software to assist me in my research. The University also provided the necessary secretarial assistance.

Finally, I am grateful to all the people, who have made this book possible. Nicole Grazioso and Heidi Burns of Peter Lang Publishing for their valuable assistance in getting this book published in a timely manner. Gratitude is also expressed to my family members, who remained patient and forgiving, when I missed some birthdays and other family events because I was away on research for the book!

Professor Emmanuel Kalenzi Twesigye, OWU

PREFACE

You are invited to join me in some exciting intellectual travels and sometimes frightening research adventures in East Africa. This book has been extensively researched in East Africa beginning in 1999 through 2009. This is a scholarly book in both its research and impartial academic analysis of the complex religio-cultural field data. However, it has been deliberately written in a simpler style in order to reach and communicate to a broader audience in the fields of Liberation Theology, African Studies, African Religion, Religion and Politics, Cultural Studies, Anthropology, Women's Studies, Religious Studies, Church History, Marian Studies, Biblical Studies, apocalyptic movements and doomsday cults.

Taking into account this intended broad scope of reading audiences, academic jargon and technical language have been either avoided or kept to a minimum. When technical language or African terms have been used, they have been explained either in the text or in a detailed endnote and glossary. For advanced readers and students detailed endnotes and sources have been provided at the end of each chapter.

In addition, some endnotes also explain some issues that could not be explained in the main text. This has been done for the sake of providing fuller information of contexts of events and possible alternative religious or cultural meanings of words, rituals or events. With the exception of the introduction, each chapter has been written to stand alone, so as to make it usable in college or university courses, by teachers, professors and students from different disciplines.

The book mainly covers new theocentric, societal, moral and cultural reformist, religio-political liberation and messianic movements in East Africa. They include the following: the *Maji Maji* in the former German East Africa (Tanzania*)*, the *Nyabingi Liberation Movement* in Western Uganda, the *East African Revival Movement* (EARM), which is also known as the *Balokole Movement;* Jomo Kenyatta's *Mau Mau Liberation Movement* in Kenya; Yoweri Museveni's *National Resistance Movement* (NRM) in Uganda, Alice Auma (*Lakwena* or Messiah)'s *Holy Spirit Movement* (HSM), and its military wing, which was called the *Holy Spirit Mobile Forces* (HSMF) in Northern and Eastern Uganda; Joseph Kony's *Lord's Resistance Army* (LRA) and the apocalyptic *Movement for the Restoration of the Ten Commandments of God* (MRTCG).

However, the book puts its main focus on the MRTCG or the Marian Movement. The book provides the first extensive academic analysis of the Marian Movement within its Catholic historical context, as well as the correlative traditional African cultural, linguistic, moral, religious, historical, political and philosophical context.

Mrs. Theresa Kibwetere's information was extremely invaluable since she was a central leader in the Marian Movement within Mbarara Catholic Diocese. She was the credible Movement's spokeswoman to the Catholic women while Joseph Kibwetere, her husband, became the Movement's spokesman to the men and tried to recruit them, especially high-ranking or respectable senior Catholic priests like the Reverend (Rev.) Fathers (Fr.) Paul Ikazire, Joseph Mary Kasapurari and Dominic Kataribabo, into the moral reformist Marian Movement. Leading Catholic priests and nuns were targeted for recruitment into this Catholic lay founded moral reformist Marian Movement in order to make it acceptable to the Catholic Church hierarchy in Mbarara.

Subsequently, Joseph Kibwetere became the public face and spokesman of Keledonia Mwerinde's Marian Moral Reform Movement which they incorporated into a religious association and descriptively named it as: *The Movement for the Restoration of the Ten Commandments of God* (MRTCG or the Movement). Mrs. Kibwetere was one of the founding and original members of the Marian Movement's inner circle, which was known as Twelve Apostles (*Entumwa*) of *The Movement for the Restoration of the Ten Commandments of God*.

Mrs. Kibwetere disclosed how the moral reformist apocalyptic Marian Movement was introduced to them by Keledonia Mwerinde and how Joseph Kibwetere, her loving and caring husband, had been converted, by Mwerinde into her new moral reformist Marian Movement. She also explained how Kibwetere was duped into becoming its figure-head in order to provide the necessary financial support and credibility to the new Marian Moral Reform Movement.

However, as the Marian Movement became better established, Mrs. Theresa Kibwetere was overshadowed and overthrown by Keledonia Mwerinde, as co-head of her household with Joseph Kibwetere, her husband. Mrs. Kibwetere resented this state of affairs in her home. Later, Mrs. Kibwetere became clinically depressed due to loss of control over her household affairs and the realization that Keledonia Mwerinde had also gained total control over Joseph, her husband, along with the family investments and economic resources. Subsequently, at the urging of Keledonia Mwerinde, and despite Theresa Kibwetere's protests, Joseph Kibwetere sold his prized exotic cattle, businesses and liquidated his investments. He did this in order to buy food and other provisions for the members of the Marian Movement, who had come and camped at his home. Mrs. Kibwetere and her children felt helpless to stop the depletion of their economic resources.

I am also indebted to the Rev. Fr. Paul Ikazire for the Marian Movement's inside information. Fr. Ikazire provided important inside information about the Marian Movement and its main leaders, including their central beliefs and main roles and activities within the secretive Marian Movement.

Fr. Ikazire's information was very invaluable for this book. He was the only surviving senior Catholic priest, who was a former key member and leader of the

Marian Movement. He was one of the original Twelve Apostles (*Entumwa*) of the apocalyptic Marian Movement. Fr. Ikazire was also a long time friend of Fr. Dominic Kataribabo, who was the main architect of the Marian Movement's theology of atonement for sins through ritual self-sacrifices, as voluntary Christian martyrdoms, and holy death, as an acceptable holy atonement and a holy sacramental religious path to God, and the attainment of eternal salvation, and peace in heaven.

I am especially indebted to Bishop John Baptist Kakubi, the retired bishop of Mbarara Catholic Diocese and Archbishop Paul Bakyenga of Mbarara Catholic Archdiocese and Western Province, for granting me audience and answering my intrusive questions concerning their role in the alienation of the new apocalyptic and moral reformist Marian Movement leaders and their followers. They provided valuable information and important pastoral letters to the Movement leaders.

Some of the material in this book has been presented at the American Academy of Religion in 2002 and 2004. Some material was presented at GLCA (Great Lakes Colleges Association) conferences in Black World Studies and some of the material was also presented to the Ohio Academy of Religion (OAR) in 1999, 2001, 2002, 2003 and 2005. Portions of data were also were presented in public lectures at Ohio Wesleyan University in 2002-2003 and 2007-2010. The feedback was invaluable for this book.

Therefore, the material presented, analysis and arguments advanced in this book have been tested and distilled by this academic process and public discourse. The book is a product of a laborious field research in East Africa and long intellectual process. Nevertheless, it remains a work in progress. I will write a second book that analyzes the teachings of the Marian Movement within a Roman Catholic theological perspective and monastic historical tradition for advanced students of Christian theology, Mariology, Church history and doomsday cults.

Many Africans are like the Haitians and other Caribbean people. Most of them still live in a world dominated by God, as the Holy, Transcendent Creative Spirit, the ancestors, spiritual beings, such as good and evil spirits. The African cosmology, ontology and world-view are almost akin to the world of the Hebrew Scriptures and in the New Testament. Prophets still see visions of God. They receive God's new revelations and demons still possess people, and they are cast out through rituals of prayers and exorcisms using consecrated holy water (*Maji*) and holy oil. Alice Lakwena's *Holy Spirit Movement*, in Northern Uganda and the Marian Movement, in Uganda, Rwanda, Burundi, and the Eastern Republic of the Congo, became popular among rural Catholics because of these healing prayers, exorcisms and traditional African religio-cultural ritual practices. These practices were meaningful and attractive to the rural Catholics.

Within the traditional Africa theocentric world-view, cosmology, and ontology, all societal distress, misfortunes, disasters, violence, diseases and premature deaths, are also traditionally religiously and culturally perceived within the African context. Subsequently, these evils or distresses are attributed to the supernatural forces. This includes God's anger, judgment and divine punishment, or as the evil results of enemies, evil-spirits, witchcraft and sorcery. As result, diseases are expected to be healed through special healing prayers, exorcisms, magic and the laying on of hands.

The African Traditional Religion, the Pentecostal Church, the Catholic Charismatic Movement and the Marian Movement are examples of these African religious groups, which explicitly confront and challenge the Devil's evil presence and destructive works in God's world. They ritually invoke the mighty cleansing, healing and restorative power of God; and in the Holy Name of God, they command the Demonic powers of the Devil and evil spirits to leave the sick or possessed people. They sing, pray and use sacred objects, including fire, Bibles, crucifixes, consecrated water, and oil to ritually cleanse them, and exorcise ritual pollution and defiling evils, and thereby, healing and curing them. These forms of faith-healing and exorcism only provide effective cures for diseases, which are evil manifestations of the demonic forces and the Devil, rather than those which are due to bacteria and viruses.

Therefore, serious medical and religious problems arise, when there is no clear method for religious leaders and their loyal followers to know or identify and distinguish the different modes of causality for the serious diseases. As a result, during the 1980s and 1990s, the prophets and charismatic leaders of the Pentecostal Church, the *Holy Spirit Movement* and the Marian Movement, among others, tragically preached that they could effectively heal and cure all diseases, including HIV/AIDS, through the patients' faith, healing prayers, exorcisms and the laying of hands. It did not work. Like magic, prayers do not cure HIV/AIDS.

Consequently, many seriously ill people needlessly died of their diseases because of their misplaced religious faith. This is also true for the members of the Marian Movement, who died self-sacrificial deaths as God's Martyrs and Mary's Saints, hoping to ascend to God, in heaven, through ritual deaths and the flames of fire in Kanungu, on holy Friday, March 17, 2000. These Marian devotees died for their faith and hope of God's salvation through the Blessed Virgin Mary's intervention and instantaneous deliverance from evil. We hope that these Marian devotees, martyrs and other saints did not believe, hope, and live holy lives in a holy quest for divine salvation, and sacrifice their lives in vain.

Emmanuel K. Twesigye, PhD
Benedicts Professor of Christian Studies;
Sharp - Davies - Trimble Professor of Religion
Ohio Wesleyan University,
Delaware, OH 43015, USA

Chapter One

AN INTRODUCTION:
GOD'S WARRIORS, LIBERATION MOVEMENTS
AND MARY'S MARTYRS

This book is based on extensive field research data from East Africa beginning in 1999 to the end of 2009.[1] The book represents a serious critical analysis of original academic field research data and its correlative scholarly approach to the study, analysis and interpretation of the data within the context of sensitive African cultural values, philosophy, the Traditional Religion, Christianity, the Holy Scriptures and history. Here, religion is functionally defined as a collective dimension of societal system of beliefs, values and ritual practices in quest of divine salvation or peace, in the presence of God, as the nameless, "Holy, Transcendent Creative Cosmic Spirit or Energy and Healing or Redeeming Holy Mystery." This is the African interrelated complex context, which has implicitly shaped the explicit religious, cultural and political data and analysis in this book. The book also both critiques and corrects some the previous erroneous theories and publications. They were intellectually misguided because they were based on inaccurate, biased, vindictive and misleading local media reports.

1. Introduction

These extensive field research data and analysis, have uncovered many serious errors and misrepresentations of religious data in many publications and media reports, articles by journalists. The errors were mainly the results of some inherent ignorance of concerning the complex symbolic nature and sacramental nature and societal functions of religion of religion in moral education, the shaping cultures, moral values and politics. Other serious errors were due to xenophobia and some inherent or unconscious religious biases and misconceptions of the traditional Catholic sacraments, strict moral codes of conduct and monastic practices, as forms of superstation, magic and cultic practices. These misconceptions led to the media false reports and allegations that the members of the Catholic Marian Movement ate real human flesh as "the body of Christ," and drank real human blood as "the blood of Christ."

In addition, there was a misunderstanding of new or messianic religious movements and radical liberationist movements. They were mistakenly labeled as dangerous "cults" in the media. These simplistic theories led to serious distortions of the African rural region-political liberationist and messianic moral perfectionist movements as "cults." As a tragic error, these complex African religio-political movements were caricatured as mere destructive evil "cults," which were led by irrational or delusional "false prophets," "false messiahs" and "evil cult leaders." However, this was both a false and tragic misrepresentation of these religio-political movements and their leaders.

Some of the movements discussed in this book have caused serious pain to the people and disruption in Kenya, Uganda, Rwanda, Tanzania, the Democratic Republic of the Congo, and Sudan. The carefully selected movements for study are both religiously and politically significant movements. They include the following: the *Maji Maji* in the former German East Africa (Tanzania*)*, the *Nyabingi Liberation Movement* in Western Uganda, the *East African Revival Movement* (EARM), which is also known as the *Balokole Movement;* Jomo Kenyatta's *Mau Mau Liberation Movement* in Kenya; Yoweri Museveni's *National Resistance Movement* (NRM) in Uganda, Alice Auma (*Lakwena* or Messiah)'s *Holy Spirit Movement* (HSM), and its military wing, which was called the *Holy Spirit Mobile Forces* (HSMF) in Northern and Eastern Uganda; Joseph Kony's *Lord's Resistance Army* (LRA) and the apocalyptic *Movement for the Restoration of the Ten Commandments of God* (MRTCG).[2]

Most of the above movements are merely outlined in their beliefs and activities. They are briefly covered in this book because there are many publications, which have extensively discussed them. For academic purposes, the primary research and main focus of this book have been deliberately placed on the more recent and less researched religio-political movements, especially the HSM, LRA and MRTCG. As a result of an extensive and careful deliberation, the present volume has been condensed and intentionally more focused on the Catholic moral reformist, religious liberationist, apocalyptic[3] and Marian doomsday *Movement for the Restoration of the Ten Commandments of God,* which is variously referred to as: "The Marian Movement" and "MRTCG."

The Marian Movement's main doomsday prophecies, apocalyptic teachings, and extreme monastic moral practices are presented and discussed within the religious, cultural, economic and political context of countries of East Africa, ᵔd the surrounding countries of Rwanda, Burundi and the Democratic Republic ᵔ Congo.[4] However, Uganda takes center stage because of recent liberation ᵔsianic movements, including the MRTTCG, HSMF and the LRA.

ᵔRTCG was founded in 1989, as God's new chosen holy Nation, the ᵔᵀganda was declared to be the Blessed Virgin Mary and God's new ᵔbal Center of Salvation. The Marian Movement was God's messianic agent of salvation for the entire world. For MRTCG or the Marian Movement leaders, Uganda replaced Israel, which was founded by the Prophet Moses based on the Ten Commandments of God. Uganda was chosen by God because of its strong witness of the Christian Martyrs to serve as God's elect Nation and chosen location of his new apocalyptic center of holiness, moral perfection, peace and divine salvation.[5]

During the 1980s and early 1990s, the NRM Government of Uganda made serious attempts to become nonsectarian, although it was predominantly filled by Anglican political elites, and thereby, covertly perpetuating the problematic British colonial structure of Anglican political hegemony. This elitist, autocratic, oppressive and sectarian Anglican hegemony had traditionally marginalized and excluded qualified Catholics, Muslims and the traditionalists from kinships and key political positions in the local and the Central Government.

Nevertheless, in 1995, the NRM Government, guided by President Yoweri Museveni formulated a new, religiously inclusive Constitution. It protected religious diversity and freedoms of conscience, religion and its practice from the interference of the State. This is an important separation of Church and State realms that is almost akin to the First Amendment of the American Constitution, which reads as follows: *"Congress shall make no law respecting an establishment of religion, or prohibiting the free exercise thereof; or abridging the freedom of speech, or of the press; or the right of the people peaceably to assemble, and to petition the Government for a redress of grievances."* In contrast, the freedoms of religion and conscience as stated in the Ugandan Constitution are broader. They are:

ARTICLE 29:
Protection of freedom of conscience, expression, movement, religion, assembly and association.
(1) Every person shall have the right to—
(a) Freedom of speech and expression which shall include freedom of the press and other media;
(b) Freedom of thought, conscience and belief which shall include academic freedom in institutions of learning;
(c) Freedom to practice any religion and manifest such practice which shall include the right to belong to and participate in the practices of any religious body or organisation in a manner consistent with this Constitution;
(d) Freedom to assemble and to demonstrate together with others peacefully and unarmed and to petition; and
(e) Freedom of association which shall include the freedom to form and join associations or unions, including trade unions and political and other civic organisations. (*The Constitution of The Republic of Uganda, 1995*)

The preparations for the above constitutional provision made it possible for the Marian Movement's application to be legally recognized and registered as a NGO (Non-Governmental Organization) in Uganda, to be accepted. The Marian

Movement's main stated objectives and purposes, included providing moral education, development and Marian devotional activities were accepted by the State of Uganda and the Marian Movement's apocalyptic religious teachings and moral activities were protected by the State despite the Mbarara Catholic bishops' protest and persecution of the Marian Movement leaders. The State had no interest in the doctrinal and moral teachings of the Marian Movement, as long as they did not break the existing laws of the country.

2. The Marian Movement as God's Agency of Redemption: Exorcism, Therapy and Healing of the Wounded World

In the 1980s there was great instability in Africa. This was particularly the case in Uganda, Rwanda, Burundi, Congo, Ethiopia, Somalia and Sudan. There were many refugees, droughts, famines and other sources of serious trauma, such as deadly diseases, which were due to the prevalence of wars, violence and abject poverty.[6] In the 1980s, when the Marian Movement emerged, there was a great prevailing existential fear or angst caused by HIV/AIDS, a dreaded new deadly disease, which had already killed several millions of people in East Africa, especially in Uganda. HIV/AIDS was dreaded mainly because it was incurable.[7] Moreover, the victims of the disease died a horrible death. The Movement leaders claimed that HIV/AIDS was God's incurable plague[8] sent into the world as punishment to people for sins and evils of homosexuality, sexual promiscuity and corruption.[9]

The apocalyptic Marian Movement leaders noted that there were new antibiotic-resistant deadly strains of tuberculosis and STDs (sexually transmitted diseases), which were part of God's punishment for the sins of economic greed leading to corruption, prostitution, theft and environmental degradation. Deforestation, as well as car and industrial emissions, which had contributed to global warming, brought malaria infested mosquitoes, malaria and West Nile fever epidemics, where they never existed before the 21st century.

Tragically, this new spread of malaria was particularly deadly because it was of a newly mutated strain of malaria that was resistant to traditional anti-malaria drugs like chloroquine and malaquine.[10] For these unfortunate people, the world seemed to have become a hostile environment, in which to live. From their predicament and pessimistic perspective and world-view, it seemed that the world was coming to an end.

In reality, for many Marian Movement members, much of life in the world was coming to an end through ritual martyrdom, as a supposed quick self-sacrificial holy path to heaven and salvation. This was also true, in as much as one looks at the dramatic manner in which it was transformed when they joined the monastic and celibate Marian Movement. It had figuratively ended for these Marian devotees, at least in the way in which they had traditionally both experienced it and known it, before joining the apocalyptic, moral reform and doomsday Marian Movement. Therefore, the Marian Movement's apocalyptic prophecies and doomsday predictions for the impending end of the world became meaningful and credible to many of these already psychologically traumatized and suffering people.

Consequently, some of these very traumatized and fear-filled people eagerly welcomed and accepted the MRTCG leaders as God's true new and apocalyptic prophets, messiahs and Apostles (*Entumwa*)[11] within a perishing world.[12] The MRTCG leaders were able to attract many Catholic followers because they claimed to heal diseases through prayers, by the laying on of holy hands and through special exorcisms. Prayers of exorcisms were a regular component of the healing services that were ritually led and sacramentally performed by Catholic priests and their trained assistants. The Marian Movement both promised and provided some components of badly needed therapy and medical treatment to the poor people in rural areas free of charge. The Marian Movement leaders also appealed to some desperate sick people, particularly, the HIV/AIDS suffers because these religious leaders claimed to have been given special powers, by God and the Blessed Virgin Mary to cure HIV/AIDS for all the people, who believed, repented all their sins, and joined the Marian Movement.

It is within these overwhelming existential conditions of angst, anxiety and serious societal, political, and socioeconomic hardships, and other anxiety-causing state of affairs, such as the intense fear for the perceived impending doomsday, at the end of the Second Millennium that constituted the main contexts, within which some liberationist movements like the HSM and LRA emerged. *The Movement for the Restoration of the Ten Commandments of God* also emerged and ministered to very anxious and needy people. This is the kind of angst and daily context of existential dread, in which the apocalyptic and doomsday Marian Movement took root and ministered to the discouraged, and both the religiously and politically marginalized traumatized, especially the traditionally politically marginalized and frustrated Catholics. This also partly explains why the doomsday Marian Movement attracted many devout Catholics, especially the poorly educated, impoverished and rural Catholic women. They needed little persuasion to believe that the world was corrupt and that it would soon come to an end as result of God's holy judgment and punishment.

This is the context of angst in which the apocalyptic and Marian Movement leaders emerged and brought God's new apocalyptic revelation of divine judgment and fiery punishment for a sinful and corrupt world and its rebellious and corrupt inhabitants, as was the case of Noah's sinful generation. Ultimately, it was in response to the above context of angst that these liberationist and radical moral reformist apocalyptic Marian Movement leaders preached God's mercy, saving grace and salvation for all the sinners, who heard God's message of warning, repented their sins, sold their property and gave the proceeds to the poor or to the leaders of the Catholic Marian Movement.

Later, these Marian devotees came and joined the Benedictine-like and cloistered Marian Movement's monastic community. They diligently lived together, in a joint holy quest for divine salvation. This holy quest was characterized by repentance and living a new reformed and simple holy life within the Marian Movement's collective, contemplative, celibate and monastic Marian Community. They also constantly strived to attain both moral virtue and spiritual perfection based on the strict observation of God's Ten Commandments.

In addition to a vow of celibacy (chastity), extreme fasting, silent contemplative prayers, and hard work, the Marian Movement members were required to take vows of obedience and contemplative prayer in holy silence (*Kusirika*). The code of holy silence transformed life within the Marian Community into a permanent silent spiritual retreat. These austere monastic measures were devised as religious and moral strategies to combat immorality, idleness and temptations to gossip and sin. They were meant as a holy path of life on the spiritual quest and journey to God, in heaven. For instance, celibacy and the code of silence promoted observation of the Ten Commandments.

Invariably, the Marian Movement leaders constantly preached that the world and its rebellious people were evil, greedy and corrupt. They warned that unless people obeyed God's message of warning and repented of their sins and reformed their lives following God's moral laws as revealed to the Prophet Moses in the form of the Ten Commandments, which the Marian Movement preached, that they were doomed to burn in God's impending fire that would come down from heaven, like a tropical thunderstorm.

Many Catholics and Anglicans in Uganda, such as the *Balokole*[13] (members of the spiritual and moral reform movement within the Anglican Church of East Africa that emerged in 1935), were already condemning corruption in State and Church affairs. As result, some of them did not perceive the MRTCG to be either strange or dangerous, as an extreme Christian moral reform and spiritual renewal movement. Therefore, these Marian Catholics, especially the devotees of the Blessed Virgin Mary welcomed the MRTCG or the new and monastic apocalyptic Marian Movement, as a new Catholic religious Order, which was also a moral equivalent and religious parallel of the traditional *Balokole Movement* within the Anglican Church.

Consequently, the Marian Moral Reform Movement, which existed within the Catholic Church, sounded as a parallel moral reform and spiritual renewal *Balokole Movement* within the Anglican Church which had now been adapted by Mwerinde and Joseph Kibwetere to the Catholic Church. The new apocalyptic Marian moral reform Movement appealed to some devout and fundamentalist Christians beyond the Catholic Church.[14] The Catholic devotees of Mary, the

Balokole and other pious Christians eagerly welcomed it.

However, the Catholic Church hierarchy denounced the MRTCG as an irregular religious Order that was founded within the Catholic Church without the bishop's or the Pope's canonical authorization and license to function within the Catholic Church. The Mbarara Diocese bishops also accused the Movement leaders of falsely claiming to have seen some visions of the Blessed Virgin Mary, and teaching extreme and dangerous moral practices and doomsday prophecies for the imminent end of the world.[15]

Nevertheless, the Movement leaders still claimed that God had given them the necessary saving grace and power to exorcize the demonic forces of the Devil in the world, to heal the possessed, or cure HIV/AIDS, and by faith and healing prayers, provide cures for the faithful, despite the fact that the Movement members were still dying from HIV/AIDS, irrespective of the healing prayers of their Movement leaders. The Movement leaders insisted that their prayers worked but the sick people lacked enough faith to be healed by God or possessed some secret sins which had not been fully repented and atoned for. Because of overwhelming unmet medical and mental needs, the MRTCG leaders were able to appeal to many devout Catholics, especially the people, who had great needs for consolation and healing.

These kinds of marginalized and needy people found it nearly irresistible not to positively respond and join the Marian Movement. They were mainly attracted to the Marian Movement by the leaders' impressive testimonies of heavenly visions, Marian apparitions. Above all, the people were impressed by the Marian Movement leaders' supernatural religious claims to possess divine power and the promises to heal the sick through prayers and exorcisms. They also won the admiration of many devout and the rural superstitious Catholics. This was accomplished by the Marian Movement leaders' convincing claims to prophesize, predict future events and to cure the dreaded HIV/AIDS. The Marian Movement leaders convinced many rural Catholics that they were able to perform these miracles by faith, exorcism and special prayers through God-given special gifts and powers of supernatural therapy or to effect cures in the holy of power of the holy Name of the Trinity: "God the Father," "the Blessed Virgin Mary" and "Jesus Christ."

Ultimately, East Africa was an African region, which had been greatly devastated and traumatized by violence, poverty, civil and genocidal wars, diseases and death. Therefore, the people in this region were physically, politically, morally and economically traumatize. As a result, they were spiritually and culturally open to God's intervention and healing of the deep collective grief, economic and social disruption, as well as deep psychological trauma and mental wounds. Healing and exorcisms provided psychotherapy and grief-counseling. These services were especially important and necessary due to the prevalent cases of post traumatic stress disorder (PTSD) and severe depression associated with brutal ethnic conflicts, genocide, destructive wars in Uganda, and the neighboring countries of Sudan, Rwanda, Burundi and the Republic of the Congo.[16]

In the absence of psychiatrists, religious leaders, such as priests, ministers, prophets, traditional doctors and faith healers (*Bafumu/Waganga*) became the main providers of counseling, therapy and supernatural agents of God's exorcism, healing and miraculous cures. The MRTCG leaders claimed to possess supernatural powers to perform exorcisms to get rid of the demonic forces or oppressive evil spirits, and to heal all diseases, including the deadly HIV/AIDS and malaria, through faith and the laying on of hands. These claims of apostolic, charismatic and divine spiritual gifts and healing practices were enthusiastically welcomed by many Christians, as the true new apocalyptic forms of God's providence, divine intervention, healing and salvation in the world.

3. Kanungu as God's New Chosen Center of Apocalyptic Revelation And Mary's Salvation in the World

The Kanungu site of the horrific Movement church inferno on March 17, 2000, was chosen because it was a refuge from persecution in Mbarara Catholic Diocese. Kanungu was located in Kabale Diocese, where the more tolerant and liberal Bishop Robert Gay[17] left the MRTCG leaders and their followers to preach, live and practice their apocalyptic teachings and experiment with living a monastic ascetic life, in peace.[18]

In addition, Mwerinde's father was another Marian devotee who left all his farm land near Kanungu to her for the purposes of supporting and promoting her divine call to serve as Mary's embodiment (*Ekyombeko*), voice (*Iraka*), visionary (*Kareebi*) and representation (*Entumwa*) in the world (*Omunsi egyi*), beginning with her family. Mwerinde's first convert was been Ursula Komuhangi, her sister. That event had made a great impression on Paul Kashaku, their father, who was a retired Catholic catechist at the neighboring Makiro Parish Church. He, too, had seen a vision of the Blessed Virgin Mary. As a devout Catholic and zealous devotee of the Blessed Virgin Mary, Kashaku became a great supporter of his favorite daughter's claims of heavenly and Marian visions, divine commissioning to God's redemptive mission and a moral crusade in the world, to save both a fallen and corrupt Church and society.[19]

The Kanungu site was also remote and rural, and therefore, it was considered ideal as a farming place that would support hundreds of the Movement's members that were housed in dormitories on the site. Because of the remote location of the site, it was also considered as an ideal place to isolate and control the Marian Movement members. The Marian Movement leaders censored the outside information that was presented to the Marian Movement members. This was partly in order to protect them from outside temptations and sins.

As a result of censorship and isolation of the Marian Movement members, whose main monastic community campus was located in a remote rural area near the border with the war-torn Democratic Republic of the Congo and Rwanda, where brutal genocide had occurred, it seemed that evil completely prevailed in God's world. Consequently, within this state of angst and ignorance, it became very easy for the Marian Movement leaders to convince the isolated people, especially in the remote African rural areas that the world was, indeed, so irredeemably evil and violent, and was therefore, coming to an imminent catastrophic or fiery end, as a result of God's righteous judgment and punishment. The MRTCG or the Marian Movement leaders attributed this apocalyptic disaster to be a result of human moral evils, and rampant sins, especially those of avarice, sexual immorality, homosexuality, corruption, violence and wars, partly because many local people were victims of many of these evils and wanted to be delivered from them, by God or God's messiah (*Lakwena*) or liberator.

Accordingly, it was easy for these marginalized and oppressed people to believe that God would punish the corrupt world and sinners, by destroying them in God's catastrophic fire as his divine retribution for disobedience, and evils or sins of: corruption, greed, violence, homosexuality, rape and other forms of moral decadence, which the Marian Movement moral crusaders strongly denounced and preached against. Hellfire had been traditionally preached by the Western Christian missionaries as God's judgment and punishment, therefore, the Marian Movement leaders, only embellished it with vivid images from Dante's *Inferno*. These images of fire were meant to scare sinners into repentance out of dread and fear of God's impending judgment and painful punishment in hell-fire.

The urgency for repentance led to the Marian Movement leaders' ill-advised and tragic device of preaching the frightening doomsday prophecies and making scaring apocalyptic predictions for the end of the corrupt era in God's purifying fire, at the end the Second Millennium. This preaching device backfired, because doomsday prophecies and predictions for the end of the world became public obsessions, which effectively overshadowed, marginalized and even negated Keledonia Mwerinde's Marian Movement's original real noble religious and moral objectives to preach repentance and implement moral reformation in both the Church and the State or the world as a whole.

As a result, these doomsday predictions became a self-fulfilling reality for the Marian Movement members, in March, 2000, when they underwent self-sacrificial ritual of atonement and martyrdom. These sacramental rituals were performed, in hope of becoming God's obedient martyrs and holy saints. They were also performed as the holy path and supernatural means to liberate the soul from the bodies and to empower it to ascend into heaven, for the attainment of God's salvation, eternal life, and everlasting happiness in the fellowship of God and the saints. Later, this code of silence made it easy for the Marian Movement leaders to plan and kill their followers in total secrecy, and then, bury them secretly without arousing the suspicion of neighbors or the local police.[20] The Kanungu MRTCG headquarters' site, where some of these Marian Movement's final martyrdoms occurred was described, in 2000,[21] by the Makerere University investigation group following the Movement's tragic deaths as follows:

(A) Two churches: The old church where members perished and the new church had just been completed before the fire.
(B) A number of residential houses:
● One fairly modern house for the leaders.
● 2 large dormitories; one for male and another for female members.
● 2 visitors' houses with a reception room.
● Kitchens and stores.
● A full-fledged primary school (with 7 classrooms).[22]
● A school dormitory and stores.
● An unfinished shrine to the Blessed Virgin Mary at the entrance of the camp.[23]
(C) A large compound with a cemetery in the middle of the site. Another cemetery is located on an adjacent hill.
(D) Fields where potatoes, bananas, pineapples and sugar-canes were grown.
(E) A dairy farm which became a model farm of about 30 Friesian cows.
(F) A poultry project.
From an estimation, the camp could host and cater for up to 300 people at anyone time.[24] However, the exact number that permanently stayed on this site cannot be ascertained since members were constantly being transferred from one site to another.[25]

The Report continues to describe the Movement headquarters campus and its architectural design as follows:

The construction of the movement's headquarters at Kanungu is in an irregular pattern. Houses are built close to each other and face in all directions. Both the old and new churches are built close to the dwelling houses. Most houses are built of mud and wattle. The rooms in some buildings are tiny. In one main house at the site, latrines are attached. There is no flowing water at the site. The kitchen, stores and school, are all part of this complex. The main residential house looks decent with over twenty small rooms. It is the same house where bodies were later discovered in pits originally meant to serve as pit latrines.[26]

In their report, the Makerere University research team's investigation also answered the important question regarding the selection of the remote Kanungu site in Kabale Catholic Diocese as the Marian Movement's new headquarters and center of operations. Kanungu was chosen, despite its location in a remote rural area with little access, either by road or telephone, and lacking in the essential facilities of electricity, clean piped water for cooking and bathing, or for plumbing and sewer systems.[27] The answer indicates that the Marian Movement wanted privacy, peace and quiet. However, the team failed to fully realize, or emphasize sufficiently, that the Kanungu site was the necessary refuge and hiding place from the apparent persecution by both Bishops John Baptist Kakubi and Paul Bakyenga of Mbarara Catholic Diocese.[28] Nevertheless, the team made some important observations concerning the selection of the Kanungu site.

The Makerere University Research Team asked and answered some important questions, like: "Why was Kanungu Chosen for the [Movement] Headquarters?" and "Why did the Marian devotees ritually kill themselves?" There are several reasons why the Movement leaders may have chosen Kanungu as their camping site. The following reasons or considerations deserve to be mentioned or analyzed:

1. The Marian Movement leaders obtained a significant gift in the form of a large piece of land from Credonia's [Keledonia's] father, which was intended to support their work. So they took this opportunity to move away from Mbarara and Ntungamo sites, which had become both too small and hostile to them and their religious activities and doctrines.

2. The group had been met with strong resistance from the Mbarara Catholic bishops and the local authorities in their previous areas of operation, as well as from the families where the Marian Movement members had gathered and camped, including Kibwetere's own family.

3. The remoteness of the place provided ample security where they [The Marian Movement leaders] would carry on their activities free from public interference.

4. Local people of the area, as well as authorities, were not hostile to them. They were hospitable. However, some kind of resistance would develop later when people started suspecting the group after hearing reports of its having been resisted in Mbarara.

5. The site seemed to be conducive to a solitary life and prayer which they preferred. It is very isolated and generally quiet and the only way of knowing what was taking place there was to actually visit the place. Located about two to three kilometers from Kanungu Trading Centre, it was only accessible by a narrow road which was constructed by the Movement members once they settled at the site. The road crosses a valley and there is a small bridge made of timber and rocks. The place resembled a monastery.[29]

The new Kanungu site for the Marian headquarters and cloistered monastic community was very remote and difficult to travel to from Mbarara. It was isolated and ideal for secrecy, religious freedom, religious excesses, despair, and therefore, conducive to the Marian Movement members' complete obedience and conviction that their leaders were telling them the truth when they claimed that the Blessed Virgin Mary had appeared to them and told them that the world was going to end at the close of 1999, in God's catastrophic and consuming holy fire, or "hellfire," as punishment for moral evil, rebellion and sin against God.[30]

The Marian Movement's headquarters in Kanungu were also both theologically and symbolically named as: *"Ishayuriro Rya Maria"* (The Place of Deliverance/Salvation by the Blessed Virgin Mary).[31] Kanungu was also considered as the global center of God's supernatural activities of revelation, grace, healing, holy pilgrimage and redemption. On March 17, 2000, it also became the venue for the Marian Movement members' final activities of holy self-sacrifices, self-martyrdom, death, cremation within the church inferno,[32] and fulfillment of the Marian Movement members' expected ascension into heaven in "Mary's flames of fire" with the assistance of God's Holy Spirit.[33]

The other important Marian Movement branch substations and camp centers in Uganda included: the Kanungu and Katojo Trading Centres in Kanungu District (Kigezi), Rutooma, Rubirizi and Rugazi in Bushenyi District (Ankole), Kamukuzi in Mbarara District (Ankole), Kyaka in Kabarole District (Toro) and Buziga in Kampala District (Buganda). Based on these major locations of the Movement's centers, it is clear that most of the Marian Movement members and victims were also predominantly the people, who came from these areas and regions, in which the Marian Movement centers were located.[34]

Therefore, the Marian Movement members were mainly composed of Banyankole, followed by the Batoro, the Banyakigezi (Bakiga, Bahororo and Banyarwanda[35]) and the Baganda. There were also many Banyarwanda, Basoga, the Congolese, and some other ethnic groups that were less heavily represented in the Marian Movement's membership.[36]

Nevertheless, the names of some of the Movement victims also clearly indicate that the majority of the members and martyrs of this tragic Apocalyptic Marian Movement were pious Catholic women, who were the traditional devotees of Mary, and their innocent children. Ultimately, although the MRTCG was founded locally in Uganda in 1989 to become God's universal,[37] apocalyptic, and inclusive messianic agency of redemption for all the people in the world, irrespective of race and religious tradition,[38] by 2000, the majority of these Marian Movement members and Christian martyrs came from regions of Ankole, Kigezi and Toro in Southern and Western Uganda.[39]

4. Problems of Field Data and Interpretation

As a detailed case study of the African messianic and liberation movements, this book will both provide and present the comprehensive socioeconomic, historical, religious, theological, philosophical, cultural and political contexts in which *The Movement for the Restoration of the Ten Commandments of God* emerged, and thrived, especially poverty, HIV/AIDS pandemic, corruption, political repression, violence and wars. It will attempt to provide the religious and theological reasons why the Marian Movement leaders, finally, committed the tragic acts of ritual killings of their most loyal followers, as acts of holy self-sacrifices and martyrdoms.

In reality, these gruesome ritual mass murders were perpetrated in order to martyr the Marian Movement members based on Fr. Dominic Kataribabo's radical Catholic theology of self-sacrificial atonement to God and salvation. Fr. Kataribabo conceived of these Marian martyrdoms as the holy means to liberate and save the Marian devotees from a hostile and perishing world. Fr. Kataribabo sought to martyr and thereby, to transform the faithful Catholic Marian devotees into angel-like spiritual beings. He wanted to transform them into saints, who would spiritually ascend to heaven in glory, to inherit God's salvation and gain the eternal life of blessedness or beatitude, happiness and peace.

A. Problems of Secrecy, Codes of Silence and Tragedy

New religious movements and cults are often very secretive in order to hide their unusual activities from the public or government officials' scrutiny. In some extreme cases, like that of the *Mau Mau* in Kenya, some paranoid leaders of secretive movements may require their members to take oaths of secrecy and silence. In the African traditional religions, there are also secretive cults and secret societies whose members take ritual oaths of secrecy and vows of silence about their activities in the movement or cult, as part of their initiation. These practices can lead to tragedy as in cases of human sacrifice, ritual rapes of virgins, political assassinations and murders of their opponents. Some of these cultic and religious practices exist in many parts of Africa today. This includes Uganda, where child-sacrifice in central Uganda, accounts for many kidnapping and ritual murders of children, for purposes of atonement to some traditional gods and God, in both religious faith and hope of miraculously acquiring divine blessings in the locally desired form of some riches.[40]

Many founding religious cult leaders and other secretive religious movements generally tend to become charismatic, totalitarian, suspicious of outsiders and paranoid. These cult-like leaders tend to distrust the public media, newspaper reporters, politicians, police and researchers. These religious leaders generally seek to impose total censorship on news and information coming from outside into their religiously, socioeconomically controlled and socially isolated communities. The Marian Movement leaders were misleadingly described by the mass media in Uganda, in the above manner.

In these cult-like religious movements and exclusive religious communities, such as the Rev. Jim Jones' *Peoples' Temple,* in Jonestown, in Guyana; and David Koresh's *Branch Davidian Community,* in Waco, Texas, the founding religious leaders had censured external news and information coming into their physically and socially isolated utopian and apocalyptic religious communities. The leaders also restricted the entry of external visitors on the movements' campuses. The movement and cult leaders also rarely permitted the members of their respective movements from visiting their families or friends back home. These observations were also true for the Marian Movement. This is one of the main reasons why some observers and the public media reporters mistook the Marian Movement for another dangerous religious cult.

These new religious movements and cult leaders' activities were designed to isolate the members of the movements and cults from the supposedly corrupting outside world and its supposed evil cultures, and society with its corrupting influences and temptations. This complete self-segregation, isolation from the world and censorship of the cult and new religious movements made it easier for the respective religious leaders to control and brainwash their isolated and co-dependent followers. In this kind of set-up, the movement and cult leaders gained the status of infallible and God-like attributes among their followers.

In the case of the ancient Christians, Jesus was hailed by his Jewish disciples as their promised Messiah (Christ), and later, the polytheistic Gentiles worshipped him as the Son of God, in the same way in which the Greek and Roman pagans had worshipped their leaders, especially the Emperors as either gods or Sons of God. For the Greeks, Zeus was believed to transform and disguise himself, in order to engage in sexual intercourse with human women and even to reproduce with them, such as Heracles. They believed that it was the same with God the Father and Jesus as his Son.

New religious movement leaders promote the absolute reliability of faith and nurture deep suspicion of reason, and secular education as the evil agencies of the demonic forces of temptations, doubt and disbelief or atheism. In many cases of cults and new religious movement, such as *The People's Temple*, HSM, LRA, and the MRTCG, the members were both spiritually and mentally controlled by their leaders. These people were conditioned and mentally programmed, or oriented into both believing and accepting whatever their religious leaders and prophets taught them, as God's revealed new apocalyptic truths, and divine instructions for living a holy life that is pleasing to God. Thus, the religious or cult leaders gained the seemingly divine or infallible power over their followers.

In some cases, this power to control of their followers led to many abuses of their followers, such as sexual and economic exploitations. In some extreme cases, some cult-like religious leaders, like the Rev. Jim Jones, Marshall Applewhite, David Koresh, Mwerinde and Kibwetere, led many of their pious followers to embrace an irrational, or religiously radical and self-sacrificial moral path of extreme self-sacrifices, and irrational self-sacrificial deaths, as the divine holy path leading them to the attainment of supernatural salvation in heaven.

As a result of this elaborate censorship and control of information and ideas, the religious founders and leaders of these communes became the main sources of their communities' information of what was supposed to be credible news within the community, and from the outside world. These religious leaders, including the Marian Movement leaders, also became God's special apocalyptic messiahs and special agents of supernatural revelations from God, mediation of God's supernatural salvation and the infallible or normative moral, religious and socioeconomic guidance for the respective communities.

The above scenario was also true for Joseph Kibwetere and Keledonia Mwerinde concerning *The Movement for the Restoration of the Ten Commandments of God.* These religious leaders served as the infallible prophets, *"messiahs," or "Christs,"* and *"popes"* for their own communities. It is also a universal problem that in many cases, when the moral reform crusaders and messianic liberationist movement leaders succeed and come into power, their reforms are short-lived. These self-appointed political messiahs and moral crusaders or reformers soon become tempted and corrupted by fame, power and wealth. Very often, the liberators or reformers succumb to these evil temptations and become the new perpetrators of the evils they had decried, and come into power to redress. The oppressed cry out to God for new messiahs or liberators.

Think about the French Revolution and the Emperor Napoleon; Joseph Stalin in Russia; Chairman Mao Tse-Tung in China; Fidel Castro in Cuba, and General Idi Amin in Uganda;[41] they all became corrupted by power. Similarly, the Marian Movement moral crusaders, messiahs and prophets, would have also changed and corrupted, after coming into power. They would have followed the examples of several previous African military self-styled liberators or political messiahs, like Bokassa, Mobutu, Gaddafi, Idi Amin, Robert Mugabe and Yoweri Museveni. They also became negatively transformed into the very evil, corrupt and totalitarian leaders, whom they had initially denounced and overthrown on charges of being: corrupt, tyrannical, autocratic, oppressive and evil.

By doing so, these messianic and liberation movement leaders inadvertently negated their own original reasons and justification for the emergence of their movement and coming into power, or the fundamental reason for being. For instance, that has been the case with the NRM (*National Resistance Movement*), or President Yoweri Museveni's Government. Whereas the NRM fought a long liberation war and came into power in 1986, in order to fight political dictatorship, electoral malpractices, and corruption, it has failed in its core moral principles and originally stated liberation objectives. On the contrary, the NRM Government has become the most corrupt government in Ugandan history.

The Movement for the Restoration of the Ten Commandments of God, as a corrective moral and spiritual renewal or reformation Marian Movement within the Catholic Church, was not given sufficient time, and the opportunities to minister and face the real temptations of power, and needs for moral, political, economic and pastoral compromises. The idealistic and moralistic MRTCG would also have eventually become corrupt, like President Yoweri Museveni's

NRM, which also originally waged a utopian Marxist political crusade for moral as well as noble democratic political reasons. Yet, the NRM became corrupted by power after coming into political office, in 1986 and many of its original noble ideals were discarded for being either too idealistic or irrelevant.

Similarly, if the Marian Movement moral crusaders had been given time and an opportunity to remain at the center of the Catholic Church, the Marian Movement would have also eventually become incorporated into the mainline Catholic Church, or become corrupted by its members and successes or the acquisitions of power. The Marian Movement would have followed the fate of other new and radical religious and moral reform movements and organizations that emerged to denounce and reform the Church, like the *Balokole Movement* in East Africa, or the historical ecclesiastical reformation movements, including Martin Luther, John Calvin, John Wesley and their various forms and traditions of the Protestant Reformation. Ultimately, if the Catholic Church hierarchy had welcomed the Marian Movement with great interest, it would have been an ideal administrative position to take. This would have been a positive strategy that would have led to the Marian Movement's initial excitement, and after blowing off steam, the Marian Movement would have run out of steam.

In time, the Marian moral reformation Movement would have naturally lost its main initial driving moral force and radical extremism for moral reform. This process would have occurred slowly as the Marian Movement leaders, being unsalaried volunteers would have run out of funds, or would have been completely overwhelmed with work. They would have been completely overwhelmed by the administrative chores of running retreats, workshops, preaching crusades and teaching missions for encouragement, and the nurturing of spiritual renewal and the moral reformation of Catholic Church and the society around them. It is conceivable that the ambitious Kibwetere, Fr. Kataribabo and Mwerinde would have been eventually corrupted by their exercise of absolute cult-like power over their followers or pride and fame.

This kind of inevitable form of eventual corruption of the Marian Movement would have gradually occurred, in time. It would have slowly taken place as these Marian Movement leaders attempted to please their new global Catholic audience, rather than seeking to please God and the Blessed Virgin Mary, as their main reason for being. They would have carried out their new moral reformation and missionary service, or redemptive mission to the world, from within the Catholic Church. However, the Mbarara Catholic bishops missed the opportunity to embrace, harness and neutralize the Marian Movement leaders and their followers. The Catholic bishops could have used them as the moral and spiritual leaven for moral revival and re-energizing the Catholic Church and its redemptive mission in the world. It would have functioned like the *Charismatic Movement*, which also promotes faith healing by ritual prayers and exorcisms.

B. Problems of Dealing with Censorship and Cult-like Silence

Some cults and secretive religious or political radical movements can be extremely hostile to the perceived intrusions or investigations by the outsiders. They can militarily seek to protect their privacy as the tragic cases of the Rev. Jim Jones' *People's Temple* and David Koresh's *Branch Davidians* clearly indicate. The researcher's venture into secretive religious movements and cults can be dangerous and tragic. The researcher can be tragically confused for a government agent, secret police informer or police criminal investigator. As a result, cooperation and information may be watched and hindered in his or her work, since the potential informers are scared away, due to fear of retribution from the respective religious or movement leaders. This was partly true in carrying out the research for this work.

Therefore, in 1999 and 2000, I was forced to find creative ways to solve this serious problem. The local police officers in Kanungu and Rukungiri were reluctant to discuss the case or release documents concerning the activities of *The Movement for the Restoration of the Ten Commandments of God.* Their refusal to cooperate fully was based on the legal technicality that the case was still under police investigation, and to release the confidential information would be unprofessional and illegal. Furthermore, that it would jeopardize any future investigation and prosecution of the religious leaders of the MRTCG on the charges of criminal endangerment of children, fraud and premeditated mass murders of their devoted religious followers. However, the police's files on the MRTCG and its tragic end were said to be missing.[42]

The field research in Kanungu, Rukungiri, Kabale, Bushenyi, Ntungamo and Mbarara districts and Kampala, Uganda, for this book in 1999-2007 was complicated by the fact that it dealt with some censored religious and state information. The field research ran into trouble because there were some close relatives of the cult victims who, did not want to cooperate, and provide needed information about the deceased members of the Marian Movement due to fear of the Mbarara Catholic Church hierarchy's disapproval of the Marian Movement. Some of informers demanded payment for their information.

However, many of them were reluctant to provide information because they were not sure how the information would be used, or if they would be held accountable for failure to advise their relatives not to join the MRTCG. However, many people, including the police officials were reluctant to disclose negative information. They claimed that they did not want the information I had gathered to be used in a negative manner that would present Uganda, as a backward African nation dominated by evil religious and political cults and murderous extremist movements, like the MRTCG, HSMF[43] and the LRA.[44]

These Ugandan patriots believed and contended that Uganda had better things to offer to the outside world, like the tourism industry, especially when it included attracting Western tourists to come and see beautiful sceneries and the rare mountain gorillas in Southern Uganda, rather than scaring the potential tourists away with frightening tales of cult ritual murders and even, cannibalism. They made it clear that they did not want my research to tarnish the good name of Uganda, by portraying its people, as superstitious religious fanatics prone to join cults, and blaming both the Catholic Church's bishops and the leaders of the Government of Uganda, especially the police that had failed to detect and prevent the MRTCG's tragic deaths.

On the other hand, my informers suggested that some corrupt Government officials and police officers may have wanted a bribe before they would release the needed information. However, since I am a law abiding citizen, a priest, and a professor of theology and ethics, I could not in good conscience participate in these cultural evils, or condone such corrupt practices. That ethical decision made it more difficult to conduct research for the book, in a timely manner. However, that was the high price for moral integrity. As such, I contend that I have earned the necessary moral experience and right to critically analyze and objectively comment on the moral values of both the Marian Movement leaders and their moral crusade against corruption and moral decadence in both the Church and State affairs in East Africa, especially in Uganda.

Unlike some foreign researchers and newspaper reporters, who do not know the local languages and cultures and make serious errors in their research reports and reports, I was born in Kambuga, Kanungu in Southern Uganda. Therefore, it is very significant to note that as a researcher, I have the rare advantage of possessing the necessary linguistic, cultural, philosophical, political historical and anthropological tools to undertake this study. I also had also taught Fr. Kataribabo, as one of students in African political, religious and cultural history, at Makerere University, in the 1970s. He was already a Catholic priest.

In addition, I had the unique opportunities open to me for having some relatives and friends, who lived in the area of the field research, and as well within the Marian Movement itself. They were extremely helpful with the research for this book. For instance, Mrs. Theresa Tibayungwa also knew Joseph Kibwetere, as a family friend, and knew the Rev. Fathers Kataribabo and Joseph Mary Kasapurari, who were some of the ordained senior Catholic priests, and the major religious leaders of the Marian Movement. Therefore, Mrs. Tibuyungwa had a unique understanding of the Marian Movement and its leadership.

As a result, Mrs. Tibayungwa was able to give me valuable information concerning their social histories, and religious lives in the Church. She had also rented her daughter's house, in Kamukuzi, to the Marian Movement leaders. They used it as both a women's residence hall and a preschool for the Movement's children until March 17, 2000, when most of them went to Kanungu, hoping to ascend to heaven, when they burned, in the church inferno.[45]

The survivors in Mbarara were violently evicted from the premises with the help of the police from the Mbarara Town Council. Fortunately, no mass graves were ever found on the site. Some of my other relatives and friends who had also rented buildings to the MRTCG leaders for a religious branch, local membership registry processing center and shop in Katojo Trading Centre, near Kambuga town, also got rid of the remaining Marian Movement's property, which the Marian devotees had not either sold or burned, before they went to Kanungu for the "Day of the Ascension" to heaven.

I was able to interview these relatives concerning the daily life, activities, beliefs and religious practices of the Movement members who lived and worked there. It was a major recruiting center for new Movement leaders and almost converted my sister-in-law, who was their neighbor. The Anglican lay leader and David Kashari, a minister at Nyarugunda Anglican Parish Church, had rented to them the Katojo house. They preached to him the need to repent of his remaining secret sins, join them and ascend to heaven with them. He said that they were very persuasive and nearly converted him to their Marian Movement, believing that it was a Catholic Church equivalent of the *Balokole Movement* of the Anglican Church, of which he was a committed member.

Subsequently, David Kashari was cordially invited to visit Kanungu, the Marian Movement's headquarters, to meet the Movement leaders. But, as a *Mulokole*[46] and a local religious leader, he said that he went there to debate and discuss the matters of Mariology and doomsday prophecies and monastic doctrines and other extreme religious practices that the Marian Movement both preached and practiced. He was particularly interested in the Marian devotees' apocalyptic beliefs concerning the imminent end of the world and the destruction of the non-Marian Movement members, who were the majority of religious and God-fearing people in the world.

As an influential *Mulokole* and religious leader in Katojo area, David Kashari was very eager to find out the reasons for the Marian Movement's mandatory requirements for selling all their members' possessions and donating all the sale proceeds to the Marian Movement. Like many people in Uganda, Kashari also considered this economic requirement for joining the Marian Movement, as an unethical form of religious exploitation and economic fraud on the part of the Marian Movement leaders.

Kashari was also curious about the Marian Movement's practices of extreme fasting, and self-sacrificial religious activities of Medieval-like monasticism. He wanted to hear the rationale for Movement's mandatory monastic practices of code of holy silence, extreme fasting and celibacy for all its members, and both the legal and religious grounds for dissolutions of existing marriages.

Like most Anglicans and other Protestants, Kashari believed that mandatory celibacy was erroneous moral obligation, since God had created Adam and Eve and wedded them to bear children and fill the Earth. He questioned their practice of selling their property and handing over all the money to the Movement's leaders without saving some money for the education of the children, and the strange teaching concerning the imminent end of the world and people perishing unless they were in the *"Obwato bwa Ruhanga bw'Okujunwa"* (God's Ark of Salvation), which they explained to him was the Movement.

However, the new and larger church building in Kanungu, which they were still in the process of building, was simply a symbolical and physical representation of Noah's Ark of Salvation. In the same way Noah built an Ark in the dry desert, the Marian Movement leaders also symbolically built a Marian holiness Movement as a symbol for God's salvation, in the middle of the African continent.[47] But the Ark of Salvation was for the redemption of the entire world.

To this end, I very carefully interviewed many relatives of the religious victims of *The Movement for the Restoration of the Ten Commandments of God,* the local police, government leaders and most important of all, I interviewed many religious leaders in Uganda. These religious leaders include: priests, bishops, archbishops and the Cardinal Emmanuel Wamala, the former Archbishop of Kampala Catholic Archdiocese and Head of the Catholic Church in Uganda. It became very clear that the Marian Movement leaders built their church building in Kanungu, as a mere symbol for God's salvation. This is the case despite the fact that they often metaphorically referred to it as the "Ark of Salvation" (*Obwato bw'Okujunwa*).

The interviews of bishops, priests, relatives, friends, and neighbors of the Marian Movement members were conducted over a period of four years (2000-2004), in order to learn how the main leaders of the Church viewed *The Movement for the Restoration of the Ten Commandments of God,* and what they did in order to warn both their followers and the government officials about it. For instance, Bishop John Ntegyereize, the Anglican Diocesan Bishop of Kinkizi, whose headquarters were located at Nyakatare, about three miles from the Marian Movement's headquarters, was involved in a land dispute with the Marian Movement leaders.

Some of the Church land shared a common land border in Kanungu with the Movement's headquarters. The land dispute concerning the dividing line of the property was difficult to resolve because of the code of silence and insistence on written communication between the two parties.[48] As a result, Bishop Ntegyereize became biased against the theology and activities of the Marian Movement because he had negatively perceived the Marian Movement to be a dangerous religious organization. Subsequently, he had warned his congregation members not to join or associate with it. Bishop Ntegyereize had condemned its doomsday teachings, and apocalyptic prophesies concerning the end of the world at midnight on December 31, 1999, or in the morning of January 1, 2000, to be completely erroneous religious teachings, "false prophecies" and even downright "dangerous doctrines" that were being preached and taught in the name of God.

These false apocalyptic teachings concerning the imminent end of the world as God's new inerrant revelations through the heavenly visions of the Blessed Virgin Mary and conversations with God caused alarm, fear and anxiety among the superstitious rural people. This included both the Catholics and some non-Catholics, particularly the *Balokole,* who had believed and taught almost similar doomsday prophecies and apocalyptic doctrines in the past. They had also claimed these teachings were God's new redemptive apocalyptic revelations and the end-of-time heavenly visions (*okushururirwa* or *okubonekyerwa).*

The *Balokole* had claimed that their apocalyptic revelations for the imminent end of the world were communicated by God the Father, to them, through Jesus Christ. In contrast, the Marian Movement leaders claimed that their own new apocalyptic revelations for the imminent end of the world were declared to come from God the Father. However, according to the Marian Movement leaders, God's new apocalyptic revelations to the world were both mediated and communicated to them through the apparitions, or visions of the Blessed Virgin Mary.

It is also important to note that the months leading to the end of 1999, were both locally and globally constituted a period of suspense that was characterized by generalized state of several stressful conditions of anxiety and dread. These stressful conditions were rooted in fear of the unknown future, general states of dread and existential anxiety. This was especially true in Uganda due to the MRTCG's apocalyptic activities and doomsday predictions for the end of the world with the closing of the decade.

As a result, many devout and other anxious religious people, including both Catholics and Protestants, went to Church for midnight mass and confessional prayers. They both fearfully and anxiously went to these sacred places of worship, churches, mosques and temples in order obtain forgiveness of sins and to wait for the end of the world just in case both Mwerinde and Kibwetere's visions and prophecies were actually true. In that case, they believed that God would find them worthy, and reward them with eternal life, if God's expected catastrophic, apocalyptic "Judgment Day," and end of the world occurred on January 1, 2000.

However, many devout Christians world-wide, especially the religious fundamentalists and the millenarians, diligently prepared themselves for the possibility of the apocalyptic end of the world and their holy ascension into heaven. The popular Evangelical religious series called "*Left Behind*" by Tim LaHaye and Jerry B. Jenkins, most effectively catered for their existential anxiety and apocalyptic beliefs and hopes for imminent ascension, into heaven. Some secular people prepared for the worst, in case the secular and religious doomsday predictions for computer-based trouble, or even the end of the world at the end of the Second Millennium were true.

Nevertheless, some Christians also believed that it was prudent to get spiritually prepared to meet God, in case the anxiety causing doomsday predictions and prophecies for the end of the world were true. They believed that they had nothing to lose, if these apocalyptic prophecies and expectations for the imminent of the world were like William Millers' 1843 and 1844 apocalyptic predictions and preparations for apocalyptic ascension into heaven, by the faithful, which turned out to be inaccurate prediction and a false prophecy and false religious alarm.

Nevertheless, many of the Christian millenarians believed that they would have nothing to lose by getting ready for the supposed impending ending of the world, and repenting their sins in readiness to face God's final Judgment Day. If it occurred, they were ready, and if it did not, they lived in a new Third Millennium, and were ready to serve God and preach repentance and divine salvation to the sinners in the world, in hope of saving them for God.

Meanwhile, in the secular Western world, there was also a serious prevailing secular apocalyptic concern and technological doomsday scenario, in the form of Y2K computer operating systems concerns. This secular doomsday scenario seemed to confirm and validate the religious doomsday predictions and apocalyptic millennial prophecies for the impending end of the world, with the dawning of a new millennium.

In the secular community, the doomsday took on a secular apocalyptic prediction of doom, at the end of the Second Millennium, unless intelligent people acted appropriately to prevent it. For instance, there was a prevailing state of anxiety and fear that computers would crash, and cause great disasters since they would not be able to read correctly and recognize the new year of 2000, unless they had been previously programmed to recognize the Third Millennium as a valid new date.

5. Treatment of Marian Ritual Murders as Christian Martyrdoms

Despite the previous common misunderstanding of the Marian Moral Reform Movement as a separatist and non-Catholic new Church denomination, the Marian Movement claimed to be Catholic and remained Catholic right to the end. Having interviewed the former Marian members and eyewitness to the monastic Marian Movement's holy life, teachings, practices and events leading to the Kanungu church inferno, it became very clear that the Marian Movement members' daily activities were carefully planned by the Marian Movement leaders, especially Keledonia Mwerinde, as the "Marian Movement's Programmer."[49] Similarly, the horrific mass murders of hundreds of apocalyptic and devout Marian Catholics, were also carefully planned and both methodically and deliberately executed ritual martyrdoms by the Rev. Fr. Dominic Kataribabo, with the assistance of some well-trusted hired outside assassins.[50]

Christian martyrdom was considered necessary, as the most redemptive, and self-sacrificial atoning holy deed. It was also considered as the most reliable and practical method to dispatch the Marian Movement's Christian holy saints, both quickly and efficiently, from this world, which they had perceived as evil, corrupt and damned. Subsequently, the final ritual martyrdoms and deaths took place on the supposed eve of the day of apocalyptic destruction, by God, through his punitive and cleansing holy fire at the end of the Second Millennium, and the early months of the Third Millennium.

The deep desire "to be saved," or to be supernaturally delivered by God from the supposed evil and perishing world, was the main driving force behind this Marian moral reformist Movement, and its radical moral activities, including ritual martyrdoms, as a guaranteed holy path to heaven. These Marian Movement spiritual renewal teachings and moral reform ideals seem to have been borrowed from the Anglican *Balokole Movement* in Uganda and the neighboring countries of East Africa, Rwanda, Burundi and eastern parts the Republic of the Congo.[51]

However, the Marian Movement was also different from the *Balokole Movement* in as much as it was both a theologically and sacramentally Catholic Church-based spiritual and moral perfectionist religious movement. As a Catholic Marian Movement, the MRTCG sought to accomplish its main mission with the direct help of the Blessed Virgin, whom they worshipped as the Mother God, the Redeemer and Mediator of human beings and God.

However, the Marian Movement leaders tragically performed mass murders as living human sacrifices, and ritual martyrdoms, by strangulation, and by poisoning their followers. Finally, the Marian Movement leaders set the remaining members on fire, during special morning Friday prayers, in their Kanungu church building.

These ritual martyrdoms were rooted in the Marian Movement's obsession with the Medieval Catholic theology of sin, penance, self-sacrifice, and atonement for sins. Within this Medieval Catholic theology of atonement and salvation, self-sacrifice for God, as a holy warrior against evil as a crusader and religious martyr, was most valued and very highly commended, as the ultimate form of self-sacrifice and atonement for sin. Christian martyrdom was positively viewed as the guarantee for sainthood and direct attainment of eternal salvation, peace and happiness in heaven, in the fellowship with God and the saints.

Finally, on March 17, 2000, the Movement leaders locked up about eight hundred of their most loyal followers in their special church building which they called the *Obwato bwa Ruhanga bw'Okujunwa* (God's Ark of Salvation), in Kanungu. After intense ritual prayers of repentance and self-purification, the Movement leaders had the Church building set on fire. The Movement leaders tragically sacrificed and ritually killed all their followers inside their "Ark of God's Salvation" as atonement to God and to transform them into God's holy saints through Christian martyrdom.

The event which had taken several months of careful planning by Fr. Dominic Kataribabo, as the Marian Movement's spiritual director, chaplain and high-priest, was meticulously executed within a few minutes. The petrol bomb fueled fire was so intense that most bodies were immediately burned to ashes. Nevertheless, these apparently tragic suicidal deaths, mass murders and martyrdoms were consistent with the Movement's teachings and practices as documented in their own handbook: *A Timely Message from Heaven: The End of the Present Times.*[52]

6. The Church Fire as Christian Mass Martyrdoms, Atonements, And a Holy Path to Heaven

Fr. Kataribabo chose fire as the preferred holy instrument to quickly kill and martyr the Movement members. He believed that fire was God's symbol that purified the world of evil by its light, heat, and consuming hot flames. Consequently, Fr. Kataribabo burned the supposed evil bodies of the Marian Movement members, so as to free the trapped souls of the saints. Death and destruction of the body were the holy means needed in order to liberate the souls from their evil imprisonment within the bodies in order to send the souls to God and his salvation in heaven.

It is significant to note that the Marian Movement had been preoccupied with fire as a means to symbolically and ritually cleanse their clothing, beddings, tools and other personal and community possessions. Subsequently, each Marian Movement member's important possessions had been discreetly branded and marked by fire, especially on the edges and fringes of clothing, beddings, utensils and tools.

On joining the Marian Movement, finger nails had been clipped, and hair was shaved off the head and the private parts. Then, these body parts were collected in a metal or ceramic container, mixed together and ceremoniously burned. The ashes had been collected and mixed with consecrated water. The mixture was then mixed with other secret ingredients. Some holy oil was added and the mixture was ritually consecrated by a priest.

Subsequently, the initiates were required to sacramentally drink and bathe in this consecrated mixture. This initiation ritual was performed in order to cleanse and exorcize the demonic spirits and evil forces from inside the body. The rest of the holy mixture, which was then referred to as "holy water," was used for ritual bathing of the whole body, or simply sprinkled on the body in the name of the Blessed Virgin Mary, the Mother of God, God the Father, the Son, and the Holy Spirit. Some of this holy water was also saved and ritually sprinkled on food or drinks before consuming them, or serving them to the other members of the Marian Movement.

This initiation ritual served like a renewal of the sacrament of Holy Baptism and was diligently performed to cleanse the body from evils associated with the body and it sensual desires, especially sexual gratification. It was performed as part of the Movement's cleansing ritual of initiation of new members into the Movement, as full members.

To the outsiders, these events were considered strange religious rituals and were used as evidence to affirm that the Marian Movement was a new deviant form of Catholicism and a dangerous Mariologist Christian cult. However, most of the outsiders and Marian Movement critics were themselves already prejudiced against the Marian leaders of the Movement and were neither culturally nor theologically well-informed on Marian traditions and rites of initiation into various religious or civic organizations, such as the *Opus Dei*, the Masons' Lodges and other secret societies.

Catholic Christians and other religious traditions, like some members of Judaism, still use sacred fires, as part of their religious symbolism, rituals and worship. But they are not considered cults. For instance, the ancient Hebrews slaughtered animals in the holy temple in Jerusalem as ritual atonements and sacrifices to God for forgiveness of sins. But Jews were not disparaged as being members of some "pagan cults." The Hebrew priests also used sacred fires and altars to perform atoning sacrifices of those animals in the holy temple. Yet, we do not degrade their practices as "pagan" or "magical cults."

Therefore, if we employ the same criteria to analyze the theologies, teachings and practices of the Catholic Church, including the MRTCG, we will become objective in our analysis of data and conclusions concerning the Marian Movement, and its teachings, practices and activities. This is especially required as one analyzes the Marian Movement's radical monastic practices, and extreme self-sacrifices in the form of celibacy, extreme fasting and ritual martyrdoms, as their ultimate holy obedience, good deeds of self-sacrifice and atonements to God for sins.

The Marian Movement's preoccupation with God's apocalyptic fire was rooted within the African Traditional Religion, philosophies and cultures. In many traditional African cultures, fire is regarded as a sacred gift from God. Therefore, according to these traditional and God-centered African cultures and world-view, fire is a sacred symbol for: God, royalty, peace (*obusingye*), warmth, divine protection, life (*amagara/kwo*[53]), spirit (*omwitsyo/Jok*[54]), and light in the darkness of life, virtue, kingship, honesty, peace, knowledge, and divine truth. The above is true in many African cultures and religions of West and East Africa.

In most areas of Uganda, *Kazooba/Cen*[55] (the Sun) is the term for God, as the ultimate heavenly Light, the cosmic Creator (*Nyamuhanga)* and fire that gives life, warmth and protection to all creation. In Nigeria, *Shango* as the God of fire and lightning is highly regarded and worshipped, as the source of light and enlightenment in the world.

In Southern Uganda, the volcanoes of the Birunga were considered the manifestations of God's sacred fires and wonders. The *Bachwezi Cult* is also symbolized by sacred fire and smoke. Mt. Ruwenzori's clouds and shining snowy caps on a clear day are also locally religiously viewed, as the divine holy symbols of God's *(Ruhanga)* presence, glory and spiritual "guiding light" to the peoples of the world. It is regarded as God's Holy Mountain, and holy temple or dwelling place, in the world.

The local people revered the Holy Mountain, in the same way, in which some Hebrews revered God on Mt Sinai, or the Masai revere God *(Ngai)* hidden in the clouds and snow of Mt. Kilimanjaro in Tanzania. As a result, the local people did not desecrate these mountains by climbing them. Instead, they both reverently prayed and worshipped God, while facing these holy mountains as God's cosmic holy temples and chosen dwelling, in the world.

Ordinary fire is also considered as a gift from God or the gods. In Uganda, as in ancient Egypt, God is associated with the Sun and its light. God is referred to as *Kazooba Nyamuhanga* (the Sun the Creative Principle/God). Like the Egyptian Pharaoh, in much of East Africa, especially in Uganda, the kings were also considered to be the temporal divine representatives of God in the world and they had sacred fires ritually lit and kept burning from their accession to the throne and throughout their reign.

These sacred royal fires were also symbolically put out when the king died. The temporarily interrupted cultural religio-political ritual of the sacred royal fire resumed when a new king was enthroned. For many Catholics, God and Christ were the new supernatural or cosmic rulers of the Church and the world. As such, their royal and sacred fire in forms of candles and holy electric lights were, ideally, to be kept lit in the sanctuaries of cathedrals, churches and wealthy homes, whose owners could afford to build sacred spaces or chapels and altars to the veneration or worship of Blessed Virgin Mary and Jesus, her son.

However, in the traditional temples, the priests were regarded as God's holy representatives in the community. They also kept sacred fires burning as God's symbol of life, guidance in the world, and protection in darkness of life, especially at night. In this respect, the sacred fire was the symbol of the Sun (*Kazooba Nyamuhanga*). Therefore, fire was a metaphor for God and holy mystical symbolism for divine revelation, truth, knowledge, and wisdom.

As a result of the above African cultural and traditional religious context, in which fire was God's symbol of holy presence, protection and guidance, the African Catholics used symbols of fire and candles, as effective symbols for

God's Holy Spirit. These symbols of fire are viewed as the visible power of God's purifying holy presence, ritual cleansing, healing, holiness, guidance, salvation and peace in the world of darkness and evil.

Subsequently, these African Catholics keep lots of candles in their homes at sacred altars at which the Blessed Virgin Mary is usually the center of illumination and attention, followed by a statue of Jesus on the cross or a crucifix. In addition, fire and firewood are essential commodities for the ordinary household. They are extremely valued by rural people because they have no access to affordable electricity.

Therefore, in rural Africa, like the Sun, fire is an essential resource for heating, lighting and cooking. Consequently, in African world view and traditions, the use of fire is a special divine gift, like language. Both fire and language are universally considered God's special divine gifts that are graciously bestowed, by God, upon human beings, and thereby, to effectively distinguish human beings, as God's own adopted children, from the rest of the animals and plants of which they were created to serve, as God's representatives and caretakers or stewards.

The above consideration was also partly why the MRTCG's monastic calls to denounce possessions and life in the physical world, as the corrupt and evil domain of the Devil, were rejected by the majority of the people. This also explains why the Marian Movement leader's apocalyptic prophecies and otherworldly sermons appealing for the rejection of the material world, were largely ineffective. The Marian Movement leaders' sermons calling sinners to obey the divine messages to repent and come to live a celibate life in the Marian Movement's monastic community, failed to attract many African Catholics. These Catholics also found the Marian Movement's vows of poverty, celibacy and rule of silence and prohibition of the use of verbal language, to be both absurd and unacceptable.

Within the traditional ontology, philosophy and world-view, language was central to humanity. It was the source of identity, information, means of communication and the basis of building social relationships, as well as a well-informed, and a viable community. In addition, like the Sun (*Eizooba*), which is the local cultural and religious symbol of God the Creator (*Kazooba Nyamuhanga*), life, and protection, fire has also gained additional mystical and symbolic value and mysteries associated with the Sun, the planets and the distant stars, almost akin to the ancient Oriental world-view and astrology. This similarity includes the African astrological system, where the planets and the stars determine some people's fate. Some people have tried to use these divine cosmic holy mysteries and mystical powers in combination with those of the African ancestral spirits in order to gain some perceived supernatural and mystical powers.

Some African traditional priests and magicians have claimed to possess the divine powers needed to perform miracles and other seemingly magical feats. These supernatural and divine religious activities include: supernatural healing by the priest's holy words, ritual healing prayers, healing by special touch, or laying of hands, and exorcism to cleanse people, livestock, homes, buildings, the community and the land from the pollution of evil, sin and witchcraft. They use their powers to cause harm to enemies and evil-doers and to heal diseases through exorcism, holy touch, prayers and medicines. Sacred water, fire and smoke are also used in exorcism.

Therefore, Fr. Kataribabo's used the traditional symbol of sacred fire, as God's fire and tool to purify the world and sinners, by burning away their perceived evil and sinful bodies. This concept was and usages of fire were also rooted in Greek dualism, Christianity and the African Traditional Religion. Fr. Kataribabo's idea and programs for the destruction of the supposed evil bodies by fire in order to cleanse and liberate the soul from evil were clearly based on his Greek dualistic philosophy and Christian dualistic theology of the body as evil and self-sacrificial death, or martyrdom as divine atonement to God.

Martyrdoms as voluntary self-sacrificial atonements to God were revered and desired as the ultimate moral and perfection that demonstrated the saints ultimate perfect love for God and absolute moral and spiritual surrender and obedience to God's will, as manifested in the self-sacrificial death of Christ on the cross. As such, the Marian Movement Catholic leaders viewed their own planned and impending self-sacrificial martyrdom, as a holy means to attain everlasting salvation and spiritual happiness, in a spiritual heaven.

The destruction of the supposed evil body was considered necessary holy procedure of liberation and redemption. Ritual martyrdoms and sacrificial destruction of the bodies were ritually performed, by Fr. Dominic Kataribabo, in order to free and cleanse the trapped souls, which were believed to be trapped or imprisoned in the evil bodies, cleanse them and send them to God in heaven. The liberated souls of the Marian Saints were sent to God, to be congratulated and rewarded with eternal life in peace and happiness. This ritual of atonement for sin through sacrificial death was also consistent with the African traditional theories of divine judgment for sin, cleansing holy punishment, human sacrifice and atonement.

These theories of atonement and rituals of sacrifice were wide-spread in pre-colonial Africa. They were central components of the African Traditional Religion. They are still practiced many Africans. They are essential components of the authentic African traditional religious, cultural values, healing procedures, peace-making, and philosophical and general African world-view. For instance, in Uganda, virgin or child sacrifice is still illegally ritually practiced, today.[56]

More importantly, self-sacrificial and ritual deaths were also accepted by some devout Marian Catholics because it was explained to them within the complex traditional Catholic theology of sin, sacrifice, atonement, martyrdom and sainthood. Consequently, these apparently new Catholic dogmas of sin and atonement made much sense to these Africans. They already believed in the traditional Catholic theological belief and Pre-Vatican II doctrine of Purgatory as a place of atonement, where the sinners had to endure the torment of God's purifying fire before they could be considered pure and morally holy enough to be admitted into heaven. In this redemptive capacity, Fr. Kataribabo was acting as God's high-priest and messiah, or agent of God's salvation, when he master-minded the program for ritual killings, self-sacrificial deaths and martyrdoms of his followers, as acceptable holy "living sacrifices"and ultimate atonements to God for sins (Rom. 12:1-2).

Within the above complex African religious and cultural context and religious understanding, it is clear that Fr. Kataribabo used sacred or "Mary's fire" as God's mediated redemptive device to save God's saints from a supposed perishing world and to instantaneously transport them from the world to God in heaven. To this end, the intense fire had been carefully planned by Fr. Kataribabo and he accelerated the fire with strategically placed crude petrol bombs and sulphuric acid containers inside the church building. He designed and planned this self-sacrificial death and martyrdom, to be as quick and painless as possible. As their spiritual guide and high-priest, Fr. Kataribabo made sure that he remained with his flock on their fiery path to Heaven.

Despite the false rumors by skeptics, and speculations by the anti-Marian Movement people that Fr. Kataribabo, along with Kibwetere and Mwerinde, had maliciously set their followers on fire and fled into exile after defrauding them of their money and possessions, it is now believed that these controversial MRTCG leaders also died along with their loyal Movement members in the Kanungu church inferno. This is now an academic debate whether the innocent members of the Movement members truly died as Christian martyrs.

Some Catholics who knew the Movement members and their leaders believe these Marian Movement members were truly Christian moral and spiritual perfectionists who lived an exemplarily holy monastic life, and finally, died as Christian martyrs for their faith. They believe that the Movement members were obedient to God's call to sacrifice their own lives as living sacrifices and holy atonements to God (Rom. 12:1-2; Mk. 8:34-9:1). Therefore, the apocalyptic Marian Movement leaders did not consider their actions as making them either guilty of murder or suicide, which would have violated their own beliefs, moral practices and one of the Ten Commandments: "Thou shall not kill."[57]

Accordingly, it is possible to view the events the Marian Movement's apparent tragic events from the Movement members' positive view the Marian Movement ritual murders as Christian self-sacrificial deaths in atonement for sins and Christian martyrdoms. From that positive perspective, one can also see how Fr. Kataribabo perceived the Kanungu church inferno as a redemptive act of God's purifying fire and tool of salvation, by burning away all human impurities.

According to the above empathetic perspective, one could probably be able to understand why Fr. Kataribabo, a well-educated and senior Catholic priest carefully planned and finally kindled on Friday morning, March 17, 2000, in order to burn away the supposed evil and sinful physical bodies. This drastic religious ritual was carried out in a Catholic sacramental faith. That is, it was sacramentally performed as an apocalyptic messianic and mystical divine attempt to liberate the souls of the saints, and to enable them to ascend to heaven and gain eternal salvation in spiritual fellowship and union with God.

The above being the case, from an objective perspective, one can then conclude that there was neither a malicious nor a criminal intent connected with the Movement's tragic activities of mass ritual martyrdoms which the public and the world have been in a rush to judge, reject, denounce and demonize in the public media as "criminal mass murders," and "cult suicides." In the future, when studies of the Marian Movement and its activities have become distanced from the present painful emotional involvement and losses of people today, it is possible that the Movement members will be reevaluated and may even, finally, become ecclesiastically accepted, appreciated and hailed as our Third Millennium Christian Martyrs.

7. African Culture, Politics and Objections to Exhume the Dead

Within the African traditional cultures and correlative religions, any unnatural deaths, such as those relating to abortion, murder, and suicide were culturally negatively viewed as great evils and thus, prohibited. In most African cultures, these kinds of activities and unnatural forms of death are still considered serious cultural, moral and religious taboos. As a result, these taboos are still feared and generally avoided. This is particularly true for both Southern and Western Ugandan traditional cultures and religious traditions where the MRTCG was originally founded. These traditions and taboos underlie the central teachings of the Marian Movement and its ritual practices.

Both Keledonia Mwerinde and Joseph Kibwetere were born into the very conservative African cultures and the Roman Catholic Church teachings, which strongly denounced the following:

- sex out of marriage covenant
- elective abortions

- homosexuality
- suicide and murders.

The above were condemned as societal evil sources of social, ritual, religious, moral and mystical pollution, defilement or uncleanliness and sins. For many

Catholics, some of these sins and evils were removed by confession, penance and rituals of atonement or indulgences. However, many of them also consulted the African traditional priests (*Bafumu/Waganga*), healers and elders in quest of ritual purifications, atonement, healing and reconciliation with God.

In many African communities, especially in the rural areas, African traditional, cultural and religious rituals were often performed to remove the perceived societal ritual pollution. It was considered necessary to ask the priests to perform rituals of atonement, cleansing and healing for the communities where these evils, especially suicide and murders had taken place. Rituals of purification and atonement were traditionally performed to cleanse the people of the cultural and moral pollution and evils, which were associated with the moral, spiritual, social and cultural state of both personal and collective defilement.[58]

For instance, in the case of the Luo, especially the Acholi, the traditional court, the *Mato Put*, was convened by the chiefs (*Rwots)* and the elders, who tried the culprits and passed sentence on the guilty party. Punishment proscribed for serious offenses, required the guilty party to pay a fine and bring atonement (*Tum)* in the form of a sacrificial goat or cow (*Gitum*), for ritual sacrifice (*Teyer*), and reconciliation with the aggrieved party, as both parties feasted together and consumed the atonement and sacrificial animal (*Gitum*).

Many well-educated African urban dwellers sometimes secretly return to their own original rural villages where they were born in quest of ritual cleansing, atonement for sins and healing by the traditional priests and healers. These educated Christians secretly perform these ritual cleansing, healing and atonement rituals, including sacrificing to God and the ancestors because they fear to be condemned by their religious leaders as superstitious Christians, who still practice the African Traditional Religion, which they denounce and derogatorily refer to as "paganism" and "ancestor worship."

Some of the well-educated people also secretly belonged to the Marian Movement. Many of these devotees of the Blessed Virgin Mary secretary traveled to Kanungu in faith and hope of miraculously ascending to heaven on March 17, 2000. As a result of the Marian Movement's desire for secrecy and censorship of information, including memberships in the Movement, we do not fully know how many people belonged to the MRTCG.

However, the membership is estimated to be between 15,000 and 20,000, including the members, who were not yet fully initiated as full members of the Marian Movement. The full members who had sold their property and given the proceeds to the poor or to the Marian Movement leaders and wanted to live a monastic life within the Movement's monastic communities were less than 6,000. Those who died in the Movement are estimated between 2,500 and 3,500.

There were also conflicting cultural, religious and political reasons, as there were many differing figures of how many people died in the Kanungu church inferno. Due to religious and political embarrassment in the public media, and for traditional cultural reasons, there was a strong political desire to keep the numbers of the dead as low as possible. Finally, this political desire drove the Government of Uganda's authorities to issue court orders to stop further police, or private exhumations of the remaining mass graves.

Furthermore, according to the traditional cultures and religions of the people in Western and Southern Uganda, suicide was regarded as a terrible moral and religious sin that polluted the person committing suicide, along with that person's respective family and community.

Consequently, not many people or organizations, including the Catholic Church, were willing to be identified with the supposed mass suicide victims. As a result, there were only a few courageous people, like Peter Bamurumba of Kakoba, Mbarara that courageously admitted that their own close family members and relatives had either perished in the Kanungu church inferno, or in other ritual deaths and martyrdoms of the Marian Movement. This reluctance to admit this reality was partly due to the fact that the Mbarara Catholic Church hierarchy and the local media had vilified the Marian Movement and its members as evil and dangerous cult members. For instance, the media first reported these Marian Movement tragic deaths on March 17, 2000, and strongly denounced them on their special and front page news headlines, as evil and "cult mass suicides."[59]

The public media, including the television, newspapers, and radio news broadcasts, sensationalized the tragic event and reported the story in special programs. They both erroneously and misleadingly reported that the MRTCG members were excommunicated Catholics, who were misled by defrocked Catholic priests. The media also misled the public by erroneously reporting that the MRTCG was a Catholic splinter church, led by Joseph Kibwetere and that it had degenerated into a "dangerous cult" and that "the cult Movement," had finally, committed mass murders and suicides.[60]

However, many of Catholics, who also venerated the Blessed Virgin Mary were very distressed and largely remained silent. However, many Ugandans were outraged by the tragic events and very strongly condemned the Marian Movement leaders for tragically misleading the followers into selling their property. They believed that the Marian Movement leaders had defrauding their followers of their money and property, and finally, killed them in an attempt to silence them. But they had allegedly deceived their loyal followers convincing them that they were being sent to salvation in heaven, of which they had been promised, when they joined the Marian Movement.

Many Catholics were in a state of denial and refused to accept that these tragic events had actually taken place within their Church. They could not believe or accept that these Marian martyrdoms were truly part of an extremist, fundamentalist and apocalyptic Marian Movement. They were willing to believe the false rumors that Fr. Kataribabo, and other Catholic priests in the Movement were actually both excommunicated and defrocked Catholic priests.

However, they had not yet been excommunicated. They still validly sacramentally functioned as Catholic priests, who consecrated and administered both true and valid Catholic sacraments. They celebrated the Eucharist and baptized many children as new Catholics and welcomed them along with their parents into the apocalyptic Marian Movement. They also built an elementary school in Kanungu to take care of the needs of these hundreds of children. Consequently, they outnumbered the adults, who died in the Marian Movement.

According to the eyewitness accounts and the Kanungu Police officers, there were several hundreds of children at the Marian Movement headquarters in Kanungu. Some of them had gone to a school there, although it had been officially closed by the State, in 1998. The school was closed for health reasons, and teaching irregular curricula, including moral education and doomsday religious revelations, at the expense of a state authorized standard school curriculum.

Subsequently, these hundreds of children, along with their parents and other relatives, also tragically died in the church inferno. However, their small and fragile skulls and those of smaller adults had been completely burned, and reduced to mere heaps of ashes. Subsequently, the eyewitness saw many uncountable small heaps of ashes. Some of these small heaps were on top of each other and were mingled together with some skulls of adults. These ashes and skulls were all over the place in the church building.

However, most of the victims' badly charred bodies and heaps of ashes were found close to the windows and doors. This tragic scene provided some evidence that some people had actually sought to flee the deadly fire, but had found the church windows nailed down and doors locked.

These heaps of uncountable ashes were not taken into account, and were not part of the officially counted and published number of 534 people, as the official number of people, who had died in the church inferno in Kanungu. It is clear that the actual number of the people, who perished in this tragic church fire, as the Marian Movement's gate to the holy path of martyrdom, salvation and quick entry into heaven, were far more than the officially estimated and published number, based on the numbers found in the register and number of intact skulls that were counted by the Kanungu police.

Handling decomposing bodies was hazardous and a health risk. Counting the dead was a gruesome, nauseating and difficult task. These were culturally troubling and gruesome tasks for which the police officers were not adequately trained or prepared to handle. The local police officers were also not properly trained or equipped to perform forensic examinations needed for identifying the dead. Moreover, they saw no point of taking the risks of handling decaying and smelly bodies, or carrying out a thorough investigation of finding out, who died and the causes of deaths, since they had already concluded that the Marian Movement members were the victims of cult mass murders. They had also speculated that the MRTCG were dangerous cult leaders, who had either both defrauded and then, killed their loyal followers, or had all committed "cult ritual mass suicides."

Many Ugandans became convinced that the Marian Movement's mass deaths were similar to those of the Rev. Jim Jones' *People's Temple* that took place in 1987, in Jonestown, Guyana. They were not interested in establishing the accuracy of the numbers of people killed, and how they actually died, or who killed them and why. They wanted to have the smelly remains of the badly charred and rapidly decomposing bodies removed and buried, without any further bureaucratic delays.

The Kanungu local area residents wanted this task to be accomplished, as soon as possible, in order to prevent a health crisis due to the overpowering stench of burned and decomposing human flesh and flies. The bodies that had been trampled and covered by others had not been completely burned and had begun to stink, as they quickly decomposed in the tropical heat.

Due to both national and international public embarrassment, the Ugandan Government, finally, and hastily ordered the remains of the Marian Movement victims to be quickly removed from the burnt-out church-building, and buried in a mass grave that had been dug nearby, on the premises using a bulldozer and prisoners, to accomplish the task quickly. The Kanungu government authorities and townspeople approved this speedy government action to remove and bury the dead.

However, during this quick process to get rid of the rotting bodies, the dead were quickly buried without any serious attempts made to make some forensic identification of the dead. There were no attempts made even to verify the alleged Marian Movement's criminal murder victims. This is mainly because the Government of Uganda and the police lacked the necessary forensic expertise to identify the Marian victims.

The Ugandan Government also lacked the necessary expertise to fully investigate how the Marian Movement members were killed, and why many of them were killed in some apparently ritualistic methods, or why they were buried naked in mass graves. They also lacked the means to preserve the bodies and body parts for identification at a later time, when such a task became feasible. What was important for the police and Kanungu Town government officials was the overriding immediate sanitary need to eliminate the sickening and overpowering stench of burnt and rotting human flesh, and to prevent an outbreak of disease in Kanungu Town and the neighboring areas.

In addition, there were no real religious, cultural or political incentives to investigate the reasons and causes of the Marian Movement members' deaths. Additionally, there were also no social or political reasons to delay the mass burial of the charred bodies. The Marian Movement members' Catholic family members and close relatives feared to come forward and claim their relatives because the Mbarara Catholic hierarchy had disowned the Marian Movement victims. They feared that they may incur Archbishop Bakyenga's disapproval and religious sanction, if they demanded church funerals for their Marian Movement Catholic victims. As a result, most of these confused Catholics decided not to show the usual emotional and customary religious and cultural care for their deceased relatives.

Given this awkward cultural, ecclesiastical or religious and social scenario, President Museveni's Government officials did not want to offend and alienate the Catholic Church leaders. Nevertheless, they did not know what to do with the unidentifiable and unclaimed human remains. Therefore, the Government buried them in one mass grave, and organized the an ecumenical religious service for the funeral service, which was attended by the Bishops Robert Gay of Kabale Catholic Diocese and three Anglican Church bishops, including Bishop Wilson Ntegyereize, of the local Kinkizi Anglican Church Diocese.

Being impoverished, the Government of Uganda had also lacked the necessary resources to hire foreign forensic experts to investigate the mass murders, and later, carefully exhume the graves and identify the bodies, body parts or other remains of the dead in order to return them to their respective families for proper funeral ceremonies and cultural or religious burial rites.

Ultimately, in Uganda, there were no qualified forensic experts that could competently carry out the needed task to identify the badly charred bodies in Kanungu, and to identify the other decomposing bodies. After the Kanungu tragedy, there was more need to identify hundreds of other Marian Movement bodies that were later found and exhumed from mass graves at different locations where the Marian Movement had residential stations and meeting camps as indicated below.

Due to a lack of the necessary funds and time, the Government of Uganda was unable to hire some expensive foreign forensic experts to come and help with the important task of carrying out the proper tests needed for the correct identification of the charred bodies and body parts. These forensic experts could have accomplished this expensive and time-consuming task by using some advanced technological tools, such as DNA sequencing and analysis, to identify the remains. This procedure would have required a lot of fiscal planning and funds to enable the process of the proper refrigeration of the human remains, cooperation and collection of samples of DNA from surviving close relatives of the fire victims and others exhumed at other Marian Movement centers and leaders' homes in Rukungiri, Bushenyi, Gaba near Kampala City.

The Government also suspended the exhumation of bodies at other sites, including Kanungu, because of the lack of safe and sanitary means to handle the bodies. The deployment of unprotected, barefooted and gloveless prisoners to dig up decaying bodies had already caused an uproar in some public circles in Uganda and much criticism from the international community.

Some vocal human rights agencies criticized the Government of Uganda for the deployment of unprotected prisoners to dig up mass graves, and handle decomposing corpses with their bare hands. The prisoners were forced to physically retrieve and handle medically hazardous, decaying, naked corpses from deep pit latrines. The police casually counted the badly decomposed and very smelly naked corpses before directing the prisoners to re-bury them, in new mass graves. Degradingly, the bodies were re-buried naked as before, without any coffins or wrapping and traditional ceremonies or prayers. They were just thrown into the pit and covered with soil.

However, those bodies that were too decomposed to pull from the pit latrines without disintegrating into pieces were left to rot there. Subsequently, these prisoners became very sick, and died of mysterious diseases. Nevertheless, the Government of Uganda refused to accept any responsibility for the alleged human rights violations, abuses and deaths of these prisoners. Some of these unfortunate prisoners had been sentenced to a few months of jail time for petty crimes such as stealing chickens and goats in the local village. But they had ended with a death sentence when they were forced to exhume dead bodies and re-bury them without proper protection, such as gloves, boots and other protective body attire.

Ultimately, both the Catholic Church leaders and the Government of Uganda officials were greatly embarrassed by the high numbers of people, who had died in the Marian Movement. They saw no point for further exhumation of bodies that had been ritually killed and buried in mass graves by the leaders of *The Movement for the Restoration of the Ten Commandments of God*. However, some political critics and skeptical members of the public in Uganda believed and voiced their feelings that the Government of Uganda was trying to cover up the fact that too many people had actually been killed by the leaders of the Marian Movement of Uganda.

Furthermore, the Government of Uganda was to some significant extent to blame as being negligent and responsible for some of the MRTCG's tragic activities. For instance, the Government of Uganda can be justifiably blamed for some of the Marian Movement's human rights abuses and mass murders. This is because the Government of Uganda ignored the warning letter of Mr. Kamacherere, the RDC (Resident District Commissioners) for Rukungiri and Kanungu, stating that the MRTCG was a dangerous cult.[61] The Government of

Uganda had both supported and officially licensed the Movement to operate officially within the country as a moral educational agent as well as both a developmental and religious organization. In addition, the government had failed to monitor and evaluate the activities of the Marian Movement, especially given the very extreme and alarming nature of the apocalyptic and doomsday teachings for the impending fiery end of the world and divine destruction of all sinners, who failed to repent and join the Marian Movement.

The critics pointed out that the Government of Uganda officials in Kampala, had unwisely licensed the MRTCG as an NGO (Non-Government Organization), despite the formal protest of Mr. Kamacherere, the District Resident Commissioner (RDC) for Rukungiri District, where the Marian Movement was officially located in 1999, before Kanungu became a separate district in 2002.[62]

Many people believed that the Government of Uganda did not want this information to come out. They believed that the Government of Uganda refused to become accountable for the Marian Movement's tragedies and failure to protect its innocent citizens, especially the children, from preventable harm and premature death. The public was critical of its government official because these horrible crimes took place without the Government of Uganda security agencies, such as the police and intelligence officers knowing about it before hand and appropriately acting, in time, to prevent the tragic deaths.

The Government of Uganda's officials were justifiably worried that the public would blame them for failing to act appropriately according to the mandates of the Constitution to protect the citizens of Uganda and prevent these mass murders, that were committed by religious extremists in the holy name of God and the attainment of salvation as a better life in heaven. In any case, the prevalence of violence and institutional or state corruption which the Movement denounced were still visible realities. As expected, many people in Uganda blamed the Government of Uganda for corruption, incompetence, and the demonstrated failure to protect the public, especially the defenseless children and the less well-educated citizens from the dangers of exploitation by:

- some new religious extremists,
- fraudulent leaders,
- economic opportunists,
- religious frauds,
- new messianic holy warriors,
- dangerous religious leaders,
- criminal cult leaders,
- child molesters,[63]
- human sacrifice,
- mass murderers and criminals.

Joseph Kony, Joseph Kibwetere and Keledonia Mwerinde were particularly singled out as these dangerous religious leaders to be protected from. Kibwetere and Mwerinde were accused of having falsely posed as God's new prophets, saints, visionaries, messiahs and agents of the Blessed Virgin Mary. They were falsely accused by the skeptical public of claiming to be God's chosen and special apocalyptic messiahs and founders of the Marian Movement or organization as the divine path of holiness, moral perfection and gate to heaven, whereas, in actuality, these leaders were merely greedy and clever religious frauds, con artists and mass murderers.

The Ugandan public, especially some aggrieved, and embarrassed devout Catholics, were relentless in the condemnation of these radical lay Catholic leaders of movements, like Alice Lakwena, Joseph Kony, Joseph Kibwetere and Keledonia Mwerinde. These Catholic Church-based violent and radical religio-political movements were disowned by the Catholic Church hierarchy because they either resulted in violence and wars, or led to self-sacrificial martyrdom and premature deaths.

There were some of the few officially identified Marian Movement's campuses as sites for investigation and exhumation of mass graves. The Movement's campuses and camps were also the locations where the Movement's secret rituals of and self-sacrificial deaths and martyrdoms took place. In these locations, some hundred of decomposing naked bodies were found or were exhumed from the Marian Movement's secret mass graves, until the exhumations were suspended and later, prohibited by the embarrassed and ashamed officials of the Government of Uganda. The official records of these exhumed bodies were recorded as follows:

- 500-800 badly charred bodies and body parts recovered from the Kanungu church after the intense fire. (The high intensity of the fire cremated children's bodies to ashes. Therefore, the accurate count was mainly for adults or registered residents. But most people who perished in Kanungu came the day before and were not registered as resident Marian Movement members in Kanungu);
- 6 naked bodies were recovered from deep and dark pit latrines in Kanungu;
- 10-20 naked bodies were too decomposed and broken up to count or recover from deep pit latrines in Kanungu;
- 20-30 naked bodies believed to be buried in the foundations of the buildings in Kanungu;
- 45-60 bodies are buried in the Movement's cemetery in Kanungu. The causes of death are not known;
- 153 naked bodies exhumed in Rutooma, Rukungiri at Verentina Busharizi's home (house floors, car-garages, and banana groves). They were classified as follows:
- 59 children
- 94 adults
- The majority of these victims were Catholic females.
- 155 naked bodies exhumed at Fr. Dominic Kataribabo's home in Bunyaruguru, Bushenyi.[64]
- The mass graves were found in Fr. Kataribabo's house floors, car garage foundation and banana plantation. The police and Uganda Human Rights Commission classified the 155 bodies found at Fr. Kataribabo's home as follows:
- 22 male adults
- 59 female adults
- 35 male juveniles

- 37 female juveniles
- 2 sex undetermined (badly decomposed bodies)
- 81 naked bodies exhumed from Joseph Nyamurinda's home in Ishaka, Bushenyi.
- 56 females (no ages provided)
- 25 males (mainly children)
- 55 naked bodies exhumed in Buziga, Kampala at Fr. Katraibabo's rented Movement house and Kampala Movement Station. The bodies were buried in the basement and car- garage floors. They were classified by the police as follows:
- 22 adult females
- 15 adult males
- 10 juvenile females
- 8 juvenile males.[65]

It is clear that if the Government of Uganda had not prohibited the identifications of other mass graves and their exhumation, the numbers of the dead members of the MRTCG would have exceeded 3,000. The total numbers of deaths within the MRTCG are the highest recorded of any Christian cult and new religious moments in history. It far exceeded the 917 people, who perished in the Rev. Jim Jones' *Peoples Temple's* tragic mass murders and suicides in 1978, in the remote rural jungles of Jonestown, in Guyana.

The police investigators, religious and political leaders, as well as the public, were stunned that the tragic deaths occurred within a Catholic Marian Movement. As a result, the Catholic Church tried to distance itself from the Movement leaders and their followers by claiming that they had been excommunicated for disobedience against the bishops and teaching false prophecies and promoting dangerous moral practices in the name of monasticism. The public was also puzzled by the fact that these ritual mass murders, or martyrdoms, both secretly and quietly took place in populated rural areas and the city of Kampala, over a period of weeks in February and early March 2000, without the police, neighbors and Marian Movement members' relatives knowing about it. They wondered and asked how these tragic events could have taken place within the community without arousing any suspicions of strange activities occurring among them.

In addition, many people were also puzzled by the fact that the Marian Movement members' deaths were self-evidently both ritualistic and cult-like. This is the case since the Marian Movement members' were ritually killed, as religious martyrs, or offered as living sacrifices to God in hope of atonement, and their bodies were stripped of all clothing. Then, they were buried completely naked,[66] and secretly at night. They were buried in hidden and unmarked mass graves, which had been secretly excavated in houses' foundations, basements, car-garages, banana groves and other secret places.

As a result of these mysterious Marian members' ritual deaths and culturally unusual burials, many Africans wondered, believed and speculated that the Marian Movement was a new Marian Catholic deadly cult and that was the main reason why these deaths had occurred, especially in this very secretive, mysterious and ritualistic manner. Later, they unconsciously believed that their speculations were the actual truths, despite the fact that there was no any credible evidence to verify and support them. But then, their curiosity was not an intellectual quest for the truth, but rather the search of meanings of the MRTCG's tragic events.

Subsequently, many people in Uganda and the global community came to the erroneous, but meaningful and even satisfying conclusion based on the mass media's distorted coverage of the Marian Movement and its activities, that in reality, the Marian "Movement was a dangerous and criminal murderous cult."[67] As such, the Marian Movement was inadvertently "exorcized" and banished from the true Catholic Church and even Christianity, as a whole. For them, the Marian Movement had ceased to be part of the true Roman Catholic Church or its traditions. But, that was an erroneous lay people's conclusion, or that of the prejudiced Catholic leadership, and did not fully take into account the complex nature of the Movement as a Marian moral reformist Movement rooted in the Benedictine monastic Catholic religious tradition. Kibwetere and Mwerinde were just Co-Abbots of the Movement and not bishops.

However, the real answers to why and how the Marian Movement members were quietly killed in a ritualistic manner, and in such great numbers, without causing commotion, or sounding an alarm, are extremely complex. The correct answers are also difficult to accept or believe. This is partly because they are rooted in the traditional Catholic Christian teachings on faith in God, sin, atonement for sin, sacrifice, martyrdom, holiness, and divine salvation as the spiritual attainment of a better and a happier life in heaven. The apocalyptic Marian devotees wanted to ascend into heaven to attain this promised divine salvation and eternal happiness which the Catholic Church preached and the MRTCG leaders promised to deliver with the help of God through the Blessed Virgin Mary.

Therefore, these Marian devotees came willingly to the Movement leaders. They wanted to be sent directly to heaven. To this end they were convinced by Fr. Kataribabo, the Movement's main theologian, Spiritual Director and chaplain, that they could attain salvation through ritual martyrdom. The adults were willing participants in this process. They may have even helped Fr. Kataribabo to perform these ritual murders as holy forms of death and martyrdom. The faithful members may have also helped to dig and bury their friends in these secret mass graves. Secondly, the Movement members were stripped naked after death in order to inspect the body from the head to the toes, in order to make sure that the member was not a secret worshipper of the Devil and the follower of the Beast who tattooed his followers with an indelible identification mark of "666."

If the evil mark of the "Beast" or Devil had been found, the Marian Movement member's body would undergo ritual cleansing through exorcism and then the body would be cremated and the ashes disposed of in a manner that would not contaminate the rest of the bodies. The other cultural and magical reason for stripping the bodies naked may have originated with Keledonia Mwerinde. Among some Bakiga traditional death rituals and superstitions, bodies were buried with some metal or other magical objects (protective charms/*orugisha*) that would prevent the resurrection of the body, and magically inhibit the separation of the spirit (*omuzimu*) from the body to return to haunt the living.

Since the Marian Movement's ritual deaths and martyrdoms were designed to kill the body and free the spirit, thus allowing it to ascend to heaven, therefore, it was considered culturally important to remove all possible physical impediments, cultural, magical or spiritual hindrances that may interfere with the liberation of the soul from the body. In order to accomplish this cultural and religious objective, the Marian Movement members' clothing and jewelry were completely removed and burned. Ideally, the body itself would have been burned or cremated in order to destroy any possible spiritual or physical impediments hidden on or in it, including the Devil's ownership symbol and tattoo of "666." However, this was difficult to do without arousing suspicion from curious neighbors and the police, except within the privacy of their Kanungu church and the inferno, on March 17, 2000.

Therefore, this careful procedure of stripping and burning of the body was carried out to ensure that the clothing or the body did not contain metal objects or other items that would accidentally serve as *orugisha* (magical protection); and thus, prevent the desired effective redemption through Christian martyrdom, and holy death, as the intended physical liberation of the soul from the body and the world, to be sent to God in heaven.

It was culturally believed that these magical devices (*engisha*) would keep the body and spirit inseparably bound together in the grave and on Earth. This magical ritual was performed by some people in Western Uganda to their hated relatives' bodies. This was done when they did not want the souls of their hateful or hated relatives to be liberated from the body and the grave, and come back into the community of the living, to haunt, retaliate and torment the living relatives, who had wronged them, before they died. Since in most African traditional religions, there was no concept of hellfire, as God's judgment and punishment for the evil-doers, the evil-doers received their judgment and hell or punishment, while they were still alive. As such, the departed had a right to return and punish the errant members of the community. That was an African form of divine judgment, justice and "living in hell."

Consequently, to prevent the dead from returning to punish the living for their sins, the *engisha*, were used to weigh them down and keep them imprisoned in their graves. The *engisha* or metal objects were magically placed on the dead body or placed in their clothing and coffins or burial mats. The magical ritual and intentions were to magically bind, confine and weigh down, what Prof. John Mbiti described in his famous book, *African Religions and Philosophy*, as the "living-dead." As such, confining and keeping the malevolent spirit or soul from being detached from the body or leaving the grave and therefore, coming to haunt the living relatives.

Therefore, according to this local African traditional cultural beliefs and religious tradition, unless the *engisha* (magical objects) were completely removed and destroyed, they would effectively prevent a spiritual process for complete separation of the soul/spirit from the body, and thereby, effectively nullify and sabotage the Marian Movement leaders' spiritual and physical efforts to liberate the soul and send it to God in heaven.

Therefore, it became a routine procedure for the MRTCG's bodies to be stripped completely naked, and searched for hidden objects, tattoos or marks of the Devil, especially the dreaded number: "666." Contaminated bodies were identified, isolated, exorcised of the demonic forces of evil, cleansed by sprinkling on of consecrated water, or ritual bath in holy water. Subsequently, the body was either burned or thrown into a deep pit.

On joining the Marian Movement members were required to remove and surrender any remaining clothing, ear rings or wedding rings, necklaces or other objects, except the crucifixes made of wood. They were given simple habits or uniforms to wear. Most of them had also surrendered their shoes and walked barefoot. When, they were ritually killed or martyred, their naked bodies were clandestinely buried in trenches dug in the ground. These naked bodies were buried without any form of covering or wrapping, such as a sheet, blanket or mat. It was a literal form of "dust to dust and ashes to ashes," which many Catholics would have heard, ceremoniously pronounced by the priest on Ash Wednesday, during the ritual of imposition of ashes on their foreheads in the form of the cross of Christ.

However, the religious leaders and politicians were embarrassed by the new apocalyptic and eschatological Marian Moral Reform Movement's radical doomsday teachings and ritual practices. They were very distressed by the Marian Movement's tragic secretive activities and tragic self-sacrificial ritual deaths. They were not ready to investigate and learn if there were some sound or acceptable religious, pastoral, political or cultural reasons for their Marian teachings, monasticism and alleged cult-like apocalyptic activities. Subsequently, the Marian Catholic Moral Reform Movement was reduced from a mainline Catholic Church affiliation and degraded to a lower and inconsequential status of a new religious sec, as well as vilified and condemned as a "cult."

Nevertheless, the erroneous vilification of the Marian Movement as a "religious cult," is damaging to the Marian tradition, but does not change the real truth and objective facts concerning Mwerinde and Kibwetere's Catholic Marian Movement in East Africa. The apocalyptic Marian Movement both started and ended as a Marian Apocalyptic Moral Reform Movement within the Catholic Church and the leaders of the Movement maintained that they were true and obedient Roman Catholics who only had conflicts with local bishops and had appealed to Rome for intervention. Since Rome did not officially act to excommunicate the Catholic priests of the Marian Movement, they believed that they were still in good standing as Catholic priests until the Pope, in Rome, had adjudicated their case.

8. New Religious and Cultural Answers for the Marian Movement's Rituals and Self-Sacrificial Deaths

Some of the main objectives for this study include providing some new important answers to the significant, but unanswered questions, which were originally raised by the Makerere University research team, in 2000, in their research report, shortly after the Kanungu inferno.[68] These important questions were raised by the Makerere Research Team and the contexts of those questions have been answered in the extensive research for this book. Their main observations and the unanswered questions were summarized and stated in their well-researched academic report as follows:

> The Kanungu cult saga leaves behind a lot to be researched. In it [The Marian Movement] we see a group of people, which started it. And it reached its climax and demised in a most tragic manner. There are a number of questions which remained unanswered:
> - Was it deliberate murder, suicide or salvation?
> - The group called itself: *The Movement for Restoration of the Ten Commandments of God.* Was it just a movement within the Catholic Church or an independent "new religion?"
> - How did Ceredonia [Keledonia] Mwerinde, a woman with such a history [as a prostitute], change overnight to be used as a vessel through which God conveyed His message of salvation to humanity?
> - How did Mwerinde, a primary four [fourth elementary school grade] dropout, manage to direct a movement composed of various people including priests and other professionals?
> - How far can we go to ascertain the truth in the Marian or other messianic or prophetic movement leaders' claims, including Lakwena, Kibwetere, Mwerinde and Kony? Were their claims God's authentic revelations or hallucinations or mere fraudulent claims?
> - Why did such a movement start and end at the time it did and in such a manner?
> - What role did corruption and the HIV/AIDS pandemic in East Africa play in the rise of religious movements in East Africa?

- What roles did corruption and political repression play in the rise and teachings of the liberation movements in East Africa?
- How can we explain the mass killings associated with the [Marian] Movement, especially the mass graves which were later found, after the gruesome tragedies of March 17, 2000?[69]

The questions posed above are important for the understanding of the Marian Movement and its mission. These are some of the central questions, which remained unanswered, by the Makerere University Research Team that have been extensively answered in this book.[70]

This book presents field research data and its analysis from a multi-disciplinary approach. The events are analyzed within their historical, cultural, political, socioeconomic moral, theological, philosophical and ecclesiastical backgrounds and contexts in order to provide some definitive and important answers to the above and other similar questions. This book was partly written to provide answers the important cultural, religious, anthropological, philosophical, political and historical questions, and hopefully solves some puzzles concerning the Marian Movement's teachings, practices and tragic self-sacrificial deaths. This field research also corrects some errors and public misrepresentations of the Marian Movement in media, especially in the sensationalist newspaper reports, and some of the earlier publications that were based on those prejudiced, erroneous and misleading newspaper reports and articles.

The Catholic Marian Movement was both misleadingly and erroneously referred to as "a cult" or "a new religion" by its enemies or the misinformed public. The Catholic hierarchy in Mbarara was reluctant to correct these errors because it had persecuted the Movement and tried to get rid of it before the Kanungu tragedies. Inadvertently, the media was effectively employed the Catholic Church hierarchy in Mbarara to accomplish what it had sought to do by interdictions of the Catholic Marian Movement in May 1992, but had failed. That was, to vilify the Marian Movement, and excommunicate the Movement and its leadership, and disassociate it from the Roman Catholic Church, of which the Catholic Marian Movement leaders and their followers had so tenaciously clung to, claiming to be its God's appointed, apocalyptic, moral and spiritual new center and reformers.[71]

In reality, it was neither of those simplistic and sensationalist silly caricatures. The Marian Movement was part of the Roman Catholic Church, and was continuing the controversial Catholic traditions of the nonconformist Marian visions and devotion. The canons and laws of the Catholic Church were also taken seriously into account, including the regulations, Episcopal and sacerdotal powers, and procedures regarding the requirement of Church's authority for administration of sacraments by Catholic priests, and the Catholic bishops' pastoral powers, including the powers for oversight of ecclesiastical procedures for disciplining the disobedient and errant priests, and the excommunication of lay Catholics and interdiction of priests. These processes were not completed by the time of the Kanungu church inferno.

Nevertheless, if the Marian Movement leaders had remained patient, their ecclesiastical status and teachings could have positively evolved and changed. Their doomsday prophecies and teachings could have been revamped or discarded, like John the Baptist, Jesus, Paul, and Peter, eventually both modified and toned down their doomsday or apocalyptic prophecies and teachings. In this evolutionary manner, the Marian Movement could have continued to exist and keep revising its failed doomsday prophecies and the unfulfilled apocalyptic predictions for the end of the world. For instance, like Jesus, St. Paul and Augustine, they could also have, finally projected these apocalyptic expectations for the divine judgment and end of the world into the infinite future of God's own time or *Kairos*.

However, the Archbishop Bakyenga was perceived as Fr. Kataribabo and the Marian Movement's relentless and implacable enemy. As such, the Marian Movement members were demoralized and became depressed. Their despair was rooted their strong belief that the Archbishop Bakyenga was vindictive Archbishop and would never let them continue to exist in peace, as a valid new apocalyptic, Marian version of the religious Benedictine Order within the Catholic Church, of which he had some canonical jurisdiction. Therefore, the desperate and clinically depressed apocalyptic Marian Movement leaders chose martyrdom in order to escape from the reach of Archbishop Bakyenga's ecclesiastical jurisdiction and interdiction, by ascending to God in heaven through martyrdom, in both strong faith and hope to attain eternal life, and live in perpetual happiness.

NOTES

1. I am grateful to the Ohio Wesleyan University and the GLCA for generous research grants and travel funds to East Africa. Ohio Wesleyan University also granted me both sabbatical and scholarship leave to do the research and to write this book. Ohio Wesleyan University also provided me with the essential secretarial support and work-students to help me with the editing and proofreading of the manuscript at its various stages. I am particularly grateful to Matthew MacKenzie for also working on the final book formatting and the index. He did an excellent job.

2. The terms for *The Movement for the Restoration of the Ten Commandments of God* (MRTCG) were many and varied. This is a factor that is reflected in the book. For instance, "The Movement" is also variously referred to as "Mary's Reform Movement," the "Marian Movement" and the like. See: MRTCG's official handbook: *A Timely Message from Heaven: The End of the Present Times*, cover and inside pages for some of the Movement's revisions and variations of the Marian visions and apocalyptic prophecies.

3. The Marian Movement was essentially a traditional Catholic Marian devotion and moral reform Movement within the Catholic Church. The Catholic Church hierarchy's opposition arose, partly because it felt morally challenged and threatened by the Marian Movement's prophetic ministry, radical moral perfectionism and a strong preoccupation with millennialism, apocalyptic and doomsday biblical literature and prophecies. The Marian Movement borrowed beliefs and practices from the Benedictine Order and the *Opus De*. They sought to ward off God's imminent judgment and doomsday, end of the sinful era, or the end of the corrupt world (*okuhwaho kw'obusingye obu*), by God's purifying holy fire.

See: *Obutumwa Bwaruga Omu Eiguru: Okuhwaho kw'Obusingye Obu*, cover page; *A Timely Message from Heaven: The End of the Present Times*, cover page, 43-55. "*Okuhwaho*" means to come to end, such as the ending of a play and the ending of a meal. The play can be resumed and a new meal can be cooked. Therefore, "*Okuhwaho*" (completion/ending) does not mean "*Okuhwerekyerera*" (destruction), as the perishing and physical destruction of the world.

4. The majority of the Marian Movement members and victims were from Uganda, Rwanda and Eastern Congo. Some names of the dead indicate that the Marian Movement most heavily recruited its members from Southern and Western Uganda, followed by Central Uganda and then Rwanda. Keledonia Mwerinde and Joseph Kibwetere, the co-founders and "Co-Abbots" of the Marian Movement were from Southern Uganda and recruited most of their followers from there. They began their mission by recruiting their family members and relatives. However, the main goal was to evangelize and redeem the whole world. See *A Timely Message from Heaven*, vi.

5. See A Timely Message from Heaven, 60. This is partly why the Marian Movement chose to call itself, The Movement for the Restoration of the Ten Commandments of God.

6. The majority of the forty-six poorest nations in the world are located in Sub-Saharan Africa. They include: Uganda and the neighboring nations like Rwanda and Burundi, whose poor people found solace in the heavenly visions and messages of the Blessed Virgin Mary as mediated by the leaders of the MRTCG as her apostles and messiahs of God's new messianic mission of salvation in the world. Jesus had preached to his impoverished and needy followers saying: "Blessed are the poor because the Kingdom of God belonged to them." (Lk. 5:20-21).

7. The Marian Movement leaders claimed to have God's power to cure HIV/AIDS for people who believed and repented all their sins. See *A Timely Message from Heaven*, 3 # 15-17. This claim to cure HIV/AIDS attracted many AIDS-patients looking for a miraculous cure.

8. *A Timely Message from Heaven*, 12 # 80.

9. *A Timely Message from Heaven*, 12 # 80. Mwerinde declared that it was God's irrevocable punishment. Only MRTCG members would be cured through faith and by God through the Movement leaders' healing prayers and exorcism. As a result, many HIV/AIDS victims joined the Movement in a quest of healing, and also died in great numbers before 2000. These deaths were not counted in the Marian Movement's mass ritual deaths and martyrdoms of March 2000. If they are counted as Movement victims, then the death toll would probably be more than 3,500.

10. Whereas HIV/AIDS has killed more than 35 million people worldwide since 1980, malaria has killed more than 100 million people, in the same period, according to World Health Organization (WHO) estimates. The WHO estimates that malaria infects 300-500 million people annually, and kills about 2.7 million, especially young children and the elderly people. About 90 percent of the malaria victims are in Sub-Saharan Africa. Tragically, they are also too poor to afford a mosquito bed net for malaria prevention. See: *www.who.int/malaria*; The WHO *World Malaria Reports: 2000 to 2006 (*Accessed on July 15, 2007). However, HIV/AIDS is economically more destructive than malaria, because it kills more skilled and productive people.

11. The term "*Entumwa*" can be used to mean "Apostles," or can loosely be used to refer to "Prophet" and "Messiah." Because of these various theological meanings of the title, and the correlative authority behind it, which the Movement leaders wished to claim for themselves, the

leaders of the MRTCG never translated it into English even in their English version of their own handbook: *A Timely Message from Heaven.*

12. A Timely Message from Heaven, 115-119.

13. The *Balokole* refers to those who claim that they are saved or "born again." It is a moral reform and spiritual renewal movement within the Anglican Church. The *Balokole* also claimed to have seen heavenly visions, and believed that Jesus' return (the *Parousia*) was very imminent and God was to end the corrupt world in their own time. They sounded like Mwerinde and Kibwetere. They also sold their properties or gave them away and gathered in selected houses to fast, pray and wait for the return of the Lord. However, they were corrected by the Anglican bishops, and went home to wait for the return of the Lord, as they lived their daily lives, in constant holiness and vigil. Tragically, the MRTCG leaders failed to learn from history. They failed to learn from the experiences of the *Balokole*. (Cf. Mk. 13: 19-23).

14. Like the *Balokole,* the MRTCG prohibited the use of alcoholic drinks, recreational drugs, tobacco products, dancing, watching or reading violent and sexually oriented materials, gossip and materialism. The MRTCG considered these practices as vices. As a result, many people considered the MRTCG as a new Catholic version of the *Balokole Movement* and referred to them as "*Catholic Balokole.*"

15. See: *A Timely Message from Heaven: The End of the Present Times* in 1991. "The book of Mary's Revelations" was revised in both 1994 and 1996. The apocalyptic prophecies and the predictions for the apocalyptic end of the world were distorted and misunderstood. In actuality, the earlier apocalyptic prophecies dealt with the end of "this era" (*Obusingye Obu*). However, the Marian apocalyptic visions kept on evolving as God and the Blessed Virgin Mary continued to reveal and communicate to them new apocalyptic messages, teachings and moral practices.

16. Uganda, Rwanda, Burundi, Sudan, Ethiopia, Somalia and the Democratic Republic of the Congo have had many years of military conflicts in which millions of people have been killed, leaving millions of orphans, and others suffering from PTSD. Tragically, the majority of these traumatized people have no access to treatment programs and professional counseling. For visual tragedies and their effects, see: *Africa's Killing Ground; The Rise and Fall of General Idi Amin*; *Hotel Rwanda*, and *The Last King of Scotland*. Joseph Kony's LRA victims and rescued school children used as "child soldiers" and sex slaves are clear examples of these cases.

17. Bishop Robert Gay is a Canadian and more liberal than African Catholic bishops. He also did not wish to get entangled in local religious administrative and theological debates and controversies. He also both attended and co-presided over the state-sponsored funeral service, on Sunday, April 2, 2000, in Kanungu. Bishop Gay's noble actions were in contrast to those of the vindictive Mbarara Catholic Diocese's bishops.

18. *The Kanungu Cult-Saga: Suicide, Murder or Salvation?* 22-23.

19. Most Ugandans were discouraged because of rampant scandals, and a prevailing culture of materialism, greed and corruption in both Church and State affairs. Many Catholic priests were accused of being greedy and sexually promiscuous instead of observing their ordination vows of poverty and chastity. Other sexual scandals in the Catholic priesthood were cited in *New Vision,* February 15, 2007, and *Orumuri*, February 16, 2007.

20. Fr. Paul Ikazire, as a former Movement leader, confirmed that it was because of the code of silence that the Movement leaders were able to control and finally, to secretly kill their followers. His observations were shared by the police and other commentators, and leaders like Mrs. Theresa Tibayungwa, Margaret Tibayungwa, Bishop Kakubi, Fr. Betungura, Dr. William Muhairwe, Bishop John Ntegyereize, the Rev. Kenneth Kanyankole, Dr. Chris Tuhirirwe and Chief John Karooro.

21. As of January 2008, the MRTCG premises in Kanungu have been ransacked, vandalized and illegally demolished by thugs and vandals. Iron sheets, doors, windows and roofing timber

were removed and stolen. Walls were torn down by vandals and bricks were stolen.

22. The school was closed in 1998 for failure to meet the required residential and curriculum education standards. Most of the teaching was religious and revolved around the Ten Commandments, sin and hellfire for sinners, especially fornicators and beer-drinkers.

23. There was also a large statue of the Blessed Virgin Mary. The statue was traditional, showing Mary as a white Caucasian woman with Middle Eastern Semitic features.

24. The MRTCG facility in Kanungu could hold more than 1,000 people on an emergency or temporary basis. The small children did not take much space and they were the majority of the victims. See *The Kanungu Cult-Saga: Suicide, Murder or Salvation?* 22-24.

25. *Ibid.*

26. *The Kanungu Cult-Saga: Suicide, Murder or Salvation?* 22-23.

27. The Makerere research team failed to appreciate the MRTCG as a Benedictine Order that practiced the vows of poverty, chastity/celibacy, obedience and contemplative silence. The Uganda Human Rights Commission Report, (2002). *The Kanungu Massacre: The Movement for the Restoration of the Ten Commandments of God*, 12-13; *A Timely Message from Heaven*,11.

28. *The Kanungu Cult-Saga: Suicide, Murder or Salvation?* 24.

29. *The Kanungu Cult-Saga: Suicide, Murder or Salvation?* 23-24.

30. See: *Sunday Vision*, March 19, 2000, p. 2. There was some confusion as to whether the world would end by drowning in a flood or by God's fire from heaven. However, an apocalyptic fire was the Marian Movement's predominant theme of God's imminent punishment and means for purifying and ending of the supposedly incurably wicked and corrupt world. See *A Timely Message from Heaven*, 75 # 41. The biblical reference to 2 Peter 3:1-14 is the key to the Marian Movement's teaching of the ending of the world both by flood and fire like Sodom (Gen. 17-18).

31. According to Muzei Bulasio Kalenzi, *"Ishayurira rya Maria"* refers to Mary's salvation from the suffocating evils, pollution and chaos of sin. But it implies that the divine intervention and salvation were like those of the days of Noah, where people perished by drowning in the flood. *"Okushayura"* is to save some from drowning in muddy waters in a swamp or quick sand. Accordingly, the Marian Movement leaders called their church building in Kanungu, *"Obwato bw'Okujunwa"* (the Ark of Salvation). Muzei Bulasio Kalenzi (93) is my own father. He is both a *Mulokole* and retired Anglican Church clergy. He was interviewed: June 29, 2001; August 4, 2006; and on July 10, 2007, in Katojo, Kambuga, Southern Uganda.

32. The famous Martyrs of Uganda had died in a fire, at Namugongo, on June 3, 1886. They too, wanted to be martyred and become God's Christian saints. See J.F. Faupel, *African Holocaust: The Story of the Uganda Martyrs*. London: St. Paul Publications-Africa, 1984 Edition. Twenty-two Catholic martyrs were canonized as Catholic saints by Pope Paul VI on Sunday, October 18, 1964 in St. Peter's Basilica, Rome.

33. *The New Vision*, Wednesday, March 22, 2000: "Kanungu Report 3."

34. See: *The Sunday Vision*, Sunday, March 26, 2000:1-2. The police identified most of the dead to have come from mainly Rukungiri and Bushenyi districts.

35. Here the term *"Banyarwanda"* refers to both the people of Rwanda and their related groups in Uganda, including the *"Banyakisoro"* or *"Bafumbira."* For instance, one family from Kigali lost 17 members in the Kanungu inferno of March, 17, 2000. See *The New Vision*, Wednesday, March 22, 2000, front page news.

36. *The Kanungu Cult-Saga: Suicide, Murder or Salvation?* 25.

37. See: *A Timely Message from Heaven*, vi-vii, 60-61. The Marian Movement leaders declared that God had revealed to them that Uganda was God's new "chosen nation and New Israel" and that "Uganda was loved by God." See: *A Timely Message from Heaven*, 60 # 69. The MRTCG perceived itself as God's second attempt to save the world, but this time through the Blessed Virgin Mary. See: *A Timely Message from Heaven*, 76-78, 119-120.

38. See: *A Timely Message from Heaven,* 30 # 102; 33 # 129. The MRTCG was God's new apocalyptic redemptive messianic mission or true Catholic Church in the world, and Uganda was proclaimed to be God's new chosen nation, and the New Israel.

39. The Marian Movement originally conducted its worship, Bible studies, Marian teachings and writings in the local language of those people. The Marian Movement's handbook was also originally written in Runyankole-Rukiga with the title: *Obutumwa Bwaruga Omu Eiguru: Okuhwaho Kw' Obusingye Obu* (Messages from Heaven: The End of this Era). The book was later translated into English as: *A Timely Message from Heaven: The End of the Present Times,* in 1991. "The book of Mary's Revelations" was revised in both 1994 and 1996. Problems of apocalyptic predictions for the end of the world were results of mistranslations of *"Okuhwaho Kw"Obusigye Obu"* (The end of this Era), as "the end of the world," by some Marian overzealous preachers and in the minds of the general public. For some answers concerning apocalyptic prophecies and Marian teachings in their own words, see: *A Timely Message from Heaven,* vi-vii, # 11, 12, 14; and 145-146.

40. Local newspapers regularly report some of these events and the bishops of Mukono Anglican Diocese and Namirembe, have condemned these human sacrifices. See *The New Vision,* Monday, 4, 2008. The Police in Entebbe arrested a man for trying to sell his nine year old son, for 3 million shillings to a local *"Mufumu"* (traditional priest) for ritual human sacrifice.

41. For instance, Gen. Idi Amin staged a military coup and overthrew Dr. Milton Obote's elected government on January 25, 1971. Gen. Amin claimed that his military government was merely temporary and a caretaker government, until national elections were held. Amin declared himself the "Lifetime President of Uganda," and the "Conqueror of the British Empire." On February 16, 1977, President Amin assassinated the Most Rev. Janani Luwum, the Anglican Archbishop of Uganda, Rwanda, Burundi and Boga-Zaire, having falsely charged him with serious crimes of sedition and treason, whose penalty was death. Amin was overthrown in 1979.

42. One of my research assistants suggested that what the police was really wanted was a bribe in order to release the files. Since no bribe was given, therefore, no files were found.

43. HSMF (*Holy Spirit Mobile Forces)* was the armed wing of the *Holy Spirit Movement* (HSM). Both the organizations were founded and headed by Alice Auma, as the Acholi *Lakwena* (Messiah or God's Messenger), in 1985. Subsequently, Alice Auma became known as "Alice *Lakwena.*" This is analogous to Jesus the Messiah (Christ).

44. The LRA (*Lord's Resistance Army*) is the continuation of the HSMF under Joseph Kony, after the defeat of the Alice Lakwena's HSMF in 1987, by the UPDF, near Jinja, and the flight of Alice Lakwena into exile in Kenya, where she died, on February 10, 2007.

45. These are some of the major eyewitness accounts and evidence that proves that not all the MRTCG members died in the Kanungu inferno or prior to that date. There were many MRTCG members who survived despite the wide-spread activities of the Marian Movement's ritual deaths, or martyrdoms and the church inferno in Kanungu, on March 17, 2000.

46. *Mulokole* is the singular of *Balokole.* He was both interested and concerned about the extreme claims and apocalyptic teachings of the Marian Movement.

47. Therefore, it is self-evident that the term: "The Ark of Salvation" (*Obwato bwa Ruhanga bw'Okujunwa*), was metaphorical for both the Marian Movement and their campus in Kanungu. It may have been used, as "the Church," which both refers to God's redemptive community.

48. The eyewitness account was provided by the Rev. Kenneth Kanyankole on behalf of Kinkizi Diocese of the Anglican Church of Uganda. All communications by Fr. Dominic Kataribabo and Joseph Kibwetere were exchanged in a written form, despite the fact that they were all sitting together face to face around a conference table. Interviewed on March 15, 2001.

49. *The Kanungu Cult-Saga: Suicide, Murder or Salvation?* 18-20.

50. Fr. Dominic Kataribabo, 63, was a well-educated senior Catholic priest. He earned

degrees from Katigondo Seminary, Makerere University, and an M.A. in Religious Studies and Education from Loyola Marymount University, California in 1987. Bishop Kakubi also believed that Fr. Kataribabo had obtained a doctoral degree in theology. There were no records to verify it.

51. *The Balokole* are members of the Anglican and other Protestant churches. They live in different countries. They all confess and testify that they are "born again" or "saved." They greet one another with singing or saying: "*Tukutendereza Yesu!*" (Praise the Lord Jesus!).

52. *A Timely Message from Heaven: The End of the Present Times*, 8-9.

53. *Amagara* is a *Bantu* term for life or vital force. According to the Rev. Beatrice Aber, "*Kwo*" is a *Luo* equivalent word for life, the soul or divine spirit, which is incarnate in each living thing. *Amagara* is a shared experience of life in the world. This includes human beings, animals and plants. Spirits are excluded from this realm of life since they are non-living.

54. *Jok* is a *Luo* word for God as the creative Spirit, which the Bantu call *Ruhanga/Katonda*. But in *Luo*, *Yamo* or wind could also be used in this sense of spirit, or spirit as the breath of life, can be called: "*Yweyo Yamo.*"

55. In *Luo* ontology *Cen,* or the Sun does not seem to create the world as *Kazooba* (the Sun) does in most Ugandan *Bantu* ontology and metaphysics. *Kazooba* and *Amen-Ra* are the same.

56. See Ismael Kasooha, "Child Sacrifices: Girl Beheaded in Ritual Murder," *The New Vision*, Monday, February 23, 2009. More than fifteen children were listed, showing how and where they were sacrificed. In 2008, in Mukono, a boy was spared by the traditional high-priest, because he was circumcised. He was regarded as mutilated and thus, unfit for ritual sacrifice.

57. Commandment number # 5 according to Catholic numbering and # 6 according to Hebrew or Mosaic numbering. The Protestants follow the Mosaic numbering and Kibwetere and Mwerinde, being Catholics, followed the Catholic numbering of the Ten Commandments. See *A Timely Message from Heaven,* 21-32.

58. "Defilement" refers to a negative state of cultural impurity, or pollution, rather than mere criminal cases of statutory rape. See: Leviticus: 18-23.

59. *The Monitor and the New Vision,* editions of Saturday 18, 2000.

60. *Ibid.*

61. The Uganda Human Rights Commission Report. *The Kanungu Massacre,* 74.

62. *Ibid.*

63. This refers to the child molesting Catholic priests, especially in North America.

64. The Uganda Human Rights Commission Report. *The Kanungu Massacre,* 20-21, 75.

65. *Ibid.*

66. They were just thrown into the trenches and pits without any wrappings and covered with soil. It was a literal understanding of: "dust to dust" and "ashes to ashes."

67. For examples see: *Sunday Vision*, March 19, 2000. Front page headline is in extra large bold capital letters with: "**SUICIDE!**" printed across the page. It had a subtitle in bold reading: "**250 to 600 Catholics Burn in Rukungiri Cult.**" The title and subtitle cover the half-page and the picture of the headquarters of the Movement covers the rest of the page. The caption for the picture reads: "**HEADQUARTERS OF DOOM: The headquarters of the Catholic cult that committed suicide at Kanungu, Kinkizi, Rukungiri, on Friday.**" See also the *Monitor Newspaper*, March 18, and issues of March 19-21.

68. *The Kanungu Cult-Saga: Suicide, Murder or Salvation?* 7-26; 56-86.

69. *The Kanungu Cult-Saga: Suicide, Murder or Salvation?* 42.

70. Since Makerere University is a respected research African university, therefore, its findings carry significant academic credibility. The Makerere researchers were right to question and reject the simplistic media sensationalist reports that the Marian Movement was a "cult."

71. *A Timely Message from Heaven*, 67-98, 140-163.

Chapter Two

PROBLEMS OF AFRICAN CULTURES, FAITH, REASON & RELIGION

Most of the major African traditional cultures, fundamental societal values, moral codes, or normative ethics, were traditionally religiously based. As such, they were essentially theocentric. Accordingly, the African traditional religious and political institutions were also traditional forms of theocracies, or "God's kingdoms" in the world. This African cultural divinization of life was also a reality for the pre-colonial, colonial and postcolonial societal hierarchies and politics.[1]

1. Divine Establishment of African Political Institutions And Theocracies

The traditionally culturally and politically venerated traditional African divine kings of pre-colonial Uganda, Rwanda, Burundi, Ghana, and the Emperor of Ethiopia, are some of the major examples of the African political hierarchies and identities, which were deeply rooted in religion. In many significant ways, these pre-colonial African monarchies were similar to the ancient Egyptian divine Pharaohs. In some case, they were also political African institutions were either direct historical descendants, in the cases of the "Nile Basin Civilizations" including Egypt, Nubia (Sudan), Uganda and Ethiopia, or closely were related in both self-definition and functions.

These traditional political institutions were essentially theocratic. The kings and their high-priests both claimed and taught that God had instituted them and their kings were God's local agents of "sons" and finite embodiments and representatives in the society, history and the world. The local creation myths included the divine institution of kingships and ordinances to govern and impose order, formulate laws and dispense justice in God's name. As a result, these traditional kingdoms, and their correlative societal, cultural religious and political institutions do not separate religion politics, medicine, education and other components of life.

African traditional cultures and traditional religion are both correlative and co-extensive or synonymous. That is, the *Ashanti, Dahomey, Ibo, Masai, Kikuyu, Kiganda, Zulu, Kinyoro, Luo, Bantu, Banyankole, Banyarwanda, Yoruba,* or *Hausa* people's traditional religions are the same as the cultures, in which they are practiced.[2]

However, despite this apparent African cultural diversity, by virtue of being African people, their traditional world-view, cultures, and religions also share major common features, such the concept of a Creator God, a hierarchy of regional gods, divine mediation through the high priests and respect for the ancestors as saints and ritual practices, such as sacrifices as atonement for sins, including human sacrifices as the highest level of sacrifice and atonement. Most of these major beliefs and sacrifices were traditionally recognized by the neighboring groups, despite local variations or differences.

In many respects, the African Religion and its main moral ideals were akin to Christianity, which manifests itself in different denominations and traditions, in the world. There was no need to convert the neighbors to one's religion because the already had a similar one. But some desirable or more powerful cults or magical practices needed for more effectively manipulating the mystical forces to heal or control natural phenomena, such as rain and fertility, could be added to existing ones.

Nevertheless, the world's religions, including Buddhism, Christianity, Islam, and some new religious movements, are still very attractive to many people in the world, including Africa. As a result, Africa has disproportionate numbers of Western Christian missionaries, especially the Anglicans, Catholics, Methodists and more recently, the Pentecostals. The traditional African rural masses and the more charismatic oriented urban dwellers are more attracted to the Christian and Muslim fundamentalist religious preachers. This factor has particularly attracted many of the scriptural literalist Christian Western missionaries to come to Africa.

This phenomenon is especially more self-evident among the less well-educated urban poor people and the semi-literate rural cattle herders and agriculturalists in the areas. This is partly because religion provides meaning and promises salvation to those facing adversity in the world. This is the kind of context in which the Marian Movement conducted its missionary activities and appealed to many fundamentalist Catholics in Uganda, Rwanda, Burundi, the Democratic Republic of the Congo and other neighboring countries. This is also why *al-Qaeda* has found fertile ground in East Africa, Sudan and other surrounding areas. It also appeals to the fundamentalists and motivates them to fight moral and religious crusades against the perceived enemies of God within the vilified secular and corrupt society.

The above being the case, redemptive religions generate the necessary positive existential faith and provide the essential human courage and power to confront and overcome the constant anxieties that are rooted in existential threats of life in a constantly changing, evolutionary finite world. This includes the transitoriness of finite life, loss, pain, suffering and the impending death. The main role of redemptive religions includes healing and assurance of faith in the inner power to overcome them in the holy name of a Creator and Redeemer God. Therefore, redemptive religions promise or offer divine power to confront life in hope of divine deliverance from evil or the attainment of supernatural salvation, as a state of fulfillment, contentment, lasting happiness, fellowship and enduring peace in a loving community.

Consequently, redemptive religions appeal to many people due to the human existential insecurities and emotional nature, such as providing the needed social, cultural and psychological support, meaning, guidance and direction to human life. These religious functions are conveyed through divine reassurance of divine providence, or protection, by providing some essential comforting ministry and consolation, especially in times of anxiety, stress, loss, including the death of a loved one, or during times of uncertainty, such as the of loss of employment and insecurities caused by war, pestilences, global climate changes, drought or floods and famine.[3] These evils were some of the dreaded conditions of angst and existential anxiety that St. John, the writer of the Book of the Apocalypse or Revelations, mythological apocalyptic "Four Horses of the Apocalypse" (Rev. 4-8), refer to as, the end of the world.

Therefore, people of war-torn, drought-stricken and HIV/AIDS traumatized East Africa could easily be convinced by doomsday prophets, like Mwerinde and Kibwetere that the end of the world was imminent, and that God's liberation and judgment day were also at hand.

2. Problems of Subjectivity and the Assignment of Cultural Or Religious Value to African Cultural Ideals and Practices

Tragically, the religious fundamentalists, such as *The Branch Davidians* and the members of *The Movement for the Restoration of Ten Commandments of God*, read these apocalyptic mythological and metaphorical imageries as literal future events, and predictions of future disasters that would culminate in the catastrophic end of this world, or at least life on the Earth.

These kinds of religious fundamentalists are not interested in learning religion based on reason, history, science or any other empirical truth, because they regard such a religious endeavor as a serious form of lack of faith, vice and a promotion of doubt, religious skepticism, and even both atheism and evil. As such, these religious fundamentalists, including many *Balokole* or the Evangelicals, are neither interested in it nor will they assist the people, who may wish to engage in such rational activities in the name of religion or research into religious teachings and moral activities. This is the basis of much religious fundamentalism in both Christianity and Islam, especially in Africa and the Middle East. The *Tabliq* Muslims, *al-Qaeda*, the *Balokole Movement* and the MRTCG are good examples of these types of people in East Africa.

The analysis of field research data and discussion of some messianic, liberation and selected new radical religio-political movements in East Africa, including their respective teachings and activities take into account local cultural perspectives, political histories, moral values and religious traditions. For instance, when we estimate the total number of people killed within *The Movement for Restoration of the Ten Commandments of God* to exceed 3,000 people, is that good or bad for East Africa? Some people want to protect Africa from negative press. But, some Catholics wanted to know if martyrdoms are ever justified for the sake of religious faith and salvation; how many people died and if they should be commended for their courage to die for their religious faith.

Murders of innocent people for the sake of God, such as the *al-Qaeda*, HSMF, LRA and MRTCG have done are not morally justified. However, according to most religious traditions, including the African Traditional Religion, Islam, Judaism and Christianity, atonement for sins, such as confessions of offenses and offering sacrifices to God, and ultimately, the pious and holy acts of self-sacrifice in the form of religious martyrdoms, represent the ultimate sacrifices to God. Martyrdom is also believed to have great redemptive value as atonement for the sins of the community. This is why Christians celebrate the self-sacrificial death of Jesus Christ on the cross, as atonement for the sins of the wicked and violent world.

Therefore, within this context, one has to reevaluate the Marian Movement ritual deaths and martyrdoms. Fr. Kataribabo, as both a Catholic priest and theologian, intended these Marian deaths to be performed as Christian martyrdoms. If these gruesome Marian Movement deaths were truly executed as some public and private manifestations of true holy obedience to God, virtue, and were forms of Christian saintly self-sacrificial martyrdoms, as living holy sacrifices offered to God by the Rev. Fr. Dominic Kataribabo, then these deaths can be said to be redemptive for the Marian Movement members. In that theological understanding, they were holy, good and atoning sacrifices according to the Marian Movement leaders and their followers.

Some of the Marian Movement's Benedictine spiritual practices, such as simplicity of a holy life, moral reforms and redemptive activities, could be appropriated by the Church, exorcized of moral and prophetic excesses, and then, carefully affirmed to be part of God's saving work by some religious fundamentalists, in the same way that the early Christians, claimed that the death of Christ on the cross was a self-sacrificial death and an atonement for the sins of the world.

The above form of moral and religious reasoning is possible depending on a fundamentalist or literalist theology of Christian martyrdom, self-sacrifice, atonement for sins and the redemptive value of good works, as the truly effective holy atonements for sins. This includes the voluntary participation in the pain of the cross and death of Jesus, martyrdom and salvation. Nevertheless, some serious questions still arise and deserve some careful theological and moral answers from the Church's hierarchy, and the Christian moral theologians, or thinkers, in Africa and rest of the international community. These questions include the following:

- Should the moral reformist Marian Movement members' deaths be both positively viewed and described as good and beneficial to Christianity, or be negatively condemned as criminal activities that destroyed human life?
- Were the victims of the MRTCG true Marian Christian martyrs, or merely gullible, ignorant and superstitious people and "cult-victims?"
- Should we positively view the Movement members' deaths as those of willing and obedient Christian martyrs and God's moral saints, even when some of their beliefs, teachings and corresponding acts were extreme, fundamentalist, erroneous and tragic?
- Do the saints and prophets have to be always right in what they teach or claim as God's work or revealed truths and apocalyptic prophecies?
- Jesus and Paul's apocalyptic prophecies were fallible and have not yet been fulfilled. Should they be rejected as false prophets?[4]

Most of the above questions cannot be directly answered by references to the MRTCG's teachings, apocalyptic prophecies, monastic practices, and radical martyrdoms of high numbers of the Christians killed in the apocalyptic Marian Movement. However, some of these important questions can be answered, when we tackle the complicated factors of intention, and the state of mind of the people, who died and those who killed them in the context of Christian theology of sin, atonement, self-sacrifice and martyrdom. This mode of Medieval Catholic theology and yet, eclectic in its Christian ethics, particularly, in relation to the infallible, holy God, and the morally authoritative teachings and definitive commandments of Jesus, as the Christ Son of Mary and the Christ of God, selected many of his moral teachings and emphasized them. As a result, the following moral teachings were emphasized some monastic virtues, as the self-evident universal Christian divine moral imperatives and heavenly virtues that all God's obedient people, everywhere and in every truly redemptive religion, especially the moral saints should aspire to attain. These virtues include the following:

- Unconditional love for all human beings
- Self-sacrifice and living a simple life for the sake of God's Kingdom
- Self-denial and renunciation of greed and pride (hubris)
- Free forgiveness of all offenses and sins, including those of our enemies
- Nonviolence, non-retaliation and free forgiveness of offenses
- Mutual respect and respect to the elders
- Coexistence and interdependence in harmony
- Mutual sharing of resources in peace. (See Matt. 5-7).

The above religious and moral concerns cannot be addressed by looking at the raw data and the numbers of the Marian devotees that were killed in the Marian Movement, without interpretation. This is because the numerical numbers or data are by themselves, essentially mute. They need a voice to bring them to public attention, or an interpreter to give them both meaning and significance.

The unprecedented numbers of deaths, are the highest ever recorded within a liberation, apocalyptic or messianic religious movement, without the involvement of war, such as in the cases of the *Maji Maji Liberation Movement*, which sought to expel the German imperialists from East Africa in 1908; *Nyabingi Movement*, which waged war to expel the British Colonial Government from Southern Uganda, in the 1910s; *Mau Mau Liberation Movement*, which waged war to expel the British imperialists from Kenya in the 1950s; the HSMF, and LRA, which waged holy wars to overthrow President Yoweri Museveni's NRM Government, in 1987, in the case of the HSMF, and from 1987-2008, in the case of Joseph Kony's LRA.

3. Perfection, Self-Sacrificial Death as Atonement

According to Christianity, Jesus, as the Christ, was the perfect and sinless human being, whose innocent and self-sacrificial death on the cross served as God's provision for the universal human being's perfect sacrifice and atonement for sin for all time. This is an extreme example of how the Early Church's Christian thinkers, philosophers and theologians creatively re-interpreted the death of one man, Jesus as the Christ (Messiah) and redeemer of the world. They affirmed that Christ's crucifixion was a self-sacrificial death, and perfect atonement for human sins. By this reinterpretation of the tragic events, the Christian thinkers intended to "redeem" and "reinterpret Jesus' tragic death on the shameful Roman cross," and positively affirm it, as the historical expression of God's universal love, and unmerited divine mission of redemption to the whole world.

Subsequently, the Christians zealously preached and proclaimed to the world that Jesus' innocent death on the Roman cross, as a moral defeat for human sins of malice, disbelief, hate and both religious (Temple) and State injustice. Christians both positively and consistently affirmed that God negated human moral evil, sins and injustice on the cross. Christians contended that God redeemed the unjust and sinful people, who unjustly condemned others and unjustly put them to death out of:

- Ignorance
- Disbelief
- Envy
- Malice
- Hate and evil
- Sadism
- Distorted values

- Bad theologies
- Cultural biases
- Misconceptions of God and evil
- Sin (Matt. 5-7).

Accordingly, Jesus' resurrection was necessary as a divine victory and the evidence of God's goodness of life over evil, especially God's divine triumph over the terrors of death. The resurrection was also proclaimed as the evidence of divine justice and God's final vindication of Jesus' spiritual and moral perfection. In reality, these Christian affirmations of faith were part of this initial Christian reconstruction and interpretation of historical data, in order to provide new religious meaning and redemptive value for the tragic events. This religious task was carried out within their new religious context and understanding of God's activities of creation and redemption within God's providence, unconditional love, nonviolence, forgiveness of sins, justice and omnipotence. This religious task became evolutionary..

The story of Jesus, as the Christ or Christology, is still evolving in the Church, today. This religious evolution occurs, as the story of the life of Jesus Christ becomes constantly retold, revised, reformulated, preached and contextualized within different cultures. This is also the process by which Mary, the holy Mother of Jesus, became slowly deified, and the Marian Movement members, finally, hailed her as fully divine, and as the "Goddess," the "Mother of God," (*Theotokos)*, the "Queen of Heaven," the "Mother of the Church," and the "Mediator of Divine Salvation."

Similarly, the stories of the MRTCG's visions and God's revelations should have been expected to evolve, develop and change as time passed. These modifications would have led the Marian Movement into becoming more established both in its teachings and monastic moral practices, within the context of an African culture, which promotes polygamy and extended families and ridicules celibacy, even when it is exercised in the name of the Blessed Virgin Mary, God, and for the sake of moral purity, religious holiness and divine redemption.

The evolution of Christology serves as an example of the model for the deification of both Mary and Jesus, her son. For instance, according to the

Gospel of St. Mark, the first Gospel to be written down by the followers of Jesus the Christ, or the Christians, the writer of the Gospel was unaware of Jesus' Virgin Birth and historical resurrection. Therefore, St. Mark omitted these Christian traditions in his own original Gospel account.

According to St. Mark, Jesus was a real man from Nazareth, who became divine, when he was adopted, as the "Son of God." The event of divine adoption takes place by virtue of his Holy Baptism in the River Jordan, by John the apocalyptic prophet. St. Mark also indicates that Jesus was adopted "Son of God," through the reception of God's supernatural gift of the Holy Spirit, at his baptism (Mk. 1:9-11). However, some Christian readers were offended, by the humanity of Jesus, and later, they edited St. Mark's original Gospel account, and added the resurrection to his account.

This Christian editorial work was carried out, not as a falsification of history, but rather as a literary or metaphorical language and symbolic religious device for their Christian expression of faith, effective narration of the story of Jesus from the point view of their religious faith, and hope for salvation and immortality. They lead to the religious interpretation of the historical data concerning the life and death of Jesus, as the true Christ of God, as the expected Jewish Messiah, because being Jews, their new Christian faith demanded it. Their own Christian faith, confession and public proclamation of their affirmations that Jesus was their promised Jewish Messiah, or the Christ, determined how the Christians selected some aspects of the historical data about the life of Jesus, told the story, and finally, wrote it down in their gospels.

Within the above respect, the Gospels are not eyewitness accounts or historical books about the life of Jesus, but rather, they are the Early Church's own public testimonies, confessions, and stories of faith in Jesus as both the expected Messiah (Christ) and God's deliverer from evil. As such, the Gospels are the formalized and conventional Christian stories of their faith and understanding of Jesus, as the Christ or Savior, and as their risen and ascended Lord. But the religious fundamentalists, including the MRTCG members, read the Gospels as actual historical records regarding the life and activities of Jesus. They also read his apocalyptic prophecies and predictions for the end of the world in a literal manner (Matt. 24-25).

Therefore, the gospels are examples of stories of faith, carefully designed and narrated, in order to promote faith that Jesus is the Messiah (Christ), rather than being historical accounts determined by mere impersonal, or empirical facts and historical events in themselves. In this case, subjectivity in the form of Christian faith, rather than objectivity in the form of historical facts and events, is the preferred paradigm of religious reporting, writing, preaching and teaching in the Church, especially in

Sunday school. To do otherwise, is strongly rejected by many fundamentalist Christians, such as the Evangelicals and the MRTCG members.

In addition to the Holy Bible, as the infallible Word of God, the MRTCG members had begun to view their own records of God's revelations through the apparitions of the Blessed Virgin Mary, in a similar revelatory and divine authoritative manner, as God's new apocalyptic, divinely revealed, and infallible Holy Word. That is one of the reasons why they were reluctant to renounce their teachings as heretical, false claims and dangerous moral teachings, when Bishop Kakubi requested the Marian Movement leaders to do so, on May 7, 1991.

The Christian fundamentalists, like the MRTCG, the Mormons and the Evangelicals, especially the more conservative members of the Southern Baptist Convention, in the USA, generally discourage intellectual religious questioning and expressions of doubt, as forms of serious sins, lack of faith, or atheism, and the sources of moral evils. They consider any questioning of God's revelation, or questioning the historical accuracy or prophetic validity of the Holy Scriptures, as both blasphemy and a sinful rejection of true Christianity.

It is also negatively viewed, as a form of atheistic doubt, secularism and a danger to the Christian faith, thus, to be opposed and eliminated from the Church scholars and its community of faith. The *Balokole* of East Africa, the MRTCG, the Mormons, and the members of the Southern Baptists in the USA are some good examples of this case. In the Muslim case of Scriptural literalism, the *al-Qaeda, Tabliq*, the Taliban, the *Wahhabi*, and the Shiite are some examples of this religious phenomenon.

It is therefore, significant to note that the Marian Movement leaders also belonged to this category of Christian fundamentalists, despite the fact that their own Catholic tradition is liberal in its approach and interpretation of the Holy Scriptures. This is another reason why they got into trouble with the Catholic bishops in Mbarara Catholic Diocese.

4. Religious Evolution, Beliefs and Mythologization of Life

Religions are evolutionary in nature. Part of this evolution is the formulation of doctrines and creation of stories and myths as teaching tools or as justifications of the religious doctrines. In the examples cited above, the stories or myths of the "adoption of Jesus as Son of God," "Virgin Birth" of Jesus, "the resurrection," and the "ascension of Jesus" into heaven are some of these central stories, which were formulated as Christianity developed, as Christianity evolved into a new religion. Similarly, the MRTCG was going through a process of religious evolution and establishment, as a Benedictine

Order, when it tragically imploded, by committing ritual martyrdoms, in order to ascend into heaven.

In the process of interviewing some eyewitnesses and other people, in Uganda, for this work, it became clear that some mythologies were already beginning to emerge in order mythologize some life-transforming events, which they had witnessed. This is a natural religious and cultural process of processing and preserving important events.

In Uganda, some of these myths emerged in order to justify the people's respective interpretation of the events surrounding the supernatural institution of *The Movement for the Restoration of the Ten Commandments of God*. They wanted to justify the Marian Movement as God's new Ark of Salvation (*Obwato*), within the perishing world. I have left out what I considered as baseless mythology, such as the allegation of human sacrifice and cannibalism. There were unfounded allegations of cannibalism rooted in ignorance and superstitions, such as witchcraft, cannibalism and vampires.

Accordingly, those malicious, misleading and sensationalist newspaper reports that the Catholic Marian Movement's leaders were killing innocent children to offer them to God, as form of holy and pure atonement for sins, were some anti-Catholic fictional stories and myths invented to vilify the Catholic Marian Movement, demoralize the Movement's supporters, and above all, they were designed to amaze, entertain the African superstitious public and sell newspapers.

The Marian Movement leaders were demonized, condemned and accused of promoting some alien, anti-social and anti-African cultural value systems and taboos, which prohibited cannibalism and witchcraft. The vicious and malicious allegations against the Marian Movement leaders included the killing and sacrificing young children; and drinking the innocent children's blood for the sacrament of the Holy Eucharist, as the sacrificial and atoning "blood of Christ."

In addition, it was falsely alleged that the Marian Movement leaders, became "evil cult leaders," who also roasted, served and ate the children's bodies, as "the sacrificed Body of Christ," during the celebrations of the sacrament of the Holy Eucharist.[5a] These allegations were also made in order to justify the fact the Marian Movement was a dangerous religious cult whose leaders were guilty of cannibalism, and were some kinds of vampires that drank real human blood for the sacrament of Holy Communion.

The claim that the blood of these innocents and their bodies were eaten as if they were the physical bread, and the blood of Christ as pure atonements that took away the sins of the world, sounded more like mere Christian mythology and fiction, rather than reality. These allegations were reminiscent of similar allegations made by the Greek and Roman pagans against the Early Church Christians, due to the misunderstanding of the sacrament of the Eucharist, in which the consecrated elements of bread and wine are believed to have been transubstantiated into the "body and blood of Christ." The Holy Communion elements are sometimes received from the priest who says: "The body of Christ and the blood of Christ." However, to the outsiders and literalists, these words may be tragically misunderstood and the Catholics may be misunderstood as cannibals, as in the case of the MRTCG Catholic priests and their followers.

Therefore, these false allegations, misleading caricatures of the Eucharist, erroneous and misrepresentations of the Medieval Catholic sacramental teachings and practices of the reformist, and apocalyptic Marian Movement, are duly both objectively and academically examined. This task is carried out in order to correct the misunderstandings of these Catholic beliefs, traditions, teachings and practices due to gross distortions and their misrepresentation in the public media.

Consequently, the Marian Movement teachings and practices are fully presented, evaluated and rejected, after a rigorous process of theological, historical, social and cultural analysis of the data, within Church history, especially in light of the Roman Catholic theological, historical and Marian traditions. They do not form part of the theological construction of the moral and theological teachings of the apocalyptic Marian Movement in this work.

We have to learn from history in order not to repeat the mistakes of the past. This includes learning some important religious lessons, so as to not repeat tragic mistakes of the past. For instance, we have to avoid mistakes, which are similar to those that resulted in the persecution of innocent Christians, as either heretics, or dangerous criminals because they were different or reformist in their radical moral teachings and nontraditional manner of worship.

Some Christians were persecuted because they were also different, or were intellectually inquisitive and innovative; "nonconformist," "liberal," "feminist," "reformist," "liberationist," "independent," and "modernist" or "postmodernist." Other Christians were also persecuted or rejected for not being "true Christians" because they advocated for some radically innovative approaches to theology, and teachings of moral values that were based on a new and a scientifically oriented understanding of the world. In short, these intellectuals were rejected or persecuted for promoting both moral and religious thinking that was fundamentally rooted within the empirical world and the sound understanding of the Natural Law and evolution. This was a new religious understanding leading the Church to adopt a new intellectual tradition that promotes sound piety, meaningful forms of healing as truly divine and redemptive practices of a wholesome religious faith.

These new forms of piety and meaningful religious faith, including relevant post-Darwinian Christianity, must be deeply rooted in the positive affirmation and true appreciation of God's revelation in nature, as God's good creation (Gen. 1:1-31), and a figurative reading and symbolic interpretation of the Holy Scriptures. This is as opposed to a literalist reading of the Holy Scriptures, as God's special revelation, in the form of an inerrant divine record of past or future events within the cosmos. This error leads to the literalist reading of the apocalyptic prophecies, such as the books of Daniel and Revelation as real and potential, or future history. Tragically, the Marian Movement leaders, also literally read the Bible, interpreted and implemented its apocalyptic prophecies for the end of the world, as God's apocalyptic instructions from heaven, as mediated through the Blessed Virgin Mary.

These Marian Movement's tragedies occurred because of the failure to understand that religion speaks in the symbolic language of myth. According to this understanding, myth includes rituals, figurative usage of language, stories, parables, poetry, music, prayers, proverbs, riddles, metaphors and symbolism. Within this complex religious world-view, apocalyptic literature and prophecies are also both metaphorically read and interpreted within this symbolic world-view in order to bring out the encoded divine meanings and moral values for the people today. Most of these religious metaphors and symbols deal with the prophetic and coded divine messages for courageously living a holy a life in this world, in face of injustice, adversity and persecution.

Similarly, the divine apocalyptic revelations and religious literature, including those of the Essenes, and the biblical books of Daniel, Ezekiel, Isaiah, Jeremiah, Micah, and Revelation (The Apocalypse of St. John) both deal with the mundane and concrete moral and religious matters of their time. These matters include:

- Disobedience and sin against God's will or Moral Law
- Violence, wars and God's imminent retribution
- Breaking the Ten Commandments, or the Covenant
- Moral decadence
- Need for repentance
- Living a new life of moral reformation

- Guidance for holiness
- Socioeconomic justice
- Concern for the poor
- Advocate for the powerless
- Concerns for peace in the community
- Promotion of peace in the world (cf. Matt. 5-7; 25:31-46).

Accordingly, Jesus, as the Christ (Messiah) of God in the world, addressed the above concerns for noble religious and civic virtues and lasting peace in the world, and gave to the world God's new prescription of godliness, and practical guidelines for lasting peace and happiness. He summed up these divine imperatives and moral obligations as follows: "Love God, and love your neighbor as you love yourself." This moral obligation for unconditional love, including the neighbors and enemies, is the main essence of Jesus' Sermon on the Mountain (Matt. 5-7).

The Early Church Christians were persecuted by the pagan Roman Emperors, most especially Nero (64-67), Domitian (81-95), Trajan (109-116), Marcus Aurelius (161-180), Decius (249-232), Valerian (253-257), Diocletian and Galerius (284-305), Maximinus (311) and Julian the Apostate (361-363). The Emperor Constantine put to an end this formal imperial persecution of Christianity by his *Edict of Milan*, in 313. The edict established Christianity as the new unifying "imperial cult" of the Roman Empire. Christianity had been persecuted as a seditious religion, which promoted the worship of Jesus as a new God and Lord, instead of pledging loyalty and worshipping the Roman emperors, as gods. In addition, the Roman citizens resented Christians as antisocial people, who refused to join others in the local and national cultural, religious and political festivities. The Christians were also hated because they were also misunderstood to be cannibals and dangerous criminals, who killed children in order to drink their blood, and eat their bodies, during the sacred mysteries of the sacrament of the Eucharist, or Holy Communion.

The Christian affirmations that the "consecrated element of bread and wine became either physically or supernaturally transformed into the real body and blood of Christ" (cf. Jn. 6:48-58), were misunderstood by both the religiously scandalized Jews and the Greco-Roman pagans. As a result, the Christians were both rejected and persecuted, as criminals and horrible cannibals.

These Hebrews and the Greco-Roman pagans misunderstood Christians because of their metaphorical language, which was taken literally by the pagans and Christians, who were former pagans. These literalist groups of religious people used their pagan philosophy and cultures to understand the Christian sacraments and references to the Christian symbolic language of eternal life and the "body of Christ," in physical terms, instead of understanding them symbolically, as mystical religious elements, which are coded in figurative and metaphorical religious language and symbols.

Consequently, the Christians of the Early Church were regarded as being members of a new secretive and dangerous cult. Subsequently, they were persecuted and put to death on false criminal allegations and charges of:

- Unpatriotic values
- Sexual immorality
- Human sacrifice

- Antisocial behavior
- Sedition
- And cannibalism.[5b]

The ancient Hebrew or Jews, as well as the pagan Greeks and the ancient superstitious Roman pagans, tragically misunderstood Christian symbolic language, rituals and sacraments. For instance, they erroneously and tragically both thought and believed that "the body of Christ and the blood of Christ," which were symbolically referred to in the celebration of the central Christian sacrament of the Eucharist, were literal and real.

The enemies of Christianity accused Christians of ritual cannibalism of their founder. They alleged that "Holy Communion" was a pagan cannibalistic ritual, in which Christians consumed illegally obtained portions of the real human bodies of infants and blood, or of young children that had been criminally sacrificed or killed in order to secure their bodies for use as the body of Christ in the Eucharistic elements. But this was a tragic pagan misrepresentation of Christianity. It was rooted in both religious prejudice and ignorance.

Christians were partly to blame for the state persecution of Christianity. For instance, they segregated themselves from the pagans. They were also secretive in their worship, metaphorical in their teachings and sometimes used coded messages and symbols to communicate with each other. However, these practices were necessary due to their own need for self-preservation and protection because of the fear rooted in the gruesome reality of the Roman imperial persecution of Christianity, as a new, evil and subversive messianic movement, which they referred to variously, including: "Jesus Messianic Movement," and the "Jesus Cult."

The Jesus Movement members refused to worship the Roman Emperor as a god. They refused to make offerings and sacrifices to his statue, because they considered it a serious sin of idolatry. Due to their obedience to the pacifist moral teachings of Jesus on the moral imperative for unconditional love, free forgiveness of offenses, nonviolence or "turning the other cheek," and peace, the Christians refused to join the Roman army, and kill the State's enemies. For those religious, moral and political reasons, the Christians were regarded as being unpatriotic, antisocial and dangerous messianic groups of subversive people.

The Christians were accused of serious crimes of treason and being antisocial due to self-segregation and refusing to participate in public civic events and festivals, which they rejected as pagan, corrupt and morally decadent. The Christians who were charged with crimes were required to renounce their supposed errant ways and sacrifice to the statues of the emperor as a national god.

When they refused to worship the emperor, saying that it was idolatry, they were accused of being unpatriotic, and charged with treason. Subsequently, these Christians were arrested, tried for treason and sedition, and condemned to death. They were publicly humiliated, and finally, executed in painful ways to serve as deterrent examples of the high price for joining Christianity, as a supposed new cult that promoted moral decadence, including secret cult rituals, secretive activities; sexual immorality, cannibalism, treason and antisocial behavior.

From the historical records, it is clear that the Roman and Greek pagans misinterpreted Christian data, teachings and rituals in order to charge the Christians with the heinous crimes of infanticide and cannibalism. Likewise, the Christian teachings on *Agape* as unconditional love for all people, including the enemies, were misinterpreted by the pagans as a promotion of an immoral life of hedonism.

The alleged Christian hedonism was thought to be a collective secretive life of sexual orgies and gross sexual immorality, where people indiscriminately had sexual intercourse with each other as part of this holy fellowship and the "Agape Meal" (Holy Communion), which secretly took place at night, in each other's houses. The ancient tragic Roman pagan cultural and religious misunderstandings of Christians, and especially the misrepresentation of Agape, and the Christian sacrament of the Holy Communion (Agape Meal), resulted in tragic Christian persecution. These religious misunderstandings of Early Church Christians were rooted in ignorance, religious prejudice, a serious distortion of information, misleading false reporting and a tragic misinterpretation of the data.

The distortion of information by the religiously prejudiced pagans, who were spies and informers for their pagan political leaders, were shaped by their own pagan beliefs, cultures and idolatrous backgrounds, as well as the perceived interests and expectations of their pagan, or idolatrous Roman and Greek superiors, employers and audiences. According to the Christian and Church history, the tragic consequences of the inaccurate information and misrepresentation of Christian teachings and practices as those of a new and dangerous doomsday or apocalyptic messianic movement, or Jesus Cult, were very tragic. Christians were singled out and officially persecuted by the State, as dangerous cult members and potentially political or religio-social criminals.

Christians were hated and falsely accused of heinous crimes they never committed. They were arrested, tortured and painfully executed. For instance, some of them were thrown into the entertainment arena unarmed, to entertain the public by fighting hungry vicious lions. The pagan emperors roared with laughter as the helpless and unarmed Christians were torn to pieces and devoured, while still alive, by the hungry beasts. Other Christians were covered with wax and set on fire to be used as torches to light the entertainment sports arenas on dark nights. Therefore, unless we are careful, we too can easily behave like these confused and malicious ancient pagan Romans and mistreat our fellow Christians.

This study indicates the need for tolerance for cultural and religious diversity. This includes constitutional formulations of provisions which grant the freedoms of religious worship and differing doctrines, and ritual or sacramental practices. We have to protect religious and cultural diversity from rejection due to our xenophobia and prejudices or because we do not approve of their practices such as the Islamic Traditions or Catholic sacramental practices including those of the Marian Movement's austere or strange monastic and apocalyptic practices. If we do that, we become like the Jews, who rejected Jesus and his apocalyptic teachings or messianic claims based on the Hebrew Scriptures and apocalyptic prophets. We also become like the intolerant pagan Romans, who crucified Jesus, and viciously persecuted his followers, as dangerous messianic cult members of the "Jesus Cult Movement," or Christianity.

In the above scenario and tragic analogy, during the 1990s, it was the Marian Movement that was vilified and persecuted as a dangerous cult, by the Roman Catholic Church hierarchy in Mbarara, and today, we are the cheering members of the public, as the public media and the academy, who continue to ridicule them, as they lay helpless, naked and dead, subject to our public viewing, analysis and interpretation of their tragic ideals, teachings and practices that led them to their despair, protests and quest for escape from persecution and the world that mocked and rejected them, while they were alive, and now, in their tragic self-sacrificial deaths to God.

The Marian Movement leaders and their followers placed the role of voluntary, obedient, and holy self-sacrificial death and martyrdom within our public, religious, and moral discourses within the academy, the Church, State and other forms of public intellectual arena. We, too, can continue to demonize them and subject them to persecution and cut them to down, or we can seek to understand them and vindicate them. We can seek to understand their Marian revelations, religious and moral teachings through a study of these elements.

This book provides some of "the insiders' cultural secrets" and essential theological and cultural keys needed to unlock the Marian Movement's reason for being, in the form of its reasons for its emergence, teachings, and practices. This task must be seriously undertaken and accomplished within their appropriate historical, religious, philosophical, political and cultural contexts, and then, weigh their merits and demerits, successes and failures, and be able to correctly identify the reasons for those factors. This process is necessary if the Christian Church worldwide and the political establishments are to learn from the tragic history of the Marian Movement in East Africa, and be able to prevent similar mistakes in handling similar religious movements in the future.

5. Constitutional Freedoms of Religion And Religious Tragedy

All messianic and liberation religious movements emerge within a complex historical, cultural, political and religious contexts. They are founded in order to remedy perceived political, religious, moral or socioeconomic evils and injustices. These are some of their main reasons for being founded. The leaders of these movements are hailed as God's sent messiahs, as in the case of Alice *Lakwena* (Messiah), and her HSM, or Joseph Kony's LRA, and God's prophets and agents of divine salvation, as in the case of Keledonia Mwerinde and Joseph Kibwetere's MRTCG.

Therefore, any research or investigation of sensitive matters concerning religion, new messianic or liberation movements, secret cults, and their associated politics, ritual mass murders, and voluntary martyrdoms, or mass suicides, is very difficult, sensitive, and can be dangerous, such as in the cases of violent, homicidal and secretive cults. These are some of the realities, which we have to become aware of as we investigate these movements and cults.

Furthermore, the study and investigation of these complex religious or political movements is made difficult by the complexities of many interrelated cultural, social, economic, moral, religious, and complex political factors. The relatives of victims, or police agents may not want to reveal secrets that may affect impending criminal procedures, investigations and prosecutions of criminals, as was the case concerning the cult-like ritual mass deaths that are associated with the radical, secretive, messianic, and religious as well as "criminal activities" of *The Movement for the Restoration of the Ten Commandments of God,* that were officially categorized by Uganda's Police and the Government of Uganda as "criminal mass murders."

Subsequently, the Marian Movement was to be fully investigated by the police for violations of human rights. The main Marian Movement leaders were also to be prosecuted according to applicable criminal laws, especially those that conform to the 1995 Constitution. The *1995 Constitution of*

Republic of Uganda grants full freedoms of: assembly, worship or "free exercise of religion," "freedom of speech" and "freedom of conscience." As such, until the Marian Movement carried out ritual murders and martyrdoms of its followers in order to send them to heaven, it legally operated within the constitutional rights provided to the people in Uganda, where the Marian Movement had its headquarters, and had also recruited most of its members.

Therefore, the Ugandan Government's case against the leaders of *The Movement for the Restoration of the Ten Commandments of God* was not based on the illegal practice of religion in Uganda. Rather, the state charges were based on human rights' abuses, especially criminal child-abuses, negligence concerning children, and the criminal activities that caused the deaths of people in several places in Uganda, where dead bodies had been dug up from hidden mass graves at the Movement's stations and around some houses owned or rented by the Marian Movement leaders. This was particularly self-evident in the Kanungu church-fire at 10:30 a.m. on Friday, March 17, 2000.

In Kanungu, the Movement's headquarters, a fire was deliberately set inside an overcrowded church building to kill hundreds of loyal members of the Marian Movement. According to the Police of Uganda, this church inferno represented a criminal act, rather than a pious and commendable act of Christian martyrdom. For the Ugandan Police, this observation was considered to be fact and evidence of premeditated crimes of mass murders by means of fire on the part of the MRTCG leaders.

Therefore, a strong conclusion was quickly reached by many people based on the popular, but erroneous view, which was strongly promoted by the sensationalist public media to sell their stories to many less well-informed people, that the MRTCG was either "a new sectarian religion" that had split from the Catholic Church, or "a new cult." This research and its findings negate the popular public and simplistic view of the Marian Movement's teachings, austere monastic practices and self-sacrificial deaths.

The above, is especially true, in regard to how the MRTCG and its teachings and activities were erroneously reported and misrepresented. This was self-evident, in the case of the prejudiced and sensationalist public media, and the publicly embarrassed Catholic Church's hierarchy of the Mbarara Catholic Diocese. For instance, the Kanungu church fire was never reported as the MRTCG intended it, namely, as radical forms of *"Opus Dei,"* or the ultimate goods of ritual sacrament of penance as: Christian obedience, holy self-sacrifices, martyrdoms, atonements to God, and ascension into heaven.

Instead of sympathetic understanding, the Marian religious protest and self-sacrificial deaths in the fire were vilified. They were negatively reported as horrible acts of ritual criminal mass murders of the MRTCG members by the Movement's criminal and greedy, evil, religious "cult leaders" and "criminal mass murderers." Consequently, there is a great theological difference between what the Marian Movement leaders intended to accomplish, by their own martyrdoms, and what was erroneously reported in the public media.

The seriously erroneous public media reports and misleading conclusions were partly based on what was considered to be concrete criminal evidence regarding the Marian Movement victims as mass murders. The allegations were that these criminal mass murders were perpetrated by the Marian Movement leaders, especially Keledonia Mwerinde, Joseph Kibwetere and Fr. Dominic Kataribabo, as the main leaders of the Marian Movement. This supposed evidence of criminal activity was cited as that the fact that the church windows were previously nailed shut with long nails, and the doors of the church-building had been both locked and barricaded prior to the beginning of the fire.

More significantly for the police investigators, was the fact that the church fire was not an accident. The fire and the Marian Movement's deaths were carefully preplanned. There was ample evidence that the destructive and tragic fire was intentionally set, and accelerated with some crude homemade petrol bombs and sulphuric acid containers that were strategically placed, at key points, inside the church building.

After the church inferno, the eyewitnesses clearly saw several burnt out kegs of gasoline and sulphuric acid containers, which had been placed around the interior of the church building, presumably, by Fr. Kataribabo and his hired assistants or the assassins. These fire bombs were made and used in order to ensure that they instantly exploded and burned with great intensity in order to cremate the Marian Movement members, as quickly and painlessly as possible.

The ultimate desired goal was to martyr the Marian devotees, by setting them on fire. They wanted to die, in the same way, in which their venerated Uganda's Christian Martyrs, who were set on fire, at Namugongo, on June 3, 1886, by the royal decrees of King Mwanga of the Kingdom of Buganda. The petrol fire bombs were used to ensure that after the initial explosions, the fire would instantaneously engulf all the worshippers and quickly burn them to ashes, before the outsiders could come and intervene.

Petrol bombs also ensured that the fire burned at very high degrees of intensity to make sure that the people were both killed quickly, and at the same time, to be completely burned to ashes; or at least, to be burned beyond recognition and proper identification. The Marian Movement leaders succeeded in these objectives. Most bodies of children and smaller adults were almost completely burned to ashes. Subsequently, it was difficult for the police to see and accurately count the people that perished in the church inferno in Kanungu, on Friday, March 17, 2000. As a result, the official figures represent a smaller number of the MRTCG's tragic deaths.

However, the intensity of the fire was also designed to make it impossible for the police, or the neighbors to break into the locked church building, in an attempt to rescue the MRTCG members from their barricaded and burning church building. It also made it futile for the police to identify the dead. The Marian Movement leaders succeeded in both intentions.

All the members of the Marian Movement that had gathered in Kanungu for the promised "Ascension Day," entered their church building (*Obwato*) and died in the inferno, as the means for the mystical and spiritual ascension, rather than a physical ascension into heaven. We know that ritual death or martyrdom was known as the path to heaven by the Marian Movement members because those who had missed the "Ascension Day," in Kanungu, tried to join their friends in heaven by replicating the Kanungu church fire, but were constantly watched and dispersed by the now more vigilant police, in order to prevent a repeat of the Kanungu tragedy.[6]

6. Economic Theory for the Marian Movement And Tragedies

Following the Marian Movement's perplexing tragic events of March 2000, millions of religious people, wanted to know what really happened, who perpetrated the events and why these tragic events were not prevented by the State police.

Subsequently, there were many differing theories and emotional speculations, which were advanced by the police, the skeptical public and perplexed politicians concerning the real nature of events and the rational attempts to provide explanations for the Marian Movement's rise, and sudden self-sacrificial tragic deaths. The prevailing theory was an economic one. Within the Ugandan culture of corruption, there was some unconscious public rush to assign an economic motive and greed, on the part of corrupt sinners, and to project these evils on to Keledonia Mwerinde and Joseph Kibwetere, and to falsely believe their own subjective and evil moral projections, as Mwerinde and Kibwetere's real reasons for founding the Marian Movement.

The above kinds of prejudiced and vindictive people made claims that the Marian Movement founders and leaders were truly economically greedy, con artists, and evil business people, who founded the MRTCG as their personal money making investment. The theory is that these criminals defrauded their followers and then killed them. But this is a faulty economic theory, and a malicious false speculation that is based on either ignorance or malice. It is designed to demonize and defame the Marian Movement and criminalize its main leaders. In reality, the Marian Movement did not have any money left, beyond that needed for daily expenses, at the time of the Marian Movement's ritual martyrdoms, in March 2000.

Nevertheless, since most of the dead were completely burned to ashes and beyond identification, it became impossible to know for sure, if the Marian Movement leaders, especially Joseph Kibwetere, Keledonia Mwerinde and the Rev. Fr. Dominic Kataribabo, were also killed in the fire, along with their loyal followers. As a result, there were many unfounded rumors and speculations that the MRTCG leaders had defrauded their followers, took their money and fled into exile, having set fire to the church building in order to kill them.

The speculations included an economic reason as the Marian Movement leaders' main motive for killing their followers. In a context of greed and corruption, an economic motive became uncritically accepted as the truth, because many people faced economic temptations in their own daily life and work. The speculation was that after the failed predictions for the end of the world, the MRTCG members became disillusioned and demanded a refund of their money and property, which had been donated or surrendered to the Movement leaders, when they joined the apocalyptic Marian Movement in hope of salvation and being transported to heaven. But when the predicted fiery end of the world failed to come at the end of the Second Millennium, some of the MRTCG doomsday enthusiasts and the impatient members of the Movement were very disappointed.

This economic theory, and allegations of corruption and fraud, became very popular as explanations of the rise and fall of the Marian Movement. They were false theories and explanations of the Marian Movement's events, but they were erroneously believed or taken for granted, by many people, as the real truth. For instance, *The Daily Monitor* editorial of Wednesday, October 10, 2007, comments on the report of the day before, in which Grace Kashemeire accused her Pentecostal Church pastor, of fraud and conning people out of millions of shillings.

The unethical, fraudulent and gain-seeking pastor asked the sick people to pay money to her, claiming that she would miraculously multiply their money, depending on the amounts donated to her church, and or cure them of HIV/AIDS through her special divine powers, exorcisms of evil spirits, as the causes of diseases, the laying of holy hands, and healing prayers. But these miracles were only supposed to occur for those, who paid her a lot of money, and came to her both in true faith and hope of God's divine healing,

and salvation. Subsequently, the people who did not get healed were told
that it was their fault. They were counseled that their problem arose because
they had either not paid enough money or lacked the necessary faith to be
healed. According to the published reports and complaints, the Pentecostal
Church pastor resorted to intimidation and blackmail in order to silence her
victims, when the promised divine miracles for the multiplication of money
and healing failed to occur. *The Daily Monitor* editorial reads as follows:

> **Arrest these criminal Pentecostal pastors:**
> The story of a Christian Ms Grace Kashemeire who was bribed and blackmailed by
> a Pentecostal church pastor to deceive other worshippers that she had been healed of
> HIV/Aids is sad. Her revelation that the pastor wanted to use her testimonies to
> extort money from Christians confirms running accusations of extortion, blackmail,
> outright fraud, sodomy and witchcraft etc, against various Born Again churches.
>
> We have heard testimonies of victims who have been conned of their money
> and property under the guise of false "sowing." Now a parishioner is revealing how
> she was used in furtherance of this racket.
>
> Hundreds and probably thousands were conned of their money in false hope
> that the pastor would cure them of their ailments including Aids. It's discernible that
> under this blackmail, many innocent worshippers could even have contracted the
> deadly virus or gotten their Aids progression accelerated, with fatal consequences.
>
> One of the victims of this pastor has already died of Aids related sickness after
> the pastor fleeced her, of millions of shillings on a pseudo-promise of a miracle
> healing. Related to this fleecing, Kashemeire's eight-year old daughter has had her
> leg broken, at the instigation of the thieving and callous pastor. The pastor wanted
> to punish her so that she spends the money she was suspected to have received from
> the deceased and declined to hand over to the church leader.
>
> The criminality in some of the Born-Again churches has burst tolerable levels.
> The government must take urgent action like it did in 2001-2003 when armed
> robberies had hit the capital and were raiding banks in broad daylight.
>
> We cannot allow a gang of criminal pastors to go on fleecing the population and
> causing deaths to people while hiding under the cloak of freedom of worship. There
> is no freedom to defraud people. That's criminal. Such criminal minded pastors
> belong to jail.
>
> In 2000 a group of thugs masquerading under religion, killed over 500 people in
> mass murder in a church in Kanungu. Later, other dead bodies were recovered from
> various sites where this Devil's church operated.
>
> But besides the government intervention, worshippers should also wake up to the
> reality of false religion and its pastors. How on earth can a person in his/her normal
> senses believe that a pastor can cure him/her of any biological infection, like AIDS
> by mere prayers or by word of mouth?[7]

The above kind of functionalist economic theory concerning false religions,
religious fraud and abuses of religious power and authority to steal from the
believers, and then, silence their victims with threats of divine retribution,
appeals to many people, especially in East Africa. The related theory that the
traditional Church or religious authority functions to support the status quo,
and that it can be used as an effective weapon by religious leaders to silence

dissent and suppress opposition, helps people to affirm that the new religious movements and churches and their leaders are corrupt and they are in reality mere economic enterprises that are disguised as religious movements, organizations and churches.

Therefore, the holders of these kinds of economic speculative theories and views about religion and its leaders are the ones who readily believed that the Marian Movement leaders killed their followers because their apocalyptic prophecies and predictions for the end of the world had failed to materialize.

In addition, there is the common speculation that the embarrassed Marian Movement leaders did not know how to handle the problem of the disillusioned Marian Movement members, who wanted their money refunded to them. There was a wide-spread belief that after the failure of the apocalyptic predictions for the end of the world, some disillusioned cloistered Marian Members wanted to defect, and to go back home to live a normal life in the world they had previously renounced as evil, and had originally left behind for being corrupt.

These speculations and theories have good reasoning to support them. But they do not explain why many hundreds of the Marian Movement members willingly came to their Movement leaders and allowed them to martyr them in order to send them to heaven.

However, there is no concrete evidence to support the commonly held view and popular speculations that the Marian Movement leaders defrauded their followers, set the fire to the church building with their followers locked inside, and fled into exile with their loot. Apart from hoaxes, nobody has actually ever seen these MRTCG leaders, alive, following the church inferno in Kanungu, on Friday March 17, 2000.

On the contrary, during the field research, we found reliable information that indicates that the Marian Movement leaders died in the church inferno along with their loyal followers.[8] This is also consistent with their own moral practices and religious teachings concerning martyrdoms as atonement for sin and salvation. Their self-sacrificial deaths are also consistent with their apocalyptic expectations for a heavenly ascension with the supernatural assistance of the Blessed Virgin Mary to attain eternal life and happiness in the fellowship of God, the Blessed Virgin Mary, Jesus, the Uganda Martyrs and the holy saints. These Marian Movement leaders truly believed in their heavenly visions and what they zealously preached, as God's new definitive apocalyptic revelations. They were willing to put both their own moral teachings and religious faith into practice, even to sacrifice their lives and die for their religious faith, as God's obedient Christian martyrs and moral saints.

7. Mary's Catholic Moral Reform Movement & Parallels To the Anglican *Balokole Movement* in East Africa

For the impartial observers, the Marian spiritual renewal and moral reformist Movement within the Catholic Church, was fascinating. This was particularly true, when it was both viewed and analyzed from a broader religious and historical context of religion and Church dynamics within East Africa. Whereas the Protestant Church tends to fracture and segment into new denominations both in North America and Africa, the Catholic Church tends to remain united by allowing the development of new religious movements and the founding of new religious orders. Fr. Dominic Kataribabo. Keledonia Mwerinde and Joseph Kibwetere believed that this was true for both the Catholic and Protestant churches, when they formally founded the MRTCG in 1991.

Therefore, it was also within this broader historical religious context, in which the leaders of the MRTCG perceived and constructed their religious and primary moral ideas, created their own apocalyptic writings, teachings and formulated their new principles for Benedictine Order-like monastic practices. My research team was also interested in the observations and comments of the Roman Catholic and the Anglican Church leaders, as well as those of the *Balokole,* about the MRTCG, as a new apocalyptic Catholic Marian Moral Movement, that was the local Catholic Church's parallel to the Anglican Church's *Balokole Movement* in Uganda and much of East Africa, Rwanda, Burundi and the Eastern Region of the Democratic Republic of the Congo. These were also the same regions from which the MRTCG recruited most of its African members.

I was interested in their observations and comments concerning the theology, teachings and practices of the Movement because the Anglican Church had encountered a similar phenomenon almost half a century before in the form of the fundamentalist movement and apocalyptic experiences of the *Balokole Movement.* They had taught nearly similar apocalyptic and eschatological doctrines.

However, the *Balokole* had taught the doctrines in the name of Jesus, instead of the Blessed Virgin Mary, as the MRTCG did. The *Balokole* were also spiritual perfectionists and moral reformists like the Marian Movement members. To some significant degree, the apocalyptic *Balokole* had preached God's impending apocalyptic judgment and for doomsday divine destruction for the unrepentant doomsday. They had also behaved like Mwerinde and Kibwetere's apocalyptic and moral reformist Marian Movement members. One of the main differences between the two moral reform and apocalyptic movements is the special Catholic and Marian elements, such as the devotion, and veneration, or "worship" of the Blessed Virgin Mary, monasticism and membership in the Roman Catholic Church.

In the 1940s and 1950s, the local *Balokole* of the Anglican Church of Uganda, particularly in Kayonza area, on the border with the Democratic Republic of the Congo (DRC), and Rwanda, had also zealously preached and taught very similar apocalyptic doctrines and doomsday scenarios. They spent all their time in collective prayer and fasting while waiting for the end of the world and their "Day of Ascension" into heaven. They completely stopped working and refused to harvest the seasonal ripe crops in their gardens, claiming that this world was ending within a few days or weeks. The *Balokole* in Kanungu had claimed that they did not have to work since they were going to heaven, where they did not need any food and drink.

However, to the great relief of many people, the *Balokole*'s doomsday prophecies and apocalyptic predictions for the end of the world had proved to be both false and biblically unfounded. These alien or Western missionary-inspired, apocalyptic and errant Christian doomsday teachings were also anxiety-causing and disruptive to the local economy and led to food shortages, among many Christian families. These erroneous apocalyptic Christian beliefs, teachings and practices were also destructive to family, and undermined traditional social security, cultural and religious stability.

Some of the people who witnessed this *Balokole* heresy, or erroneous religious teaching, including those who had believed those teachings or taught them, were still alive, and some Anglican bishops, like the Rt. Rev. John W. Ntegyereize, did not want these *Balokole* and their devout religious congregation members to be misled by Mwerinde and Kibwetere's moral reformation and spiritual revivalist apocalyptic revelations and teachings. They also did not want them to be worried about the predicted imminent doomsday and apocalyptic end of the world in God's catastrophic fire, at the end of the Second Millennium.

Mwerinde and Kibwetere's apocalyptic prophecies and doomsday predictions, in addition to their prophetic preaching of the urgency for the repentance of sins, compulsive obsessions for promotion of moral perfections, piety, holiness of life, and moral integrity, sounded familiar. They were borrowed from the local the Anglican *Balokole Movement.* This was confusing to some influential people within the Catholic Church hierarchy because the Marian Movement claimed to be a reform Movement within the Catholic Church, based on the Marian apparitions.

However, the Marian Movement also both promoted and practiced some antiquated medieval traditions, and both appropriated and practices some Anglican *Balokole*-like apocalyptic, puritanical moral teachings and austere practices. This is partly because the MRTCG and the *Balokole* sounded almost the same in their testimonies, preaching repentance of sin, "Evangelical-like" zeal for personal and collective moral holiness of life as evidence of true repentance, divine obedience and piety.

The Marian Movement members also shared some *Balokole*-like moral teachings, such as: moral reformation as spiritual perfection, apocalyptic beliefs, simplicity of life, and austere moral practices.[9] This is very significant to note, especially when given the fact that both Joseph Kibwetere and Keledonia Mwerinde were devoted Marian Catholics. As a result, the Marian Movement leaders attributed their special divine revelations to God through the Blessed Virgin Mary, instead of attributing them to Jesus and the Holy Spirit, as the Anglican *Balokole* had done during the 1940s and 1950s.

In this Anglican crisis of the errant apocalyptic *Balokole* in Southern Uganda, the crisis was peacefully mediated and tactfully resolved. The Anglican bishop was located in Mbarara, and without good means of transportation, he thought it was too far to travel on foot to Kayonza. Therefore, requested the Archdeacon of Kabale, the Rev. M. Mutanga, to handle the crisis. In turn, Rev. Mutanga dispatched Mr. Yokana Bakebwa, a respected and "an outstanding Evangelist and Lay Leader," from Kinkizi area, to go on his behalf, and in the name of God and the Anglican Church's orthodoxy, to persuade the errant Christians to renounce their errors.

Yokana Bakebwa, most effectively used, his diplomacy and administrative skills to peacefully neutralize and squash," the new apocalyptic and Pentecostal religious movement," within the local Anglican Church, as an errant religious teaching (*Edini y'obuhabe*), and "dangerous heresy." Mr. Bakebwa appealed to his religious "errant brethren" (*empabe*) and sisters to repent of their sins and to renounce their heresies (*obuhabe*). Bakebwa gained the *Balokole's* trust, because he was one of them, and his mission was a great success, because it was conducted within the spirit of mutual understanding, love, trust, respect and compassionate pastoral care.

The errant apocalyptic *Balokole* had stopped working in their gardens. They abandoned the essential tasks of farming, such as tending farm animals and harvesting of ripe crops, to pray and wait for the Lord's return (*Parusia*), on what they believed to be an impending "Day of the Ascension." Work ceased because the *Balokole* and their families were spending all their time in self-purification through confessions of sin, fasting, Bible-study, fellowship and prayer while they diligently kept vigil and waited for the immediate return of Christ and the end of this world. In heaven, there was no eating or drinking. Accordingly, work in the food gardens and planting new crops or harvesting those already planted had been stopped as evidence of faith in God's new apocalyptic revelations for the imminent end of the world.

Remarkably, nearly half a century later, the Marian and apocalyptic MRTCG, also emerged in the same region. Like the previous apocalyptic *Balokole Movement*, the Marian Movement apocalyptic leaders also nearly taught these kinds of imminent apocalyptic doomsday beliefs, and practices. However, unlike the *Balokole,* who were successfully persuaded to renounce their own errant apocalyptic teachings, the Main Movement members were not persuaded to renounce, or constructively modify their own errant apocalyptic teachings, by their own Catholic bishops.

Consequently, when the MRTCG members gathered at their respective Marian Movement centers for the final purposes of self-sacrificial atonement, martyrdom and ascension into heaven, there was nobody to dissuade them from their mission. As a result, they actually went through with their tragic apocalyptic plans. As such, they only went a step further than the previous errant and apocalyptic *Balokole* of Kigezi, in Southern Uganda, during the 1950s.

It is ironic that the apocalyptic MRTCG leaders built their headquarters, and finally, died in the same region, where the *Balokole* had, initially, recruited their own members, and nearly sent them to heaven, during the 1950s. The apocalyptic *Balokole,* as the holy saints of Jesus the Christ, believed in an imminent end of the world. In 1948, the *Balokole* of Kigezi in Southern Uganda, were invited by their leader to come and gather in some selected holy mountain places and churches, and wait for arrival of the predicted "Day of the Ascension" into heaven.

Many fundamentalist and apocalyptic *Balokole* strongly believed that their generation was also God's time for final divine judgment of sinners, and the tragic end of the world (*okuhwerekyerera kwe ensi egi*). Others were sure that it was a kind of "*Parusia.*" That is, the *Balokole* would ascend into heaven, leaving sinners behind to live in the violent, war-prone and dangerous world, for another millennium, when God would, finally, destroy this supposed corrupt and evil world that is believed to be dominated by the Devil. And then, God would establish his own perfect Kingdom on the Earth, as "Heaven on Earth," and God's apocalyptic restoration for the primordial "Garden of Eden" (Gen. 1:1-31).

The apocalyptic and doomsday *Balokole* had also expected Jesus' visible physical return to take them up physically into heaven. Like the doomsday *Balokole,* the apocalyptic and doomsday MRTCG members also expected an imminent end of the world, and spiritual ascension into heaven. However, unlike the *Balokole*, who did not know how they could physically fly, or miraculously ascend into heaven, without wings like the angels, were traditionally presumed to have, the MRTCG leaders taught that in their spiritual glorious ascension, they would be assisted by the Blessed Virgin Mary.

Unlike the *Balokole,* who seemed to believe in a physical ascension to heaven with their physical bodies, the MRTCG leaders were completely dualistic in their Greek philosophy, and taught that the bodies would be discarded before the souls' ascension into heaven. This was believed to be the case, since the Marian Movement leaders taught that only the disembodied souls, as spirits, were believed to be akin to God, and able to associate with God, and inherit eternal life of salvation, spiritual fellowship with God, in heaven.[10]

The Marian Movement leaders' teachings on this topic of how people would go to heaven and what kind of equipment that they would need, was a complex system of Catholic theology of salvation (*soteriology*), eschatology (end of time teachings), and philosophical metaphysics (theory of life and being), which were almost incomprehensible to the lay members of the Marian Movement and were complete mysteries to most outsiders.

Therefore, the *Balokole* expected to experience a real bodily ascension into heaven, just like helium balloons float upwards into the blue sky above, on a clear warm day. The *Balokole* believed that they would ascend into the sky like the risen Christ was reported to have done according to the accounts of the Apostles as found in the Holy Scriptures. He is believed to have both physically and gloriously ascended into heaven (the sky) while his Apostles looked on in complete wonder (Acts 1:9-11).

The ancient people's cosmology was so crude that they believed that God, the angels and the saints were physical beings that lived in heaven (paradise). They believed that heaven was a physical place like a glorious palace of gold and lavishly watered green gardens located in the sky above the earth. They had no idea that the space above was too cold and hostile to support life and that the Earth was more like heaven, when compared to living on the life-less moon or the neighboring planets, like the cold and frozen Mars and Venus, which is boiling hot, and has a toxic and corrosive atmosphere filled with sulfuric acid.

Nevertheless, the *Balokole* and the Marian Movement members were almost like *The Heaven's Gate* cult people, who believed that life in heaven was better, and was located on another planet. They also erroneously believed that heaven was in some place in the sky or space, and the believers could travel to heaven in a spaceship or comet.[11] Unlike the ancient Egyptians, who sought to take their treasures to heaven with them, these apocalyptic groups gave away their treasure, or sold their possessions and gave the money to their leaders, or to charity in preparation for their spiritual ascension into heaven, where the material, or earthly possessions, such as money, food, minerals and wealth were not needed.

Bishop Ntegyereize also condemned the sales of land and family property by Movement members as a mandatory requirement for joining the apocalyptic Marian Movement. The bishop said that this practice was socioeconomically dangerous, and disruptive to the peace and well-being of the community. The African traditional families hold land and property in common. Therefore, by an individual's decision and action of selling these collective possessions and surrendering all the proceeds to the Marian Movement's leaders in Kanungu, without provision for the upkeep of the family members, or considerations for the education of the children, was completely irresponsible, unethical and an unacceptable indirect form of economic fraud on the part of Keledonia Mwerinde and Joseph Kibwetere. The Rt. Rev. John Wilson Ntegyereize, the Kinkizi Anglican Bishop, duly warned the local religious leaders of other religious affiliations, and the government officials to that effect.

However, Yorokam Kamacerere, as the RDC (Resident District Commissioner), and main government's officer for Rukungiri area, which at the time included the Kanungu area as its sub-district, objected to the recommendation that the Marian Movement should be recognized and registered as NGO (Non-Government Organization). This was in contrast to his morally weak and probably more easily bribed and corrupted subordinates, in Kanungu, who zealously recommended the apocalyptic Marian Movement to be officially recognized and registered by the Government of Uganda, as a civic moral educational and development oriented NGO.

Mr. Kamacherere was a man of sound and great personal moral integrity, and therefore, could not be corrupted by bribes, or expensive presents, such as cows and money. Subsequently, he remained opposed to the questionable beliefs, ethics and moral practices of the leaders of *The Movement for the Restoration of the Ten Commandments of God*. He refused to support the Marian Movement, Kamacherere wrote an administrative letter to President Museveni opposing the Movement's application for registration as a moral education, developmental and a charitable NGO (Non-Government Organization), with its headquarters in Kanungu.

In his letter, Mr. Kamacherere both described and referred to the Marian Movement as "a dangerous cult." He based this judgment on the observation of the Movement's monastic practices and doomsday teachings. He objected to the Marian Movement's own preoccupation with otherworldly visions and concerns, as stated in their articles of incorporation.[12] For instance, in those articles, the main duties of the officers were to record and teach moral reformation based on the heavenly visions, and revelations from God through the Blessed Virgin Mary.[13]

In addition, as the RDC for Rukungiri District, Mr. Kamacherere, as a devout Anglican, took seriously the Anglican and Catholic bishops' concerns about the anxiety causing apocalyptic doctrines, extreme monastic practices and panic-inducing prophecies, by the apocalyptic and leaders of the MRTCG. Fear and existential anxiety were related to the Marian Movement leaders' doomsday prophecies and apocalyptic predictions for the imminent end of the world, in a catastrophic fire, as God's punishment for sins of sexual immorality and corruption.

Unlike the Rev. Richard Mutazindwa, who was the ARDC (Assistant Resident District Commission) for Kanungu, who was allegedly given extravagant gifts by the Marian Movement leaders, including several Friesian milking cows, as the price for his official support for their Marian Movement's activities, Kamacherere was incorruptible. Kamacerere opposed the registration and State licensing of the MRTCG as an NGO, while the Rev. Mutazindwa, his administrative assistant, supported the Marian Movement's registration. Mr. Kamacherere also heeded the warnings of the bishops in both Mbarara and Kanungu, and took their warnings and rejection of the Marian Movement seriously enough to pass them on to President Yoweri Museveni. Kamacherere, as an Anglican, was not being anti-Catholic, by his refusal to support the Catholic Marian Movement.

However, many Anglicans gave their political and religious support to the Catholic Marian moral reform and apocalyptic Movement because they considered it as a convenient political strategy. They were not interested in the efficacy or validity of the Marian apparitions or Catholic theology and the Marian Movement leaders' claims and teachings or practices. Conversely, these opportunistic Anglican politicians wanted to demonstrate that they were both politically and religiously impartial. They sought to avoid pitfalls of sectarian politics. This position was deemed ideal since the main opponents of the Marian Movement and its leaders were predominantly Catholics, especially the more conservative, and intolerant priests. This was particularly true for those priests, who were personally or professionally allied with the conservative bishops of Mbarara Catholic Diocese.

In 1994, as the RDC for Rukungiri District, Mr. Kamacherere wrote to President Yoweri Museveni an official letter stating some serious administrative concerns, and religious objections concerning the dangers posed by the MRTCG, as an extremist Marian Movement. He strongly believed that the Marian Movement leaders exhibited some excessive and religiously unhealthy moral and religious fanatical and compulsive moral obsessions for the attainment of perfection in the holy name of the Blessed Virgin Mary as "the Holy Mother of God" and "Queen of Heaven."

Kamacherere's cultural, religious and political assessment of the Marian Movement's self-evident compulsive obsessions for preaching of God's apocalyptic judgment and imminent cosmic doom in God's cleansing holy fire, was negative. He was of the impression that the Marian Movement was "a Catholic doomsday cult." In part, Mr. Kamacherere's assessment was based on the observations that the Marian Movement enthusiastically proclaimed that God would soon judge people and that God would burn all sinful people in the world, unless they repented of their sins and joined the apocalyptic monastic Marian Movement. He was also alarmed by the fact that this moral reformist and apocalyptic Marian Movement manifested new special extremist and fundamentalist religious and moral obsessions for personal moral purity and collective moral and political perfection.

These Marian Movement members' compulsive moral and religious obsessions for perfection, as manifested in the attainment of heavenly virtues, as well as the societal, religious and moral attainment of a saintly life in the world, were unrealistic. He noted that the economic requirement for the Marian Movement members to sell their property, and give all proceeds to the Marian Movement leaders, were cult-like and posed a real threat to the economic well-being and security of the Marian Movement members, as well as endangering the people in the entire region. In his letter, Kamacherere called for an immediate official Government criminal investigation into the clandestine activities of the Marian Movement.

However, not much was done by the local government authorities, partly because the Rev. Richard Mutazindwa was friendly to the Marian Movement leaders and wrote an opposing report and supported the recognition of the Marian Movement as a Non-Governmental Organization (NGO) for economic development, religious activities and moral education. The newspapers and the Kanungu people alleged that this friendship was rooted in corruption, since the Rev. Mutazindwa was the alleged recipient of major gifts from the leaders of the Marian Movement, including three highly prized Friesian milking cows, he was favorably socialized to accept them as good neighbors and to write positive letters of recommendations concerning their supposed good, and the beneficial religious, educational and charitable projects within the community and the nation as a whole. On the other hand, the Rev. Richard Mutazindwa was an Anglican priest and Assistant RDC for Kanungu. As such, he did not wish to be accused of being a sectarian or anti-Catholic. Subsequently, he did not investigate the concerns raised by Kamacherere, another Anglican, who was the RDC of Rukungiri District and his boss.

Therefore, it is conceivable that if the RDC for Rukungiri and his Kanungu assistant had been Catholics, the MRTCG leadership in Kanungu would have been subjected to an appropriate closer scrutiny and vigilance, at the request of Bishop John Baptist Kakubi of Mbarara Diocese, since both Joseph Kibwetere and Fr. Dominic Kataribabo were from his diocese. These measures would have probably prevented the Marian Movement's eventual tragic mass self-sacrificial deaths in 2000.

However, the predominantly Anglican political and administrative leadership in both Rukungiri and Kanungu was tolerant of the MRTCG, and its apocalyptic teachings and extreme monastic activities for fear of being accused of being anti-Catholic. These political and religious factors are some of the main reasons for Rev. Mutazindwa's decision to support Joseph Kibwetere and Keledonia Mwerinde's Marian, holiness, moral and spiritual renewal Catholic Marian Movement. This is true, irrespective of the allegations that the Rev. Mutazindwa was corrupt, and had been bribed by the Marian Movement leaders with some Frisian cows, and free domestic labor in order to win and maintain his political favor and administrative support.

In reality, the Rev. Mutazindwa welcomed the Marian Movement in his impoverished Kanungu area, as a positive religious organization that promoted moral education, economic development, and both housed and fed the poor. He was not concerned about the Marian Movement's apocalyptic Marian visions and doomsday predictions of an imminent end of the world. He knew that those of the doomsday *Balokole* had failed to materialize, and saw no reason for causing panic. He supported the Marian Movement leaders because he wanted to use the Marian Movement for his political and economic agenda. He wanted to use them to develop the rural area and town of Kanungu. In turn, the Marian Movement leaders also had their own political agenda. In turn, the Marian Movement leaders sought to use him to obtain his valuable political and administrative support and needed endorsement to gain legitimacy, as a beneficial Catholic, educational, developmental and charitable organization in the area. As RDC for Kanungu, the Rev. Mutazindwa gave to them, the necessary administrative and political support, and they were grateful to him.

In addition, many Anglicans positively viewed the moral reformist and apocalyptic Marian Movement or the MRTCG, as a religious organizational equivalent of "a Catholic *Balokole Movement*" within the Catholic Church. As such, they saw no real legal or political reasons to investigate, limit or prohibit the Marian Movement's religious, educational and economic activities in the community as the Mbarara Catholic bishops, Bishop John Ntegyereize[14] of the Anglican Diocese of Kinkizi, and Kamacherere, the

Rukungiri RDC demanded. Furthermore, the Rev. Mutazindwa also had no personal, ecclesiastical, political and administrative reasons, or incentive to obey Bishop John Ntegyereize's wishes or directives. Rev. Mutazindwa strongly believed that Bishop John Ntegyereize, as the local Anglican Bishop of Kinkizi Diocese of the Anglican Church of Uganda, had deliberately both ecclesiastically marginalized and isolated him.

Subsequently, when the Rev. Mutazindwa was given attention or political respect by the Catholic Marian Movement leaders, he responded accordingly, having felt rejected by Bishop Ntegyereize.[15] The Rev. Mutazindwa embraced the Catholic Marian leaders for having most eagerly and reverently welcomed him. They had accorded to him the necessary cultural, customary religious and political recognition, which he craved. In turn, he gave them his political and administrative support, which they badly needed. As a result, they were allowed to carry out their activities, both good and evil, without police surveillance and the government's intervention. Consequently, the Government of Uganda was unable to detect and prevent the self-sacrificial secret ritual deaths and the tragic church inferno, in Kanungu, on Friday, March 17, 2000, and thereby, preventing the hundreds of Marian devotees' deaths that took place before the Kanungu church fire.

NOTES

1. See: John Mbiti, *African Religions and Philosophy*; Emmanuel Twesigye, *African Religion, Philosophy, and Christianity in Logos Christ: Common Ground Revisited*; *God Race, Myth and Power: An African Corrective Research Analysis.*

2. *Ibid.*

3. God and functions or religion are realities for them. Their existential experiences negate Sigmund Freud's assumption that God was an illusion. See *The Future of Illusion.*

4. These questions are answered in various chapters of the book. The data presented and its analysis or arguments are made to support a particular position, and they are components of these answers

5a. See the misleading and damaging false accusation of cannibalism and sensational front page news headline: "**CULT LEADERS DRANK BLOOD**," *The New Vision*, Tuesday, March 28, 2000. The story was also carried by *The Uganda Monitor* and other local newspapers. This mode of sensational reporting distorted the Marian Movement.

5b. See Philip Schaff, *History of the Christian Church* (Grand Rapids: Eerdmans Publishing Company, 1980), Vol. 1, 380-390; Justo L. Gonzalez, *A History of Christian Thought* (Nashville: Abingdon: 1970), Vol. 1, 60-235.

6. For instance, see *New Vision*, Wednesday, March 29, 2000: "Kanungu Report 4." The police conducted surveillance by State directives on some suspected MRTCG active members.

This was done in order to preempt voluntary ritual mass murders or martyrdoms in an attempt to gains salvation and ascend into heaven.

7. For the full coverage of these stories, see: *The Daily Monitor* of Tuesday, October 9, 2007 and Editorial of *The Daily Monitor*, Wednesday, October 10, 2007.

8. I interviewed many relatives and eyewitnesses and they all affirmed that the Marian Movement leaders were at the Banquet and were present in the church building with their followers on the "Day of Ascension." Some of the body remains resembled the Marian Movement leaders, especially the skulls and insignia rings for the leaders. These are pieces of evidence which contradict Mrs. Kibwetere views and assumptions that Mr. Kibwetere, her husband, was killed by Keledonia Mwerinde during the 1990s, due to HIV/AIDS-infection.

9. Yokana Bakebwa and Blasio Kalenzi read the MRTCG's handbook, and declared that Mwerinde and Kibwetere had plagiarized their own teachings from the *Balokole*, but had given them to their own followers as God's revelations through the Virgin Mary, instead of Jesus Christ. March 20, 2002.

10. *A Timely Message from Heaven*, 19-20.

11. Since religion is faith-based, therefore, there are many people, who reject science and reason. They reject evolution and the reality that the Earth is the best planet to live on.

12. The Uganda Human Rights Commission Report (2002). *The Kanungu Massacre: The Movement for the Restoration of the Ten Commandments of God,* 75-84.

13. *Ibid.* 75.

14. Bishop John Wilson Ntegyereize was hostile to the Marian Movement. He said that they scared people with false doomsday prophecies, and engaged in dangerous economic, cultural and moral practices, like selling all possessions. It also attracted some *Balokole.* See: *The Kanungu Massacre,* 41. Bishop Ntegyereize was interviewed, on August, 17, 2004.

15. Bishop Ntegyereize had trouble dealing with the priests, whom he could not control. Rev. Richard Mutazindwa and Rev. Canon Hamlet Kabushenga, the former Member of Uganda Parliament, for Kinkizi East, are two Anglican examples of this case.

Chapter Three

CHURCH AUTHORITY, STATE POWER AND RESISTANCE MOVEMENTS

Any well-organized and sound organization, including the Church and the State, must have well-defined constitutions, or clearly formulated and well publicized governing laws and codes of normative ethics, or professional conduct for both its respective officials and members or citizens, as a whole. The institutions that seek to endure and last for a long time must also create benevolent and good structures, which have well formulated delineations of powers of the leadership or hierarchy and the rest of the officials.

1. Introduction

The above also applies to the traditional institutions of divine monarchies and their correlative institutions of the priesthood, as well as the definition and assignments of State power and Church/Mosque/Temple moral or religious authority, as part of God's special revelations, holy institutions and mandates. According to Prof. John Mbiti's research that is well documented in his book, *African Religions and Philosophy*, it is clear that the hundreds of the African traditional creation myths are part of these theocentric traditional societal methods for the holy formulation and institution of ordered societies and divine kingships in the world.

A careful study of main creation stories and myths of the institution of divine kingships as theocratic monarchies in Uganda, Rwanda, Burundi, Ethiopia, and Ghana will clearly reveal how these African traditional societies had carefully defined religious and political institutions, as God's divinely instituted holy institutions for the ordering of society and maintenance of harmony and peace within the society and the world, as God's Kingdom on Earth.

Accordingly, Queen Muhumuza's *Nyabingi Liberation Movement*, Alice Lakwena's *Holy Spirit Movement*, Joseph Kony's *Lord's Resistance Army,* and Mwerinde's *Movement for the Restoration of the Ten Commandments of God* as well as the *Muslim Allied Democratic Forces,* are theocratic religio-political movements, which are rooted within this African culture, Traditional Religion and politics. As such, these are valid African religio-liberation movements, and not evil "cults."

In the African traditional divine kingdoms and churches or religious establishments, powers and authority come down directly from God and not from the people, who are governed, on God's behalf. That is, traditionally, the absolute divine kings, emperors and high-priests were only answerable to God. But the kings or emperors could use their political and military powers to coerce and force the religious leaders, such as the prophets and high-priests to obey them, or be banished, executed and martyred, as in the cases of the Hebrew prophets, including John the Baptizer and Jesus. In the case of Uganda, the Christian Martyrs, including the Anglican Archbishop Janani Luwum, who was assassinated by President Idi Amin, on February 17, 1977, clearly illustrate the nature of this deadly form of Church and State conflicts, even in the modern era.

However, for truly democratically elected governments, civic organizations and charitable societies, both power and authority, are defined differently, and they also come from different sources. Accordingly, any true and effective earthly kingdoms, empires and political governments have police and military forces, as a form of coercive power. The president or king's orders are to be obeyed and enforced by police or military force. Their real authority and power come from the respective offices which they hold and the constitution that authorizes and empowers them to carry out defined political, economic, social, public, legal and military actions for the welfare, security, service, defense and common good of the citizens and the nation. In more democratic and just nations, the leaders are indicted, tried, punished and deposed when they misuse and abuse their offices.

However, for the traditional Christian Church, true authority and power come from God. Authority and power do not flow from the constitution or come from the people whom they lead. Authority and power in the Catholic Church and related churches come from God, through Christ and the Holy Spirit. These forms of grace are imparted onto the Church by Christ. Christ chose the Twelve Apostles, trained them, and finally, ordained them, as his apostles (Jn. 20:16-20). He gave them power to go into the world and teach people to repent of their sins, to love and forgive unconditionally in the same way God has forgiven them and to enter God's Kingdom of Unconditional Love, free forgiveness of sins and peace. To Peter, Jesus gave the power of the keys to open heaven for the repentant sinners and hell for those, who fail to heed the message of God's "good news" of free invitation to enter the Kingdom of God.

According to Augustine and Thomas Aquinas, God is the ultimate source of both Church and State powers and authority. However, they subordinated the state power to that of the Church's authority because the Church was God's direct agency of grace, revelation and salvation in the world. The

Christian Holy Roman Empire was the result of this political theology. The Pope was supreme. He could depose the divine kings of Europe. The Inquisition was the tragic result. King Henry VIII of England finally staged a political and religious coup against the Pope in the sixteenth century. He declared himself the new Head of the Church of England. He subordinated the Church to the State.

However, with a traditional Roman Catholic theology and political theory, the Church remains superior to the state. This is a form of theocracy for a modern Catholic society. The Church's superior divine authority and power come from God, through Jesus the Christ, and the anointing of the Holy Spirit. It does not consist in the laity's majority vote for their leaders as it is the case with secular institutions, organizations and governments, such as the Prime Minister of Britain, or the President of the USA. For instance, Jesus was not elected as the Christ, or Messiah, by his disciples.

Similarly, within the Catholic Church tradition, the laity does not elect their priests, bishops, and the Popes. According to the Catholic religious traditions and teachings, religious and supernatural power and authority are mediated from God to Christ, the world through the Church through the Pope, bishops, priests, and finally, the lay religious leaders.

In this divine religious hierarchy, the role of the power of grace, divine election, the guidance of the Holy Spirit through training, prayer and holy ordination is important and vital. *The Movement for the Restoration of the Ten Commandments of God* realized these factors. As a result, Joseph Kibwetere and Keledonia Mwerinde worked extremely hard to persuade the duly trained Catholic priests and nuns to join the Marian Movement.

Mwerinde recruited well-known male leaders into her predominantly female populated Marian Movement because she wanted use them for her political, social, and economic agenda. Mwerinde needed Joseph Kibwetere and Fr. Dominic Kataribabo in order to provide pastoral and spiritual care, as well as giving both credibility and validity to the Marian Movement, as a Catholic organization, or Marian Movement within the established Catholic Church. She did not found the Marian Movement as a separatist movement, or association that was outside or removed from the Catholic Church.

The leaders of the Catholic Marian Movement were also part of the conservative Catholic right wing, who still affirmed that the ancient exclusive Catholic Church's dogma of *"Extra Ecclesiam Nulla Salus* (outside the [Catholic] Church there is no salvation), which is still the normative religious and theological normative principle for many conservative Christians. But in this case, they still interpreted the term "Church" in an exclusive Pre-Vatican II manner, to refer to the physical and historical "Roman Catholic Church."

As such, for most of these theologically Pre-Vatican II theologians, priests and their conservative devoted Catholic followers, the faithful members of *The Movement for the Restoration of the Ten Commandments of God* perished and went to hell, since they died in a state of ecclesiastical sanction of the Church by virtue of Bishop Kakubi's letter of suspension of Joseph Kibwetere, his associates and followers from receiving Church sacraments, and in the case of the priests' suspension from the celebration and administration of the sacraments, including saying mass in public or private houses and hearing confessions of sins.

The Episcopal decree of suspension by Bishop Kakubi did not amount to excommunication, as the papers had erroneously stated, in many articles published by *The Monitor* and *New Vision*, during the years of 2000-2002. According to the Archbishop Paul Bakyenga,[1] the Holy Father, Pope John Paul II did not excommunicate the members of *The Movement for the Restoration of the Ten Commandments of God*, their leaders or the priests involved in the rebellious Marian movement.

Nevertheless, many Catholic lay people in Mbarara Archdiocese and other Catholic dioceses in Uganda strongly believe that the priests involved in the Movement, particularly, Frs. Kataribabo, Ikazire and Kasapurari, were interdicted and threatened with excommunication by the hierarchy of the Catholic Church. However, the decrees of suspension issued to them by Bishop Kakubi, on May 7, 1991, and put into a written form on May 12, 1991, clearly indicate that the priests are suspended from their sacramental and other priestly duties for disobeying him as their Diocesan Bishop and canonical superior and chief pastor. The suspension was to remain in effect until they repented and decided to obey him as their Diocesan Bishop, as the canon laws require.

In technical, legal and theological terms, the Catholic Church's decrees had serious implications for social, religious, moral and posthumous consequences for the Marian Movement members, their relatives and supporters. Nevertheless, there is a major distinction between suspension from duty and reception of sacraments and excommunication. Excommunication means that the person or people excommunicated are delivered to hellfire and eternal damnation in hell. There is no hope for salvation, unless they are restored to fellowship with God through the Church as their "Mother" and "Ark of Salvation."

However, if *The Movement for the Restoration of Ten Commandments of God* severed links with Bishop Kakubi, but had not retained their links with the Catholic Church and the Pope, there would be a period of grace or suspension of Bishop Kakubi's interdiction. Then, canonically speaking, the Catholic Church and its hierarchy, in Mbarara would no longer possess the necessary canonical power, and pastoral means to exercise an ecclesiastical jurisdiction over them, until the Pope had acted on the Marian Movement leaders' appeal.

Accordingly, the Catholic Church hierarchy in Mbarara would not have the canonical jurisdiction and power to excommunicate the Marian Movement leaders and their members, even if it wanted to do so. However, in this case, it clear that the Catholic Church hierarchy in both Mbarara and Rome did not seek or wish to excommunicate the errant Marian Movement priests, despite the Marian Movement's strange doomsday prophecies for an imminent divine judgment and fiery end of the world. The Mbarara bishops had also both rejected and discouraged the Marian Movement's extreme monastic teachings concerning holy obedience and moral perfection, as complete detachment from earthly life, in terms of possessions, education, sex, and family ties.

No viable Church, State, community, organization, association or society can continue to exist meaningfully, and survive for a long time, while discouraging its members from the individual or private ownership of property, and strongly prohibiting sexual intercourse and the development of any caring, family or friendship ties. On the contrary, the ideal Church, State or civic organizations are those, which strongly promote these economic, political, and wholesome moral and social values. And try to show people how to most meaningfully engage in the activities of life in the community, society and the world both joyfully and peacefully. This moral instruction is essential in order to promote and bring about positive development, which does not exploit people, or both pollute and degrade the environment. This integrated and comprehensive approach will promote developments, which result in positive conditions of:

- social harmony
- productive team work
- equitable sharing of scarce resources

- socioeconomic justice
- peaceful mutual coexistence in harmony
- joy and happiness.

These are the existential factors, which most effectively transform the world into God's Kingdom. These moral and social values are part of the keys for building God's Kingdom and the establishment of heaven on Earth. This positive acceptance of human life and this world, and despite its imperfections, suffering and pain, is necessary in order to live a good and happy life in the world, instead of seeking to flee from it, as the members of the MRTCG tragically did, in March 2000. This religious approach is a more constructive and positive affirmation of life and the evolutionary world, as God's good creations to be protected and improved. This is in direct opposition to those misguided radical theological dualists, who rejected the body and the physical world as evil entities because they are not spirit or perfect. This includes the leaders of the MRTCG and similar groups. These Christians have to be reminded that this is the same world that God loved so much that he sent his own beloved Son to come and save, instead of destroying it (Jn. 3:16-20).

Therefore, these kinds of otherworldly and misguided escapist religious leaders and people, like the members of *The People's Temple, Heaven's Gate, Branch Davidians,* and the MRTCG, have to be instructed to accept life and the world. They have to be taught to appreciate finite life within this world, as God's wonderful miracle and special free divine gift, despite its imperfections. These otherworldly oriented religious escapists, have to be converted to true religion and divine truth, which accepts the world, as God's good creation, and to see it, as the true Garden of Eden, which needs human care, preservation, healing and divine restoration.

The above approach leads to the glorious appreciation and praise or worship of God, as the Creator of life and the wonderful world, rather than seeking to get rid of the world or to flee from it. Then, God's people can wage a moral crusade, or holy war against the human-made moral evils of corruption and moral, social, economic and political pollution that defile God's good world, and transform it into a violent place. This is a better approach than merely condemning the world as an evil domain of the Devil, and then, seeking to escape from it, and ascend into heaven, as Kibwetere and Keledonia's holiness and apocalyptic Marian Movement erroneously sought to do by killing its loyal followers in order to deliver them directly to heaven.

Ultimately, God created human beings in the world to live there and not in the sky. God created humanity to live in the world in fellowship with him or her, as their gracious primordial Ancestor or Parent (Origin), as their ever present "Creator," "Sustainer" and "Redeemer." The world was at the same time also simultaneously the Garden of Eden, the Kingdom of God and Heaven. Tragically, the leaders for *The Movement for the Restoration of the Ten Commandments of God* were not theologically sophisticated enough to be able to realize that this is an important theological truth.

The Marian Movement was dominated, by fundamentalist Catholic lay people, and was by its religious nature, simplistic in terms of a literalist reading and interpretation of the Holy Scriptures. Fr. Kataribabo made some important liturgical innovations, but failed to make necessary theological reforms, except in matters of sacramental confession, and the administration of the Eucharist, according to Pre-Vatican procedures that required the penitent to receive the host on the tongue, while devoutly kneeling.

2. Religion, Politics, Dissent and Persecution

In many African traditional and the Muslim theocratic, or God-centered nations and societies, religion is both deeply and inseparably intertwined with politics. It is the most effective tool for education, moral agency, information, political and social-economic mobilization and social control.

Concepts of God-centered values and political laws of theocracy are most clearly visible, in cases of some Islamic countries, like Saudi Arabia, Iran, Egypt, Libya, Sudan and Pakistan. The centrality of religion permeates all the main arenas of life. In these countries, the religious power is the foundation of moral values, economics, laws and government.

According to theocracy, religious dissent is persecuted because it threatens the political and religious establishment. Within this theocentric system, religious dissent is negatively viewed, as political opposition and social deviance. As such, religious dissent is treated more harshly, as a form of religious heresy, societal vice, rebellion, lack of patriotism and treason.

Accordingly, religious dissent is viewed negatively, as also being both social and political dissent and rebellion. Consequently, in most theocratic societies, especially Muslim and Catholic nations, religious dissent is often persecuted and its members are both socially and politically marginalized, discriminated against and treated, as social and religious outcasts. In some cases, laws are enacted to ban and outlaw new religious sects, as forms of unacceptable organized religious dissent and political protest.

In Uganda, religion had been used as a destructive sectarian and divisive political tool. Anglicanism was the religious, royalist and aristocratic political tool, which was employed to mobilize the elitist Anglicans to consolidate political power, and rule all the kingdoms and the nation of Uganda.

The Anglican royal power and political hegemony in Uganda was a direct result of the Anglican royalist missionary and political strategy of Bishop Alfred Tucker. Bishop Tucker was the second bishop, to be appointed for the Anglican Equatorial African Province, of which Uganda was the central location of the Anglican Province and its main Christian missionary operations.

Bishop Tucker succeeded Bishop James Hannington, who was martyred, in 1885, by King Mwanga, because he came through Busoga, which was culturally considered the backdoor to Buganda Kingdom, only to be used by friends or with the king's prior permission. Bishop Tucker understood the cultural, political, military and religious power and value of the African kings and chiefs.

Subsequently, as a result, Bishop Tucker carefully devised the "royalist," or "aristocratic," religio-political missionary strategy for Uganda, and especially for its five main kingdoms, including Busoga. Bishop Tucker's religious and political main missionary objectives were to establish both an Anglican Church and an Anglican political hegemony in Uganda. This was also his Anglican missionary mission and strategy for the Anglican missionary work, within the surrounding British territories and the countries of East Africa, of which he had jurisdiction, as the Anglican Bishop for the Equatorial Province.

Bishop Tucker's royal strategy was to convert all the kings in Uganda and their prime-ministers and major chiefs to Anglicanism. Then, he persuaded and informally commissioned local Anglican kings and chiefs, as some kinds of lay royal Anglican Christian ambassadors and local missionaries to preach and convert their own households, loyal chiefs and their subjects. Failure to follow the religious call of the king and chiefs to join their religion was viewed negatively, as religious and political dissent. In the Kingdom of Buganda, this religious dissent led to the tragedy of royal Christian persecution, mass arrests, murders, State executions and martyrdoms of Christians in the years of 1886-1887.

Those courageous faithful Baganda Christians, who refused to obey the royal decree of King Mwanga to abandon Christianity, as a foreign, or European colonial religion, and revert to the African Traditional Religion, or the *Kiganda* religion of the ancestors, were mercilessly hunted down, as dangerous political rebels, anti-cultural values and unpatriotic criminals. This State Christian persecution was later abandoned by King Mwanga. This was partly due to the fact that among the religious rebels, and therefore, cultural and religious political dissenters, were the privileged young sons of major chiefs and future political leaders, who were serving, as political interns in King Mwanga's own palace. Nevertheless, some of these courageous Christians were arrested, and summarily sentenced to death for treason and disobedience to the king.

The Christians were charged by the State, with the crimes of disrespect, abandonment of cultural traditions, lack of patriotism and treason, of which they could not successfully defend themselves, without renouncing their new religious faith, and abandoning the practices of Christianity. These Christians were facing charges of serious State and religious crimes. Some of these crimes were considered capital offenses, which were punishable by death, such as public hanging, or being burned alive.

The Christians were accused of treason because they were converted into membership of foreign religions, which preached the supremacy of the Christian loyalty to their new, absolute and powerful King Jesus, as the Lord (*Kabaka/Mukama*). The Christians also claimed that it was more important to obey God and the Lord Jesus, than to yield to the requirements of their cultures, the Traditional Religion and the mandatory traditional obedience and loyalty to King Mwanga, or other kings and chiefs. Above all, these "Christians became dual citizens." They belonged both to the Kingdom of God, through their allegiance to Jesus Christ, as their Lord, and yet, they were still Baganda, who belonged to their local Kingdom of Buganda with the *Kabaka*, as their earthly king.

However, as citizens of God's Kingdom, they were willing to defy the decrees and values of King Mwanga and suffer the political, physical and military consequences for their choice to rebel against their divinely instituted earthly king. They were, subsequently, hastily tried for treason and burned at Namugongo by King Mwanga's *Mujansi* (Military General), who was known and feared by Alexander Mackay and other European Christian missionaries for being nationalistic and viciously anti-European. He was opposed to the presence of the European Christian missionaries. He was vilified for being anti-Christian for opposing the culturally alienating Western Christianity, and its intrinsic foreign moral, colonial, cultural values, and political influences.

Characteristically, these alien values and Western imperialism had come along with the European Christian missionaries. Christianity, as a tool of Western cultural, religious and political imperialism, was antithetical to the African Traditional Religion. It was opposed to the African cultural values and cultural practices, such as the highly valued cultural practice of polygamy. Consequently, Christianity and its correlative foreign European cultural values were negatively evaluated and rejected by the traditionalist Baganda, as a colonial, corrupt, immoral and secular religion when compared to the traditional one, which was very theocratic.

These alien Christian values included rejection and disobedience to ancestral Kiganda customs, religious ideals and normative values, such as absolute obedience to the king (*Kabaka*) by all his royal subjects, including royal requests for sexual encounters, regardless of gender, age, marital status and other sexual commitments. This was supposed to be a sign of royal favor and source of pride for the people fortunate to be chosen by the king. But Christianity condemned these traditional religious and cultural values and practices, as unacceptable forms of "primitive conduct," "heathenism" and sexual immorality.

Homosexuality, which had been introduced at the king's palace by Muslim Arab traders from the East African coast, was viciously attacked by the Christian missionaries as an abomination to God. Some of the royal pages or political interns, who had been engaged in homosexual acts with King Mwanga, before their conversion to Christianity, had renounced homosexuality as a grave moral evil.

Subsequently, they rejected King Mwanga's homosexual advances, and thereby, caused his great rage and hostility against them. His anger was directed against both the Christian converts and their Christian European missionaries, along with Christianity, as a whole. For the king, Christianity was a foreign and destructive moral, religious, political, and cultural force which had to be directly confronted, fought and eliminated from the country. King Mwanga believed that he had the moral and political obligation to destroy Christianity before it's correlative imperialist forces could destroy him, neutralize his political power and take-over his kingdom and declare it a new British Christian colony at the heart of Africa.

King Mwanga was perceptive and correct to equate religious dissent with political dissent. This factor was responsible for causing a civil war in Buganda, in 1892. In reality, the Anglicans and Catholics were armed religious, military and political parties. They were mutually hostile and intolerant of each others' existence. The Anglicans and Catholics hated each other in the holy name of God, Christ, salvation and religious orthodoxy. They never realized the irony that Jesus, as the Christ, or Messiah, was actually Jewish. Like God, Jesus the Christ was historically never a Christian that was either Catholic or Anglican.

Nevertheless, the European Christian missionaries made it appear as if Jesus, as the Christ, as their "Lord and King" (*Kabaka/Mukama*), was a European emperor or great divine king. This approach made it erroneously appear as if Jesus, the Christ, was either an Anglican (member of the Church of England), or a Roman Catholic monarch, in the case of the Roman Catholic missionaries. These European missionaries also preached that the "Lord's Kingdom," excluded nonmembers as non citizens of God's Kingdom. The Anglicans alleged that Roman Catholicism was a false, corrupt and idolatrous "Papist religion." These bigoted Anglican British Christian missionaries alleged that Catholics were heretics and that Roman Catholicism was a false religion, whose members worshipped images and saints, instead of worshipping God.

The French Roman Catholic missionaries also claimed that God did not accept Anglican Christians in heaven and found extreme arguments to persuade King Mutesa to reject and evict the British Anglican missionaries from his kingdom. These cantankerous Christian missionaries believed that there were no redemptive merits in Anglicanism, or any other Protestant denominations. They vilified Anglicanism as a false religion that did not save its members, but only led to painful eternal hell-fire. They argued this was the case, since Anglicanism was not founded by God, but was rather founded by the rebellious and sinful King Henry VIII of England.

The Catholic missionaries emphasized the fact that King Henry VIII was a religious rebel, who was excommunicated by the Pope, in the 16th century, for unlawfully divorcing Catherine, his wife, without the Pope's permission and due process for the marriage annulment. But King Mutesa was a polygamist, who did not care about European cultural, religious and political controversies regarding their royal marriage conflicts and political or religious consequences of King Henry VIII's sexual exploits. He thought that these were trivial matters to occupy his time, to require either moral or religious judgment about the presence of the Anglican Christian missionaries based on these seemingly trivial European cultural and religious matters.

The French Catholic missionaries begged King Mutesa I to expel the Anglican Christian missionaries, whom they decried as dangerous heretics, and wanted his help to eliminate them from his kingdom. However, the enraged British Anglican missionaries also implored the perplexed King Mutesa that to expel the French Catholic missionaries as "evil people" and "false Christians," who were "Papists" and idol-worshippers.

However, the cantankerous French Catholic missionaries were relentless in their vilification of the Anglican missionaries and insistence that the King Mutesa must expel the allegedly heretical, damned and spiritually dangerous Anglican missionaries, if the king and his subjects wanted to be saved, by God, and to go to heaven, when they died. That was a mistake because the African Traditional Religion emphasized living a good and a peaceful life, in the present, as God's blessing, rather than postponing living in the present, by mere focusing attention on the future and looking for God's rewards or blessings in the future life, after death. For them, heaven was here, and they were already living joyfully in it. They cared little for a life with God in heaven, apart from this world. As such, they were not going to expel any Christian missionaries out of the land, unless, it was for a serious political or military reason.

These annoying, vicious, sectarian and relentless European quarrels between the Anglican and Catholic Christian missionaries, which regularly took place at King Mutesa's palace, had amused, entertained and both amazed and greatly puzzled the king and his chiefs. After some discussion of the rude and cantankerous behavior of European sectarian Christian missionaries, King Mutesa and his major chiefs had prudently and wisely concluded that Islam and the Traditional Religion had more merits than the sectarian, divisive and religiously intolerant Christianity. Furthermore, the Arab Muslims had also warned King Mutesa and his chiefs that European Christianity was a political tool and the vanguard of the European imperialist and colonialist powers, which would come and conquer their country and enslave them. These Arab Muslims were aware of the British imperial and colonialist activities in Egypt, the East African Coast, South Africa and India.

Theologically, the Arab Muslims also denounced the European Anglican and Catholic Christianity, alike, as forms of an idolatrous, corrupt, imperialist and false religion. The Arab Muslims contended that the Christians falsely deified and worshipped a man called Jesus, who was mere a Prophet of God. The Arab Muslims alleged that the Christians were idolaters and promoted a false religion. They declared that the Christians were misguided Europeans, who blasphemously worshipped the messenger or prophet of God, instead of worshipping God, who had sent him, to warn people against the very sins of idolatry and the worship of false gods.

It was believed and hoped that the African kings and their chiefs were more inclined to heed the warnings of the traditionalists and Muslims, especially since the European Christian missionaries were divided and hostile to each other. More importantly, the European Christian missionaries could not agree on Christianity's central redemptive truths, teachings, practices and values.

Subsequently, the sectarian and feuding Anglican and Catholic European missionaries, also deliberately taught and misled their African Christian converts, to hate and fight each other, in the holy name of God, Christ, the true Church and salvation. In this manner, the trusting and naive fundamentalist African Christian converts blindly inherited the vices of religious intolerance sectarianism from their sectarian and intolerant European Christian missionaries. The legacy of these European historical ethnic conflicts and the vices includes:

- Christian sectarianism
- religious prejudices
- bigotry
- hostility
- religious intolerance
- religious violence
- religious divisions
- and military conflicts.

Although the Christian Church has experienced divisions, ever since it was founded by Christ (Acts 15; 1-35; 1 Cor. 1:10-4:21), these European Christian conflicts and vices were relatively new. Historically, they went as far back, as the European Christian Reformation, in the sixteenth century. Nevertheless, they were destructive because this was also the era of European imperialism, expansionism, and renewed Christian missionary activity, to convert the people in the new colonial or imperial territories.

As a result of the Western sectarian Christian missionary work, along with their correlative destructive bitter rivalry, hostility and sectarian examples of the European Christian Missionaries, African, especially the Ugandan history has become permanently sectarian and violent. As a consequence of religious intolerance bigotry, conflicts, violence and religious wars of 1892, the Catholics, in Uganda, were militarily defeated. Subsequently, they were politically marginalized and repressed by the Anglicans, for more than a century. These are some of the tragic results and sad legacy of the European Christian missionaries and the British colonial agents in colonial Uganda.

This tragic Christian legacy is historically rooted in the European Christian missionary imperfections, evils and sins. Ultimately, the European Christian missionaries were seriously morally, socially, and politically contaminated with their European sectarian religious and political history, such as that of Northern Ireland. These European imperialists and Christian missionaries were rooted in their own experiences of sectarianism, religious bigoted and intolerant history and cultures of Europe, going back to the conflicts of the Protestant Reformation.

Subsequently, much of Uganda's past and present history of movements and military conflicts is the result of the deep-rooted evils of moral, religious bitter rivalry and sectarianism, which were inseparable from these Christian missionaries' ordinary European life, culture and history. These were some of the major societal factors which both consciously and unconsciously both shaped and influenced the European Christians and their activities, including missionary work and education in Africa, including East Africa. This is most especially true for Uganda.

The negative influence included the Christian missionaries' vicious religious rivalry and the sowing the destructive religious vices and political evil seeds of religious bigotry, sectarianism, religious intolerance, division and violence, along the historical sectarian models of Ireland and Northern Ireland. It is clear that the European Christian missionaries carried with them these destructive evils of religious violence and religious mutual exclusiveness. They brought these vices and destructive sectarian practices to Uganda, as part of their own European culture and sectarian religion. Tragically, these mutually hateful European and intolerant European Christian missionaries nearly managed to transform Uganda into another kind of Northern Ireland.[2]

The European Christian missionaries, tactlessly vilified each other before King Mutesa and his bemused chiefs, and inadvertently taught the Africans, that religion was a political tool, for political mobilization and conquest of their enemies. But the Africans also learned that the State was supreme and controlled religion, including the Christian Church itself. The African rulers, including President Idi Amin, also realized that Christianity was divided, and as long as the Christians were divided and fighting each other, the king or the ruler had the power over them all, as their arbiter, and peace-maker.

The sectarian history for both the Catholic and Anglican missionaries and their converts was destructive. The African Christian converts were recruited and converted to both mutually exclusive and intolerant Catholic and Evangelical Anglican denominations, in the case of Uganda. Both the Catholic and Anglican European missionaries, along with their African converts, both enthusiastically and vehemently repudiated each other, as heretics and missionaries of non-redemptive and false religions. This major, negative, historical sectarian Christian missionary factor is still the main root-cause of much of the contemporary evils of religious sectarianism and political instability in Uganda, when compared to Kenya, Tanzania, Zambia, South Africa, Ghana and Nigeria.[3]

The intolerant, sectarian and quarrelsome European Christian missionaries sowed their deadly seeds of Christian rivalry, sectarianism, religious bigotry, political violence and religious sectarianism, which took root and yields most of its abundance of evil fruits in Uganda. Alice Lakwena's HSM and Kony's LRA are part of this Christian missionary colonial tradition of religious sectarianism, intolerance, violence and quest for a Catholic theocracy.

The nineteenth century European Christian missionaries in Uganda were religiously and politically destructive to the local kingdoms, religions and cultures in Uganda. This is true in as much as these European Christian missionaries were the fore-runners of European imperialism and colonialism in Africa, especially East Africa. They were also divisive because they were deeply entrenched in their religious history of religious bigotry, intolerance between the Catholics and the Protestants, the Baganda.

The African Anglicans and the Roman Catholics, who innocently inherited these religious, moral and political evils from their European missionary teachers and mentors, also erroneously and tragically believed that these vices were true and core components of their respective Christian denominations. They, too, ignorantly contracted this deadly and serious moral and spiritual disease of mutual religious and social hatred, discrimination, intolerance, division, sectarianism and violence.

Consequently, in 1977, President Amin, a Muslim, banned about twenty seven small Christian denominations and missionary agencies in Uganda, leaving the Anglican, Catholic and Orthodox churches as the State recognized "religions," in addition to Islam. However, President Amin also pointed out that many had Africans ignorantly inherited the corrupt Western religious traditions, which were both socially and politically destructive to Uganda.

President Idi Amin, a fanatic Muslim, also strongly believed that Anglicanism in Uganda was a part of destructive British form of imperialism. He also believed Christianity was a defective form of European cultural religion (*Edini*), colonialism, and was an invisible, but an effective covert tool of Western imperialism and espionage, in Africa. He also believed that Christianity, promoted horrible religious prejudices against Muslims and also preached hellish vices of mutual religious intolerance, discrimination, segregation and violence. He also believed that these evils were tools of Western missionaries, colonialists and imperialists to divide and conquer the peoples of Africa, and to rule them as obedient subjects.

The corrupting and destructive evils and vices of the European Christian missionaries in Africa, particularly Uganda, include colonialism, imperialism, sectarianism, intolerance, racism, bigotry and violence that were perpetrated in the name of Christ. Subsequently, they viciously militarily confronted each other in a sectarian religious war in February 1892. This sectarian military confrontation was also a Catholic military and political struggle to gain political power and dominance in the kingdom, and the rest of the country. The outnumbered Anglicans, being the allies of the British imperialists, in the country, finally, emerged militarily victorious, and subsequently, became politically dominant in both Buganda and later, in the rest of the country. This was because Buganda provided the political paradigm, as well as, the social, and religious role model for the rest the nation, to follow. Bishop Tucker and the English Colonial Government officials in East Africa were very much aware of these important East African religious, political and cultural dynamics. They both employed and exploited them to their religious and political advantage.

This traditional correlation between religion and politics is best illustrated by a case study of the Kingdom of Ankole. In East Africa, it became common for the politically oppressed and marginalized groups to use religion as a tool for protest and dissent, or even military mobilization as in the cases of *Maji Maji Liberation Movement*, in German East Africa, in 1906; the *Nyabingi Movement*, in Southern Uganda, in 1912; the *Mau Mau Liberation Movement* in Kenya, in the 1950s; Alice Lakwena's *Holy Spirit Movement* in Uganda, in 1987; and Joseph Kony's *Lord's Resistance Army*, 1987-2008 in Uganda, clearly illustrate this point. It is also self-evident in the Kingdom of Ankole that religion was used as a tool of the oppressed to seek redress and justice, in the form of the *Bagyendanwa* Royal Drum Cult.

The politically oppressed *Bairu* brought their grievances to the high-priest of the Royal Drum (*Bagyendanwa*). In turn, as God's royal agent and local voice and instrument of God's grace, mercy and justice, in cases of grievous offenses and injustice, the royal high-priest co grievances both to the Drum and the *Omugabe* (King).

The *Omugabe* was supposed to be magnanimous and

information provided to alleviate the problem. The system provided checks and balances to the autocratic power of the king and his leading chiefs. However, this system of checks and balances was not understood by the English Christian missionaries. As a result, the Anglican missionaries, who resided and worked in the king's palace, condemned the institution of *Bagyendanwa* as a pagan and superstitious institution to be eliminated by the Christian king.

Subsequently, this traditional religio-political institution changed, when Christianity was introduced in Ankole. Tragically, this good and ideal traditional God-centered system devised in God's name to provide effective political, moral, socioeconomic, religious and cultural checks and balances of non-democratic royal power, and to effectively redress cases of gross injustice and buses of power was abolished. This is one example of cultural and religious misunderstandings of good cultural, moral and religious institutions by misguided Christian outsiders.

In this unfortunate case, the European Christian missionaries condemned the *Bagyendanwa* Royal Drum Cult, as paganism and divination. From that time, the *Omugabe's* royal institution was under political assault by aggrieved *Bairu* subjects, who now lacked an effective method to mediate and conciliate their political and other grievances, especially those against the monarchy itself.

The kingdom was, finally abolished, by the aggrieved *Bairu* Catholics, in the 1990s, when they resisted its restoration, by President Yoweri Museveni. However, what President Museveni overlooked was that the Ankole Kingdom was never a democratic institution, and as such, its restoration did not need a majority democratic vote for its approval! It needed the right royal prince (*Omuhinda*) and some few devoted royal supporters, as well the state approval and support. Monarchies are invaluable historical, cultural, and political institutions. They are sources of great national cultural historical heritage and pride.

In the traditional Ankole Kingdom, the *Bairu* peasants (*Bakopi*), or the subsistence agriculturists, were traditionally both politically and religiously marginalized. Later, these traditional agriculturalists, found their own effective political voice, legal weapon of political protest, and nonviolent rebellion against the *Mugabe* (King), an Anglican patron, and whose monarchy was dominated, by the Anglican *Bahima* royal aristocrats and cattle-keepers, by joining the Roman Catholic Church.

Ruhara, was one of the highly respected and rare prominent *Mwiru* chiefs, in King Kahaya's *Bahima* royal cabinet. He boldly sought to assert his uniqueness, different religious identity, and a form of political independence or dissent by adopting Roman Catholicism. As a result, Ruhara became the chief protector of the French Catholic missionaries and the Catholic converts, within the Ankole Kingdom. But by so doing, the Catholics, inadvertently, both politically and religiously became second class citizens, like Ruhara, who was their *Mwiru* chief and main patron.

Since the *Omugabe* granted the Anglicans royal welcome, and a place to build a royal church in his palace, at Kamukuzi, Ruhara, as the main local convert to Catholicism, also finally granted the French Catholic missionaries a large piece of land, at Nyamitanga, in his area of chieftaincy.

On Nyamitanga hill, the Catholic missionaries built their own church. It became the Catholic Church headquarters within the Ankole Kingdom and the surrounding areas of Kigezi and Mpororo. Subsequently, the Banyankole *Bairu* peasants eagerly looked up to Ruhara, their fellow *Mwiru* and powerful chief, for both political and religious leadership, as well as, the ideal role-model in matters of religion and politics, also eagerly followed Ruhara, their beloved and respected both chief and champion, or hero into Roman Catholicism.

In contrast to the *Bairu* peasants or agriculturalists, most *Bahima* chiefs, and the aristocratic ruling class of cattle-keeping *Bahima,* being ethnically akin to the *Mugabe* (king), naturally adopted Anglicanism, as their preferred royal and privileged religious tradition, within their ethnically and religiously divided precarious kingdom. Similarly, other Banyankole people, who wished to become politically significant, or needed the political favors of the *Omugabe*, followed their king into Anglicanism. In this manner, Anglicanism became the established Church in the Kingdom of Ankole, and the Anglicans gained political hegemony over the more numerous Catholics.

King Kahaya and Nuha Mbaguta, his Prime Minister, were both more anti-Catholic, than they were *anti-Bairu.* As a result, in 1901, King Kahaya and his newly Anglicanized Bahima cabinet unanimously passed a decree outlawing, and banning Roman Catholicism from their "Anglican Ankole Kingdom." Even Ruhara, the *Mwiru* chief and patron of the Catholics, fearing for his position and life, signed the decree banning the Catholics from working in the kingdom, despite the fact that he had welcomed them and unsuccessfully tried to protect them.

Ultimately, only the *Mugabe* (king) could provide the necessary effective legal, moral and economic support for the work of the Christian missionaries in his kingdom, unless the British took-over the administration of the kingdom and imposed the policy of religious neutrality and impartiality in terms of missionary access and protection of their mission stations and converts. This Catholic missionary protest took place, in 1902.

Subsequently, the British Colonial Administration wished to appear religiously neutral on this matter, and reversed King Kahaya's decree of

1901, which banned the Catholic missionary activities in Ankole Kingdom, which both King Kahaya and, Nuha Mbaguta, his loyal *Enganzi* (Prime Minister) had, effectively transformed into an "Anglican Kingdom," with an established Anglican royal Church.

The both religiously and politically marginalized and excluded Catholics within Ankole Kingdom, resented this sectarian royal favor for the Anglican Church and promotion of the Anglican Church establishment and hegemonic political power. They regarded it as being politically discriminatory, and an unwise royal promotion of Anglican sectarian politics that alienated the majority of the Catholics. Notably, these marginalized and aggrieved Catholics were predominantly *Bairu*.

As such, they were also members of the traditionally aggrieved and socioeconomically despised and marginalized class, in Ankole Kingdom. Their grievances were ignored by the Anglican *Bahima* aristocrats, despite the fact that they were the ethnic majority. In a democratic institution, these marginalized and aggrieved Catholics would have seized power and become the real dominant religious group and political force in the kingdom. They, too, could have transformed the kingdom into a Catholic Kingdom, as the Catholics in Buganda had militarily tried to do, in February of 1892.[4]

As the powerful economic and political patron and defender of both a religiously marginalized Catholic and politically disenfranchised *Bairu* group, once again, Ruhara welcomed the Catholic French missionaries and served, as their local guardian, provider and political protector. This religio-political move by the *Bairu,* was a form of religious dissent, with direct political consequences, for both themselves, and their hated Anglican *Bahima* monarchy. The *Bairu* being the majority in Ankole, and Catholic, or the followers of Ruhara and the French Catholic missionaries, had serious consequences for the monarchy.

This is because the monarchy was Anglican in its religious establishment. It was also dominated by the aristocratic *Bahima* ethnic and minority political group. As a result, in the 1990s, the Anglican elitist monarchy was, eventually abolished, by the formerly marginalized, disenfranchised, despised, oppressed and aggrieved majority ethnic *Bairu* Catholics. They were an irreconcilable aggrieved political group, because most of its members were previously dehumanized, systematically oppressed, and discriminated against by the *Bahima* Anglican monarchy, and its hegemonic power.

This political and religious repression occurred, despite the fact that *Bairu* Catholics were the majority of the citizens of Ankole Kingdom. As such, it was both dehumanizing and politically destabilizing that within this Ankole Anglican Kingdom, the *Bairu* and Catholics were deliberately singled out, marginalized and systematically both politically and economically disenfranchised, as an inferior and undesirable religio-political group, within the kingdom.[5]

The Catholics, like Mr. Francis Tibayungwa, a *Mwiru*, or *omwambari* (a privileged cattle keeping *Mwiru*), who was appointed to the lofty position of *Kihimba* (Deputy Prime-Minister), and who was later appointed the new Administrative Secretary of Ankole Kingdom, were given a few political tokens of goodwill, by the *Bahima* dominated Anglican establishment. These political tokens were extended to the Catholic *Bairu* majority, who were their subjects, with the hope to appease them and keep them compliant. However, these religious and political tokens were too few and too small to achieve their intended political and religious objectives.

Ultimately, Ruhara's many *Bairu* were proud to belong to Ruhara's religious-political party. They were often heard to have proudly declared, "*Itwe nitushoma Ediini ya Ruhara*" (We follow/read/worship according to Ruhara's religion).[6] This was in contrast to the Anglicans, who despised the Catholics and also declared: "*Itwe nitushoma eky'Ediini y'Omugabe*" (We follow/read/worship according to the religion of the king/*Omugabe*).[7]

Ruhara's Catholic religious-political party was composed of the *Bairu,* and finally, the *Bairu* majority by the decision of its own majority political power, passed its own informal decree, a century later, and banned the Anglican monarchy, by refusing to have it reinstated, in 1994.

The predominantly Roman Catholic *Bairu,* in Ankole, reasoned that the *Bahima* Anglican-based monarchy in Ankole had excluded and oppressed them for being both *Bairu* and Catholic. They also noted that the Anglican Church-based monarchy had once tried to ban Catholicism from the kingdom. When that strategy failed, the royal and aristocratic political Anglican hegemony and its power structures had systematically politically excluded and marginalized them. The Catholic *Bairu* strongly believed that the Anglican political hegemony had actually tried to destroy them economically, in the years after 1902.[8] This *Bairu* Catholic majority religio-political group also happened to be heavily *Democratic Party* (DP) and anti-monarchy. The monarchy, being Anglican Church-based had also become associated with *Uganda Peoples Congress* (UPC).

Therefore, the Anglican-based monarchy had little chance of survival, given the prevalent state of religious and political sectarianism in Ankole, in which there were many discontented Catholic *Bairu* as the majority of the citizens and voters. Therefore, unlike the Kingdom of Buganda, where people were homogeneous and nationalistic, the Ankole Kingdom was a *Bahima* empire imposed on the majority of the *Bairu* agriculturalists. And they revolted against their aristocratic rulers and oppressors, whom they despised, as being underdeveloped and less intelligent cattle-keepers.

Ironically, in this bitter sectarian and tense religio-political atmosphere in Ankole, the powerless, but more numerous Catholics, finally, used their great numbers, and the new democratic process to seize power in the Ankole Kingdom. However, democracy and election of a king (*Omugabe*) was not a solution to the predicament of the ancient institution of the monarchy and divine kingship of the politically endangered Ankole Kingdom. A democratic election of the king was impossible, since the *Bairu* class could not become part of the hereditary traditional royal *Bahinda* clan and become traditional kings (*Abagabe*), and since the divine institution of the monarchy was a hereditary one.

Therefore, it could not be legitimately accessed by election and a democratic vote, as the *Bairu,* had demanded. As a result, the *Bairu* Catholics, finally, decided to destroy the hated institution of the monarchy, which had excluded them from power and oppressed them for being both the *Bairu* and Catholics.

In addition, President Museveni, a formerly marginalized Munyankole, as a lower class *Muhima,* or a non-*Muhinda* (non-royal clan) did little to help the Anglican former royal *Bahima* and *Bahinda* ruling family to come back into power and regain the cultural grandeur and religious mystic of their ancient throne. This was partly because he did not have room for two kings, namely, himself in Rwakitura, and another true king, to whom he would pledge allegiance, in Kamukuzi. But that political consideration was self-centered, as well as being both culturally and politically short-sighted.

Joseph Kibwetere, as a frustrated and failed Catholic and DP politician, also realized the powerful effect of employing religious loyalties and sectarianism as effective local tools for political, social and religious effective mobilization, protest and rebellion. Kibwetere's role as the co-founder of *The Movement for the Restoration of the Ten Commandments of God,* was a part of this phenomenon. He succeeded in co-founding an organization with both a national and an international attraction, in which he was the supreme religious, political and a spiritual leader, as the publicly recognized supreme Prophet, Voice of God and Head or Spokesman of the Marian Movement. Kibwetere rebelled against the laws of the state by consenting and giving assistance to Fr. Dominic Kataribabo to kill hundreds of innocent people in order to send them to God, in heaven, as his obedient martyrs and saints.

Kibwetere also rebelled against the Roman Catholic Church leadership which he accused it of corruption and failure to preach the true Gospel of God and the strict need to repent of sins, greed, sexual immorality, materialism and apathy concerning the plight of the poor and the immorality of the religious leaders, including the priests. Being the prophet and cofounder of the Marian Movement, Kibwetere also gained the necessary religious, social, political recognition, and the fulfillment, which he had failed to obtain as an educator, businessman, politician, husband and a father.

Kibwetere was admired by the Marian Movement members. He was highly esteemed as a holy man, who became both the redemptive agent of God and the Blessed Virgin Mary's apocalyptic prophet. He is especially remembered for his most controversial and frightening doomsday prophecies and sermons, in which he appealed for urgent repentance, and moral reformation, based on the observation of the Ten Commandments of God, in order to avoid God's wrath, judgment and punishment in God's cleansing fire, at the dawning of the new millennium, and the end of this corrupt era, in the world. His followers also found similar spiritual, moral and social satisfaction. They were all escapists from the real world, in which God had created, and placed them to live most fully, and meaningfully all their lives.

This is the same world that the Evangelist John positively affirms as being both good and worthy of God's Incarnation and redemption, rather than destruction. He writes: "God so loved the world so much that he sent his beloved Son that whoever believes in him would not perish but have everlasting life" (John 3:16). Unfortunately, many followers of Jesus have tragically failed to realize that this is the very world that God loves and seeks to redeem through the work of unconditional love, unmerited grace and free forgiveness of sins (Matt. 5-7), as they are concretely expressed in the world, through the Divine Incarnation of God in the world, and the explicit religious and moral teachings of Jesus, as the Christ, and as the definitively perfect Incarnation of God in humanity, and the historical processes of the world.

3. Alice Lakwena's Holy Spirit Movement & Protest In Northern Uganda

In many ways, the rise, rituals and operation of Alice Lakwena's *Holy Spirit Movement* (HSM)[9] in the 1980s in Northern Uganda are reminiscent of the rise and operation of the *Maji Maji Movement* in 1908-1909, against the Germans in the former German East Africa, which is today called Tanzania, and the *Mau Mau Liberation Movement,* during the 1950s, in Kenya.[10] Alice Auma as "*Lakwena*" ("Messiah" or "Savior") was the self-proclaimed divinely called the "prophetess of God," and supernaturally commissioned God's Messiah for the Acholi people.[11]

Auma successfully convinced her fellow Luo pe᷉ actually God's chosen and commissioned Messiah, and P₁ to save them from evil, the domination of evil spirits and the Devil. These were the allegedly evil forces and the demonic powers of the Devil of which President Museveni and his supposed oppressive troops were believed to be the real physical local destructive manifestations and evil incarnations in the world. Therefore, these evil forces of the Devil were to be ritually killed off and completely eliminated from the region in order to cleanse the land of defilement and ritual pollution.

Subsequently, both Lakwena and Kony engaged in what seemed to be religious and magical rituals designed to cleanse the Acholi-land from this moral, political and military evil and pollution of the land caused by the occupation of foreign troops from the South and the shedding of innocent blood. These inclusive and theocratic political, military, moral, spiritual doctrines and practices were fashioned out of their Catholic faith, the African Traditional Religion, Luo religious and traditional political cultural norms and values. In Northern Uganda, where there are no kingdoms, these political values, include tribal exclusive ethnic identity, militarism and traditional grass-roots mass participatory democracy led by a chief (*Rwot*) or an outstanding military hero and cultural leader.

The Catholics, being traditionally marginalized and excluded from positions of political power, were also members of the marginalized communities and political groups or associations. As a result, they were the ideal members of marginalized and disenfranchised groups and communities from which to recruit political or armed rebels, like the Lakwena's HSM and Kony's LRA. Naturally, these were some of the politically and economically frustrated people, who were opposed to traditionally Anglican-based governments in Uganda.

Therefore, it is not surprising that Alice Auma, who became *Lakwena* or Messiah, was a Roman Catholic, and most of her followers were also disenfranchised Catholics, or that after her own defeat, Joseph Kony, a former Catholic catechist, succeeded her, and formed the infamous, armed and violent *Lord's Resistance Army* (LRA).[12]

Subsequently, as both a religious and a political messiah, Alice Lakwena's divine agenda and mandate were comprehensive. Her own explicitly stated divine messianic mission was to deliver and save people from the perceived Devil inspired demonic invasion, and oppression of the Acholi-land in Northern Uganda by the foreigners. In reality, the perceived foreign invaders and oppressors were not foreigners at all. They were fellow Ugandans, namely, President Yoweri Museveni and his predominantly Banyankole, or the *Bantu* dominated *National Resistance Movement* (NRM) Government and troops, the UPDF (*Uganda Peoples Defense Forces*).

Alice Auma, as "*Lakwena,*" or the Acholi Messiah (*Lakwena*) and the Catholic founder of the HSM, being an uneducated woman, was essentially, akin to Keledonia Mwerinde. Having never studied African history, or the African Traditional Religion, Christian theology and ethics, they simply improvised their religious teachings and practices, which they based on supernatural Marian visions and heavenly revelations. These women claimed to be God's new chosen messiahs, and agents of God's salvation, in their respective communities. Subsequently, they taught their heavenly visions, and new understanding of God, as God's Special Revelation through the Holy Spirit, in the case of Lakwena, who founded the *Holy Spirit Movement*, and in the case of Mwerinde, who founded MRTCG, because of the apparitions of the Blessed Virgin Mary.

First, Alice Lakwena sought to save Uganda, and after that, she wanted to save the rest of the world from the governance of what she considered corrupt, sinful and secular governments. She wanted God's rule, or divine theocracy, to prevail in the world, with the Pope presiding over it. Joseph Kony sought to do the same, but wanted to accomplish this divine theocracy though a holy war conducted by the *Lord's Resistance Army* (LRA), to impose the theocracy based on the strict observance of the Ten Commandments of God.

Similarly, Keledonia Mwerinde, another poorly educated Catholic lay woman in Southern Uganda, also tried to do the same thing as Lakwena was doing in Northern Uganda, but in a more peaceful manner. The main difference with Lakwena is that Mwerinde was both pacifist and claimed that her own teaching came from God through the revelations communicated to her through the Blessed Virgin Mary. Both women were driven by the same ideals, namely to reform the corrupt moral values of both the Catholic Church and establish God's holy theocracy based on conversion, repentance, holiness, ritual drinking or bathing in consecrated holy water and the observation of the Ten Commandments.

Alice Lakwena was unaware of the historical existence and failed military religio-political operations of the *Maji Maji Movement,* in the former German Tanganyika, which was later, renamed Tanzania by President Julius Nyerere, after independence, in 1961. The *Maji Maji Movement* had failed in its political and military objectives to liberate East Africa from the German invaders and imperialists, because of its leaders' reliance on religion, and beliefs in its powers of supernatural faith and the magical powers of the consecrated holy water to fully armor them, and protect them against the deadly effects of the German rifle bullets and artillery fire. They both tragically believed and taught that when one is a fully committed believer in the power of God and bathes in holy water that he becomes bulletproof.

Similarly, the *Maji Maji* leaders had also taught the magical and protective properties of consecrated holy water and oil. They had tragically believed and taught that not only were the believers impermeable to bullets, but the bullets shot at these holy warriors would also be both miraculously stopped by the ancestral spirits, and transformed into mere harmless water. In addition to both faith in God's power and miraculous protection, the holy warriors were also required to pray, and offer sacrifices to the ancestral spirits for divine protection.

There were elaborate rituals for purification and diligently bathing in consecrated holy water while reciting magical prayers to ensure proper and full protection of God's Holy Spirit, and also for the traditional magical protections in the future battles. These Africans engaged in a holy war against better armed German colonialists. For these conquered and oppressed Africans, their holy wars were wars of liberation. They were not acts of holy and self-sacrificial mass suicides and martyrdoms, for the sake of defense of God, religious doctrines, or for the sake of attainment of eternal life in heaven, like the *al-Qaeda* teaches its holy warriors, before they undertake suicidal military missions, as holy war (*jihad*) and holy self-sacrificial act for God, that would be generously rewarded by God with salvation and life of eternal bliss, in heaven. Rather, for these Africans, it was undertaken, as some religio-political holy war to liberate the people, and expel the invaders.

These holy wars were also fought in a ritualistic and religious manner in order to cleanse the land from foreigners' ritual pollution that was associated with their desecrating presence in the land. They sought to drive out the German imperialists as the supposed agents of evil, ritual pollution, as well as being oppressive foreign colonial oppressors. They also sought to kill the German's local African collaborators, since they could not be driven out along with their foreign masters. The African colonial collaborators were considered to be dangerous traitors to the people. Therefore, they were rejected and subject to capital punishment as a form of exorcism and ritual cleansing of the community from moral, spiritual and social pollution which these people had brought upon the community and its members.

Like the *Maji Maji Movement,* members had become mobilized and trained to become the formidable holy warriors to fight the German invaders. The peaceful members of Lakwena's *Holy Spirit Movement* were also effectively politically and militarily transformed into God's holy crusaders as the *Holy Spirit Mobile Forces* (HSMF), who were mobilized to fight the supposed evil invading military forces of President Yoweri Museveni's NRM Government that was considered to be alien to the people in Northern Uganda, in as much as it was heavily dominated by the Bantu people from Southern and Central Uganda.

Again, like the *Maji Maji* holy warriors, the HSMF were also, primarily armed with deep religious faith, and hate for the foreign invaders as agents of the Devil, whose troops were evil spirits that could be successfully fought with the weapons of religious faith, prayers, singing hymns, the sprinkling holy water on them in the Name of God and Jesus in order to perform exorcisms on them and drive out the evil spirits that possessed them.

Accordingly, it was believed that the Devil or evil-spirit possessed people carry out acts of violence and injustice against the people of Northern Uganda. As such, Lakwena believed that her moral crusade was an essentially spiritual warfare, in which she had the power of the Holy Spirit to exercise the evil-spirits from the Devil-possessed people, who were co-opted as the physical soldiers of the Devil in the world. They had to be cleansed from evil by the power of God through the Holy Spirit, which were incarnated in her as the *Lakwena* or the Messiah.

Nevertheless, despite Lakwena's deep faith in God and the power of the Holy Spirit, like the *Maji Maji*, who were defeated by the German colonial troops in the former German East Africa, in 1908, Alice Lakwena and her HSMF holy warriors were also finally defeated, in 1987, by President Museveni's better armed troops. In both cases, the holy warriors' moral crusade or liberation wars and their weapons of magic, religious faith in God and the ancestors, and the mystical armor of consecrated water were no match for the German bullets and artillery fire.

The military failure of the *Maji Maji* war and subsequent tragic destruction of the Movement's faithful holy warriors as the German troops carried out a bloody military massacres of the *Maji Maji* holy warriors, later also became the tragic fate of the HSMF when it waged a similar holy war against the troops of the Government of Uganda in 1987.[13] Like the *Maji Maji* holy warriors, Alice Lakwena's consecrated holy water, prayers and magic failed to protect the HSMF holy warriors against the UPDF bullets.

Like the *Maji Maji* holy warriors, the HSMF holy warriors were also massacred, despite their deep faith in God, the armor of holy water and the promises of the Alice Lakwena that the Holy Spirit would protect them. Lakwena's prophecies, charismatic promises and emphatic religious assurances of faith that the Holy Spirit and baptisms or ritual baths in magical holy water would make them invincible and victorious against their enemies, who were vilified as foreign demonic forces and troops of the Devil (President Museveni), failed to materialize.

Like the poorly armed *Maji Maji* holy warriors, the both unarmed and poorly armed holy warriors of the Holy Spirit Movement Forces (HSMF) were also both brutally defeated and exterminated, in 1987, by President Yoweri Museveni's Government's better armed troops, the NRA (*National Resistance Army*). The NRA was militarily confronted, by the HSMF holy warriors, who were merely armed with hymns, sticks, holy water, holy oil (*moya*) and stones for supernatural weapons, as faith-operated spiritual or supernatural (magical) explosive hand grenades, and a few old rifles. But more importantly, they believed they were God's holy warriors, who were invincible because they were supernaturally armed with a deep religious faith in God, ritual baths in holy oil (*moya*), baptisms in consecrated holy water (*Maji*), and the practice of magic, which tragically proved to be inadequate religious weapons to wage a military war against better armed government troops, regardless of whether the soldiers believed in God or not.

Ultimately, what really mattered or worked during a conventional war, including holy wars or military moral and religious crusades, were not the depth of religious faith, holiness and moral perfection of the troops and moral crusaders, like the HSMF and the LRA preached, at first. Rather, what truly worked during the battle was military reality, as opposed to faith and magic alone. What worked best in war was military experience and good military preparation.

The outcomes of the battle depended not on faith in God, but rather, on the quality and nature of military training of the troops; the quality of weapons, with which the troops were equipped, and the quality of the military surveillance and logistics, which were provided to the field military leaders. Unlike Alice Lakwena's unarmed HSMF's unwise and fatal decision to engage in a conventional war against the UPDF, in 1987, in which the HSMF holy warriors were ruthlessly massacred, the poorly equipped LRA and ADF rebel soldiers and resistance or liberation movement fighters learned not to repeat the HSMF's tragic military mistake.

Subsequently, the leaders of the LRA and the ADF often chose to avoid conventional military confrontations and direct battles with the UPDF, in which either they would have been completely exterminated or lost the battles. Instead of conventional battles, both the LRA and ADF chose to engage in the indirect and informal warfare, in the form of protracted guerrilla war and terrorism.

However, Alice Lakwena and her holy warriors of the HSMF were completely blinded by their fundamentalist, fanatical and literalist religious faith in God's providence and redemption. They strongly believed God would intervene and save all his obedient saints, from evil and harm's way, including bullets fired at them, by the Government of Uganda's troops.

Therefore, they most tragically, as well as both ignorantly and foolishly, chose to engage in a direct military confrontation with President Museveni's perceived evil Government of Uganda and its troops, to destroy them, in a holy war of exorcism. This holy war was designed as both a religious and cultural sacramental means to liberate, heal and cleanse the land of evil and ritual pollution, by foreign troops and their evils of mass murders, rapes and defilement. Alice Lakwena and her HSMF holy warriors considered President Museveni, his NRM Government and troops, as true visible evil embodiments and demonic incarnations of the evil spirits and the Devil, within their supposedly "holy land."

Therefore, Alice Lakwena, as God's new apocalyptic prophetess and messiah in the world, and the HSMF, as God's holy warriors, would be able to confront these perceived demonic evil forces and could successfully exorcize them, by holy healing chants, faith and the sprinkling of holy water on those evil demonic forces to drive out the Devil, and to exorcise the evil spirits from them. They also did it in order to reclaim, purify and ritually cleanse the land, which the foreigners and their armies had plundered, defiled and culturally polluted. This was an Acholi cultural form of *mat oput* (holy justice, punishment and reconciliation). The holy warriors, who died heroically in the battle, were treated as heroes. They were also religiously revered and hailed God's martyrs as holy sacrifices (*Gitum/Gityer*)[14] and holy atonements (*Tum*)[15] for sins.

Armed with holy oil (*moya*) and holy water (*Maji*), deep religious faith, and strong hopes that God would directly intervene, on their behalf, defeat and supernaturally or magically exterminate the supposed demonic forces of the Devil in the form of the defiling presence of the oppressive NRA troops, they waged a holy war against President Museveni's NRM Government. They also wanted to ritually cleanse the NRA/UPDF troops, and exorcise the evil spirits from them. They sought to accomplish this religious and cultural objective by sprinkling holy water on the NRM Government troops, in order to save them from the demonic possession of the Devil, and overthrow the NRM Government of President Museveni.

The HSMF, was formed out of the HSM, as its military wing. Like the HSM, the HSMF was headed by Alice Lakwena as the Holy Spirit's embodiment and God's Supreme Commander. The HSMF operated on the moral and religious principles of the HSM. Both the HSM and the HSMF were completely under Alice Lakwena's religious, spiritual, moral, political and military command, as their Messiah (*Lakwena*).

HSMF's main tasks were to defend the HSM unarmed members and to kill God's enemies, so as to establish a divine theocracy. It was to this main goal that Alice Lakwena, as God's Messiah, mobilized her holy warriors, the HSFM to wage a moral and military crusade against the evil forces in the world, beginning with President Museveni's NRM Government and its military. Therefore, in 1987, the HSMF marched into battle against the troops of the Government of Uganda, without the necessary fire arms, or protection. These fundamentalist holy warriors strongly believed that they were completely armored and made bullet-proof, by the invisible and invincible supernatural powers of the Holy Spirit and the magical powers of prayer, faith and ritual baths in holy oil and consecrated holy water.

However, during the holy war, God failed to appear and fight on their side of the HSMF, as they had been promised by the Prophet Alice Lakwena. As a result, the HSMF holy warriors were mercilessly slaughtered as self-sacrificial Christian martyrs. Subsequently, the defeated Alice Lakwena fled to Kenya, where she lived in political exile. Due to hardship, distress, and unhygienic conditions in the refugee camp, Lakwena fell sick and finally died in the refugee camp, on January 27, 2007. By 2004, Alice Lakwena had lost the power of the Holy Spirit. As a result, she was no longer, the formidable God's apocalyptic Acholi *Lakwena* (Messiah).

Subsequently, she tried to return to Uganda, as Alice Auma, and as a mere citizen, without any covert political or military ambitions. But, after a protracted process of diplomatic negotiation of a permanent truce and reconciliation between the NRM Government of Uganda and some of Lakwena's surviving HSMF followers, who had also fled with Alice Lakwena to Kenya, the negotiations broke-down. The militant members of the HSM were still considered as a major threat to the Government of Uganda and socioeconomic stability in Northern Uganda. Kony's LRA was causing havoc in several districts in both Northern and Eastern Uganda.

Therefore, initially, the Government of Uganda wanted to entice and persuade Lakwena's remaining HSMF holy warriors to renounce war, sign a peace treaty, be granted amnesty and come back home to Uganda, as free and peace-loving citizens. The Government of Uganda was eager to negotiate with them because they had not joined Joseph Kony's *Lord's Resistance Army* (LRA).

The Government of Uganda was interested in preventing them from joining Kony's LRA, which had become the violent and vicious military successor to the HSMF. But, in contrast to the LRA, the HSM and the HSMF had been more peaceful, religio-political, and messianic. The HSMF was also largely unarmed, or poorly armed since it was primarily a religious liberation movement headed by the Prophetess and Supreme Commander Alice Lakwena, serving as God's Messiah, and the *Holy Spirit Mobile Forces*, serving as God means to establish and maintain his theocracy.[16]

Having learned from Alice Lakwena's HSMF military failures, which he attributed to her folly and tragic reliance on religious faith in God, and the magical or supernatural powers of consecrated holy water and practices of magic, as her main weapons to fight a holy war against the demonic forces, including their evil manifestations as the NRA, Joseph Kony decided to wage a conventional guerrilla war. He wanted to continue and accomplish Alice Lakwena's religious, military and political objectives. Originally,

Joseph Kony wanted to establish a holy theocracy, which was based on the strict observation of the Ten Commandments.

To this end, Joseph Kony mobilized Lakwena's remaining troops, and revamped Alice Lakwena's military and religious ideologies, which had had manifested themselves in the tragic failures of Lakwena's more peaceful and unarmed holy warriors leading to the NRA's defeat of the HSMF. He believed that these weaknesses led to the HSMF's failure to defeat and overthrow President Museveni's NRM Government, and the better armed NRA as the Uganda Government's troops.

Consequently, Joseph Kony decided to acquire military weapons and train his holy warriors of the *Lord's Resistance Army* how to use them effectively to inflict great casualties on President Museveni's Government officials, troops and all his perceived enemies, including the civilians in Northern Uganda, who cooperated with foreigners and supported President Museveni and his NRM Government, and its oppressive troops, that occupied Northern Uganda.

Kony believed in ethnic cleansing, whereby, he tortured, maimed and killed off thousands of innocent Acholi people, especially those, who cooperated with the foreign invaders. Kony planned and sought to replace them with what he perceived, as a new "ethnically purer" generation of proud, strong and "ethnically patriotic Acholi people," of whom the majority would be his own descendents. Subsequently, he raided Northern Uganda and kidnapped hundreds of young school girls to be transformed into his wives, and others to be given to his commanders, as gifts, to be used as wives, concubines or sex slaves.

As a result of Joseph Kony's change in philosophy from Alice Lakwena's nonviolence and peaceful spiritual military strategy, to a more violent military one which employed real military weapons, similar to those of the NRA, the LRA waged the most brutal ("savage"), indiscriminate, and destructive "holy war" that resulted in great evils and tragedies, in Northern Uganda. These great evils have included religious, political, and economic disruption and military terror directed against the Government of Uganda and the innocent civilian populations in Northern Uganda, since 1987. The LRA's "terrorist holy war" of liberation, has also resulted in the most heinous crimes and abuses of human rights, anywhere, in the modern world. As such, both Alice Lakwena and Joseph Kony were disowned, by their own Catholic Church.

The Catholic Church leaders have sided with the leaders of the Government of Uganda and condemned these violent movement leaders as evil-doers, sinful abusers of human rights, and misguided violent people. The bishops of the Catholic Church have also condemned Alice Lakwena and

Kony for misunderstanding and misusing the Catholic faith, and then, erroneously inflicting serious harm, on the people.

Furthermore, engaging in abuses of human rights in the name of God and the Catholic Church, in a quest to overthrow, what they believed to be a corrupt NRM Government, in order to establish a holy Catholic theocracy in Uganda. For Joseph Kony, Joseph Kibwetere and Keledonia Mwerinde, the Catholic theocracy, would be based on the strict observance of the sacraments, and moral and spiritual perfection, based on the fulfillment of the Ten Commandments.

Within this turbulent historical, religious, moral, spiritual, political and military respect and *Acholi* cultural understanding, Joseph Kony became the successor of Alice Lakwena. Like Alice Lakwena, Joseph Kony drew his spiritual, political and moral inspiration from the Catholic tradition, the Acholi African Traditional Religion, traditional magic, heavenly visions of God and strong religious faith and conviction that he was God's new chosen apocalyptic messiah (*Lakwena*), who was sent to redeem and deliver the Acholi people, and the rest of the Ugandans from the evil and oppressive regime of President Yoweri Museveni and his NRM Government and predominantly Bantu troops from Central and Southern Uganda.

Traditionally, the Government of Uganda and its troops had been predominantly Luo; and mainly composed of the Acholi and Langi people of Northern Uganda. With the NRM's successful liberation war, and the military overthrow of traditionally Northern Uganda-based governments, along with their troops, the people of Northern Uganda had felt that they were a conquered and disenfranchised people, who were ethnically and politically discriminated against, by their military conquerors.

After President Museveni came to power, most of the defeated troops of Idi Amin and Tito Okello from Northern Uganda and West Nile ran into exile. Others were distrusted, disarmed and discharged. They were discriminated against and largely left out of the new military, which was dominated by the *Bantu* people of Western Uganda and President Museveni's NRM Government for political and security reasons. As a result, these soldiers from Northern Uganda and West Nile justifiably felt marginalized and oppressed. Subsequently, they joined the Alice Lakwena's HSMF and Joseph Kony's LRA because they were aggrieved and wanted to reverse these undesirable conditions and recover the lost power and its privileges. Therefore, the NRM Government's troops definitive military defeat of Alice Lakwena, in 1987, near Jinja would not be the end of the Acholi attempts to regain power in Uganda.[17]

The poor, unemployed and disenfranchised *Acholi,* especially the traditionally marginalized and disgruntled Catholics, had most willingly and positively answered Joseph Kony's call in the Name of God to come, join him and continue Alice Lakwena's moral and military crusade. That is, the LRA waged a holy war, in order to overthrow President Museveni's NRM Government, and to establish God's Kingdom and theocracy, which was to be based on the observation of the Ten Commandments of God.

Many politically marginalized, unemployed and oppressed Acholi people willingly heeded Kony's appeal to take up arms, and go to the bush, to wage a new "holy war" against the President Museveni's NRM Government as the perceived Devil, and political personification of the destructive corrupt rulers, oppressors and the evils spirits.

Like Alice Lakwena, Joseph Kony also preached that in reality, the Devil and evil spirits existed, and both oppressed and possessed people. He argued that the local embodiments of the Devil, and the evil spirits existed in Acholi and the country the form of President Yoweri Museveni, as the Devil, his NRM Government and troops, the UPDF, as the incarnations of the evil spirits. As such, they had to be fought and exorcised in order to cleanse and heal the land of their moral defiling evils and ritual pollution.

Subsequently, the LRA *(Lord's Resistance Army)* was formed, as a religio-political holy war. It was a moral crusade, and an Acholi political military movement. Like Alice Lakwena's HSMF, the LRA's main mission objectives were also both religious and political, namely, to overthrow the NRM Government; and to establish a theocracy, with Joseph Kony, as God's appointed political Messiah, divine representative and ruler.[18]

Consequently, the most successful and meaningful practical response to Kony's LRA must also be double edged. That is, the correct and permanent solutions to the LRA's and Lakwena's HSM grievances must be both religious in scope and political, in their formulation, implantation and societal or community outreach. If these practical solutions are to work, they must have the necessary corresponding positive and accompanying economic, moral and cultural benefits that facilitate the economic, religious, educational, agricultural, social, cultural and political rehabilitation of the currently displaced, impoverished, terrorized and disenfranchised people of Northern Uganda.

Otherwise a permanent state of dread, existential anxiety, despair, political, economic, and cultural chaos will continue to prevail in Northern Uganda, or other affected areas. When this happens, there will always be a need for God's direct intervention and need of a military and political messiah (*Lakwena*) to deliver the oppressed people of God from their oppressors, degradation and to lead them to freedom and peace. As such, religious-political and military revolutionaries, such as Alice Lakwena and Joseph Kony, will always arise in the name of God, as God's appointed messiahs, who are sent to deliver or save the oppressed people. Religious people expect God to save them from their state of oppression, poverty, discrimination, disenfranchisement and despair.

Therefore, many oppressed religious people will always welcome and follow these kinds of real or false messiahs in faith and hope that they are God's true messiahs sent to redeem them from their oppressive conditions of poverty, disease, discrimination and lack of access to the national economic and political resources in order to develop, and uplift themselves from their state of economic and political weakness and despair.[19] As such, the African leaders must resolve these oppressive conditions of angst, if they wish to establish stable governments, democracy and peace within their own countries.

Ultimately, happy and satisfied people have no need of military, political or economic messiahs, such as Gen. Idi Amin, Gen. Yoweri Museveni, Alice Lakwena, Joseph Kony, Keledonia Mwerinde and Joseph Kibwetere, who have emerged, at different times in Uganda, since January 25, 1971, when Gen Idi Amin, staged a military coup and overthrew the oppressive UPC Government of President Milton Obote, and then, claimed to be Uganda's long awaited political and economic messiah. But then, when he expelled the Asians, he drove the country into an economic and political crisis. He declared himself a life president; and persecuted the Christians, especially the Anglican political elites. Later, on tragic night of February 16, 1977, President Amin assassinated the Anglican Archbishop Janani Luwum, the Head of the Anglican Church Province of Uganda, Rwanda, Burundi and Boga-Zaire.

As a result, other political and military messiahs, like Yoweri Museveni, arose to liberate the oppressed Ugandans from President Amin's repression, and later, to overthrow President Milton Obote, accusing him of electoral malpractices in 1980. However, other messiahs, especially Alice Lakwena and Joseph Kony, emerged in Northern Uganda, after Museveni had, in 1986, militarily overthrown governments that were militarily based in Northern Uganda.

4. Joseph Kony's Lord's Resistance Army (LRA) In Northern Uganda

Alice Lakwena's *Holy Spirit Mobile Forces* were, finally, military defeated by the NRA troops, near the city of Jinja, in 1987. Following the HSMF's complete military defeat, Joseph Kony, Alice Lakwena's cousin, who was another disgruntled, marginalized and angry Catholic, decided to reorganize the remnants of the Lakwena's HSMF. He wanted to continue Lakwena's holy war against President Museveni's NRM Government and his NRA troops, which later, was renamed, as the UPDF (*Uganda Peoples Defense Forces*).

Joseph Kony was a former fundamentalist Catholic catechist. He was slightly better educated than, Alice Lakwena, his cousin. Like Lakwena, Kony was also very charismatic. As a result, he attracted great interest, among the disenfranchised *Acholi,* especially as he resolved to carry on Lakwena's religio-political crusade against the UPDF. But this time, a militant Joseph Kony decided to wage an effective war, with a better trained, well armed, loyal group of disciplined and fighting holy warriors. He trained them to fight in a well-organized military guerrilla manner for an effective protracted warfare.

Prophet Kony, as the religio-political successor of Alice Lakwena was the Acholi's new Messiah (*Lakwena*). He also wanted to liberate the Acholi people, and his messianic mission, and main political objective were to overthrow President Yoweri Museveni's NRM Government and destroy the oppressive UPDF. He claimed that God had sent him to establish a new theocracy under the Pope, and the divine theocracy would be governed by God through the people's observation of the Ten Commandments.

Like Lakwena, Joseph Kony also condemned President Museveni and his NRM Government for being an oppressive, corrupt and evil system. He stated that these were some of the main reasons why he wanted to engage in a holy war and to overthrow the tyrannical regime and to establish God's theocracy, in its place.

At the beginning, Joseph Kony claimed that his new theocracy would be characterized by justice, harmony and godly virtues. This was because it would be based on the observation of the Ten Commandments of God, and also both the moral authority of God, as based on the Bible and the Pope's encyclicals and pastoral guidance. To this end, Joseph Kony gathered together the remnants of Lakwena's HSMF scattered members. He trained and forged them into a new armed liberationist and formidable Catholic nationalist fighting machine, called the *Lord's Resistance Army* (LRA).

Mainly due to its poorly educated leadership, the LRA did not formulate a clear religious or political agenda, in terms of a manifesto. As a result, the movement did not receive the necessary positive religious or political reception, either from the Catholic Church's elite leadership, or the larger community. The LRA's leadership and objectives were distorted and seriously misunderstood by the public, the *Acholi* elders and the Catholic Church, whom it sought support from.

Later, the LRA retaliated against the local Acholi people and the Church for their failure to support their liberation movement and holy war as against the perceived oppressive NRM Government. Subsequently, the LRA leaders were condemned, and LRA was classified by the USA as "a terrorist organization." Finally, after LRA's mass murders of civilians in Northern Uganda, Sudan and Democratic Republic of the Congo, Joseph Kony along with Raska Lukwiya, Okot Odiambo, Vincent Otti, and Dominic Ongwen, his military generals, were indicted by the ICC (International Criminal Court), on October 13, 2005. As of 2010, Kony was still in hiding.

The LRA's original stated major goal was to impose a Catholic Government on the Ugandan people, based on the strict observation of the Ten Commandments. There were no details of how this theocracy would function, and whether, it would respect human rights. But when it became clear that the LRA was not a movement, whose leaders and holy warriors respected human rights and the strict moral teachings of the Catholic Church, the public became very skeptical.

Later, the public and the State vilified the LRA, when it became clear that Joseph Kony would not obey the directives of the Catholic bishops in Northern Uganda, then, the Catholic Church hierarchy in Uganda, very diligently and prudently dissociated itself from Joseph Kony and his LRA. The LRA as a radical Acholi messianic and liberation movement was condemned, especially for its criminal acts and gross abuses of human rights, including the following:

- Kidnapping of children, and women.
- Armed highway robbery.
- Slavery and holding young girls as sexual slaves.
- Mass murders of suspected opponents.
- Collective punishment of people and communities who are suspected of being Government supporters or collaborators.
- Assassinations of teachers, doctors, politicians and priests.
- Setting houses, food stores and villages on fire as punishment for collaboration with the NRM Government.
- Sadistic tortures and maiming of innocent people and cutting lips, noses and ears of their victims to terrorize the community.
- Committing genocide in order to "cleanse the land of evil people."
- Rapes of girls and women as infliction of collective cultural degradations.
- Collective punishment, public humiliation of people and terrorizing the local community.
- Using HIV/AIDS infected soldiers as weapons of biological mass destruction; sending them to rape women and girls so as to infect them and their community with HIV/AIDS.
- Vandalism and destruction of property, livestock and crops.
- Savage acts of brutality, killing, and maiming of helpless and defenseless villagers.
- Protracted brutal guerrilla warfare and terrorism.
- Refusal to negotiate terms of peace because the NRM Government and

President Museveni were equated with the Devil and evil to be destroyed rather than compromised with by God's holy warriors and liberators (messiah).
- Pain and prolonged suffering in Northern Uganda.[20]

Ironically, the self-righteous leaders of the LRA and their followers as the publicly self-confessed moral and religious crusaders under the banner of the *Lord's Resistance Army* also both publicly and grossly, committed heinous crimes against humanity, abused human rights, violated traditional cultural moral norms, and ultimately violated nearly all God's Moral Law and the Ten Commandments, which they sought to impose on the country of Uganda, to serve as both the Nation's Constitution and Civil Law Code.

As a result of gross abuses of human rights, committing heinous crimes and great atrocities including maiming, rape, torture, robbery and mass murders, the LRA lost public credibility in its supposed noble religious and political goals in its protracted war to overthrow the elected Government of Uganda following the national elections of 2001.

Due to its horrible crimes of mass murders and other forms of gross abuses of human rapes, including rapes and mutilations of innocent civilians, the LRA has been negatively classified and labeled as one of the world's evil and terrorist organizations, by the UN, and the governments of Uganda and the USA. This official vilification of the LRA has made it difficult for the religious leaders in Uganda and other foreign diplomats to engage in the constructive peaceful process needed for a peaceful and lasting negotiation of truce and reconciliation between the LRA and the NRM Government of Uganda.[21]

Some warlike and violent people in Uganda still strongly believe in the laws of retaliation, as a form of justice and deterrence to future crime. The followers of the Mosaic Law of *Lex talionis,* which is often summed-up as: "tooth for a tooth, and an eye for an eye" (Exod. 21:24), or the advocates of retaliation and targeted violence, as justice and deterrence to further crimes, fail to correctly observe and realize, as Jesus the Christ, correctly did that it is an immoral law, which does not promote peace, in the community or the world.

Violence is by its intrinsic nature antithetical to peace. As such, the process of retaliation and counter-retaliation is unable to produce lasting or meaningful peace. The Middle-East provides ample evidence for this religious, moral, military and political truth. If violence was an ideal moral, political or military tool to establish lasting peace, the Middle East and Africa would have been the most peaceful and stable regions of the world, since brutal forms of violence dominate political affairs in these regions.

Ultimately, violence, including just wars, crusades, jihads or holy wars, is evil and by itself cannot produce lasting peace. This is because violence in itself is antithetical to love, mercy, goodness, forgiveness and peace. For instance, the pre-Christian Mosaic Law and its popular form of retribution creates an evil system that is composed of a seemingly vicious cycle of violence and counter-violence, based on the law of *karma* or cause and effect.

This is a tragic vicious cycle of violence, which is rooted in the antiquated Mosaic Law of *Lex talionis* (equal retaliation). It goes on without ending, unless one group completely defeats and exterminates the other group, as their unforgivable and irreconcilable enemies. Genocide is this deplorable method to achieve that absolute goal. Adolph Hitler tried to exterminate the Jews, and Rwanda's oppressed majority *Hutu* group tried to exterminate their Tutsi minority rulers and oppressors, in 1994.

In his famous political discourse, *The Prince*, Machiavelli outlined the dilemma of the use of military power to build a dictatorship or an empire. A good example is that of the Israelis and the Palestinians, who have both erroneously and tragically followed the path of violence and the Mosaic Law to resolve their land disputes and political problems, for many years, without success or resolution of their conflicts. Ultimately, they will also, finally learn from sages and prophets of nonviolence and peace, such as the Buddha, Jesus Christ, Gandhi, Martin Luther King, Bishop Festo Kivengere, and the Archbishops Janani Luwum and Desmond Tutu that wars and violence are intrinsically evil and destructive.

These above prophets and teachers of nonviolence both reject and renounce violence and war as constructive methods for the establishment of any ideal national or international conditions of governance, justice, harmony and lasting peace. This is because violence and war are agents of violence, coercion, destruction and death. Therefore, they can never be effective and morally acceptable tools for the establishment or maintenance of lasting peace. They fail to work because they are antithetical to love, forgiveness, trust, peace and nonviolence, which are the true foundations and ingredients of societal harmony, mutual tolerance of diversity, forgiveness and true mutual peaceful coexistence in society, nation and the world. If wars ever brought peace, the Middle East, Sudan, Congo and Uganda would been the most peaceful places in the world.

These errant advocates of the laws of "*Lex talionis,*" or equal retaliations are found in the Mosaic Law, which the HSMF and the LRA sought to impose on the Ugandans, have made it difficult to have a truly meaningful program of national reconciliation in Uganda and Rwanda following the crimes of civil wars and genocide.

Therefore, South Africa's Peace and Reconciliation Commission should serve as an ideal model for the establishment of peace and reconciliation in

Uganda and Rwanda. In Uganda, hundreds of thousands of people were killed and others were traumatized by the brutal and oppressive regimes of Idi Amin, Milton Obote, and Yoweri Museveni. Thousands of people were also the vicious victims of the liberation movements of Yoweri Museveni's NRM, Alice Lakwena's HSMF, Joseph Kony's LRA, the ADF (Allied Democratic Forces), and the apocalyptic and escapist Keledonia Mwerinde and Joseph Kibwetere's *Movement for the Restoration of the Ten Commandments of God.*[22]

5. The Islamic Allied Democratic Forces (ADF) in Western Uganda

The *Allied Democratic Forces* (ADF) were a rebellious Muslim political, and violent military group, which emerged in the 1980s and worked with *al-Qaeda*[23] in order to overthrow President Museveni's NRM Government. Radical Muslims and Catholics resented the NRM Government, which was perceived to be a disguised continuation of the tradition of the Anglican hegemony, which had traditionally marginalized both the Catholics and Muslims in Uganda.

The Catholics had been unfairly discriminated against and treated by the Anglican ruling elites, as "Second Class Citizens," whereas the Muslims had been treated as "Third Class" and the Traditionalists or "pagans" had been relegated to the "Fourth Class" and treated with disdain by the Christians and Muslims. Yet, many Christians and Muslims were hypocrites, who secretly still practiced many of the African traditional main religious rituals and cultural elements, such as healing through magic (*kubandwa*), prophecy (*okuranga*) and divination (*kuragura*), which they denounced in public. Alice Lakwena's HSM and Kony's LRA had celibately included both Christianity and the African religion, so as to attract and minister to poorly educated people in the rural areas.

However, by doing so, they had offended the urban and Westernized Christians, who subsequently, rejected and vilified them as new religious cults that invalidly claimed to be new religious or messianic liberation movements whose main goal was the establishment of God's holy theocracy. The Muslim extremists also wanted to establish a Muslim theocracy in Uganda. But the Christian and Muslim advocates of a divine theocracy never united in their holy wars and moral crusades to establish a divine theocracy because the Muslims wanted to base it on the *Shari'a* or Islamic law and ideals whereas the Christian moral crusaders wanted to base their theocracy on the Ten Commandments and Christian moral ideals.

The militant *Tabliq* Muslim leaders who were reported to be behind the ADF Movement were part of the Muslim extremists in Uganda. This fundamentalist, extremist and exclusive Muslim movement wanted to impose the rule of *Shari'a,* the Islamic Law, in East Africa, beginning with Uganda. In this respect, the *Tabliq* was a Muslim parallel to Joseph Kony's *Lord's Resistance Army,* which was a Catholic-based military liberationist movement waging a supposed Christian "holy war" in Northern Uganda. The LRA stated that their primary "holy objective and mission" was to overthrow President Museveni's *Bantu*[24] and Anglican-based Government of Uganda.

The LRA wanted to replace it with a Catholic theocracy based on the strict observation of the Ten Commandments of God, whereas the ADF, wanted to overthrow the NRM Government in order to replace it with Islamic theocracy, based on the *Shari'a.* In reality, both the ADF and the LRA were both fundamentalist religious liberation movements, fighting the Government of Uganda for similar basic objectives, namely, to overthrow President Yoweri Museveni and his Anglican Church oriented NRM Government of Uganda, and to replace it with a theocracy, or God's Kingdom. One of the main differences between the LRA and the ADF was that fact the ADF was a radical Muslim extremist religio-political military movement, whereas the LRA was Christian messianic religio-political military liberation movement. Consequently, the ADF sought to base God's Kingdom in Uganda on a strict observation of the Islamic Law or *Shari'a,* whereas the LRA sought to impose on the people the observation of the *Torah* or the Law of Moses.

Both the *Torah* and the *Shari'a* were considered, as the true and sound practical moral, religious and political basis of God's Reign in the world, moral guidance for the visible establishment of God's Kingdom, as the divine redemption and cleansing of the supposedly secular and corrupt world. Obviously, this scenario sounds as if these religious extremists and fundamentalists in Uganda, wanted to transform the country into a new Middle East, where Muslims, and Jews are constantly and tragically fighting "holy wars" (*jihads* and crusades), and brutally killing each other in the name of God and God's holy laws, honor and in defense of what is considered God's revealed infallible and inerrant sacred Scriptures; the *Torah,* in the case of Judaism, and the *Qur'an,* in the case of Islam.[25]

Having been perceived as evil people, President Museveni and his UPDF were supposed to be annihilated, as destructive evil demonic forces in the world, rather than compromised or negotiated with. This being the case, the main goal for moral and religious crusades, is both to completely destroy and annihilate all the perceived evil people, as the evil embodiments and the demonic soldiers of the Devil and the evil demonic forces in the world. This is clearly seen in Lakwena's *Holy Spirit Mobile Forces (*HSMF), and the

Lord's Resistance Army's (LRA) doctrines and holy wars against the troops of the Government of Uganda.[26]

Alice Lakwena proclaimed the NRM Government to be the expression of the Devil's governance and dominion in the world, and President Yoweri Museveni as a demonic embodiment of the Devil. That is mainly why Lakwena preached that God's HSMF as holy warriors could defeat the NRM Government and its UPDF (*Uganda Peoples Defense Forces*), by ritually bathing in consecrated holy water and smearing themselves with peanut and soy bean butter to become bulletproof having been armored and bullet-proofed by deep faith in God, their ritual piety and God's work of providence through the Holy Spirit.

Lakwena preached that the Holy Spirit was going to fight on their behalf and destroy the Devil's evil forces — President Museveni, NRM Government and the UPDF.[27] Lakwena also told her unarmed holy warriors to sing holy songs and to throw stones and twigs at "the UPDF, as the demonic forces of the Devil and infidels, or enemies of God" in faith and hope that God would magically transform the stones and twigs into hand-grenades and bombs, which would devastate God's enemies, and by the invincible power of the Holy Spirit, completely destroy the Devil's forces.[28]

The same extreme religious and radical moral doctrines are seen in Bin Laden's religious and moral teachings and the *al-Qaeda's* religious and moral crusades (jihads and holy wars) against America, especially the tragic events that are connected with the "Attack on America" on September 11, 2001, in which thousands of innocent people were killed, and their property was destroyed. Similar religious, moral and political doctrines of mutual hatred and intolerance are the strong foundations and indefatigable energizing force behind the never-ending destructive violence and brutal wars between the Muslim Arab Palestinians and the Israelis, who wish to build a Zionist Jewish State in Israel. That is why it is difficult for them to live together in harmony and peace or find a nonviolent compromise for their military conflicts and cultures of violence.

This is partly because some of them are moral and religious extremists, who believe that they are the chosen people of God. And as God's people, or faithful servants and saints, they also believe that they cannot negotiate a truce or compromise with the evil-doers or the supposed evil outsiders. This erroneous view is rooted in the religious belief that to negotiate a truce with the enemies amounts to dealing with evil and negotiation with the enemies of God or the Devil. This idea and moral principle of non-negotiation with evil-doers is almost similar to the American policy of non-negotiation with the organizations and people, who have been identified or classified as terrorists.

This rigid moral principle and public policy position of non-negotiation with the supposed evil-doers does not work because it merely alienates the supposed enemies, even more and leaves no room for peaceful conflict resolution, or persuasion of the errant party to repent, renounce error, be reformed, fully rehabilitated and re-integrated into the peaceful Global Community. The ancient Hebrew prophetic tradition presumed that the State was a theocracy. Consequently, God's Moral Law was supreme, non-negotiable and could not be compromised without committing the sins of moral revolt against God and idolatry. As such, the liberationist leaders of the LRA and the radical moral crusaders of the MRTCG were like Moses.

Therefore, in this prophetic tradition, in which the Hebrew prophets, including John the Baptist and Jesus, chose to die, rather than compromise with evil political or religious establishments, there no compromises with what is believed to be evil. As a result, most prophetic and messianic movements, like the HSM, the LRA and the MRTCG shun outside influences, which may lead them to negotiation and comprise.

Both negotiation and compromise are often despised and rejected as evil practices and corrupting agencies of the Devil. This is partly because negation and compromise are also negatively regarded, as the institutional tools for corrupting God's prophets and morally upright people, by persuading them to compromise with evil, or the Devil that are represented by a corrupt State or Church. These moral purists believed that they are corrupted by negotiation through either association, or acceptance of the offer to share power, or by participation in the power and economic affairs of the State or the Church, which were originally deemed to be evil and corrupting, and were denounced, as such.

Negotiation is the antithesis of a revolution. Most revolutions, such as the French Revolution, are often violent and non-negotiable. In addition, these violent revolutions also cause abrupt and radical changes that completely destroy much of the infrastructure and societal systems, in order to eliminate what is considered evil or oppressive, including cultures, traditions, regimes and other establishments, including religious institutions.

In contrast, the ideal goal of negotiation change, reformation or conflict resolution, is supposed to reach a reasonable compromise, which is acceptable to the parties, in conflict. For Kony, negotiation was not fully embraced, until 2008, when he was almost completely surrounded and his troops annihilated, by multinational forces of Uganda, Sudan and the Democratic Republic of the Congo.

As a prophet and a messianic movement leader like the Prophet Moses, he did not wish to negotiate terms of surrender. Nevertheless, due to his precarious situation, Joseph Kony very reluctantly agreed to negotiate terms of surrender, but refused to sign the negotiated Peace Treaty between the

LRA and NRM Government of President Museveni, on April 10 and 11, 2008. The previously scheduled signing dates, on March 16, 2008, and other subsequent dates were also proposed, but not honored by Kony.

The real reason why Kony did not sign these approved treaties was that he saw himself as God's messiah, who could not compromise with what he still believed to be an evil NRM Government. As a stalling tactic, at the end of 2009, Kony requested for another political mediator so that he can continue to negotiate to have the ICC indictments revoked as a condition for signing the Peace Treaty, in 2010 or later. However, Kony gave other reasons, such as the indictment by ICC, which he wanted withdrawn first, before he could sign the Peace Treaty. Nevertheless, the fate of all God's self-appointed prophets and messiahs, will finally, catch-up with him, too.

The fact that Joseph Kony was a reluctant participant in the negotiation of a lasting Peace Treaty, are clear. In October 2007, Kony killed Gen. Vincent Otti, his second in command. He killed him because Otti agreed to negotiate a compromise and a Peace Treaty with President Museveni's NRM Government.

Kony despised President Museveni's NRM Government and alleged that the UPDF were the destructive, genocidal and corrupting demonic forces of Devil and embodiments of evil-spirits or other of evils in God's world. As such, General Kony preferred continuing to wage a holy war against them, in hope to completely destroy them, in God's holy name, instead of negotiation of a compromise or a Peace Treaty, with them.

This idea that negotiation and democracy are incompatible with God's will, moral holiness and the Ten Commandments or the Shari'a is the major source of moral crusades, holy wars and jihads. This religio-political position rejects any moral justification and political validity of negotiation of compromises and Peace Treaties, sources of political, moral or religious evils, and apostasy.

Therefore, moral crusaders treat these processes with moral skepticism and as evils to be shunned, or destroyed by God's true prophets, moral saints and the incorruptible holy warriors. This is because the negotiations require compromise, with what they believe to be evils. This is also the basic reason why many compulsive moral perfectionists, radical and extreme religious fundamentalists refuse to negotiate terms of peace with people and regimes, which they perceive as evil. They prefer to destroy those people and regimes as the embodiments of evil or the agents of the Devil.

Thee religious fundamentalists, like the HSMF, LRA, the *Balokole*, the Mormons, the Jehovah's Witnesses, Evangelicals, the MRTCG, *Opus Dei*, and the *al-Qaeda*, constantly choose obedience to God, rather than choosing obedience to human rulers, or powers. They also diligently seek to destroy the perceived evil people, corrupt governments and supposed communist regimes, in self-sacrificial acts of holy wars and destructive violence, affirming them to be both God's will, and divine justice, and morally just as divine retribution.[29]

Ultimately, in any moral crusade, God's holy forces feel that they have the divine mandate to persevere and defeat the Devil's evil forces. This was also the USA's President George Bush's dilemma with the war, in Iraq. In 2001, President Bush had characterized President Saddam and his country as a major component of "an axis of evil in the world." Having vilified Saddam and his troops, President Bush was compelled to destroy him and exterminate his troops as supposed evil agents of violence and sponsors of terrorism in the world.[30]

False charges of illegal possessions of weapons of mass destruction against President Saddam were trumped-up, as a moral justification and strategy to mobilize both political and military support at home. Therefore, President Bush could not allow the UN inspectors to complete the inspections in Iraq. This is because they had not found any alleged weapons of mass destruction, and the American administration did not want to lose support for the invasion of Iraq, by having the UN discredit the American stated public excuses for the war. The war was previously planned as a continuation of the original American-led military invasion and war in Iraq, under President William Bush, Sr. just a decade earlier.[31]

Like Bin Laden's religious, moral and military crusade against America, President Bush's war in Iraq was implicitly, and sometimes, explicitly fought, as a moral and religious crusade against the evil forces of tyranny and Islamic extremism. President George Bush's stated objectives for waging the war included the regime change in Iraq and Afghanistan, in order to promote both democracy and human rights. These objectives include women's liberation and to institute the rule of law that fosters the respect for human rights, for all people, irrespective of religious affiliation, age, class, gender, race, color and nationality.

The regime change included getting rid of Saddam Hussein, as a dangerous dictator, who threatened to destroy the world with weapons of mass destruction. President Bush found out after invading Iraq that the United Nations' investigators were correct in their findings, prior to the American invasion of Iraq, in 2003, in their statements that affirmed that the weapons of mass destruction did not exist, in Iraq. In any case, China, Israel, North Korea, India and Pakistan, among other nations, possess weapons of mass destruction, and yet were not attacked. Therefore, the Arab Muslims believed that Bush wanted to get oil and defend Israel from Arab aggression and used the excuse of weapons of mass destruction for waging his war for his own hidden agenda.

Since the USA is the main super power in the world today, and the chief democratic role- model for many emerging democracies in the world, including those in Asia, the Middle East, and Africa, one can therefore, validly ask the following moral, religious and political questions about the American decision to wage war and attack Iraq, instead of Saudi Arabia, where most of the attackers on America came from on September 11, 2001:

- Why Saudi Arabia was not attacked, and yet, Iraq which did not have weapons of mass destruction, was attacked, whereas Israel, Pakistan, India, France and North Korea, which had real nuclear weapons and other weapons of mass destruction, were not attacked?
- Was it because Saddam and Iraq more actively supplied weapons to the Palestinians whereas the USA supplied weapons to the Israeli government?
- In this moral crusade in the Middle East, was Saddam Hussein and Iraq punished for supporting the Arab Muslim religious jihad, whereas most Christians in the USA supported the Israeli moral and religious holy war against the Palestinian holy warriors (*jihadists*), or moral crusaders?[32]
- If this is the case, then, is it not possible that the USA has entered the dangerous realm of religious conflicts and crusades where the depth of faith in God and one's cause are the main power and driving forces in the holy war rather than superiority of intellectual decision, military might, and superiority of technology?[33]

Extreme religious zeal, bigotry and intolerance are some of the causes of moral, religious, political, cultural, and military holy wars, or crusades and jihads, in the world both in the past and in some regions of the world today, particularly the Middle East, Northern Ireland, Sudan and Uganda. Therefore, religious fundamentalism, bigotry, intolerance and imperialism can be called the source of terrorism in the world. President Museveni has, fought similar kinds of religiously inspired terrorism, military and messianic religious-political liberation movements in Uganda, for more than twenty-two years. These messianic and liberation movements in Uganda and the surrounding countries, such as Sudan and the Democratic Republic of the Congo, include the ADF, HSMF, and the LRA. They are not easily defeated by the Government troops and military might.[34]

The ADF was a small Muslim group supported by *al-Qaeda,* and many Ugandans could not tell the difference between the two radical, intolerant and militant movements. As a result, the ADF was accused of being an *al-Qaeda* terrorist organization. With the Muslim's hope to return former dictator Idi Amin to power due to his failing health, in the 1990s and later, his death, on August 16, 2003, the ADF lost its morale and could not recruit many new members into the movement. The ADF was, finally, militarily conquered and silenced, in 2004. But it only lays both politically and religiously dormant, and will re-awaken, when the political, religious and military conditions are most favorable.[35]

Due to some strong sectarian religious, historical and political reasons, the ADF leaders did not actively seek to recruit politically, or economically disgruntled Catholics to join the ADF Movement. Had they done so, the ADF-Catholic military coalition would have overthrown President Museveni's NRM Government which became increasingly unpopular in many areas of the country. This was because the NRM Government had failed to become sufficiently religiously, ethnically and politically inclusive, in its senior ranks in the military, cabinet and key appointments in both political and civil service sectors. The Anglicans and the Bantu people from Central, Southern and Western Uganda dominated the top ranks and positions in President Yoweri Museveni's NRM Government.[36]

However, there was a conscious attempt on President Museveni's part to become more inclusive and diverse in his appointments. To that end, President Museveni appointed Dr. Speciosa Kazibwe, a Catholic and later Prof. Gilbert Bukenya, another Catholic, as President Museveni's Vice-Presidents.[37] This was a token attempt to appease the Catholics, and prevent their bid for a radical quest for true democracy, by joining the *Democratic Party* (DP), and agitating for a return to multiparty politics, which they would dominate, by virtue of being statistically the religious majority and citizens in the country.[38]

Nevertheless, the Muslim ADF leaders both politically and militarily miscalculated, when they hoped that most of the politically and economically marginalized, and disgruntled Catholics in Uganda would support them, or remain politically neutral. Thereby, the ADF leaders hoped that the Catholics inadvertently would enable them to overthrow the NRM Government. Gen Idi Amin had employed the same strategy, in 1971, and had successfully overthrown President Milton Obote's predominantly Anglican-based government. The Catholics had supported the military coup hoping that they would come into power since the Muslims were a small religious minority without the necessary educated people to run the government.

However, Gen. Idi Amin was a fundamentalist Muslim with some hidden Islamist agenda,[39] and was not keen on sharing power with the Catholics. With President Muammar Gaddafi of Libya's strategic help and fiscal assistance, President Idi Amin wanted to transform Uganda, a predominantly Christian country, into an Islamic nation that was aligned with the Muslim nations of North Africa and the Middle East.[40] He had filled his government with some semi-illiterate Muslims, and had killed the Benedicto Kiwanuka, a leading Catholic politician and High Court Judge, who had briefly served, as the first elected Prime Minister of Uganda in 1961, as the leader of the DP.[41]

The Catholics were not going to make a similar political mistake. As a result, the ADF was not supported by the local people in Western Uganda and Kampala, where it was based for most of its operations. MRTCG was a non-violent Catholic protest and pacifist version of the failed Alice Lakwena's HSM[42] and Joseph Kony's armed and violent LRA.[43] It is very significant to note that it was not a mere coincidence that all these radical religio-political movements were founded by politically, religiously and socioeconomically marginalized and disgruntled lay Catholics.

As such, these liberation and messianic political movements were also intrinsically crude, liberationist, and different rural forms of lay Catholics' political and religious protest movements, which sought to establish God's reign of justice, holiness, equity, and peace or theocracy.[44] This divine theocracy, as God's Kingdom on the Earth was to be based on the strict observation of God's moral laws, especially as explicitly found in the Ten Commandments of God that were both revealed and given to the world through the Prophet Moses (Exod. 20).[45]

The Catholic Church leadership and Catholic political elites found it necessary to distance themselves from these rural area forms of crude and violent Catholic religious movements, political and economic protests. This was partly because these well-educated Catholic leaders knew that these rural area Catholic political and messianic movements would not succeed in overthrowing the government.

These Catholic political elites knew that these crude rural Catholic grass-roots political protest movements were, instead very embarrassing to the Catholic Church and its elite membership,[46] especially in the urban areas, particularly, those sophisticated Catholics in the cities of Mbarara and Kampala. The Catholic political elite wanted to gain political power through legitimate, democratic, and national electoral processes. To this ideal, democratic and peaceful political end, DP (*Democratic Party*), was considered, as a better, more effective, nonviolent, democratic and ideal political tool.[47]

NOTES

1. Based on the interview conducted, on August 5, 2003, in the Archbishop Bakyenga's office in Nyamitanga, Mbarara Archdiocese Headquarters by this researcher and writer (Prof. Emmanuel Kalenzi Twesigye).

2. Following the definitive religious wars of February 1892, in which the Catholics were completely defeated and humiliated, by the Anglicans, even when they were more numero⟨...⟩ and were supported by King Mwanga, some of the aggrieved European Catholic missio⟨...⟩

suggested to divide the Kingdom of Buganda into two Christian kingdoms. Their proposal was sectarian and it required the Kingdom of Buganda to be split into an Anglican kingdom ruled by an Anglican king, and a Catholic Kingdom of Buganda, to be created.

3. Semmakula Kiwaunka, *A History of Buganda from Early Times to 1900*: 67-139.

4. See: Samwiri Karugire, *A Political History of Uganda*, 49-98; Semmakula Kiwaunka, *A History of Buganda from Early Times to 1900*: 67-139; Hansen, *Mission, Church and State in a Colonial Setting: Uganda 1890-1925*: 29-65. This was the beginning of destructive religious sectarianism and political polarization in Uganda. The scholarship on this period tends to become sectarian, and prejudiced in its data analysis. The religious wars continue within politics, as well as schools and the academy.

5. Samwiri Karugire, *A History of the Kingdom of Ankore in Western Uganda* (London: Clarendon Press, 1971), 106-125; Peter Kasenene, *Religion and Politics in Ankore*, 41-55.

6. *Ibid.*

7. *Ibid.*

8. *Ibid.*

9. Heike Behred, "The Holy Spirit Movement & the Forces of Nature," in Hansen and Twaddle (edited), *Religion and Politics in East Africa,* 59-71.

10. See: F. B. Welbourn, *The East African Rebels* (London: SCM Press, 1961); F. B. Welbourn, *Religion and Politics in Uganda, 1952-1962* (Nairobi: Oxford Press, 1967).

11. See: Tarsis B. Kabwegyere, *The Politics of State Formation and Destruction* (Kampala: Fountain, 1990), 19-48, 61-93, 218-234; Holger Bern Hansen and Michael Twaddle (edited), *Religion and Politics in East Africa*; F. B. Welbourn, *The East African Rebels* (London: SCM Press, 1961); F. B. Welbourn, *Religion and Politics in Uganda, 1952-1962* (Nairobi: Oxford Press,1967).

12. Heike Behred, "The Holy Spirit Movement & the Forces of Nature," in Holger Bern Hansen and Michael Twaddle (edited), *Religion and Politics in East Africa,* 59-71. Joseph Kony, Alice Lakwena's cousin, mobilized her HSMF remnants and transformed them into the deadly, armed LRA.

13. *Maji* in Swahili language means water and the *Maji Maji* revolt against the German imperialists in former German Tanganyika utilized magic and African Religion, as tools for political and military mobilization against a perceived evil occupying foreign German colonial forces. They were well organized and well-motivated, but poorly armed. The HSMF, who were similar to the *Maji Maji* in religious beliefs, in as much, as both believed that bathing in holy water and anointing themselves with holy oil (*Moya*), they would become bulletproof. They believed that bullets fired at them would magically be neutralized, and transformed by God into harmless water (*Maji*).

14. Information provided by Rev. Beatrice Aber of Kitgum, Uganda, on January 6, 2008.

15. *Ibid.*

16. See note 13, above.

17. *Ibid.*

18. *Ibid.*

19. *Ibid.*

20. The LRA leaders were finally indicted by the ICC on October 14, 2005. They were indicted for crimes of mass murders, rape, human rights abuses, torture, slavery, kidnapping, against humanity. This was the first warrant of arrest issued by ICC 1989. In March 2008, the ICC refused to rescind its indictments of desperate appeal, as a condition for signing the final peace treaty ganda.

Kiwanuka, *A History of Buganda*, 1-117; Twesigye, *Common*

Ground: Christianity, African Religion and Philosophy, 1-41, 83-128; Twesigye, "Religion and Politics of Independence in Uganda," *Occasional Research Papers*, Makerere University, 1971; Tarsis B. Kabwegyere, *The Politics of State Formation and Destruction*, 19-48, 61-93, 218-234; Hansen and Twaddle (edited), *Religion and Politics in East Africa*, 106-142; F. B. Welbourn, *The East African Rebels*; Welbourn, *Religion and Politics in Uganda, 1952-1962*.

23. *Al-Qaeda* is a worldwide Muslim organization to promote Islam and defend the faith. It is particularly opposed to Western cultural and religious (Judeo-Christian) imperialism in the Arab and Muslim regions of the world, particularly in the Middle East. The 1989 bombings of the American embassies in Kenya and Tanzania, and the September 11, 2001 *al-Qaeda* terrorist Muslim attacks on the World Trade Center and the Pentagon, are some of these jihads against the USA, for being an ally of Israel.

24. Most of the key cabinet members and high military officers were appointed by President Yoweri Museveni, based on his loyalty to his *Bahima*, or other *Bantu* groups, and especially the members of his Anglican Church of Uganda.

25. Hansen and Twaddle (edited), *Religion and Politics in East Africa*, 1-58.

26. Heike Behred, "The Holy Spirit Movement & the Forces of Nature," in Hansen and Twaddle (edited), *Religion and Politics in East Africa*, 59-71.

27. Alice Auma had visions of God and the Holy Spirit in which she was appointed Messiah (*Lakwena*) and in the same vision she saw the enemies of Acholi people as the Anti-Christ embodied in President Yoweri Museveni and his UPDF troops as the demonic forces of the Devil or the incarnation of the evil spirits, that polluted the Acholi land and could be vanquished through a spiritual warfare by exorcisms and ritual cleansing by washing with consecrated holy water.

28. *Ibid.*

29. This is the kind of moral theology and philosophy, which is subscribed to, by radical liberation groups, like the *Hezbollah, al-Qaeda,* HSMF, LRA, MRTCG and the ADF.

30. Holy wars, such as jihads and crusades, each combatant and violent religious or holy warrior group, such as George Bush's wars and Bin Laden's *al-Qaeda,* claims to be more justified and holier before God than the other side, which is vilified as evil or the apocalyptic embodiment of the Devil/Great Satan, or the "Beast" and the "Anti-Christ," whose Christian symbol is "666" (Rev. 13: 16-18). Like the *al-Qaeda*, the HSM and LRA were also religious and moral armed crusaders to change the world into God's holy theocracy.

31. President George Bush's war in Iraq was more of a moral crusade against what he perceived as a moral evil, dictatorship and Islamic threat to democracy, free trade and capitalism.

32. Bin Laden reversed this trend on September 11, 2001 by attacking the US for supporting Israel in their conflicts with Muslim Arabs. This was one of bin Laden's publicly stated main grievances for waging a holy war on America.

33. These questions and similar ones yield different answers depending on the person's nationality, race, gender, religious affiliation, age and education. Most of them side with Israel against the Palestinians because they share either an ethnic or religious affinity to the Jews as opposed to Muslim Arabs. For instance, the Christians use the Hebrew Bible rather than the Qur'an.

34. See: Heike Behred, "The Holy Spirit Movement & the Forces of Nature," in Hansen and Twaddle (edited), *Religion and Politics in East Africa*, 59-71.

35. Hansen and Twaddle (edited), *Religion and Politics in East Africa*, 1-58.

36. This was one main reason why many people were against the NRM Government and President Museveni's quest to amend the Constitution in 2004 and 2005, and his bid for "Third Term" in office.

37. The balancing of religious Anglican and Catholic political power and ethnicity has

led President Museveni to appoint Professor Apollo Nsibambi, an Anglican and a Muganda, as his Prime Minister, whereas reserving the position for Vice-President for a Catholic from either Buganda or Busoga.

See: Semakula Kiwanuka, *A History of Buganda*, 1-117; Twesigye, *Common Ground: Christianity, African Religion and Philosophy*, 1-41, 83-128; Twesigye, "Religion and Politics of Independence in Uganda," *Occasional Research Papers*, Makerere University, 1971; Tarsis B. Kabwegyere, *The Politics of State Formation and Destruction*, 19-48, 61-93, 218-234; Hansen and Twaddle (edited), *Religion and Politics in East Africa*; F. B. Welbourn, *The East African Rebels;* F. B. Welbourn, *Religion and Politics in Uganda, 1952-1962*.

38. Cardinal Emmanuel Wamala, former head of the Catholic Church in Uganda, constantly challenged the NRM Government to adopt true democracy based on multiparty politics. He believed that if the Catholics united and voted for a DP presidential candidate, then, the traditional Anglican political hegemony would be permanently overthrown.

39. Omari H. Kokole, "Idi Amin, 'the Nubi' & Islam in Ugandan Politics," in Hansen and Twaddle (edited), *Religion and Politics in East Africa*, 45-58.

40. See: Fountain, *Uganda 30 Years 1962-1992*, 49-53; Kiddhu Makubuya, *et al*, editors, *Uganda: Thirty Years of Independence 1962-1992*, 143-152; 384-387; Holger Bern Hansen and Michael Twaddle (edited), *Religion and Politics in East Africa*, 45-58.

41. Samwiri Karugire, *A Political History of Uganda*, 186-191.

42. Heike Behred, "The Holy Spirit Movement & the Forces of Nature," in Hansen and Twaddle (edited), *Religion and Politics in East Africa*, 59-71. This represents a religious distortion of the HSM.

43. *Ibid.*

44. Hansen and Twaddle (edited), *Religion and Politics in East Africa*, 45-71.

45. *A Timely Message from Heaven*, 1-33, 59-61.

46. There were well-educated Acholi people, who for ethnic, economic and political self-interest supported these rural Catholic political movements, regardless of religious tradition or occupation.

47. As a result, some of the main critics of the HSMF, LRA, and MRTCG, are the Catholic Church leaders and the Catholic political elites. They are the ones, who have a lot to lose, if these violent and radical liberation movements are not neutralized.

Chapter Four

ANGLICAN HEGEMONY, CATHOLIC MARGINALIZATION AND PROTEST MOVEMENTS

In Uganda, the Anglican Church has traditionally politically and socially served as the politically semi-established Church of Uganda. Colonial Uganda was to some deliberate extent covertly trying to follow the traditional religio-political model of the Church of England, of which it was a religious and political missionary product and a political colonial descendent, through the royalist missionary of Bishop Alfred Tucker.

Bishop Tucker's British colonial missionary strategy was to convert all major African kings, and their principal chiefs, along with the leading clan heads to the Anglican Church. He hoped that their loyal subjects would follow the religious example of their kings and chiefs and convert to the Anglican Church. By doing so, Bishop Tucker transformed the Anglican Church in East Africa, especially Uganda, into an elitist and royal Anglican Church.[1] For many British Anglican missionaries in Africa, the established Church of England served as the ideal Anglican political and religious model for the Anglican Church in Uganda and the rest of British colonial Africa.

1. Systematic Catholic Marginalization

The Anglican elites, in Uganda, have by this British colonial missionary design, traditionally monopolized the local and national political power. Conversely, these Anglican kings, chiefs and their political followers have also often deliberately autocratic and anti-democratic.

By political design, the royalist Anglican hegemony, deliberately politically and economically marginalized and oppressed the numerically stronger Catholics. As a result, in the absence of true democracy and effective multiparty political systems, the Roman Catholic Church has, by default, emerged as the main voice of the powerless masses and well-organized forum for expressions of social and political critique of the Anglican-based government.

In 1954, the formation of the Catholic based Democratic Party (DP), clearly indicated, the Catholic Church positively served as the real main religio-political institution, whose traditional role was to serve as the checks and balance of power in Uganda. In this respect, the Catholic Church served as the political organ for dissent, and political opposition of the traditional

Anglican hegemonic power.

Consequently, the Catholic Church has by default, effectively served the Uganda people as an effective opposition political party. In this religio-political role, the Catholic Church and its clerical hierarchy have served as the prophetic voice for the oppressed and political protest of the marginalized or powerless masses. To this end, the Catholic Church has resisted the tyranny and oppression of the traditional autocratic Anglican elitist aristocratic rulers, oppressive royal and hegemonic power.[2]

It was a religious, political and historical reality that the Catholic religious, political, economic marginalization and discrimination by the ruling Anglican elites and frustrations had led to some serious religious, political and military protests and wars in Uganda. In 1892, the Anglicans and Catholics had fought a civil war in the Kingdom of Buganda in quest for total religious, political, and economic control, power, hegemony and dominance in the land.

However, helped by their British allies, the Anglicans had won the war and established an Anglican hegemonic power in Buganda and the rest of Uganda. This Anglican hegemony remained viable into the turbulent post-colonial history of Uganda. It became the root of Uganda's political discontent and instability since the majority of the citizens of Uganda claimed a Catholic religious affiliation, especially in the Ankole Kingdom, leading to its eventual abolition, in the 1990's, by angry and formerly politically marginalized *Bairu* Catholics, who constituted a majority of the citizens of Ankole Kingdom.

Catholic religious, political and economic frustration had continued to grow and fester. The founding of DP (*Democratic Party*) in 1954 was designed as an effective public national religio-political forum for protest, and legal device to publicly discuss and vent this Catholic frustration. It was also the instrument to find a political solution in the independence elections of 1962. Instead, the Anglican Church-based UPC (Uganda Peoples Congress), working with the Anglican kings of Uganda, including the nationally and internationally notable *Kabaka* Edward Frederick Mutesa II of Buganda, won the national elections and continued the Anglican hegemonic power in Uganda at the expense of the more numerous Catholics.

Initially, many Catholics in Uganda naively welcomed President Idi Amin's military coup, on January 25, 1971. This was mainly because these politically marginalized and aggrieved Catholics wrongly believed and thought that Idi Amin, being also a marginalized Muslim, would be more sympathetic to other traditional religiously marginalized groups, such as the Roman Catholics. They erroneously expected to share political power with Gen. Idi Amin's Muslim Party, at the expense of the Anglicans, who had previously marginalized and oppressed them, since the fateful religio-political war of 1892, in the Kingdom of Buganda.

However, President Idi Amin became a Christian persecutor, who tragically killed many Christians, in order to transform Uganda into an Islamic country, despite the fact that it was, overwhelmingly, a Christian nation. In 1971, Muslims were only seven percent of the total population of Uganda. The Anglican and Catholics accounted for more than 80 percent of the Ugandans. But tragically, as the new President of Uganda, Gen. Idi Amin first persecuted the former ruling Anglican elites. He brutally persecuted and killed thousands of them, including their religious leaders.

Thousands of Christians, along with many bishops and the priests, were forced to flee the country and live in exile in Kenya, Tanzania, South Africa, Zambia, Europe and North America. Later, President Amin viciously turned against the Catholics, who had supported his military coup. He began to persecute and kill them, too. Like their Anglican compatriots, many Catholic were also forced to flee, into exile.

Therefore, expected messianic deliverance of the Catholics from religious marginalization and persecution by the Anglican hegemony, failed to materialize under President Idi Amin's military regime. Instead of liberation, President Idi Amin established a "reign of terror" 1971-1979, from which President Julius Nyerere of Tanzania and Yoweri Museveni's liberation troops, militarily delivered them from, by overthrowing President Idi Amin, in 1979. President Yoweri Museveni's NRM (*National Resistance Movement*) seemed to be both religiously and politically inclusive enough to permit the appointment of Dr. Specioza Kazibwe as Uganda's Vice-President in 1995 and Dr. Gilbert Bukenya as her successor, following her abrupt resignation in April 2003.

Following President Idi Amin's "Reign of Terror", many politically and economically frustrated Catholics have, from time to time, strongly protested and founded political protest parties, like DP and liberation movements, such as the HSM, LRA and the messianic and apocalyptic MRTCG. The military protest movements, like Alice Lakwena's *Holy Spirit Movement* (HSM), in 1988-87, and Joseph Kony's notorious *Lord's Resistance Army* (LRA),[3] 1987-2005, are more radical forms of rural and poorly educated Catholic protest movements in Northern Uganda.

The resistance movements have survived because they had some political sympathizers and support, especially among some more educated Catholics, and people from Northern Uganda. They were the real political beneficiaries of these movements and protests. Before the rise of these armed Catholic movements in Uganda, the Democratic Party (DP) founded, in 1954, by Catholics in Buganda, with the active assistance of the Catholic bishops at Rubaga, had been the traditional, and nonviolent Catholic political protest party and a mobilization platform for most Catholics in Uganda, particularly, those in Buganda, Ankole, Bunyoro, Busoga, Kigezi, Toro and Tororo areas. Northern Uganda seemed to have transcended religiously based politics in preference to ethnicity.

Christianity was supposed to be less strongly rooted in these Northern Region areas, as compared to both the Southern and Central regions, where most people tended to identify themselves more along the religious and political affiliations than ethnic ones. This observation was generally true with major exception of the Baganda.

The Baganda political and cultural nationalists were inherently sectarian along ethnic lines rather than religious lines. According to Ugandan political history, in general, the Baganda ethnic cultural and political nationalists preferred to be identified with the Kabaka and Buganda Kingdom, at the expense of the rest of Uganda, with some notable exceptions like Benedicto Kiwanuka and Dr. Paul Semmogerere, the main DP Catholic and Ugandan nationalists. In rejection of both the DP and UPC, the Baganda ethnic cultural and political nationalists had formed an important, religiously inclusive, Baganda ethnic political party, in 1962.

This ethnically Baganda sectarian political party was called *"Kabaka Yekka"* (The Buganda King Alone).The Baganda sectarian cultural and political party rejected national multiparty politics. In 1966, it led to the Kingdom of Buganda's tragic secessionist resolution by the kingdom's *Lukiko* (Parliament) of May 20, 1966, directing Uganda's Federal Government of Prime Minister Milton Obote to leave the territory of the Kingdom of Buganda, by the end of that month.

The Kingdom of Buganda wanted to become a separate country, with Mengo, as its headquarters and Bulange Parliament, at Mengo, as its national parliament.[4] Instead of the anticipated national independence for the Kingdom of Buganda, Milton Obote, the Prime Minister of Uganda, as the head of state, responded in alarm, arresting leading Baganda chiefs on May 23, 1966, and when a riot started at the palace, on May 24, 1966, Obote, the executive Prime Minister, sent Gen. Idi Amin to quell the Baganda revolt. Gen. Idi Amin, as Obote's hatchet-man, used great military brutality to storm King Edward Mutesa II's Palace. He killed the rebels and deposed the king (Kabaka), who ran to hide at Bishop Joseph Kiwanuka's residence Rubaga Catholic Cathedral.

Subsequently, King Mutesa fled into exile in England for the second time and died there on November 21, 1969, under mysterious circumstances. Many anti-Obote Baganda ethnic nationalists strongly believed that Obote followed him there with secret agents who secretly poisoned their king, but this allegation was never proved by medical or criminal forensics. On September 17, 1967, the Kingdom of Buganda and the other three main kingdoms were officially dissolved by the irate Dr. Milton Obote, the Prime Minister and head of state of Uganda. These kingdoms and their respective kings were restored in 1986, by President Yoweri Museveni, as cultural institutions. The cultural nationalists, especially the Baganda, were overjoyed.

The less culturally united, politically divided and religiously sectarian Banyankole were unable to restore their monarchy. They were unable to overcome their deep cleavages of traditional religious and political divisions along the Anglican ruling *Bahima,* aristocrats, and the predominant agriculturalist Catholic *Bairu,* as the oppressed subjects and the ruled majority population group, with the "Anglican *Bahima* Ankole Kingdom." They used their great numbers to reject the monarchy as an antiquated and oppressive sectarian institution. This negative *Banyankole* experience, majority hatred of the monarchy and the *Bahima* Anglican aristocratic class was unique to the Ankole Kingdom.

Cultural and ethnic nationalism in kingdoms of Buganda, Bunyoro and Toro transcended the problem of traditional Anglican hegemony in these kingdoms. The founding of *Kabaka Yekka,* in Buganda, was great evidence for this ethnic nationalism and political unity based on it that transcended traditional tendencies of religious sectarianism and resentment for Anglican political hegemony.

However, Bishop Joseph Kiwanuka, the nationally politically influential Catholic Bishop of Rubaga, favored national politics based on a Catholic majority, such as DP. Therefore, Bishop Kiwanuka strongly opposed and protested against the Catholic Baganda's joining the *Kabaka Yekka,* at the expense of DP, which was the legitimate Catholic political party.

DP was a national political party, which would be weakened by *Kabaka Yekka,* and therefore, unlikely to have the sufficient numbers required to beat UPC (*Uganda Peoples Congress*) Party, which was an Anglican sponsored political party with a large support of Uganda's Muslims and other non-Catholics who looked at the Anglican monarchies and the Anglican ruling elite, as great leaders to be maintained in power by their own votes. The latter preferred the status quo and the peace that they knew and resented change of governments and the uncertainties that those radical changes were bound to bring.

Perhaps more significantly for Keledonia Mwerinde and other Catholics who later joined the MRTCG, Kibwetere was a well-known Catholic politician and member of the *Democratic Party* (DP). The *Democratic Party* had become a political party for angry, frustrated and disgruntled Catholics of all classes and ethnic groups in Uganda. This was partly rooted in the party's historical past, agenda, values and objectives.

Inevitably, the *Democratic Party* had become politically and religiously identified with the Roman Catholic Church, whose members had become politically marginalized in Uganda. The Catholics were politically marginalized irrespective of the fact that the Catholics constituted a numerical majority in Uganda. Catholics were a majority, when compared to the Anglicans, who had ruled them since the destructive religious war of 1892. This definitive religious and political war was viciously fought between the Anglicans *"Bangereza"* and the Catholics *"Bafaransa,"* in the Kingdom of Buganda.

Subsequently, the religio-political definitive between the *"Bangereza"* (Anglicans), and the *"Bafaransa"* (French Catholics) permanently polarized the country of Uganda into permanent religious sectarianism and hostile political religio-parties. For instance, the ruling aristocratic, hegemonic Anglicans and the mass of the ruled people composed mainly of disenfranchised Catholics, particularly in the kingdoms of Ankole, Buganda, Bunyoro and Toro.

The religious conflicts in the Kingdom of Buganda, and the victory of the Anglican political party over the more numerous Catholics set the political model for Anglican hegemony for the other kingdoms and rest of Uganda. Sectarian schools also reflected this Anglican political hegemony in their objectives of education and the curriculum. That is, the Anglicans schools were established to educate and train the children of kings and chiefs to rule the country and serve as the colonial agents of British indirect rule in Uganda.

This Anglican hegemony in Uganda started, in 1892, and still continues today. But it exists in some disguised forms, like President Yoweri Meseveni's NRM Government and the UPDF. Backed by their British allies in the form of Captain Lugard, and his Nubian Muslim mercenaries from the Sudan, the Anglicans won the religious war and from that time onwards, all Ugandan kings and their major chiefs had become converted to Anglicanism and the Anglican Church had indirectly become the royal and politically established "Church of Uganda." Henceforth, the Roman Catholics had become both politically and socially marginalized and disenfranchised people in Uganda, particularly, in the kingdoms of Ankole, Buganda, Busoga, Bunyoro and Toro.

The Roman Catholic Church and its hierarchy found itself serving as the default opposition political party to the elitist, royalist and autocratic Anglican ruling class as symbolized by the Anglican monarchies, prime-ministers and most of their cabinet members in the various kingdoms of

Uganda. Ultimately, since no Muslim or Catholic princes could become king in Uganda, the politically marginalized and aggrieved non-Anglican political groups, especially the Catholics, actively sought to abolish these ancient "Anglicanized monarchies of Uganda."

This radical anti-monarchist movement, especially in Ankole, justified itself on the basis of Western ideas of democracy and freedom. The abolition of the traditional institution of the monarchy was promoted in order to gain freedom and democratic power. In the case of the Ankole Kingdom, the anti-monarchist *Bairu* Catholics constituted the majority of the citizens who were also the subjects or the ruled masses.

Therefore, unless they could elect a king (*Mugabe*) from their non-aristocratic (*Bairu*) Catholic ranks, then, they did not want another Anglican *Muhima* for a king to rule over them, and probably oppress or discriminate against them. They promoted republican ideals and wanted the nation to become a republic. The more moderate Catholic politicians were willing to retain monarchies in Uganda but with limited political powers. They were willing to support constitutional amendments that would effectively transform the traditional Anglican kings into mere cultural figure heads without real administrative and political power to affect any national political or economic agenda, including the constitutional power and authority to either appoint any chiefs or dismiss them from his or her cabinet.

As a result of this Catholic political marginalization and oppression, by the elitist and royal Anglican class, the Catholics felt angry and demoralized. They looked for a nonviolent and political method to reverse political history and gain political power in a legitimate democratic manner. Subsequently, in order to negate Anglican political hegemony, reverse the colonial culture of political oppression and improve the general social state of affairs for the marginalized Catholics, the DP was founded in 1954. Understandably, DP was the religious, political weapon, and legal tool to accomplish these desired political, religious, social and economic objectives. As such, it is essential to note that modern multi-party politics cannot be understood, unless one understands that DP was originally historically founded as a Catholic religio-political protest against Anglican political hegemony.

Subsequently, DP has historically attracted some disgruntled Roman Catholics, such as Benedicto Kiwanuka and Joseph Kibwetere. As a result, DP was employed and used as a political vehicle for Catholic political mobilization and protest, against the traditional Anglican ruling aristocracy, and hegemony. This Catholic Church-based democratic process of protest was publicly visible in all the four kingdoms of Uganda, namely, Ankole, Buganda, Bunyoro and Toro, as well as within Uganda's Federal Government and its regional administration at District levels, especially in

Kigezi. In the 1980's, Joseph Kibwetere became the leader of the *Democratic Party* in Ntungamo District, a former political division of the Ankole Kingdom and Mbarara District.[5]

Kibwetere failed to unseat the Anglican political candidate, who was a UPC (*Uganda Peoples Congress*) member. Kibwetere got very frustrated by political injustice, which the Roman Catholics in Uganda suffered at the hands of the Anglican aristocratic ruling elites. These Anglican ruling elites resented true democracy and fair multiparty political elections in the kingdoms and the rest of the country since this democratic electoral process would lead to either sharing political power with the Catholics, being abolished, in the case of hereditary Anglican monarchies as in the case of the Kingdom of Ankole, or being constitutionally overthrown and replaced by the Catholics.

Understandably, Joseph Kibwetere was deeply aggrieved by the prevailing destructive religiously based and sectarian politics in Uganda. He was familiar with the political experience of mutual intolerance and deeply entrenched political divisions that were traditionally rooted in Uganda's turbulent history.

Uganda's violent past history was characterized by traditional ethnic conflicts and vicious sectarian religious conflicts between the British-allied ruling Anglican aristocracy and the disenfranchised Roman Catholics, who constituted the majority of the politically marginalized people in Uganda. Kibwetere's heavenly visions of the Virgin Mary directed him to repent and prepare himself to become God's new prophet and messenger in the world.

Like Mwerinde, Kibwetere's prophetic duty, redemptive and apocalyptic messianic mission were also to reveal God's new will for the world. The other duties were to represent the Marian Movement to the outsiders. In addition, all the Twelve Apostles of the Blessed Virgin Mary and Christ (*Entumwa za Bikira Maria na Yezu*)[6] had to teach and preach, to the world, God's redemptive message for the imminent end of the world and the doom of sinners in God's fire from heaven.

Therefore, the core of the Movement's message and preaching were prophetic. That is, they were more concerned with the history and current events which they reinterpreted in apocalyptic terms. They read the present signs of evil, as portrayed in the apocalyptic Book of Revelation, in current events as the harbingers of the end of the present era and possibly, the end of the world, itself. For instance, they saw the destructive effects and signs of global warming, climate changes, the threat of new deadly diseases like HIV/AIDS, cases of widespread drought, famine, destructive hurricanes, floods, and the destructive wars of genocide and renewed threats of nuclear wars as the apocalyptic signs the world was coming to an end.

The apocalyptic biblical Book of Revelation was used as the reference manual for their sermons and interpretation of history. Therefore, the Movement leaders proclaimed God's warning to repent and renounce sins and evils of sexual immorality, greed, materialism, pride, corruption, violence and disobedience to God's Ten Commandments.

2. Joseph Kibwetere and Keledonia Mwerinde Form A Marian Devotion Leadership Team

In 1988, Joseph Kibwetere and Keledonia Mwerinde heard about each other and knew of their common interest in Marian devotion. This was a result of their holy pilgrimage to the Nyabugoto sacred caves, in Nyarushanje. It was believed by many Catholic devotees of the Blessed Virgin Mary, Nyabugoto was a holy mountain, where the apparitions of the Blessed Virgin Mary could be experienced by some of her most favored and chosen devotees.

At the Nyabugoto Holy Mountain, the local Catholic Marian devotees had formed a women's prayer club to worship the Blessed Virgin Mary as a Goddess. The Marian Prayer Club held regular monthly meetings headed by Gauda Kamushwa, the founder of the Marian Prayer Club. Mwerinde was one of her followers.

However, this scenario changed when Mwerinde and Kibwetere met at these meetings. Kibwetere advised the women to form a more business like Marian Club, so as to attract Marian pilgrims to the Holy Mountain, and maybe charge an entrance fee to enable them to develop the site into an attractive Marian tourist site, like the European Marian sites, such as Fatima in Portugal, Lourdes in France, and Guadalupe in Mexico. Most importantly, Mwerinde and Kibwetere shared a common religious experience. They shared an important mystical spiritual bond because of their mutual, or shared mystical devotion to the Blessed Virgin Mary and having received the heavenly beatific visions of God and the Blessed Virgin Mary.[7] It seemed to them as if their meeting was preordained and they were brought together by some powerful divine providence, or God, for a specific task, namely, to serve the Blessed Virgin Mary and save the world.

The Marian Movement leaders interpreted their Marian pilgrimages and seemingly accidental encounter at Nyabugoto Holy Mountain, in 1988, as true divine providence and holy mystery that worked as some kind of invisible divine guidance, or mystical force. For some people, this is simply called "predestination" or "fate." In this case, both Mwerinde and Kibwetere met and changed history, when Kibwetere came and brought along some Marian nuns from Mbarara, and visited the sacred caves of Nyabugoto, in Nyakishenyi to see and venerate the Blessed Virgin Mary.

These caves had become well-known in Kigezi and Ankole areas among the Roman Catholics as holy ground to come to, on a pilgrimage, especially during the holy and penitential season of Lent. Many local Marian women reverently came to these caves in order to venerate the Blessed Virgin Mary who was supposed to have appeared there to the shepherds and the local women; the best known among them being Gauda Kamushwa, a local trader in used clothing. This is the holy ground where Gauda Kamushwa and other Catholic women had cleaned, according to local custom, and furnished with special local beautiful grass (*engunga*). The *engunga* was traditionally used in Western and Southern Uganda to adorn traditional shrines, temples and royal houses or palaces in Kigezi and the Kingdom of Ankole. Thus, these Catholic women transformed the Nyabugoto caves into holy shrines for the veneration and worship of the Blessed Virgin Mary, and Jesus, her son.

The Nyabugoto women's original Marian "Worship and Prayer Group" was led by the local Catholic Marian devotee and pious woman called Gauda Kamushwa. She, too, thought that the Blessed Virgin Mary had visited her and commissioned her to preach her message of salvation to save the world, in her name, but had lacked the resources and organization to carry out her divine mandate. Therefore, she was overjoyed when Keledonia Mwerinde picked up the mantle and founded the necessary Marian Movement to preach repentance and save the world. These lay Catholic women were informal, but well-organized, for Marian devotional activities in the sacred caves on the Nyabugoto Holy Mountain. They regularly came together, and climbed the mountain and then "ascended" into these "holy cave temples," near the top of the mountain cliffs to venerate the Virgin Mary who was supposed to have appeared to the local shepherds.

However, some skeptics alleged that having no religious reference in which to understand the life comforting apparition or vision of the Blessed Virgin Mary, the shepherds had apparently mistaken the Virgin Mary's apparition to be both a visual illusion and a mental delusion (*waringa*) caused by fatigue, and hallucination from many hours of staring at the rocks. Originally, the shepherds were forced to seek refuge in the caves because of rain and thunder outside.

There is also a lack of light, within the caves behind the rock, which looks like a human being and resembles the curved statutes of the Blessed Virgin Mary. Nevertheless, the shepherds and the women of Nyakishenyi, who came to visit these awe inducing, sacred and mysterious caves, strongly believed that the Blessed Virgin Mary had taken form in the rock and appeared to them, high up, in the quiet rocky mountain caves. Kamushwa claimed that she had been visited by the apparition of the Blessed Virgin Mary, who had directed her to repent of her sins, and to obey her commissioning (calling) to preach God's consolation and her message of grace, salvation, unconditional love and protection for the oppressed, the powerless and the poor.

In addition, Kamushwa claimed that the Virgin Mary had directed her to raise funds to help and provide for the impoverished and needy people.[8] But, due to poverty and lack of skills to transform her commissioning into action, Kamushwa had failed to fulfill both her divine calling and mandate as Mary's agent of redemption in the community and the world.

3. The Blessed Virgin Mary Chooses Her New Agents of Redemption

Not yet known to each other, and by some mysterious spiritual forces that some people may variously choose to call "divine providence," "predestination," "fate" or "coincidence," both Keledonia Mwerinde and Joseph Kibwetere had each gone separately to the Nyabugoto sacred caves to venerate the Blessed Virgin Mary, whose apparition was reported to be constantly taking place in these sacred caves for her faithful local devotees and other devoted followers, who came there in deep faith, reverence and in the quest of the Blessed Virgin Mary's blessings and hope to see her life-transforming apparitions.

At the beginning of 1989, Keledonia Mwerinde and Ursula Komuhangi, her sister and religious convert, went to the Mbarara Catholic Archdiocese at Nyamitanga to declare to the Church hierarchy their beatific and life transforming experiences of God's calling, receptions of divine new urgent revelations and the apparitions of the Blessed Virgin Mary, in the Nyabugoto sacred caves. These devotees of the Blessed Virgin Mary and leaders of her Marian Movement truly believed that they were fulfilling God's redemptive mission in the world. They believed that God had entrusted, to them, this divine mandate and commissioning, through the mediation of the Blessed Virgin Mary.

The Marian Movement leaders both testified to God and proclaimed to the world that, through the Blessed Virgin Mary's glorious apparitions, and life-transforming holy visions, they had personally and individually been chosen, and called to serve God in a new way. They had received God's divine calling, consecration and commissioning to go into the world to testify and preach the new urgent messages of God, to the world as given to them by the Blessed Virgin Mary.

Many nuns and several professionally frustrated, disgruntled and unhappy priests were upset and angry with the Catholic hierarchy. And due to their religious marginalization and poor treatment by the Church leaders, these Catholic women very eagerly believed Mwerinde and Kibwetere's visions and revelations of God, through the Blessed Virgin Mary. For them, it was received as God's provision for the true liberation of women from their husbands, other male oppressors and the patriarchal Church leaders that continued to marginalize them. They also welcomed the MRTCG leaders' new moral and spiritual reformist messages and promotion of celibacy.

Consequently, many of these oppressed and impoverished Catholic women joined the MRTCG leaders and participated in their moral crusade. For these liberated Catholic women, joining the Marian Movement and its monastic and celibate collective community was like joining a traditional Catholic religious order and becoming a nun. Their vows of obedience, poverty, celibacy and silence were positively viewed as becoming real nuns. When they adorned the traditional nuns' uniforms and veils, to them, it was not a mere act of wearing a uniform, or costume. For these Marian Movement devotees, it was regarded as a true public and personal expression, that they were indeed, real nuns of the Catholic Church.

Many Catholic lay people also believed the Movement leaders' preaching and God's new apocalyptic messages, warning against evil and sin and urgent need for repentance, as timely and important. Therefore, they positively affirmed the Movement leader's redemptive mission and the validity of their heavenly visions of God and the Blessed Virgin Mary. Among the Movement's original leaders, the better educated and influential lay Catholics were Joseph Kibwetere and his wife Theresa Kibwetere, whereas the Rev. Fr. Dominic Kataribabo was the most highly educated priest and leader of the Movement. As a result, Joseph Kibwetere and Fr. Dominic Kataribabo became the external symbols and representatives of the Movement. This was important in terms of the Movement's credibility and appeal to both the lay and professionally trained and ordained members of the Catholic Church.

As if directed by God and the Blessed Virgin Mary, of whom they were great devotees, Theresa and Joseph Kibwetere invited both Keledonia Mwerinde and Ursula Komuhangi to come and stay with them, at their home at Kibumba, in Ntungamo. Thus, the original Marian Movement was later modified to become a broader based developmental, religious and moral education "association" (*Ekigombe*). The new "association" and moral crusade movement was legally founded as a Non-Governmental Organization (NGO) with the new name of: *The Movement for the Restoration of the Ten Commandments of God* (*Ekigombe Ky'Okujumura Ebiragiro Ikumi Bya Ruhanga*) as a new coalition and partnership of both Keledonia Mwerinde and Joseph Kibwetere.

Mwerinde provided most of the heavenly visions and spiritual direction of the Movement whereas Kibwetere provided the fiscal resources and administrative direction. Later, the Rev. Dominic Kataribabo joined and provided the theological and liturgical direction of the Movement, including the secret ritual confessions and ritual deaths or murders of the Movement members, especially, the climatic church inferno, in Kanungu, on March 17, 2000, in which more than seven hundred people were fire bombed and incinerated to ashes.

The skulls of children and small adults were particularly the ones burned to complete ashes. According to eyewitnesses, the children were also the majority of the people that were in the MRTCG camp and those Movement victims that perished in the church building fire. Therefore, the actual death toll in this fire is also much higher than the original 534 skulls that survived the fire. In reality, the death toll in Kanungu is estimated to be higher than eight hundred people.[9]

Before the tragic ritual deaths of the hundreds of members of the Marian Movement, at the MRTCG's centers in Kampala, Bushenyi, Rugazi and finally, and prior to the Marian Movement's horrendous church fire, in Kanungu, on March 17, 2000, the Marian Movement had become popular, among the Catholic devotees of the Blessed Virgin Mary, in East Africa, Rwanda, Burundi and the Eastern Region of the Democratic Republic of the Congo. Nevertheless, it is politically and religiously significant to note that, like Alice Lakwena's *Holy Spirit Movement* and Joseph Kony's *Lord's Resistance Army,* in Northern Uganda, *The Movement for the Restoration of the Ten Commandments of God*, was also Roman Catholic both in its origin and leadership. It drew most of its membership, mainly, from some relatively politically disenfranchised and frustrated Roman Catholics.

Therefore, it is not surprising that these politically marginalized, socioeconomically oppressed or discouraged, ecclesiastically alienated fundamentalist apocalyptic Catholic Christians had eagerly expected to ascend to heaven and leave the world behind, in which they felt marginalized, oppressed, persecuted and alienated. This is the distressing profile of most of the people within the Marian movement, who most eagerly anticipated the fiery end of this supposedly evil and corrupt world, in which their sinful and corrupt oppressors, would be judged and sentenced to death in a painful fire, as God's vengeance and vindication for the oppressed of the holy Saints of the Blessed Virgin Mary.

Based on the field research data, it became self-evident that these Marian devotees truly hoped for their divine vindication and supernatural deliverance, or divine liberation and salvation to come with the apocalyptic end of the era, at the Second Millennium, on December 31, 1999, at midnight. They were not sure how this event would occur. Nevertheless, they both hoped and believed that it would mark a happy and glorious dawning of the Third Millennium, as the mystical and spiritual beginning of a New Era of God's Kingdom, in the cleansed and renewed world, or Heaven.[10]

4. The Movement's Membership and Catholic Religious Affiliation

The Movement for the Restoration of the Ten Commandments of God was predominantly Roman Catholic, in its ecclesiastical origins, leadership, main membership, central beliefs, monastic teachings, moral values and sacramental or liturgical practices. The complete historical study and comparative analysis of the Marian Movement's main teachings, beliefs, sacramental procedures, worship and moral practices revels that they were overwhelmingly Roman Catholic, especially in its medieval traditions, moral ideals or teachings and ritual or sacramental procedures. This is especially true when we compare the Marian Movement central moral teachings and monastic practices within the Catholic traditions and practices as found within the medieval religious Orders, and particularly, the Benedictine monastic Order. The Marian Movement was so Catholic that its conservative priests deliberately revived the Pre-Vatican II exclusive dogmatic doctrines of the Catholic Church and salvation, as well as sacramental confessions of individual sins before a priest and the Eucharist in one kind for the laity, received on the tongue while kneeling.

Most importantly, the leaders of the Movement and their followers called themselves the true, repentant, morally reformed and spiritually renewed, God-fearing loyal Catholics. Their redemptive divine mission was to convert the rest of the Catholic Church and its hierarchy to this moral crusade, repentance, obedience to God's moral law and living a new life of moral and spiritual renewal and holiness based on the strict observance of the Ten Commandments of God.

By the year 2000, the Marian Movement had more than seven thousand members nationwide. There were also converts to the Movement from Rwanda, Burundi, Congo and Kenya. These MRTCG members were predominantly disillusioned and unhappy Catholics who came from all classes and many ethnic groups.

However, the majority of the apocalyptic Marian Movement members were the poorly educated women who were the most dedicated devotees of the Marian Movement in Uganda and the surrounding countries of Rwanda, Burundi, Tanzania, Kenya and the Democratic Republic of Congo during the 1990's. In the years of 1998 and 1999, other Marian devotees were reported to have come from, Austria, France, Italy, Portugal and Germany, for brief visits, and to investigate Joseph Kibwetere and Keledonia Mwerinde's reports of regular visions of the Blessed Virgin Mary and to hear the special messages which had been revealed from Heaven concerning the imminent end of the world and the beatific ascension into heaven by the faithful Christians on the night, on December 31, 1999, at the end of the millennium.

Without sacrificing both its originality and integrity of the message and independence, the Movement had, subsequently, developed important religious, theological and personal ties with the Marians in these countries and sought their fiscal support in the construction of a new Church building, improvement of their crop and animal farms and other proposed development projects (*The New Vision*, Monday, March 20, 2000:1- 4). Asuman Mugyenyi, the Uganda Government Police spokesman, on March 20, 2000, declared to the nation and the world, which was still puzzled and mourning, the supposed "Kanungu Cult mass suicides," and that the "Cult" had international links. Accordingly he declared that: "The Cult had ties with France, Austria, Italy and Germany."[11]

The Movement had also made this claim in its handbook as it declared that its divine revelation from God, Christ and the Blessed Virgin Mary was similar and in continuity with God's message as revealed through the Virgin Mary and her special apparitions to selected people in special places in Europe and other parts of the world. As such, the visions of the Blessed Virgin Mary to Keledonia Mwerinde and Joseph Kibwetere were neither unique religious experiences nor delusions. They were part of the Catholic tradition and Marian devotion.

However, the apocalyptic messages that were declared to be revealed by the Blessed Virgin Mary were themselves, unique and non-traditional. Bishop Kakubi said that he found them false. He said that, in most cases, the reported Marian apparitions and messages from heaven sounded too excessive or too fantastic. They sounded like artificial inventions and fiction. As a result, they were a challenge to traditional Catholic faith. And they were too much to be believed by the traditional and conservative Roman Catholic Church hierarchy, especially, Bishop John Baptist Kakubi and Bishop Paul Bakyenga of the Mbarara Diocese.[12]

As a matter of fact, the Mbarara Catholic bishops negatively viewed and harshly treated the religious claims that Joseph Kibwetere and Keledonia Mwerinde had received God's special revelations through the regular appearances of the Blessed Virgin Mary. The Catholic bishops of Mbarara Diocese treated these religious claims as pious frauds, delusions, erroneous beliefs and dangerous claims to be renounced and rejected by all the faithful Catholics. Subsequently, they were warned to desist in such claims and practices in relationship to the Blessed Virgin Mary. They were subsequently, officially interdicted, along with their followers, in 1991.

The lay leaders of *The Movement for the Restoration of the Commandments of God* were officially suspended from taking the Eucharist until they obeyed the bishops, renounced their errors and returned to the traditional Catholic Church's teachings and practices. The Catholic priests within the Movement, especially Fr. Dominic Kataribabo, Fr. Paul Ikazire and Fr. Joseph Mary Kasapurari, were also formally interdicted by Bishop Kakubi.[13] These priests were prohibited from celebration of the Eucharist for the public or in private homes. They were forbidden to hear confessions until they had renounced their errors and decided to obey Bishop Kakubi as their local Diocesan Bishop. In response, the Movement moved its headquarters to the remote rural area of Kanungu, in Kabale Diocese, partly to avoid Bishop Kakubi's interdiction as the Mbarara Diocesan bishop.

The Marian Movement's migration and physical relocation of the Movement's headquarters to Kanungu within the Kabale Catholic Diocese was canonically ideal. It was desired by the Movement leaders and their followers in order to avoid the administrative harassment of the Mbarara bishops. The Movement relocated in Kabale Catholic Diocese where Joseph Kibwetere and Fr. Dominic Kataribabo, were non-controversial religious leaders, in Kabale Catholic Diocese. Therefore, the Marian Movement's definitive migration to Kanungu was an important symbolic religious action. It was calculated to maximize the religious activities of the Marian Movement without close observation, or supervision, ecclesiastical pastoral direction, and Episcopal administrative interference, by Bishops Kakubi and Bakyenga of Mbarara Catholic Diocese.

However, problems were revived for the Movement leaders in 1999 when Bishop Paul Bakyenga became the new Archbishop of Mbarara Archdiocese which included the jurisdiction of Kabale Diocese and Fort Portal Diocese. In addition to the Mbarara Diocese, these were the two Catholic dioceses where the Movement was most active and had recruited most of its loyal members.[14]

The above were some of complex factors that constituted a very hostile environment, oppressive, and extremely stressful religious conditions for the Marian Movement's religious leaders. The Marian Movement leaders' stress, paranoia and despair were deeply rooted within the negative view that the Catholic Bishops in Mbarara had of them and their Marian Movement.[15] The Mbarara Catholic bishops had publicly expressed hostility to the Marian Movement leaders. The bishops rejected the Marian Movement leaders' main testimonies, and central or fundamental religious claims of having received special heavenly visions and having seen the apparitions of the

Blessed Virgin Mary.

The Marian Movement leaders claimed that God had through the apparitions of the Blessed Virgin Mary, divinely chosen, commissioned and granted them a special status both within the Church, and his special redemptive mission in the world. The Marian Movement leaders claimed that God had really called, through the power, and mediation of the Blessed Virgin Mary, consecrated and granted to them the divine power to become his new agents of the Blessed Virgin Mary and God the Father's new apocalyptic revelations, and supernatural rescue mission to provide salvation in the perishing world.

The Marian Movement leaders claimed that these events were true and should not be doubted or questioned by the Catholic bishops if they were faithful to God and not corrupted by materialism, and sins of greed and sexual immorality, in as much as they condoned both among the priests and their congregation members, especially the rich business people, politicians and government officials.

According to Bishop Kakubi, the Mbarara Catholic bishops rejected these Marian Movement leaders' religious claims, for being excessive, false, and erroneous. They reaffirmed that the Catholic Church and its traditional hierarchy and chain of mediation, were the only ones valid, as God's true agencies, and means of God's true revelation, mediation of redemptive grace to the world, divine channels for the forgiveness of sins and salvation. Bishop Kakubi affirmed that Joseph Kibwetere and Keledonia Mwerinde could not have ascended to heaven to have a dialogue with God, as if God were another mighty human being, or great king residing in some kind of royal palace in the sky, or heaven.

Bishop Kakubi strongly believed that these Marian Movement leaders were delusional and dangerous false prophets, who misled many faithful Catholics, especially the poorly educated, superstitious and trusting devotees of the Blessed Virgin Mary. As a result, he waged a counter moral crusade against the Marian Movement, through education of the Catholics, so as to be better informed and avoid being seduced by false prophets and heretics, like Joseph Kibwetere, Fr. Dominic Kataribabo and Keledonia Mwerinde. Bishop Kakubi affirmed that he chose to denounce them and wage war against their religious teachings and moral practices because they were extreme, dangerous and had defied his authority, as their bishop. Consequently, the Marian Movement leaders were correct, when they felt that they were being attacked by the Catholic Church, especially the Mbarara Catholic hierarchy.

Therefore, the Marian Movement leaders' view of the hostile Catholic hierarchical authority in Mbarara Archdiocese must be taken into account as part of the negative public context, religious pressures and psychological trauma that came to seriously bear upon Fr. Dominic Kataribabo and Joseph Kibwetere who negatively viewed the Archbishop Paul Bakyenga as their insurmountable great enemy.

These paranoid Marian Movement leaders wrongly believed that Archbishop Bakyenga wanted to have them, formally excommunicated, by the Holy Father, the Roman Pontiff, and therefore, completely eliminated from the Catholic Church and destroyed. But during the Archbishop Bakyenga's meeting with Pope John Paul II, in August 1999, although the matter of the apocalyptic Marian Movement came up, the Pope did not seek to excommunicate the priests, within the controversial Marian Movement. In 1993, the Pope had not acted on the Marian Movement's priests and their appeal, and he never did.

The Holy Father, Pope John Paul II, had very wisely counseled the Archbishop Paul Bakyenga that he wanted the Church to be patient. He wanted to wait and see if the Marian Movement's apocalyptic prophecies and predictions for the end of the world at the end 1999, or early in 2000, would be fulfilled by God. For Pope John Paul II, it was important to wait and see, since the Marian Movement leaders had claimed that their prophecies were God's true end-time or apocalyptic messages for the entire Church and the world. Furthermore, these apocalyptic prophecies were delivered to the Church and the world as God's new and timely holy revelations communicated to them, through the apparitions of the Blessed Virgin Mary. The prophecies failed to materialize. But before the Pope could formally act on their case, the Marian Movement members martyred themselves, in order to flee from the hostile world, the Catholic Church hierarchy, which had rejected and persecuted them, and to ascend to heaven.

However, the leaders of the Marian Movement became isolated, depressed and paranoid. They were afraid to face the world beyond their community in Kanungu, which they had taught the people to believe that it was God's new provision for "Noah's Ark of Salvation" (*Obwato*)[16] in the corrupt and perishing world of sinful skeptics and violators of God's Ten Commandments.

Finally, it was also primarily due to despair when Bishop Paul Bakyenga, their perceived chief enemy, became the new Archbishop of Western Province, that they quickly realized their dilemma in that they had no real geographical and religious refuge, in Kanungu, in which to hide from to the hostility and crushing ecclesiastical powers of the Roman Catholic Church hierarchy, in Mbarara.

5. Escapism, Apocalyptic Religious Teachings And Doomsday Tragedy

Tragically, it was the promotion of Bishop Bakyenga to the position of the newly created position of Archbishop of Mbarara Archdiocese and the Western Region that caused a new crisis for the Marian Movement. Archbishop Bakyenga represented the same hostile Roman Catholic ecclesiastical power and authority, in Mbarara, which the embattled Marian Movement leaders had originally sought to escape from both canonically and geographically, in early 1993, which now exercised canonical power over their refuge in Kabale Catholic Diocese.

These Marian Movement members had attempted to escape by physically relocating their main headquarters and center of operations from Joseph Kibwetere's home at Kabumba, in Ntungamo District and Fr. Dominic Kataribabo's home, in Bushenyi District, which were both canonically and geographically located within the ecclesiastical jurisdiction of Mbarara Catholic Diocese to Kanungu in Kabale Catholic Diocese.

With the new Mbarara Archdiocese, came the old administrative canonical and religious problems. The priests and their lay people were forced to reevaluate their Catholic Church membership, and consider their willingness to accept the Catholic hierarchical authority, as the Church discipline and canons required. An extreme moral reformist and Protestant-like radical consideration would have been to rebel against the directives of the Catholic bishops, like the Rev. Prof. Martin Luther, had done, in the sixteenth century, renounce their canonical obedience to the Catholic Church hierarchy and form their own new independent Church, which would not be affiliated to the traditional Roman Catholic Church.

However, that was too radical to be accepted as a good option. As a result, it was rejected because it was more Protestant-like and objectionable to the devout Catholic Marian devotees, whose main objective was to bring moral and spiritual renewal and reformation to the Catholic Church, which they truly treasured and loved; and did not wish to abandon.

Nevertheless, these Marian Movement moral reformers strongly believed that their Roman Catholic Church should be urgently morally reformed because it had become corrupted by grave evils and sins of greed, materialism and sexual immorality. As such, they did not wish to abandon the Catholic Church, because to do so, negated their own reason for being as God's redemptive agents, or as a reformist and Marian group within the Catholic Church, as they correctly viewed themselves, despite their own eclectic version of the Medieval, apocalyptic and new radical version of the ancient Benedictine monastic Catholicism and Mariology.

The Marian Movement's disillusionment and renewed serious religious and ecclesiastical problems were deeply rooted within the realization that the Marian Movement had no local place where to flee, in order to hide. It was extremely depressing for the desperate and persecuted Marian Movement leaders that they could no longer physically escape the ecclesiastical jurisdiction and interdiction of the Catholic Church hierarchy, in Mbarara. There was the fact that with the new ecclesiastical creation of the new Archdiocese of Mbarara, by Rome with Bishop Paul Bakyenga, as the new Archbishop. This was the proverbial "last straw which broke the camel's back."

With the appointment of Bishop Paul Bakyenga, as the new Archbishop of Mbarara and the Western Province, the old ecclesiastical problems and conflicts would also resurface. It is fundamental to realize that Bishop Bakyenga, who had been promoted to the new position of Archbishop of the newly created Mbarara Catholic Archdiocese, was the very man, whom Fr. Dominic Kataribabo had resented as his professional rival for the position of bishop, and now truly hated, as his tireless nemesis and ecclesiastical superior.

Fr. Dominic Kataribabo still regarded Archbishop Paul Bakyenga, as a ruthless enemy, who wished to have him excommunicated, in order to destroy him and his moral reformist Marian Movement. These factors of intense mutual professional competition, antagonism and ecclesiastical hostility between Fr. Dominic Kataribabo and Archbishop Paul Bakyenga provide the necessary foundations for unlocking the mysteries of the Marian Movement and tragic martyrdoms.

By the time of the Marian Movement's tragic self-sacrificial deaths and martyrdoms, in March 2000, Fr. Kataribabo still resented Archbishop Bakyenga as his former religious rival, to whom he lost his quiet bid for the position of Bishop of Mbarara Diocese. However, as the new Archbishop of Mbarara and the Western Province, Archbishop Bakyenga, had now gained the ecclesiastical power to exercise canonical jurisdiction over them, in Kanungu, since Kabale Catholic Diocese, was within his jurisdiction. Therefore, the paranoid Marian leaders believed and feared that the Mbarara bishops' original canonical interdiction of the Marian Movement and its leaders, especially the priests, would become reactivated, by Archbishop Bakyenga, as their relentless nemesis.

Tragically, Fr. Kataribabo was unable to both accept and forgive Archbishop Bakyenga for some perceived pastoral and administrative malice or wrongs directed against him and the Marian Movement by the Mbarara Catholic hierarchy. In addition, Fr. Kataribabo was also both his envious and resentful of Archbishop Bakyenga's successes and successive promotions. Paul Bakyenga was appointed Mbarara Catholic Diocese's Bishop Coadjutor in 1988; and then, he was appointed the Diocesan Bishop, in 1995. In 1999, Bishop Bakyenga was both promoted and appointed as the new Archbishop of Mbarara and the Western Region.

It was the elevation of Bishop Bakyenga, in 1999, to the position of the Archbishop of the Western Catholic Province of Uganda, which finally, drove Fr. Kataribabo to complete despair and clinical depression. Tragically, Fr. Kataribabo saw Archbishop Bakyenga, as his implacable enemy. He also believed that Bishop Paul Bakyenga had taken his place.

Fr. Kataribabo was compulsively obsessed with the consideration that he could have been the person enjoying these successes and promotions had Bishop John Kakubi not bypassed him for promotion, to the initial position of Coadjutor Bishop of Mbarara, in 1988. Due to these unhealthy compulsive obsessions, disillusionment and professional dissatisfaction, Fr. Dominic Kataribabo became very desperate. He sank into a severe and deep state of clinical depression, at the beginning of the year 2000.

Without treatment, Fr. Kataribabo became convinced that God was speaking to him and commanding him to sacrifice his followers to him as both holy atonements and as the holy path for them to become God's holy martyrs and Mary's saints. Fr. Kataribabo heard voices inside his head due to his delusional state. But he strongly believed that they came from God through the apparitions of the Blessed Virgin Mary. The visions were confirmed by Kibwetere and Mwerinde, who were also very depressed and probably suicidal.

Subsequently, Fr. Kataribabo began to ritually kill the members of the Marian Movement, partly, as a form of Christian martyrdom, and as a means to redeem and deliver them from the Catholic Church that had rejected them. It is also possible that from a medical and psychiatric point of view, that one could also partly contend that Fr. Kataribabo was a clinically depressed, and a mentally ill, and a suicidal Catholic priest. Subsequently, one can also validly argue that Fr. Kataribabo, effectively, both planned and executed these gruesome Christian martyrdoms and living sacrifices to God for atonement of sins and guilt, because he was mentally ill.

Therefore, it is most likely that many of these absurd rituals of self-sacrifices and horrifying martyrdoms were tragically carried out because of his theology of martyrdom and atonement, which was rooted in mental illness, which believed to be the real directives of God the Father, through the heavenly visions and apparitions of the Blessed Virgin Mary. His mental illness, including depression and the apparitions of the Blessed Virgin Mary were expressed in real religious delusions, and hallucinations, which he were convincing to him that he was both Mary's and God's special servant, chosen high priest and apocalyptic messiah (*Entumwa ya Ruhanga na Bikira Maria*). Yet, these phenomena are also common characteristics of some mental illnesses.

In addition, self-sacrificial deaths and martyrdoms can also be medically explained, as being the real tragic results of some suicidal impulses that are sometimes aggravated by severe states of clinical depression.[17]

6. Despair and Depression Led to the Marian Mass Murders and Martyrdoms

Ultimately, it was due to overwhelming despair, or angst, and untreated clinical depression, on the part of both Joseph Kibwetere and Fr. Dominic Kataribabo, that plans for martyrdom were implemented, in March 2000. In addition, Keledonia Mwerinde had also run out of money and viable options after the failure of the prophecy for the end of the supposed corrupt world, at the end of the year 1999, and beginning of 2000. Fr. Kataribabo, their theologian and spiritual advisor, was unable to help them think of new religious solutions to their theological, moral and prophetic crisis.

If Fr. Kataribabo had not become depressed and suicidal, he could have advised them to proclaim that God had out of his mercy and unconditional love for the sinners, extended the period of his free saving grace into open future, in order to offer more time to sinners to hear his messages of warning, repent and observe the Ten Commandments. Tragically, both the Catholic Church hierarchy and Fr. Kataribabo failed to offer this kind of the essential and timely intervention, in terms of theological, pastoral and prophetic guidance to the Marian Movement leaders and their followers, who depended on this needed religious guidance, pastoral counseling and spiritual direction, when they needed it most.

Furthermore, some of the Marian Movement's own faithful followers were also disillusioned and discontented and because of the failed apocalyptic and doomsday prophecies for the tragic end of the world, at the beginning of the Third Millennium. Some of them are believed to have demanded a refund of their money and property in order to return to a normal life outside the Marian Movement's Community. Yet, the money had already been spent on food and building projects, radical and practical solutions had to be soon found, in order to end all these serious and irritating problems. The Marian Movement leaders could have told them that the money was already used and could not be refunded. Therefore, the economic theory does not explain the Marian Movement's martyrdoms, and the attempts of those, who were left behind to try and arrange for their own martyrdoms, so as to ascend into heaven, and to join their Marian friends and saints in heaven.

The Marian Movement's leaders originally promised their followers peace, and salvation and sure deliverance from the sinful world to a peaceful life with God in heaven. These problems demanded action and urgent deliverance from an apparently evil, hostile and sinful world. Finally, they committed ritual martyrdom, as their religious and perceived holy path and permanent escape from their own Catholic Church, and its perceived corrupt hierarchy that had rejected, them, and then, also vilified and persecuted them. They were, like cornered beasts, which had the options to stay and fight or try, by all means, to flee to safety.

Tragically, the Marian Movement's leaders chose to flee from the world, and leave behind its problems of rejection, ridicule and persecution. Subsequently, in the second week of March, 2000, they invited their loyal followers to bid farewell to their friends, family members and relatives, and come to Kanungu, where they would ascend to heaven. They would be delivered to heaven with the assistance of the Blessed Virgin Mary. They strongly believed that they were leaving both the evil and corrupt world and the Church that persecuted them behind. They also believed that God would vindicate them, judge the world and perish sinners and their corrupt world, in God's own heavenly fire, which would come down as tropical thunderstorms and lightning. Nevertheless, there was some mystery and vagueness concerning the doomsday prophecies and predictions for God's arrival of the apocalyptic appointed judgment day and hellfire.[18]

However, in order to permanently escape the Catholic Church hierarchy and its perceived unjustified persecution, the Movement leaders quietly dispatched their faithful followers to Heaven and finally did so publicly on the morning of Friday, March 17, 2000, by means of petrol bombs that quickly engulfed the faithful members of The Movement for the Restoration of the Ten Commandments of God in a church inferno.

Of course, there were other important factors which contributed to this tragedy. But a compassionate and caring Catholic hierarchy and more tactful Catholic ecclesiastical administration in Mbarara probably would have prevented the Kanungu tragedy.[19]

An administratively constructive, flexible, inclusive, tolerant and patient Catholic hierarchy in Mbarara would have exercised ecclesiastical tolerance for religious pluralism in beliefs and worship, along with good pastoral care, unconditional love and inclusiveness of these errant Marians. This could have been tactfully carried out and accomplished in the same manner in which the "Charismatic groups" have been tolerated, and successfully integrated within the Catholic Church worldwide, including Uganda.

The Catholic Church could have accomplished this ecclesiastical delicate process for the integration of the Catholic Marian devotees, spiritual perfectionist and moral crusaders, in the same way, that the Anglican bishops of the Church of Uganda, constructively tolerated, and successfully integrated the disruptive members of the, apparently, heretical and separatist, "revival and holiness movement," locally called "The *Balokole*" (the saved ones). If the Catholic bishops in Mbarara had done this, they would have most effectively prevented the Marian Movement leaders' extreme views, despair and desperation to save themselves and their members, through ritual mass murders and finally, an apparent mass suicide.

Is it a significant factor that the Catholic members, who out of traditional Catholic expressions of piety and devotion to the Blessed Virgin Mary, joined *The Movement for the Restoration of the Ten Commandments of God* as a monastic form of a spiritual and chosen religious path to God and salvation became rejected by their own Catholic Church? Subsequently, these Marian Catholics experienced unexpected Church condemnation and ecclesiastical abandonment.[20]

Invariably, they all felt both vilified and rejected, by their own Catholic Church hierarchy and ridiculed by the membership of the Catholic Church which they loved so much and were willing to die for as its martyrs. They strongly believed in the divine mediation and miraculous intervention of God through the Blessed Virgin Mary and the fire of the Holy Spirit to purify them from their sins and the contamination of the world.

Like all other religious dualists, such as Plato, Jesus, Paul and Augustine,[21] the Marian Movement leaders also believed in two parallel, but interrelated realms of matter and spirit (mind), which express themselves in both life and existence. The body was considered evil and unredeemable. Therefore, the body could be starved, burned and killed. This was because of its evil desires, impulses and senses including: sexual drives, speech, hearing, touch and needs for food, drink and sleep which had to be tamed, minimized and both denied physical and mental expression in order to avoid sinning against God or breaking God's moral, spiritual and natural laws.

Most of those laws were summarized by the Ten Commandments of God as revealed to Prophet Moses. Life based on God's obedience and true holiness was to be rooted in the observance of the Ten Commandments and to serve as the true universal measure of any true religion, holiness or true spirituality and a good moral life.

Regardless of the name of the religious tradition, all forms of true and effectively redemptive religions in the world, including Christianity and the Roman Catholic Church in particular, have to be ultimately measured by how well it taught people, especially its followers, to obey God's Moral Law and Special Revelation. These moral teachings are based on Natural Law and

Holy Scriptures, tradition, and reason as components of Special Revelation. The obedient moral agents, and especially the Christians, have to be instructed and learn how to most diligently live a simple, righteous and holy life that is both in harmony with the neighbor and pleasing to God.

Ultimately, it is very significant to note that in many cases, the European Christian missionaries working in Africa were to some extent "colonialist," "Eurocentric" or "White-supremacist" in their Western imperialist cultural values, missionary strategy, missionary education and religious ideals. As a result, they chose to over-simplify the fundamental doctrines and ethics of Christianity, since they condescendingly regarded the African natives as simple, ignorant and illiterate. This led the missionaries to work under the racist and destructive assumption that the Africans were unable to understand the complex basic theological dogmas and ethics of Christianity.

Consequently, European missionaries chose to teach that such a holy life was based on the diligent observation of the Ten Commandments of God as well as the universal ethics of non-violence, unconditional love for the neighbor and free forgiveness of offenses. The sacrament of confession was itself based on confession of specific sins as breaches, or moral infractions and cultural violations of the Ten Commandments of God.

The sacrament of Baptism was understood in Evangelical traditions as a symbolic removal of sins, whereas for many Catholics it was understood as the removal of Adam's Original Sin and the social initiation rite into the Church as God's religio-political community in the world. The sacrament of Baptism was also a voluntary public pledge to renounce sins, vices and the Devil as characterized by evil ways of life. They took a sacred oath to obey God and live a redeemed holy life based on the observance of the Ten Commandments of God.

The consecrated holy water for Baptism was presented to the traditional Africans as God's magical water that had been infused with God's power of prayer and the Holy Spirit, and as a result, the consecrated water had now gained special supernatural magical powers to wash away sins, exorcise evil demons, and be used to heal the sick by sprinkling it on the holy water on the sick people in the holy name of God the Father, Son and Holy Spirit. As such, both Alice Lakwena's *Holy Spirit Movement* and Keledonia Mwerinde's *Movement for the Restoration of the Ten Commandments of God* were following this colonial Catholic Missionary tradition and religious practice to use consecrated holy water to exercise evil spirits and heal the sick.

The religious debates concerning the nature of the holy path to God, heaven and salvation are important when we study the history of Muslim and Western Christian missionaries in Africa and what their followers learned from these foreign religious missionaries and teachers. For instance, for the Catholics, including the Marian Movement leaders, and for the Anglican *Balokole* and the Methodists, salvation depended on the diligent obedience to God and the holiness of life, or piety which resulted from it.

According to the moral perfectionist Marian Movement leaders, piety was visible as a public testimony to one's inner state of moral and spiritual perfection (*okuhikirira*). This state of holiness or perfection could be achieved through "*Opus Dei*" as obedience to God's Moral Law, holy will and Grace or the intuitive positive power of disciplined moral and spiritual inner deployment of God's free inherent supernatural gift of his saving grace to live a holy life and learn to move toward spiritual and moral perfection, by voluntarily performing self-sacrificial good works of charity and justice in the community and the world.

Ultimately, for most Catholics, including the MRTCG members, the redemptive good and holy works of self-sacrifice, atonement, and piety were constituted by the diligent observations of the Ten Commandments, reading the Holy Scriptures, and studying the apocalyptic and prophetic books, such as the books of Daniel, Amos and the Book of the Revelation. In addition, they read and studied the Marian Movement's handbook of the new apocalyptic revelations and warnings of God to sinners in the world, through the Blessed Virgin Mary.

These divine and Marian revelations addressed human moral evils, corruption, and sexual immorality and called for the urgency of repentance and moral reformation or rehabilitation. To this end *The Restoration of the Ten Commandments of God* was Mary's Society, which was designed to become an Africanized version of the medieval Catholic Benedictine holy contemplative cloistered life, which was to be daily lived in the strict observance of holy silence, prayer and diligent hard-work as a form of sound spirituality, when combined with regular devout prayers, Bible-study, and silent constant reciting of "Hail Mary" or the rosary.[22]

NOTES

1. For instance see: Holger Bernt Hansen, *Mission, Church and State in a Colonial Setting: Uganda 1890-1925* (New York: St, Martin's Press, 1984); Roland Oliver, *The Missionary Factor in East Africa* (London: Longman, 1957); Samwiri R. Karugire, *A Political History of Uganda* (Nairobi: Heinemann, 1980); E. R. Norman, *Church and Society in England 1770-1970: A Historical Study* (Oxford: Oxford University Press, 1976); D. A. Low and R.C. Pratt, *The British and British Overrule* (Oxford: Oxford University Press, 1960); A. R. Tucker, *Eighteen Years in Uganda*

and East Africa (London: Edward Arnold, 1908); Hansen and Twaddle, *Religion & Politics in East Africa* (Athens, Ohio University press, 1995). As a result of this colonial legacy of the historical political alliance of the British Colonial Government and the Anglican Church in Uganda, the Anglican Church still and identifies itself as the established Church and calls itself: "The Church of Uganda."

2. Ibid.

3. The Roman Catholic Church has wisely dissociated itself from these radical Catholic movements. It has done so, in the same way, that mainline Islam has disowned *al-Qaeda,* for fear of political and economic retaliation by the powerful state leaders, such as those of the USA, who regard these radical movements and their supporters, as dangerous people or terrorists. Crusades, jihads and holy wars to establish divine theocracies are negatively perceived by democratic institutions, as unacceptable forms of politics and liberation theologies.

Theocracies reject secular democratic ideals. They are sometimes negatively viewed and labeled as forms of Medieval-like tyranny, by the authoritarian clerics, or some radical, despotic and fundamentalist religious leaders, in the holy name of God. The Pope as the head of the Holy Christian Empire is now a mere utopian apocalyptic dream. The same is true for apocalyptic hopes of a utopian Islamic worldwide holy Caliphate, or divine theocracy ruled by an Ayatollah, or the Caliph, who would impose a theocracy on the people, based the strict observations of all the tenets of the *Shari'a.*

4. Ironically, as if some ethnic Baganda nationalist politicians had not learned from the tragic secessionist attempt, of 1966, that had resulted in the abolition of the kingdom, there were similar calls for Buganda's session in the *Lukiko* (Parliament), in 2006 and 2007. This time, unlike his father, King Ronald Mutebi was wise enough to reject these destructive and suicidal calls for Buganda's political secession to form a separate and new country of Buganda Kingdom.

5. See: James Mujuni, "Who is Joseph Kibwetere?" *The New Vision,* Wednesday, March 22, 2000; Henri E. Cauvin, "Fateful Meeting Led to Founding of the Cult [MRTCG] in Uganda," *New York Times,* March, 2000; Kabazzi- Kisirinya, et el., *The Kanungu Cult-Saga: Suicide, Murder or Salvation?,* 17-18; Uganda Human Rights Commission, *The Kanungu Massacre: The Movement for the Restoration of the Ten Commandments of God,* 12.

6. *A Timely Message from Heaven,* 119-121.

7. *A Timely Message from Heaven,* 1 and 21.

8. See Rev. Kenneth Kanyankole, *The Historical Origins, Beliefs and Practices of Kanungu Cult,* 3.

9. Dr. Sam Birungi, the local pathologist, confirmed that it was difficult for him to count the number of the dead and the scene was chaotic and unsecured by the police. Interview on October, 14, 2001. He said that by looking at remaining fragments and identifiable body parts, and mounds of ashes, the number of the dead people could be higher than 1,000, since it was standing room only, for those inside the church building.

10. Many Christians, as well as members of the MRTCG, went to their churches for midnight prayers and vigils. They went to their places of worship, in order to

await either the end of the world, or the arrival of the new millennium, at midnight, on December 31, 1999. Most of them were relieved that nothing drastic had happened. "They wanted to live." John Karooro: an interview, March 20, 2002.

11. *The New Vision*, Monday, March 20, 2000: 4.

12. See *A Timely Message from Heaven*, iv-vi, 67-98.

13. Bishop Kakubi's decree of May 7, 1991 and letter of May 9, 1991.

14. The MRTCG leaders, who had fled to Kanungu, in Kabale Catholic Diocese to escape the Mbarara bishops, now felt cornered, trapped (*Bashanga bataine obuhungiro. Bakeyita*), and ritually killed their followers, as living sacrifices to God, and thereby, martyred them. In their own despair and depression, the Marian Movement leaders perpetrated these activities, in order to transform them into God's saints and to send them directly to heaven. This was the tragic insight of the Marian Movement, as gained from an interview with Fr. Paul Ikazire, on August, 3, 2003. This is the main reason why the MRTCG was denounced as a dangerous cult. See: John Kakande, "Kanungu Horror: Who is to Blame?" *The New Vision* (Talk of the Town IV), Wednesday, March 22, 2000.

15. As a result, the MRTCG leaders felt cornered, trapped and desperate. This scenario led ritual killings and martyrdoms of their loyal followers. See: John Kakande, "Kanungu Horror: Who is to Blame?" *The New Vision* (Talk of the Town IV), Wednesday, March 22, 2000. For more detail, see note 34, above.

16. *A Timely Message from Heaven*, 65.

17. See: Kabazzi- Kisirinya, et el., *The Kanungu Cult-Saga: Suicide, Murder or Salvation?* 17-18; John Kakande, "Kanungu Horror: Who is to Blame?" *The New Vision* (Talk of the Town IV), Wednesday, March 22, 2000; Matthias Mugisha and James Mujuni, "Kataribabo with his Doctorate in Theology, was the Brain behind the Cult's Liturgy: The Priest Who Became a Killer," People: *The New Vision*, Monday, April 3, 2000.

16. A careful reading of *A Timely Message from Heaven* indicates that the doomsday prophecies were modeled after the Book of Revelations and *Balokole* apocalyptic theology, and that the dates were not important. What was important was the desired effect and repentance to avoid destruction in hell-fire.

19. The *Balokole* were successfully integrated into the Anglican Church by patient bishops and priests. Following the Anglican bishops' tolerance and administrative flexibility would have resulted in the eventual MRTCG's peaceful and beneficial reintegration into the Catholic Church. Ultimately, if the Mbarara bishops were also as liberal, tolerant and flexible as Bishop Robert Gay of Kabale Catholic Diocese, to which the embattled Marian Movement members had taken refuge, until 1999, when Bishop Bakyenga was appointed the new Archbishop of The Western Province, the MRTCG would have been successfully integrated in the Catholic Church.

20. See *A Timely Message from Heaven*, 1-21, 67-98.

21. As examples, see Paul: Romans 6-8; Gal. 4-6; Augustine, *Confessions; The City of God.*

22. *A Timely Message from Heaven*, 1-21, 67-98, 157-159.

Chapter Five

MARY'S APPARITIONS & CALL FOR MORAL TRANSFORMATION OF THE CHURCH & WORLD

Whereas the *Balokole Movement* was predominantly an Anglican Church-based and a Christ-centered, apocalyptic moral reformation movement within East Africa, the moral reformist and apocalyptic Marian Movement was a parallel African founded Christian moral reformation movement within the East African Catholic Church, especially Uganda.

1.Introduction

The *Balokole Movement* and the Marian Movement were apocalyptic moral renewal Christian movements, which were both founded and led by devout African lay Christians within their own respective Anglican and Catholic Church traditions. Similarly, both religious movements condemned the status quo and denounced the perceived moral decadence within their religious traditions, including the moral imperfections of bishops and the clergy. Because of these movement leaders' condemnation of the Church, as a corrupt and sinful institution, these moral reformist movements were also both strongly opposed, and resisted by the Church and its hierarchy.

The belligerent moral reformist movement leaders contended that the historical Church of Christ, was now, completely corrupted by the corrupt and sinful world, in which it was instituted by God to serve. They lamented that the Church, which it had been originally instituted by God through his Christ, to convert to God's holiness by preaching repentance and moral reformation. However, the Church hierarchy opposed the reformist moral movements and tried to eliminate them from the Church.

Nevertheless, there were positive and practical reasons of inclusiveness the Anglican bishops conciliatory and attempts at full inclusiveness of the belligerent *Balokole* moral reformist leaders and apocalyptic their followers. The Anglican bishops were tolerant of the *East African Revival Movement* or the *Balokole Movement* in order to placate them. By doing so, the Anglican Church bishops wanted to avert the looming possibility of Anglican Church schism into an Evangelical *Balokole* Church and the traditionalist Anglican Church, the more tolerant and flexible Anglican bishops decided to reconcile the moral radical and theologically errant *Balokole* leaders.

Subsequently, after some prayers for repentance and quest for God's guidance, the Anglican bishops became conciliatory. They became administratively flexible, consciously inclusive and decided. Subsequently, they decided to strike a compromise position and accepted to incorporate the uncompromising apocalyptic leaders of the *East African Revival Movement* (*Balokole*) into the Anglican Church leadership.

In contrast to the Anglican bishops, the Catholic bishops failed administratively to become flexible and conciliatory, when the belligerent moral reformist leaders of the Marian Movement confronted them. Consequently, the Catholic bishops tragically failed to incorporate the moral crusading and reformist Marian Movement leaders into the Catholic Church leadership. Ultimately, this Catholic bishops' administrative hard-line position led to the Marian tragic self-sacrificial deaths and martyrdoms. This is true, in as much as the Marian Movement's self-sacrificial deaths, were sacramentally performed, by Fr. Kataribabo, as holy self-sacrifices and martyrdoms, and as the holy means to escape from the local Catholic ecclesiastical persecution, by ascending into heaven, as Mary's Christian martyrs.[1]

2. Keledonia Mwerinde's Conversion, Changed Life And New Dress Code as a Nun

The moral reformist and apocalyptic Marian Movement leaders were in reality akin to the *Balokole*, or the members of the *East African Revival Movement,* who enthusiastically testified to the world that they were converted or "born again," and invited the other people to do the same claiming that the world would soon come to an end, in God's apocalyptic judgment. As a result, the Marian Movement members were sometimes mistaken for the *Balokole*. Keledonia Mwerinde and Joseph Kibwetere most zealously testified of their religious conversions and life-transforming religious visions of the Blessed Virgin Mary. They also testified of their encounters with the risen Christ through the Holy Spirit.

Both Keledonia Mwerinde and Kibwetere claimed that they had personal encounters with God, which were mediated to them, through the apparitions of the Blessed Virgin Mary. These heavenly experiences led to spiritual, moral and religious conversion and a correlative transformation of life.

Testimonies of notorious sinner's religious conversions, or repentance and subsequent complete transformation of life, are not unique to Keledonia Mwerinde. The famous biblical examples of these religious cases include Mary Magdalene. Traditionally, many Christians believed that Mary was converted from a life of prostitution, and her life was transformed to that of a Christian saint.

Likewise, Saul was also miraculously converted by God, from a life of Christian persecutor (Acts 8-9), transformed the greatest Christian Apostle and missionary to the Gentile Greek and Roman pagan world. These are some examples chosen from the New Testament to illustrate how true religious conversions may lead to a complete new mode of life and a new set of moral values. These biblical stories clearly show how a notorious sinner, or an evil person, can actually be converted or repent of evil ways of life, and become God's reformed and obedient saint and servant in the world.

However, the main problem remains how to devise an effective strategy for missionary activities, in order to convert the sinners in the world, and reform them into God's saints. Yet, to accomplish this noble task without scaring them with God's unquenchable and catastrophic apocalyptic hellfire, like the MRTCG leaders did. Yet, unlike in Islam, and some fundamentalist forms of Christianity, scare tactics are not considered by some well-informed Christian thinkers as appropriate Christian tools and missionary strategies, or evangelistic methods to be employed by God's truly loving and compassionate, Christian missionaries and servants, in order to accomplish God's work.

Nevertheless, many Catholics, Evangelicals and Muslims employ scare tactics as part of preaching to sinners in order to frighten them into repentance, due to fear and dread of hellfire. Some varying versions of Dante's *Inferno* or hell were verbally reproduced in the Marian Movement's sermons. Imageries of judgment and unrepentant sinners burning in dreadful agony in hell-fire were vividly painted in order to frighten sinners into conversion and repentance of sins, due to dread or fear of divine punishment.

Dante's *Inferno* was implicitly adopted by the Marian Movement leaders as part of God's new apocalyptic revelation. Dante's *Inferno* and the Book of Revelation were used as God's divinely inspired resources to illustrate many of the Marian Movement's apocalyptic and judgment sermons. Like the *Balokole,* the Marian Movement leaders strategically preached these dreadful "fire and brimstone" sermons order to frighten people into repentance. This was part of their main preaching method and missionary teaching strategy deigned to frighten sinners, and thereby, hoping to convert them.

Subsequently, the Marian Movement leaders were like the *Balokole* religious leaders, in both theology and apocalyptic teachings. The *Balokole* initially successfully employed the tool of the fear of God, which was rooted in apocalyptic theology and prophecies for the imminent end of the world, to convert many sinners to their revival movement. Accordingly, the Marian Movement leaders followed the *Balokole's* preaching techniques and teaching methods to covert Catholics to their Marian Movement.

Consequently, from an academic perspective, it becomes self-evident that the Marian Movement leaders carefully designed their frightening apocalyptic prophecies and doomsday judgment and fire, and did formulated them in the name of God, as God's new apocalyptic revelations, in order to be able to accomplish their religious divine mission for the redemption of sinners in the world. This is partly because for true Christianity, as originally proclaimed by Jesus as the Christ, God is essentially a Loving *"Abba,"* Compassionate, and Forgiving heavenly Parent.

Accordingly, God as a loving heavenly Parent should be loved and not feared. God should be lovingly worshipped as an appropriate human reciprocal response to God's activities of unconditional love, creation, life, unmerited redemptive grace, free forgiveness of sins, and goodness, rather than to be feared as a merciless heavenly Judge, or to be merely worshipped out of fear (Matt. 5-7).

Once fear is gone, then, the people who believed in God, or did good works, primarily due to the fear of God, or to avoid present and future, or the apocalyptic divine retribution and punishment, eventually become godless skeptics, humanistic and scornful atheists. Therefore, the traditional Evangelical, or the American Southern Baptist-like, methods of preaching God's imminent or apocalyptic "fire and brimstone," or threatening people with hellfire, is accepted by many Christians, as a valid method to convert sinners, and led them to repentance of sins.

These alienating and frightening new Evangelical preaching methods and apocalyptic Christian missionary strategies were both adopted and most effectively used, by the *Balokole* of the *East African Revival Movement.*[2] Later, these Evangelical methods were also adopted by the Marian Movement leaders, as instruments and methods for preaching and teaching their moral reform agenda.

The moral crusaders and reformist leaders of the MRTCG were familiar with the *Balokole Movement of East Africa,* and adopted effective Evangelical or *Balokole* preaching and missionary style in order to convert the rebellious, corrupt and notorious sinners in the world, beginning with Uganda. They adopted this *Balokole* preaching method of preaching, not to become a branch of the Protestant Church, but rather, in order to scare local sinners into repentance.

However, this missionary method is counterproductive and a bad missionary strategy, especially if one wishes to convert well-educated people. This is because this Evangelical missionary or preaching method relies on ignorance, inducing guilt, and religious emotion, especially the fear for fire in hell or anxiety concerning divine judgment and eternal damnation.

Subsequently, most results of this negative Christian missionary approach, theology and preaching are negative. In most cases, the positive results, such as the joys of emotional religious conversions, do not last long. In some cases, these religious feelings are transitory or temporary experiences, which need regular reinforcements. This is the one of the reasons why the Evangelical preachers and Catholic priests continually reinforced their messages and sermons, by calls to repent all sins, or to undergo regular spiritual self-examinations of confessions. In extreme cases the preachers resort to God's threats of torture in hellfire, excommunication and damnation of sinners, who fail to repent and observe the Commandments of God.

As such, the MRTCG failed to devise more loving missionary strategies for effectively preaching God's messages of salvation, and converting evil people, in the world, and leading them to a positive divine transformation of life, like that which was experienced by Mary Magdalene, Paul, Constantine, Augustine and Mwerinde, among others. They all testified that their own lives were positively transformed because of their experience of the encounter with the loving God, in Christ, rather than being threatened with divine justice, judgment and torture in hellfire. The fear of God does not produce a true love of God and peace in the sinner or worshippers of God. This was one of the major weaknesses in the teaching of the Marian Movement and life within its holy, silent and contemplative monastic community.

The missionary challenge to convert sinners, or evil people in the world, and both to reform and transform them into good, or God's holy people and obedient saints, are the ultimate strategic missionary and pedagogical (instructional) challenges of most leaders of all revealed, or major religions. This includes the Prophet Moses, the Buddha, Jesus as the Christ, and the Prophet Muhammad.

Ultimately, this central religious goal and religious missionary objective constitutes the fundamental redemptive mission and main objective of most mainline religions, including missionary forms of Buddhism, Christianity, Judaism and Islam. In the fulfillment of this divine missionary and redemptive mission, some religious traditions have even claimed that their religious tradition was the only true divine revelation, truth and redemptive path to God and salvation.

Judaism, Christianity and Islam have been guilty of this kind of religious bigotry, and exclusive claims of being the only universal true divine vehicles of God's revelation, truth and salvation. Keledonia Mwerinde's MRTCG, as a Catholic Marian Movement, also claimed to be the only true path to God's new revelation, the channel of God's redemptive grace and salvation from her Catholic Church's religious and doctrinal heritage. Mwerinde was part of the traditional religious quest for holiness, human societal transformation and divine redemption. There were similar movements before her and some of the movements were non-Christian.

To this end, Siddhartha Gautama's enlightenment process serves as the paradigm and role model for religious reformation and quest for holiness that led to the rejection of materialism and renunciation of human bodily desires, wealth, comfort and pleasure in order to live a simple holy life of fasting, silence and contemplative prayer. Siddhartha became the Buddha (the enlightened one) and the founder of Buddhism. Similarly, Prophet Moses serves as a divinely enlightened founder of Judaism, whereas Jesus as the Christ is treated as the main embodiment, *theophany,* or revealer of God, and the founder of Christianity.

St. Paul and St. Augustine serve as good reformers of Christianity and Prophet Muhammad serves as the main agent of God's revelation to the Arabs and founder of Islam. All these religious founders and teachers underwent life-transforming religious experiences, or encounters with God that resulted in a definitive conversion experience, similar to that of which Keledonia Mwerinde also claimed to have undergone. This conversion experience was similar to the one, of which the *Balokole* testified, and recommended to others, who wished to experience a life-transforming encounter with God, or desired to establish a direct personal relationship with God.

These kinds of special spiritual encounters with God, and life-transforming moral and spiritual conversion experiences are also variously referred to, especially by the *Balokole* of East Africa*,* as " a new spiritual birth;" "being born again," or "being saved" (*kulokoka/okujunwa*), and a "spiritual renewal." This holy conversion experience, is supposed to lead to its implicitly necessary, or accompanying spiritual renewal and moral reformation. These forms of transformations of life are supposed to occur, as the true moral and spiritual fruits of conversion. These moral and religious reforms of life are the external evidence of the inner state of grace and salvation, which are the main religious objectives and intended moral goals for the divine redemptive mission and reason for the existence of the *"Balokole Movement,"* or the *East African Evangelical Revival Movement.* Later, these also became the same general objective for the Marian moral reformist *Movement for the Restoration of the Ten Commandments of God.*

The Balokole Movement also preached moral reformation and spiritual renewal to both the Anglican Church religious leaders, such as the bishops and clergy, in the same way it preached to the ordinary lay people. As fundamentalist Protestant Christians, the members of the *East African*

Evangelical Revival Movement both believe and teach that the religious leaders and lay people are alike and equal before God. They believe that they are all equally sinful in the sight of God and both equally live and exist in real need of God's grace, repentance, conversion and spiritual transformation from sinful lives to live new holy lives as God's obedient saints and servants in the world.

Therefore, like the *Balokole* or other redeemed saints of God like St. Paul and St. Augustine, Keledonia Mwerinde had experienced deep, personal, inner religious and moral conversion. Her experience of personal, spiritual and moral conversion was also locally akin to that commonly experienced and testified to, by the Ugandan Anglican *Balokole*. Despite some religious skeptics, Mwerinde's religious experience of conversion was real and transforming. Ursula Komuhangi, her sister, was one of the first people to realize that Keledonia Mwerinde had become positively both spiritually and morally transformed. She morally became a new person.

Subsequently, Komuhangi became Mwerinde's first convert and member of the MRTCG. This transformation occurred, when Mwerinde repented and obeyed the Marian apparitions and Mary's directives to become her messenger (Messiah and Voice of revelation and instruction) and the new apocalyptic divine instrument of God's salvation through the Blessed Virgin Mary in the world. In obedience, Mwerinde began her new life and divine ministry of preaching and calling other sinners like her to repent, come back to God and live a new holy life of moral and spiritual reformation based on the strict observation of the Ten Commandments of God.

In order to demonstrate her transformed life and piety to her fellow Roman Catholics, Mwerinde tried to display and communicate to them of her own inner, deep religious and moral conversion, by borrowing the religious language and symbols of the *Balokole* with which they were familiar. However, being Catholic and speaking to Catholics, Mwerinde also had to speak and testify to them in the familiar Catholic language of devotion to the Blessed Virgin Mary and sacramental prayer.

Ultimately, for effective communication purposes, Mwerinde had to creatively employ and use the most familiar and effective Catholic symbols, in order to accomplish this religious task most effectively, meaningfully and relevant within the Catholic context. Subsequently, she had both tried to formulate her spiritual experience in understandable concrete images and to express her conversion in those concrete religious Marian images and metaphors of her visions of the Blessed Virgin Mary to the rural Catholic masses.

By doing so, Mwerinde also wanted to prove the reality and religious validity of her new and supernaturally transformed religious life to her fellow

Roman Catholics. Mwerinde, most especially, wanted to demonstrate the reality of her new moral and religious life to the people in Kanungu in the Makiro Parish and the neighboring areas of Rugyeyo, Kambuga and Nyakishenyi. This was important for Mwerinde because some of these local people had known her before her life-transforming religious conversion as another beer-seller and prostitute in Kanungu.

As such, Mwerinde's conversion and transformed life were to be regarded as some of the Blessed Virgin Mary's concrete miracles. Mwerinde also wanted to challenge the people to have faith to see, believe and accept by faith that the Blessed Virgin Mary. She affirmed that the Virgin Mary had, indeed, appeared to her changed her life, and chosen her to serve as her "Messiah," or special agent and Apostle *(Entumwa)* of salvation in the world. It was only through faith that these Marian events and claims could be accepted as God's redemptive works and revelations in the world. Nevertheless, for the many skeptics, Mwerinde's testimonies of Mary's heavenly apparitions were rejected as delusions.

The enemies of the Marian Movement dismissed the central claims of the Marian apparitions and regarded them as clever forms of religious deception. These skeptics maintained that the Marian visions were invented in order to deceive superstitious Catholics. They claimed that the real reason behind these supposedly fraudulent religious Marian apparitions as God's apocalyptic special revelations, was actually economic.

This false and slanderous economic theory and motive for the emergence of the Marian Movement was designed as the means of absolute religious rejection, negation and vilification of the Marian Movement's stated religious objectives or mission of public moral education and reformation. These kinds of skeptics including the sensationalist reporters of *The New Vision* and T*he Monitor Newspaper*, amusingly speculated that Mwerinde and Kibwetere were shrewd business people, who fraudulently sought to gain access to the wealth of their unsuspecting gullible religious followers.

The local reporters for the public media had speculated that the Marian Movement leaders wanted to secure positions in the community that would lead to some personal economic, political and religious benefits. Some of these speculations were false. However, some of these speculations were based on the observations that claims of religious conversions had in some cases resulted in appointments to leadership positions that had led to possibilities of some economic gain, or prestige, such as a evangelist, pastor, or bishop, in the cases of the *Balokole*.

Being dissatisfied with Gauda Kamushwa's Nyabugoto Marian Prayer Group, in Nyakishenyi, and also desiring to found their own more global Marian Movement, in August 1988, Keledonia Mwerinde and Ursula

Komuhangi, her sister and loyal convert, went to Mbarara. They went there, in order to testify, preach and publicize their new revelations and messages to the Church and the world. Mbarara, rather than nearby Kabale, was the chosen destination and focus of their missionary task to convert the Catholics to the veneration of the Blessed Virgin Mary, who required, a new strict moral, holiness, religious and political code based on the strict obedience of the Ten Commandments of God.

Mwerinde considered Mbarara ideal for her religious and moral reform agenda. It was the main center of Roman Catholicism in Southern and Western Uganda. However, since Mwerinde did not know the people in Mbarara, she looked for Joseph Kibwetere to assist her with accommodation, finances, transportation, preaching her Marian message and communication of her visions of the Blessed Virgin Mary to the traditional and conservative patriarchal Catholic Church and its hierarchy, in Mbarara.

Kibwetere personally knew the Mbarara Catholic bishops and the influential priests in Mbarara, whereas Mwerinde did not. As a result, Mwerinde instinctively knew that she needed Kibwetere's support in order to succeed in her for calling and religious task of establishing a viable Marian Movement and to carry out a successful moral crusade to save and reform sinners, both within the Catholic Church and the corrupt world.

3. Keledonia Mwerinde Appointed Male Leaders to Deal with Patriarchy

Keledonia Mwerinde as the Blessed Virgin's prophetess and servant looked for Joseph Kibwetere and converted him to her Marian Movement. She outlined her own religious ideas, visions of the Blessed Virgin Mary, and her being commissioned by the Blessed Virgin Mary, to preach her messages of salvation, repentance, and moral reformation to the Church and the world. Mwerinde told Kibwetere that the Blessed Virgin Mary had commanded her to seek for him to help her establish the Marian moral reformation Movement.

Finally, Mwerinde persuaded Kibwetere to join her moral and spiritual crusade to reform the Catholic Church and save the world. She eventually succeeded in persuading him to head the new Marian Movement and religious moral crusade, in order to most effectively utilize his religious, social, political connections and influence needed to make this Catholic moral and religious revival and Marian Movement viable and successful within a patriarchal Catholic Church and a patriarchal Africa culture and male-dominated society and world .

Although Keledonia Mwerinde was the real founder of *The Movement for the Restoration of the Ten Commandments of God*, she had the political and economic humility to appoint Joseph Kibwetere, the more politically, religiously and economically powerful, and both locally and nationally known Catholic lay leader, politician and educator, as the Administrator and figurehead of the Marian Movement. However, Mwerinde remained the real spiritual leader, Mother and Programmer of *The Movement for the Restoration of the Ten Commandments of God.*

Therefore, to the outsiders, Joseph Kibwetere appeared, as the founder and leader of *The Movement for the Restoration of the Commandments of God* and the Movement's Spokesman, but the insiders and those, who knew the Marian Movement well, knew the truth to be different. They knew the fact that Keledonia Mwerinde was the real powerful leader and powerful founder of *The Movement for the Restoration of the Ten Commandments of God.* They also knew that Mwerinde was the real invisible power behind the Marian Movement, and that she acted firmly as its leader behind closed doors, though to the public she projected Joseph Kibwetere and Fr. Kataribabo, as the main leaders of the Marian Movement.

In reality, Joseph Kibwetere was Keledonia Mwerinde's chosen and appointed administrative, social, political and economic Movement leader. He was her instrument or fiscal and political tool for her Marian Movement's success in dealing with a prejudiced patriarchal culture and male-oriented Catholic Church. Subsequently, Kibwetere became molded into Mwerinde's ideal puppet.[3] He became her very effective public representative in a local African patriarchal culture, which marginalizes women.

Within the traditional context of the African patriarchal cultures in both Church and the secular world, men's authority and teachings are more easily accepted and assigned a higher value and credibility than taught by women. As such, Mwerinde appointed men as symbolic public political, social and religious leaders, of her Marian Movement, both within the community and in the Church. In any case, Mwerinde's main target was the conversion of the patriarchal Catholic Church hierarchy in Mbarara, and Catholics, who have been traditionally taught to accept the male-priesthood, as a true representative of the male Christ and God, the Father.

The male priesthood and male priests were theologically explained as essential agents of God, the Father, and Christ, his Son, as God's Mediator of special divine redemptive mission in the world. Mwerinde sought to subvert this traditional patriarchy by appeal to the Blessed Virgin Mary as the "Mother of God" and "Queen of Heaven." Mary was elevated to full divinity on the basis that if Jesus is the Christ, the "Son of God," and God, then Mary as her Mother, has also to be God, since only God and a Goddess, could give birth to God.

The Church's traditional perception of God, as a male being, who worked through the patriarchal Catholic Church priesthood to recreate and redeem the "fallen and sinful world," made it difficult for the Catholic Church to ordain women as priests, and to recognize them, as official agents of God's work of revelation, and supernatural redemption or salvation. Therefore, it was easier and necessary for Mwerinde, a marginalized Catholic woman, to appoint both Joseph Kibwetere and the Rev. Fr. Dominic Kataribabo, as her special Team Leaders and public representatives and public relations officers for the Marian Movement. Kibwetere and Fr. Kataribabo's public role was especially most vital in the Marian Movement's dealings with the conservative patriarchal Catholic Church hierarchy in Mbarara and to the Government of Uganda officials, who were also predominantly male.

Consequently, Keledonia Mwerinde was ready and eager to bestow on her male co-leaders of the Movement some of her powers, visions and messages. This was her calculated strategy to turn her mission into a real viable movement, successful organization and moral crusade, within a patriarchal society. Mwerinde recruited the men to serve, as the public leaders of her "Movement of Mary," which was officially known, as *The Movement for the Restoration of the Ten Commandments of God,* in order to build a credible Christian organization within the Catholic Church.

Mwerinde believed that the male leaders would effectively lead and serve the Marian Movement, since male leaders would be more acceptable than female leaders, to the Catholic Marian Movement members, and most especially, to the conservative traditional Catholic Church's patriarchal hierarchy. Mwerinde also strongly believed that within the given African traditional context of patriarchal culture, the officials of the Government of Uganda would find it more acceptable to deal with men, rather dealing with her as a woman.

It was mainly due to this traditional African cultural factor and consideration that Mwerinde both discreetly recruited and promoted male leaders Joseph Kibwetere and Fr. Kataribabo as co-leaders of her Marian Movement. Mwerinde wisely promoted her male co-leaders to serve as her religious, legal, political, economic and social officers of the Marian Movement in matters of the establishment, function and governance of *The Movement for the Restoration of the Ten Commandments of God* as an independent NGO (Non Governmental Organization), instead of dealing with her, as an unknown and poorly educated woman.

Keledonia Mwerinde knew her strengths and weaknesses, and that made her a great leader of her Marian Movement. Mwerinde was definitely a shrewd strategist, opportunist, and skillful leader, and a clever manipulator of people, both within and outside her Marian Movement. These are some of the reasons and societal factors why some people, who knew Keledonia Mwerinde, before here religious conversion, remained skeptical about the authenticity of her religious conversion.

Likewise, they also doubted and questioned the authenticity of her claims of the visions and apparitions of the Blessed Virgin Mary. They were also skeptical about both Mwerinde and Kibwetere's revelations from God and his doomsday prophecies and predictions concerning the apocalyptic prophecies for the impending end of the "Present Era" (*Obusingye obu*) or world, in a catastrophic fire. For most people, they believed that this doomsday prophecy would materialize on December 31, 1999, at midnight, or early in the year 2000.[4]

There were mandatory Marian Movement's requirements for new members to take a vow of poverty and for its most loyal members to sell property and give all the money to both Mwerinde and Kibwetere to promote the Marian Movement's redemptive mission. The money was used to feed the Marian Movement members, rent offices in Kampala, Mbarara, Fort-Portal, and Katojo. The rest of the funds were used to build the Marian Movement's school and headquarters in Kanungu.

However, many outsiders mistakenly believed that the Marian Movement leaders were very rich and their Marian Movement had immense fiscal resources. In fact, the Marian Movement members fasted a great deal, partly because the Marian Movement leaders did not have enough funds to buy sufficient food for their followers.

Unlike Jesus who is believed to have fed five thousand by multiplying two loves fish and five little loaves of bread, the leaders of the Marian Movement did not possess the miraculous powers to stretch meager funds to feed thousands of their followers, for many years. Therefore, it is understandable why they wanted the world to end with end of the last century. That was how far they could stretch their funds to feed their followers, and meet their major fiscal obligations, without disgracefully declaring to the world that they were actually, bankrupt.

Ultimately, the Marian Movement entry fees, proceeds from sales of possessions and donated money were not enough. The Marian Movement leaders needed more funds for to pay for the ambitious Marian projects. The Marian Movement leaders were trying to secure more funds from Marian devotees in Europe and other places, when they decided to undergo martyrdom and ritual self-sacrificial atonement for the sins of the world on March 17, 2000.

The Marian Movement members also hoped to discard their physical bodies by ritual death or in purifying flames of the fire. The Marian

Movement's leaders burned the bodies of their followers, not to murder them, but rather, to set them free, from the supposed evil bondage of the body, in which the souls were believed to be imprisoned and subjected to evil sensual temptations. Getting rid of the body was considered good, since it was the preferred method of voluntary self-sacrifice to God, in atonement for sins. It was also regarded as the means for sharing in the atonement of Christ, and thereby, liberate the souls trapped within the physical bodies, to enable them to ascend spiritually, to heaven,

However, these Marian Movement's requirements were considered by the police, and some people, as clear evidence needed to discredit and that prove that the Marian Movement's key leaders were mere clever criminals and fraudulent evil people, who deceived and defrauded their innocent pious followers. These kinds of skeptics alleged that the apocalyptic and monastic Marian Movement leaders were engaged in the evil practices of theft and fraud under the guise of religion, piety, vows of poverty, communalism and monasticism.

These skeptics, including the Catholic Church leadership and the public media also constantly alleged in the public media that these Marian Movement leaders were, in reality, very evil people. They completely vilified the Marian Movement and its leadership. They slanderously contended that the Marian Movement leaders were evil people, who were cunning religious leaders, and who blasphemously used the holy name of God and the heavenly visions of the Blessed Virgin Mary to enrich themselves.

Furthermore, the enemies of the Marian Movement and some intellectual or religious skeptics alleged that the well-publicized Marian apocalyptic prophecies, and God's mediated new revelations through the apparitions of the Blessed Virgin Mary, were deceitfully conjured up, by Mwerinde and Kibwetere, in order to deceive the unsuspecting and defraud the faithful Catholics of their money and possessions. These skeptics believed that this strategy worked well among the devout Catholics and especially the poorly educated, superstitious and the rural Catholic devotees of the Blessed Virgin Mary. These skeptics alleged that religion, and especially, promises of God's supernatural healing prayers and the Marian visions were used, as a means to attract and defraud other religious people, especially the devout Catholics in rural areas.

In any case, many people in Eastern Africa and the surrounding countries were already mentally, politically and socioeconomically traumatized and destabilized. Many of them were scared and suffering from existential anxiety because of having witnessed atrocities of genocide, horrendous deaths caused by HIV/AIDS, and civil wars. There were several millions of internally displaced people and refugees because of civil wars, and genocide in neighboring countries. Other millions of people were victims of rampant state corruption, armed robberies and the prevailing culture of violence that characterized the hellish state of affairs in Africa's Great Lakes Region.

The most affected countries by these evils of wars, instability and violence were the Democratic Republic of the Congo, Uganda, Rwanda, Burundi and Sudan. Eritrea, Somalia and Ethiopia also experienced severe forms of violence during this period. As such, it was easy for many rural masses to be convinced by errant apocalyptic preachers like Mwerinde and Kibwetere that the world was soon coming to a catastrophic end, in God's cleansing fire.

It was also easy to recruit liberation armies, such as those of Yoweri Museveni, Alice Lakwena and Joseph Kony, if the charismatic leader claimed to be God's chosen and sent messiah to liberate and save from their prevailing hellish conditions. Promises of peace and prosperity, such as the establishment of just governments and theocracies, were noble ideals to fight and die for, especially, if they were considered as God's will and holy mandates.

These are the same kinds of angst or economically, socially and politically desperate states of affairs, which breed crimes of opportunism, greed, exploitation, dictatorships as well as false prophets, and false messiahs, who falsely promise divine intervention as deliverance for the faithful. The above evils are also similar conditions of angst, chaos and despair, which characterized both spiritual and moral desperation that gave rise to the MRTCG. These evil conditions of despair and the threat of death troubled many Africans, including many Ugandans.

These prevailing states angst and despair, explain why especially the traumatized and devout rural Catholics, were ready to accept Keledonia Mwerinde and Joseph Kibwetere as God's prophets, and God's messiahs or agents of liberation from the perceived evil and seemingly perishing corrupt world. Mwerinde and Kibwetere's claimed that they had received special heavenly Marian apparitions and visions, These Marian apparitions and visions were accepted as evidence that both Mwerinde and Kibwetere were, indeed they were the truly chosen apocalyptic agents of God's new special revelations and redemption.

As such, thousands of pious Marian Catholics were attracted by Mwerinde and Kibwetere's piety, Marian teachings and moral reformation strategies for the Nation and the world. They rejected the unfounded allegations that these new prophets and messiahs were merely dangerous criminals, who were con-artists, false prophets, and false messiahs. From their own personal knowledge of Mwerinde and Kibwetere, the Marian Movement members and their neighbors, knew that they were slandered and falsely accused of being economically greedy as criminals, who were trying to fool people and defraud them of their important possessions, wealth and money in order to enrich themselves.[5]

However, most loyal followers and new Movement converts saw the surrender of their possessions, wealth and money as a form of self-sacrifice for the support and promotion of the Movement's work as it sought to convert people and bring them into the Kingdom of God. Most of these MRTCG members correctly realized that the money had been used to build the Kanungu headquarters, to buy exotic cattle for the farm, buy tools and farm equipment. In addition, the funds were also used to buy food to feed the many hundreds of people, who lived within the Marian Movement's monastic community in Kanungu, Bushenyi, Mbarara, Katojo, Kampala, Kasese and Fort Portal. In early 2000, the Marian Movement paid for some prime air-time on Radio Toro, in order to preach, teach and promote its apocalyptic teachings and practices to the people in Western Uganda. The broadcasts were in the local *Lutoro* and *Runyankole-Rukiga* vernacular languages.

Keledonia Mwerinde felt compelled and empowered by God and the Blessed Virgin Mary to testify and preach to her fellow Catholics and not to the Anglicans or other Protestants, since she was Roman Catholic and perceived that Catholics were her main initial religious audience and primary targets for preaching and conversion. Although she later declared that her main mission and message was for the whole world, she also realized that her visions about the Blessed Virgin Mary and the message entrusted to her by God, through the Blessed Virgin Mary, were most meaningful and relevant to Roman Catholics.

The non-Catholics were preached to irrespective of religious affiliation. They were all invited to God's salvation through faith and obedience to God's Ten Commandments. They were invited to repent, come and join the holiness and apocalyptic Marian Movement, or Catholic reformist and religious revival Movement, which was akin to the familiar *Balokole* Movement within the Anglican Church of Uganda. *The Movement for Restoration of the Ten Commandments of God* was founded with the help of Joseph Kibwetere, as Keledonia Mwerinde decided to accomplish her divine commission and religious task in Uganda and the rest of the world, in a traditional Catholic religious manner, with Marian symbolic spirituality and monastic methodology.

To this end, Keledonia Mwerinde symbolically dressed in a simple habit and veil like the Roman Catholic nuns at her local Makiro Catholic Church Parish, Kanungu, whom she had strongly admired and respected since her youth. Her father had been a catechist at Makiro Parish. Mwerinde's family lived at Katate, the near Makiro Parish Church, where she was born, grew up and also later, died.

Ultimately, Mwerinde wanted to establish a new religious Marian Order, along the lines of that of St. Benedict. Subsequently, when Mwerinde made some converts, she also asked them to dress like nuns if they were women, and to dress in long black pants and white shirts, like monks, if they were men. But all the Marian Movement members gave up their own clothes and dressed in long, simple uniforms. One of the main objectives for dressing simply in these uniforms, was to promote holiness and equality, by removing all the barriers and temptations of economic class differentiation, materialism, individuality and pride.

Mwerinde also sought to imitate the nuns' lives and work schedules, within the convent. She adorned a large crucifix and remained in silent prayer. She broke her life of silence, in order to testify to her Marian visions and preach the prophetic messages of repentance, life based on the obedience to the Ten Commandments of God, God's wrath against sin, and sinners and his impending punishment of the sinners and their corrupt world by destruction. Mwerinde both strongly believed, and preached the following:

- That God was a holy and righteous God.
- That holy God was interested in people's moral and spiritual purity.
- Human holiness and spiritual perfections were regarded as the extensions of God's own holiness and perfection. They were historically incarnate in the people, as God's spiritual mirrors and moral agents or representatives in the world. Therefore, both holiness and perfection were attained through the gradual processes of divinization, or *theosis,* and they were manifested in the obedient people that God created to become his own adopted children (*imago Dei).* To this end, God has freely endowed human beings with the necessary potential, mental, moral, spiritual, mystical powers and virtues.
- God's obedient Church or redeemed community has God's mandate to redeem lost sinners (*kujuna/kushayura*) and transform them into God's obedient saints. They are to become nurtured and developed by the ideal and godly community (or the Church, Temple and Mosque) into godly people. The religious and moral community has the divine mandate to nurture and transform its members into the truly intelligent moral agents as God's representatives in the world. God's community is charged with the divine moral mandate to create all its members into intelligent, well-informed, thinking, creative, peace-loving and responsible free moral agents in the world of non-thinking and lesser intelligent creatures in the world.
- God had instituted the Ten Commandments to guide the people's daily lives in order to live according to God's moral law and fulfill God's requirements of moral perfection and holiness.
- God was extremely angry because human beings had rebelled against God's moral law and had broken the Ten Commandments.
- Therefore, because of their sins, God would punish them by sending them into the painful hellfire.

- Being angry at human rebellion, sin, corruption and sexual immorality, the holy and righteous God would send divine punishment for sin in the form hellfire whose hot flames would flare and come down like rain in a severe tropical thunderstorm.
- God's holy fire would consume these rebellious sinners in this cosmic purifying holy fire.
- God would destroy and bring this world to a catastrophic end.
- God would bring this world to a fiery end, or cleanse the world of sin and purge the world of sinners, in order to transform it into God's holy kingdom.
- No sinner would escape destruction in this hellfire except those, who had accepted her message and repented of their sins, renounced greed, materialism, and disobedience to God's revealed cosmic moral, as handed down by God, to the world, in the form of the Ten Commandments through the Prophet Moses, and therefore, either explicitly or implicitly, having become members of *The Movement for the Restoration of the Ten Commandments of God.*[6]

Within this religious understanding, one could positively affirm that Keledonia Mwerinde had a clear revelation in her own mind that she had been selected, by God's unmerited grace to become God's special apocalyptic Messiah and servant of the Blessed Virgin Mary and God the Father, to redeem the world. She was to begin her redemptive ministry with her own family, the people of Kanungu and the nation of Uganda, which was now also perceived as God's new chosen nation to redeem the world, just like God had previously chosen Israel. This divine election of Mwerinde and commissioning as her special redemptive agent or Messiah in the world had been carried out by God, through the mediation of the Blessed Virgin Mary.

Subsequently, Mwerinde had proclaimed to the Ugandans and the rest of the world that God had through the Blessed Virgin Mary, selected her. Mwerinde both believed and testified that the Blessed Virgin Mary had consecrated and commissioned her for her special redemptive work in the world. Mwerinde claimed that the Blessed Virgin Mary had, then sent her out, into the world, to serve as Mary's embodiment (*Ekyombeko*), voice (*Iraka*) and redemptive agent or Apostle (*Entumwa*).

According to Mwerinde's self-understanding God, the Father, Mary had chosen her to become their special servant, prophetess and redemptive agent (*Entumwa*), in the world. Within this understanding, Mwerinde's both divine commission and mission were to become God's new apocalyptic agent of God's salvation, within the rebellious, corrupt and perishing contemporary world. This was the world, in which the traditional Catholic Church and its hierarchy, had become disobedient to God.

The Marian Movement members believed that the Church (*Ecclesia*), including the Catholic Church and its hierarchy, had become sinful, morally corrupt and ineffective as the agents of God's redemptive grace and salvation in the world. These greedy and materialist people had become part of the evil and oppressive demonic forces, in God's world. They had become evildoers and agents of evil, instead of being the positive, obedient and loving holy agents of God's grace, healing power and supernatural redemptive forces, or agents of God's forgiveness, salvation and peace in the sinful, evil, oppressive, corrupt, and violent world.

According to the writings of *The Movement for the Restoration of the Ten Commandments of God* and testimonies by the Marian Movement members, Keledonia Mwerinde most remorsefully repented of her many public and private sins, especially those of past sexual immorality. She adopted the Blessed Virgin Mary and St. Mary Magdalene as personal saints and ultimate role models. St. Magdalene was significant, as Mwerinde's role model, because she, too, like Mwerinde, had a notorious past as a prostitute. Yet, despite her sinful past, Magdalene had become a saint in Christ's Church. Mwerinde also wanted to become God's redeemed and reformed sinner, obedient saint and redemptive servant in the world.

It was self-evident that Keledonia Mwerinde aspired to be like Mary Magdalene and like her, to become God's saint. In this noble religious quest, Mwerinde sought the help of the Blessed Virgin Mary, and ultimately believed that she had been chosen by God, through the mediation of the Blessed Virgin Mary herself. She believed that her divine mission was to become God's special servant and agent of new apocalyptic divine revelations concerning the imminent end of the world as God's punishment for breaking of his Ten Commandments and other sins.

These radical new revelations concerning God's wrath for human sins, disobedience and punishment, including HIV/AIDS, imminent doom and a fiery end of the world, were for the Church and the whole world, and not just a few Marian Catholics, in South-Western Uganda. Accordingly, these divine revelations of God, the Father, were mediated and communicated to Mwerinde and through Mwerinde to the entire world through the visions of the Blessed Virgin Mary.

Mwerinde did not allow her notorious past history to stand in the way of God's calling to become a new person, transformed by God's saving grace to become God's saint and apocalyptic Messiah, through the Blessed Virgin Mary's intervention. Having become transformed into God's servant, as well as both Christ's and Mary's Apostle (*Entumwa)*, Mwerinde was prepared to do God's work of grace, revelation and redemption of the world through her and her followers, especially Joseph Kibwetere and Fr. Dominic Kataribabo.

Like Mwerinde, Magdalene had been a prostitute, before her encounter with Jesus the Christ, and subsequent conversion. Because of her encounter with Christ and the experience of his unconditional love (*Agape*) and free forgiveness, she had been converted and transformed. Mwerinde also had a similar conversion experience.

Subsequently, she emphasized God's moral holiness and need for obedience and repentance. Mwerinde adopted both Magdalene and the Blessed Virgin Mary as her personal role models and guiding saints. They were her main sources of moral courage and inspiration. She sought to imitate their holy lives and to become like them. Eventually, Mwerinde having experienced several visions of the Blessed Virgin Mary, she claimed to have become the local embodiment of the Blessed Virgin Mary (*Ekyombeko kya Bikira Maria*) and her Voice (*Iraka*), Prophetess (*Omurangi*) and Messiah (*Entumwa*) or saving agent in the world.[7]

At first, Mwerinde's central moral and religious teachings were based on the core moral teachings of Jesus that emphasized obedience to God, repentance of sins, unconditional love (*Agape*) and free grace. This redemptive process is characterized by the unlimited and free forgiveness of sins by God and the saints, or those obedient people that were called to become his obedient followers.

Like the many *Balokole* of the Anglican Church of Uganda that Mwerinde knew from her childhood, who believed in the transforming power of faith and the sacrament of repentance, from a past life of moral and spiritual wretchedness to that of a moral saint, Mwerinde also truly believed that she could be "born again" through repentance of her sins. Like the *Balokole*, Mwerinde also strongly believed that, by God's power and saving grace, she could also be truly transformed into God's true saint. She hoped that after her moral transformation, she become empowered or commissioned by God to become the Blessed virgin Mar's special moral agent, Apostle and missionary of redemption and change in the world.

Subsequently, as a Marian devotee, and visionary, Mwerinde believed that she had received a special vision or the apparition of the Blessed Virgin Mary. She testified that through the apparitions, the Blessed Virgin Mary had chosen and commissioned her to serve as her apocalyptic Messiah and Prophetess in the world. Thus, Keledonia Mwerinde became transformed into God and Mary's Messiah, Prophetess and missionary in the world. She testified that this redemptive mission was conferred upon her due to the Blessed Virgin Mary's saving grace, her obedience, deep faith in God, complete devotion to the Blessed Virgin Mary and by the complete repentance of her past sins.[8]

Again, like the *Balokole,* Mwerinde was also determined to live a simple holy life based on the observance of the Ten Commandments. But as a Roman Catholic, she sought to live her new spiritual life based on the Catholic faith, teachings, moral and spiritual practices, especially the spiritual graces and special merits which were supposed to be accrued by devotion to the Blessed Virgin Mary and constant silent prayer based on the silent recitation of the rosary.

Subsequently, the repentant Mwerinde tried hard to live a holy life pleasing to the Blessed Virgin Mary, Jesus Christ, her beloved son and God, his Father. Mwerinde desired to behave like a saint, and finally, to become one. She also wanted to impress the people of Kanungu with her reformed and new life of holiness and obedience to God, which was in contrast to the violent and immoral life she had lived in Kanungu Township as a notorious beer-seller, bar-owner and prostitute.

Mwerinde's life was reorganized and transformed according to the revelation she had received from the Virgin Mary. She lived in holy silent meditation on the lives of the saints that she knew and engaged in serious contemplative prayer. Her hope and desire were to become a pure vessel as God's new messiah, or apocalyptic agent of new revelation, redemptive grace and salvation in the world.

4. Mwerinde Recruits Kibwetere Guided by Marian Visions

Remarkably, at the same time that Keledonia Mwerinde was having visions of the Blessed Virgin Mary in Kabale Catholic Diocese, Joseph Kibwetere of Mbarara Catholic Diocese was also having visions of the Blessed Virgin Mary independently of Keledonia Mwerinde's own apparitions. The two visionaries and Marians would later meet in 1988 and form an effective Marian Movement that was given the name of *The Movement for the Restoration of the Ten Commandments of God (*MRTCG*),* which was successfully registered as an NGO in 1993.

This MRTCG's formal recognition and registration as NGO, was a respectable national status. It was granted to the Marian Movement by the State, despite some serious official opposition from Yorokam Kamacherere, the Rukungiri District Administrative Commissioner. He had serious concerns regarding the Marian Movement's true objectives, and warned that the Marian Movement was a "Mariologist doomsday cult," which had the potential to cause serious harm to its members, or the other members of the community. The Government of Uganda failed to heed the warnings of its own senior administrator in favor of his subordinate's more positive recommendation for registration of the Movement as an NGO.

Mr. Kamacherere's unscrupulous and corrupt subordinate had been bribed by the Movement's leaders. As a result, he ignored the publicly obvious danger signs of the Movement and its leaders. For instance, he ignored the Movement's dangerous activities and the Marian Movement's leaders' excessive preoccupation with secrecy that was more cult-like in nature. The MRTCG's preoccupation with secrecy for its leaders and members greatly exceeded that of the traditional Catholic Church's hierarchy and sacerdotal need for confidentiality of confessions, silent retreats, prayer and meditation.

There was a need for the correlative religious provision for "sacred space." This required the Marian Movement leaders to build its religious campus (monastery) in Kanungu. Kanungu was a quiet place, which was located far away from a big and noisy city, like Kampala. The Marian Movement's new headquarters were initially designed to become the Marian Movement's private holy retreat center, and main campus.

Kanungu was designed to become the global focus of the salvation and the renewed Christian world. It was intended to become the hideaway for contemplative and silent retreats. In Kanungu, it was already revered as a holy praying community that had been carefully designed to become the center for local silent and saintly people. The Marian Movement's Kanungu headquarters were planned to become part of a symbolic holy isolation, distant from people and the world in order to fast and pray during the times of retreat and silence.

It is true that Kanungu provided some special features. It was designed and built as a silent Benedictine monastic farming community. There was a school, two church buildings, and both a dairy and food-crops' farm. The members of the Marian Movement were required to sell all their property and personal possessions and give all the proceeds to the leaders of the Marian Movement.

Apart from the male leaders, the Marian Movement members, having surrendered all their personal clothing, were required to wear simple uniforms as nuns and monks. The Marian Movement taught strange dangerous doctrines that the world was about to come to a tragic end. They discouraged ownership of personal property, personal success, personal identity, marriage, sex, public speech, speaking, and even discouraged education for the children, despite the contradiction of the existence of a school in the MRTCG community or camp, in Kanungu.

Furthermore, for the leaders of the MRTCG, every day seemed to be a silent day of prayer, retreat and fasting in isolation from the world. Having been effectively corrupted, silenced and blinded by bribes, as the Government of Uganda officials later realized, following the Kanungu inferno, the Rev. Richard Mutazindwa, who was the Assistant Resident Commissioner (ADC) for Kanungu, had been administratively and politically negligent.

As an Anglican clergyman, who was trained in pastoral care and counseling, he failed to recognize serious signs of depression. He ignored the

Marian Movement leaders' excessive manifestations of symptoms of paranoia, and escapism from the world. He also tragically ignored the Marian Movement's excessive dogmatic, dangerous and apparently neurotic claims, which were constantly made by the MRTCG leaders that they had heard God's voice or seen God, who had directly revealed to them that the world was so corrupt and would soon be destroyed by God's consuming and cleansing holy fires.

However, if the Marian Movement leaders had access to nuclear or other weapons of mass destruction, the Rev. Mutazindwa and other government leaders would have taken seriously preventive measures to avoid an apocalyptic disaster. This would have occurred, at the time when the Marian Movement leaders preached that the world would soon catastrophically end, by God's fire because of God's divine judgment and punishment for human greed, corruption, homosexuality, violence and other heinous sins.

To some extent, the Rev. Mutazindwa was in agreement with some of the teaching of the Marian Movement, such as the deplorable prevailing state of both hedonistic materialism and moral decadence in the country and much of the world. The destructive allegations of Catholic priests sexual immorality and molestation of children made some religious people pay attention to some portions of the Marian Movement's moral warnings and teachings. They paid attention to the Marian Movement leaders' urgent call for the Church's moral reformation, beginning with the Church's priestly hierarchy, which was denounced as being morally corrupt and spiritually bankrupt.

As God's new prophets and prophetesses, the Movement leaders claimed that God had revealed to them that the end of the world was imminent and was going to come at the end of the year 1999 because of God's punishment for sinful human beings, who committed adultery, were corrupt and joyfully broke other commandments of God. Many religious leaders were against the Movement's official recognition because the leaders also demanded that their followers had to sell all their belongings, and take their own children out of school and come to live in a monastic and celibate commune in Kanungu.

These unorthodox and radical new teachings of celibacy, communal living in an isolated community of silence and prayer became standard within the apocalyptic Marian Movement. In addition, there was a religious requirement for all the Marian Movement members to sell all personal and family properties, and to donate all the money to the Marian Movement. Many people found this monastic practice to be both religiously questionable and socioeconomically disruptive to both families and the community.

The Marian Movement broke up families and impoverished the rest of the family members because of the sale of family properties and giving all the proceeds to the Movement's leaders. For religious leaders and government officials, *The Movement for the Restoration of the Ten Commandments of God* was a new and dangerous religious cult, although its founders were devoted Roman Catholic Marian lay people and well-educated Catholic priests in good standing at the time of the foundation of the Marian Movement, within the Catholic Church, in 1989.

Meanwhile, according to the documents of *The Movement for the Restoration of the Ten Commandments of God*, on April 25, 1984, the Blessed Virgin Mary also appeared to another Roman Catholic layperson by the name of Joseph Kibwetere. This testimony found great credibility among the Catholics of Mbarara Diocese, who knew him as an exemplary pious Catholic.

However, after the Kanungu inferno, and subsequent discovery of several mass graves in different areas of the country containing hundreds of naked bodies belonging to the Marian Movement members, the general perception of Kibwetere changed suddenly. He became extremely vilified and overwhelmingly negatively portrayed by the public media, as a greedy opportunist, cunning business-man and a conman, rather than being a respectable devout Catholic religious leader, an outstanding educator, a respectable politician and businessman.

This was mainly due to an extreme overreaction by the Church, the State and the public media to the Marian Movement's shocking horrors of voluntary self-sacrificial deaths and martyrdoms, which took place in March, 2000. Joseph Kibwetere, Keledonia Mwerinde and Fr. Dominic Kataribabo became the convenient scapegoats for the Marian Movement's radical departure from true Catholic doctrines and virtues of moderation, especially the radical and tragic liberation theologies and ritualistic self-sacrificial deaths, as Christian martyrdoms.

Previously, Joseph Kibwetere was both well-known and respected as an exemplary citizen, by most of his neighbors, the Mbarara Catholic Diocese hierarchy and priests, as a very devout Catholic, generous businessman, DP politician, an outstanding lay Catholic leader, administrator, and a Catholic educator. As a well-established Catholic educator, administrator and lay leader, Kibwetere had been appointed the headmaster of Kishariro Catholic Primary School, in 1957. And because of his administrative skills and piety, as a Catholic layman, in 1958, Kibwetere was appointed to the enviable position of Assistant Supervisor of Catholic Schools, in the Mbarara Catholic Diocese. He served in this capacity until 1962.

Kibwetere was one of the few outstanding and devout Catholics, who had both local and national religious and political recognition. For instance, he had been a Catholic DP (*Democratic Party*) politician and a lay-religious leader, who had the resources, zeal and need to go to Rome in 1984 on religious pilgrimage and try to see the Pope. The Kibwetere valued this holy pilgrimage to Rome, even when he was present as a member of a traditional public mass audience of pilgrims in St. Peter's Basilica court area, where the Holy Father, the pope, often appeared in the Basilica's window to greet the masses of Catholic pilgrims, and others in the courtyard below the window. For Kibwetere, that was a beatific vision of heaven on earth.

Furthermore, Kibwetere's religious faith, personal dedication and loyalty to the Catholic Church are clearly demonstrated by his professional life, fiscal, political and fiscal support for the Catholic Church. His outstanding leadership as a Catholic teacher and supervisor of Catholic schools in Mbarara Catholic Diocese are some of the objective factors as evidence of his being a staunch and good Catholic layperson. For instance, there was the fact that he had also built a good permanent Catholic Church building for his home parish church a few hundred yards away from his own house.

In 1963, Kibwetere had also built Nyakazinga Secondary School, as a pioneer independent Catholic secondary school, in the Mbarara Catholic Diocese. Again, the Catholic secondary school was located near his home in Ntungamo. This private secondary school, which was founded by Kibwetere, did not succeed. This was mainly, due to the fact, that it did not receive the necessary Catholic hierarchy's moral and fiscal support from the Mbarara Catholic Diocese. Part of the Church's failure to help him secure funds for the secondary school was rooted in jealousy and suspicion that Joseph Kibwetere had started the school as a profitable business venture to enrich himself rather than to serve Catholic students and the Church.

Later, the founding of an independent Catholic high school and its failure, were unfairly, used by some members of the public and the Catholic Church's hierarchy in Mbarara, to discredit Joseph Kibwetere and Keledonia Mwerinde, as economically greedy and opportunistic entrepreneurs. Subsequently, they were vilified as a religious frauds and con-artists, when their *Movement for the Restoration of the Ten Commandments of God* began asking admission fees to help with the Movement's increasing expenses and fiscal needs. Finally, the Marian Movement leaders decided that since the Marian Movement was a voluntary religious association with expenses to pay, they would charge the following one time organizational modest dues and modest admission fees to help with the living and other expenses:

- 5,000 Uganda shillings[9] or children
- 8,000 shillings for the youths
- 25, 000 shillings for adults,
- and there was free admission for the very poor. [10]

In addition, the leaders of the Movement required all the members to sell all their properties and personal possessions and bring all the proceeds to them as part of their required self-sacrifices to God, to support the Movement and its various local and national outreach operations. This included preaching missions, paying for radio time on Toro Radio in 1999 and 2000, payments for rental properties in Katojo, Kanungu, Mbarara, Buziga-Kampala, and building projects at its headquarters, in Kanungu.

However, any visit to Kanungu would have proved, to both the outsiders and the skeptics that Kibwetere and Mwerinde did not misuse the Marian Movement's funds. There is no evidence that they used the money obtained from their own followers for their own profit, but rather, used the money to buy cattle, feed thousands of their followers that came to camp at Kanungu and used the rest to erect elaborate buildings at their headquarters at Kanungu. These buildings included a completed school block for students from primary one to primary four, two big church buildings, two large dormitories, and a large residential house for the Marian Movement's leaders, a guesthouse and a number of smaller houses.

The rest of the money went to the purchase of supplies and provision of transportation of the Marian Movements' members and leaders. Fuel costs in Uganda are very high, and yet, the Marian Movement leaders traveled constantly between the headquarters and the many substations of the Movement, which were located in many parts of the country, particularly in Rukungiri, Bushenyi, Ntungamo, Kasese, Mbarara, Fort Portal and Kampala districts of Uganda. In all these areas, the MRTCG attracted mainly devout Catholics.

These Marian Movement devotees were predominantly poorly educated, impoverished rural women and their children. Nevertheless, the economically and politically disgruntled Catholic men, like Joseph Kibwetere and Fr. Dominic Kataribabo also joined the women's original simple Marian Movement for their own religious and political agenda. Their various agenda included search of meaning, power, recognition, as well as quest for moral perfection, solace and peace. In addition, Fr. Kataribabo wanted to use the Marian Movement as the tool to publicly unmask, criticize and condemn the perceived corruption and immorality of the Catholic Church and its hierarchy.

Ultimately, the Marian Movement members wanted to escape from what they believed and experienced or perceived as a corrupt and hostile world. Some of the Marian Movement members believed that both the Church and the world, or the nation, had both marginalized and victimized them. Some of these people believed that the corrupted Church and the evil world had either directly rejected or persecuted them.

Many Catholic women, who joined the Marian Movement, had personally experienced some dehumanizing incidents of marginalization and oppression for being women within a patriarchal hegemonic world. Other members of the Marian Movement, also strongly believed that the society and the world, had discriminated against them, dehumanized them, marginalized and oppressed them for being Catholics. In the case of Uganda, they also alleged that they were oppressed for being members of a disfranchised political party, namely, the traditional Catholic-based *Democratic Party*. These oppressive existential religio-political factors were, especially true, in the case of Joseph Kibwetere. This is one of the main reasons why the public erroneously believed that Kibwetere was both the founder and absolute leader of the MRTCG.

As a result of either prejudice or misinformation, many people erroneously believed that Kibwetere was a failed politician and businessman, who had founded the MRTCG as his revenge on the political world against the Catholic Church. They erroneously believed that Kibwetere wanted to embarrass the Mbarara Catholic Church and the bishops, who had failed to recognize and reward his political and administrative gifts and to value his contributions to the community, Nation and the Catholic Church.

Ultimately, the Catholics and other people, who did not know the role of an Abbot as head of a Marian Movement as a new African Benedictine Order, misunderstood him to be a pope of a new separatist Catholic Church. This tragic misunderstanding of Catholic Church traditions and polity, could not allow these outsiders to view the Marian Movement as a new religious Benedictine Order, with Kibwetere as Co-Abbot and co-head of the MRTCG.

The articles of MRTCG's incorporation clearly indicate the MRTCG was a new religious Order, which was founded with the main objective being to reform and purify the perceived corrupt Catholic Church. Consequently, the public, including the Mbarara Catholic bishops tragically failed to both appreciate and assist the MRTCG as a truly beneficial religious organization (*Ekigombe*) and moral reform Marian Movement. They also failed to accept the reality that the Marian Movement was a true new Catholic moral crusade and Marian devotion organization.

Most significantly, they also failed to understand the true prophetic and positive religious mission of the Marian Movement, which aspired to operate within the local Catholic Church (*Ecclesia*), despite the resistance of the Catholic Church's hierarchy. Like the Hebrew prophets who were both rejected and persecuted by the traditional religious establishment, the new apocalyptic prophets of the Marian Movement were also rejected and persecuted by the Roman Catholic Church to whom they were sent by God and the Blessed Virgin Mary. Likewise, the Catholic church hierarchy sought to persecute and silence the Marian Movement's mission and role as a real moral crusade and prophetic voice or instrument for God's divine moral indictment, judgment and challenge to the corrupted Church, corrupt materialistic community, nation and the supposedly perishing corrupt or evil world (*Ensi egi*),[11]

NOTES

1. This was the overwhelming finding of 10 years of my field research and the inside insights and views of many Marian former members. As a result, the Government of Uganda banned the Marian Movement. Subsequently, the police officers were employed to both investigate and conduct effective surveillance over the MRTCG members, and to foil any assemblies, plans and attempts by the remaining MRTCG members from physical self-sacrifices to God and self-martyrdoms, in their deep religious faith and hope to ascend into heaven, to join their ascended friends and relatives. That finding has shaped the theology, ethics and presentation of the research data in this book.

2. Hell-fire or *Gehena,* it was locally called, was a form of everlasting painful torture by God in Godly holy fire, which had to be avoided at all costs. Many sinners repented of their sins and joined the *Balokole Movement* due to fear of God's judgment and punishment. See Twesigye, the "The *Balokole* Movement," STM Thesis, University of the South, 1979.

3. There were local speculations that Mwerinde used magic to brainwash (*kuroga*) and control her followers, including Joseph Kibwetere and Fr. Dominic Kataribabo. However, I found no evidence for these widely held beliefs and defamatory allegations.

4. According to Fr. Paul Ikazire, the prophecy for the apocalyptic end of the world was part of the scare tactic by the Marian Movement leaders in order to scare sinners to repent. It had been previously fixed and moved three times according to convenience. *A Timely Message from Heaven,* Prophet Kibwetere makes it clear that the present era would end, and a new one would begin with the new millennium.

5. These were malicious, defamatory and damaging perceptions and allegations, which were made by the Marian Movement's jealous or embarrassed opponents and enemies. However, these false allegations dominated the mass media and distorted the reports on the Marian Movement, their ideals and self-sacrificial deaths as atonements to God rather than cult suicides. See *A Timely Message from Heaven*, 80-115.

6. *A Timely Message from Heaven*, 3, 12, 16-17.

7. This is based on the information provided by Fr. Paul Ikazire, one of the former leaders of the Marian Movement and the people of Kanungu, who knew Mwerinde and the Marian Movement members. The MRTCG was a local part of the religious community.

8. See *A Timely Message from Heaven*, 1-25.

9. That was about $2.50 in the USA currency. It was not much money. However, since Uganda is an impoverished nation, some misinformed members of the public being also poor, erroneously thought and believed that this small fee was much money that made the Marian Movement leaders rich people. The reality was the Marian Movement leaders did not have

sufficient funds to keep the Marian Movement members properly housed, fed and clothed. Therefore, severe fasting was partly devised in order to alleviate the dilemma caused by lack of funds and food shortages. They by necessity lived an extremely austere and simple monastic life.

10. The MRTCG was an association with set minimum entry fees. See: Kabazzi-Kisirinya, *et el.*, *The Kanungu Cult-Saga: Suicide, Murder or Salvation?* 31. Yet, some people complained that the Marian Movement was for the rich who could afford the entry fees. See Patrick Mugumya, "Cult Membership was Reserved for the Rich," *The New Vision*, Saturday, April 1, 2000.

10. This was a confusing apocalyptic reference. As a result, the Marian Movement leaders' apocalyptic prophecies were tragically misunderstood, by both the outsiders and some scriptural literalist members of the Marian Movement. These literalists literally interpreted the apocalyptic references to mean the total end of the world rather than the passing of an era (*Okuhwaho kw'Obusingye obu*). See: *A Timely Message from Heaven*, 20-65.

Chapter Six

MARY'S APOSTLES OF SALVATION AND PROPHETS OF DOOM

The Movement for the Restoration of the Ten Commandments of God started informally, in the early 1980s, as a rural Catholic Marian Women's Prayer Group in the Kabale Catholic Church Diocese. These Mary's devotion prayer meetings were led by Gauda Kamushwa in the sacred mountain caves of Nyabugoto, in Nyakishenyi, but they attracted little national attention. This situation changed in 1988, when Joseph Kibwetere and two nuns from the Nyamitanga Cathedral in Mbarara Catholic Diocese, visited the Nyabugoto sacred mountains, to venerate the stone statue of the Blessed Virgin Mary, and met Keledonia Mwerinde.[1]

Joseph Kibwetere impressed the impoverished Marian devotees with his wealth and ideas. He suggested that the Marian Women's Prayer Club could be more effective if it were better organized, as an association, whose primary mission and objectives were to promote holy pilgrimage to the Nyabugoto Holy Mountain, personal holiness and devotion to the Blessed Virgin Mary. The Catholic Women Marian devotees were already carrying out this mission, but in an informal and less effective manner.

1. Introduction

In January 1989, Keledonia Mwerinde, one of Kamushwa's disciples, decided to go to Mbarara to look for Joseph Kibwetere and to seek his assistance in forming a formal Marian Devotion Association within the Catholic Church. She needed his fiscal resources and administrative skills to help her transform her Mary's informal devotion prayer group into an effective formal reformist religious association (*Ekigombe),* within the Roman Catholic Church (*Ekelesia*), in Uganda, Rwanda and other countries.[2] Some influential nuns and priests in Mbarara Catholic Diocese, including Fr. Dominic Kataribabo and Fr. Paul Ikazire, were recruited into the Marian Movement. The intention was to use them, in order to become formally established and recognized as a true Catholic, new moral reform Marian organization within the Catholic Church. They also needed the priests' assistance, to enable them to more effectively promote their Marian moral reform, and spiritual renewal Movement, within the Catholic Church.[3]

Therefore, Mary's Moral Movement was not conceived and founded as a separatist sect or new the Catholic Church. It was founded as a Mary's devotion, and reformist Marian Movement within the Catholic Church, to serve as the new moral conscience for the Church. Its mission was to promote repentance, moral and spiritual reform within the Church's hierarchy (bishops and priests) and lay membership. The founders of the Marian Movement believed that the Catholic Church and its hierarchy, as well as lay membership, were corrupt, sinful and materialistic. Therefore, they needed to repent of their sins, and live a new holy life based on the strict observation of God's Ten Commandments.[4]

It is extremely important to note that the Kanungu people, especially the Catholics, knew the Movement members and respected them for being Catholic moral perfectionists and "spiritual revivalists." They referred to them as Mary's devotees and worshippers: *"Aba Nyabugoto."*[5] This is a local reference to the Marian Movement members as the organized group of devotees of the Blessed Virgin Mary that originated in the Nyabugoto holy Mountain. They were the new and better organized component of the Marian tradition in Southern Uganda, and the neighboring Rwanda.

The traditional devotees of Mary had regularly performed their holy pilgrimage to the Nyabugoto holy Mountain, in Nyakishenyi, to both venerate and worship[6] the Blessed Virgin Mary, inside the sacred cave, where God had mysteriously carved her statue, in the mountain rock. The local Catholics and the Protestants did not view the Marian Movement as a new Church. They treated the Marian Movement's headquarters, in the same way, in which they positively perceived and treated a Catholic monastery, or convent. The members of the Marian Movement dressed like traditional nuns and monks, and behaved like them. As a result, the Marian Movement members were accorded the honor and respect that were traditionally bestowed on Catholic nuns and monks by their neighbors and the people in the local communities.[7]

However, the Catholic Church hierarchy in Mbarara Diocese misunderstood the real nature and positive role of the new radical, moral and spiritual reformist Marian Movement within the Catholic Church. The Marian Movement had started operating without the permission and license of the Catholic bishops, especially since among its objectives, was the promotion of religious moral education, sound religious values and building a Catholic model school, in Kanungu, at the Movement's headquarters.

Therefore, the Mbarara Catholic hierarchy felt ecclesiastically belittled, spurned and bypassed by the overzealous, compulsive moral-spiritual perfectionist, contemptuous and self-righteous Marian Movement leaders. This was, especially noted, to be true in the Marian Movement leaders' process of planning, founding and operating the new MRTCG, as a Catholic association, or Marian Movement, within the Catholic Church, of which these bishops were the local leaders. Yet, these Marian Movement leaders never had the courtesy to either consult or inform these bishops, of their intentions and plans, prior to the founding of the Marian Movement. Understandably, these bishops felt slighted and were upset.

Subsequently, the offended and enraged Mbarara Catholic bishops took what they considered appropriate and timely canonical steps to stop the activities of the Marian Movement, and kill the organization. The offended Mbarara Catholic bishops sought appropriate canonical, and public relations measures designed to cause a complete destruction and elimination of the MRTCG's troubling presence, and disruption of the traditional work of the Catholic Church.

The Mbarara Catholic bishops completely misunderstood the Marian Movement's work and mission. As a result, they vigorously opposed, persecuted, and tried to stop, exorcize, and eliminate the MRTCG and its activities, considering them to be some evil works and demonic results of the Devil's work to divide, and discredit the redemptive work of the Catholic Church. Fr. Father Betungura strongly believed that the work and doctrines of the Marian Movement were contemptuous of the moral authority of the Catholic bishops and divisive; and therefore, the Marian Movement leaders were possessed, by the demonic forces that led them to do evil and rebel against their Catholic bishops.

According to Fr. Betungura, the Marian moral and spiritual revolt against their Mbarara Catholic bishops meant that, the Marian Movement's reformist leaders were new rebellious and evil schismatics, heretics and Protestants, who were no longer true Catholics. These were the negative observations and convictions of Ponsiano Betungura, a disillusioned former colleague of Fr. Kataribabo of Mbarara Diocese. He did not want to discuss the Marian Movement leaders' indictment and condemnation of the Catholic priests for their violations of the vows of celibacy.

Nevertheless, Fr. Betungura, very explicitly, stated that he strongly believed that Fr. Kataribabo and Joseph Kibwetere were evil people, who had really become possessed by the Devil. And as a result, they became diabolical "cult-leaders," and both the effective agents and evil instruments of the "dark forces" of the Devil, and evil-spirits that led to both death, and destruction, instead of the salvation, which they enthusiastically preached and sought to attain.[8]

Based on Fr. Betungura's detailed recollection, negative report, but yet, a careful ecclesiastical religious analysis and insightful theological understanding of the radical and tragic events within the Marian Movement, it becomes clear that Fr. Kataribabo was disliked by some of the Catholic priests, as well as the bishops. Accordingly, the Mbarara bishops' hostile response and treatment of the Marian Movement, its leaders and members, were based on serious mutual prejudices and understandings. It became very clear that the Marian Movement and its moral reformation mission had been seriously distorted, misunderstood and subsequently misrepresented by the Mbarara Catholic bishops and many of the Catholic priests. In brief, the Marian Movement was portrayed and misrepresented to many Catholics, as the work of the Devil, which must be shunned by obedient Catholics.

As a result, there was also a misleading emphasis concerning the Marian Movement's leaders' moral, religious and ecclesiastical revolt against the Catholic Church, as a whole. There was also a false claim that the priests had been excommunicated and the lay Marian Movement leaders, especially Kibwetere and Mwerinde had decided to separate themselves from the Roman Catholic Church, to form a new schismatic Catholic Church, or an apocalyptic Protestant denomination. The truth was that they were being canonically, or ecclesiastically (legally) forced out of the Catholic Church, by the less flexible, conservative and intolerant Catholic hierarchy, in the Mbarara Diocese, which later became the center of the new Archdiocese of the Western Province of Uganda.

In the aftermath of the Kanungu tragedy, on March 17, 2000, the Catholic Church hierarchy, in Mbarara, has consistently, maintained that in its dealings with the newspapers and interviews, it did everything possible, to persuade the errant and dissident priests, and their Marian followers, to return to the true faith, within the mainline Catholic Church. The belligerent moral reformist and radical Marian priests were implored to abandon their pietistic and reformist moral Catholic crusade within the Catholic Church. They were commanded to obey their Catholic bishops, in all prescribed matters of traditional doctrines, or matters concerning the Catholic Church's orthodox faith, moral values and practices.

The threat of excommunications failed to lead a more constructive handling of the Marian Movement's leaders. The Catholic bishops' hard-line was not conducive to a more peaceful pastoral care or persuasion of the Marian Movement leaders to a moderate position, that would have led to the necessary positive modification of the moral and renewal teachings of the Marian Movement. This kind of constructive Episcopal pastoral approach would have, eventually, led to the peaceful reintegration of the alienated Marian Movement leaders and their followers, back into the full communion of the local Catholic Church. This would have been the ideal ecclesiastical approach to deal with the belligerent and radical moral reformist Marian Movement leaders, rather than threatening them, or canonically and forcefully seeking to throw them out of the Roman Catholic Church.

Nevertheless, it was to this confrontational and tragic end, that the Catholic bishops in Mbarara effectively employed the Episcopal powers and the mighty weapons of the Church canons. They employed their constitutional, or ecclesiastical and traditional Episcopal powers to interdict any defiant, or errant priests, within their dioceses, and to appeal to the Pope, in Rome, through the *Papal Nuncio* (Ambassador), for jurisdiction and action, if excommunication of the priests is warranted. But the canons confer full ecclesiastical powers upon the local Catholic bishops to both interdict and excommunicate any errant, or defiant lay Catholics, within their ecclesiastical and diocesan jurisdiction.

As such, Bishop Kakubi had the canonical power to excommunicate Joseph Kibwetere, because he was a lay Catholic within his own diocese, over which Bishop Kakubi exercised his ecclesiastical jurisdiction, until 1992, when Kibwetere fled to Kanungu, in quest of ecclesiastical refuge, in Kabale Catholic Diocese. However, Bishop Kakubi had no ecclesiastical authority, or canonical power to excommunicate Keledonia Mwerinde, because she was from Kabale Catholic Diocese, and therefore, resided outside his ecclesiastical jurisdiction.

Similarly, Bishop Kakubi had the power to interdict the Mbarara Catholic Diocesan priests, within Marian Movement, like Frs. Kataribabo, Ikazire, Kasapurari and Kamagara, but had not power to excommunicate them, since only the Pope could excommunicate and defrock Catholic priests, despite the fact that they had been trained and ordained by the local bishops, on behalf of the Catholic Church.

This global papal jurisdiction is important as the focal point, Special Revelation, Truth and symbolic power for unifying divine redemptive grace, ecclesiastical unity, Catholic priesthood, effective ministry, redemptive mission, pastoral function and administration of effective sacraments. It also protects Catholic priests from any abuses stemming from the arbitrary decisions, discipline and administrative incompetence of their local bishops.

Fr. Dominic Kataribabo, Joseph Kibwetere and Keledonia Mwerinde experienced these Church canons, as destructive Episcopal instruments and ecclesiastical weapons, which they had to dodge, in order to avoid being administratively, professionally, personally, and spiritually harmed.[9] That is one of the major reasons, why the Marian Movement leaders moved the MRTCG's headquarters to Kanungu, in Kabale Catholic Diocese, where they were not under interdiction, and the frightening Catholic threat of excommunication.

Bishop Robert Gay, of the Kabale Catholic Diocese, was a liberal Canadian expatriate, who did not care about the local theological squabbles about the validity of the Marian visions, and claims of new apocalyptic divine revelations, through the Blessed Virgin. If the visions and the apocalyptic revelations were true, then, they would soon materialize, and the world would come to an end. If the doomsday prophecies were false, then, the world would not end, and the MRTCG members would either go back home, or decide to remain, and live a holy life, as part of the godly, Catholic monastic community.

Nevertheless, unlike the liberal and tolerant hierarchy of Kabale Catholic Diocese, the Mbarara Catholic Diocese was most affected by the activities of the Marian Movement. It had lost a lot of Catholics, and all the Catholic priests of the MRTCG were from Mbarara Diocese, and none came from the Kabale Diocese, and therefore, Bishop Gay did not have to act against them. However, he did not stop them from celebrating sacraments in his own diocese, in the same way Bishop Kakubi had decreed, in Mbarara Catholic Diocese.

Therefore, there was an urgent need for the hierarchy in the Mbarara Catholic Diocese to explain why it rejected the MRTCG. This was because it was seriously embarrassed, because of the defections to the Marian Movement, of some influential Catholic priests, such as the Rev. Fr. Dominic Kataribabo, former Kitabi Seminary Rector, whom many people, including Bishop John Kakubi believed to be extremely well-educated, and according to Bishop Kakubi, to have even acquired a doctorate degree in Catholic theology,[10] and the Marian Movement's leadership under Joseph Kibwetere, a very influential DP politician, educator and Catholic layman in Mbarara Diocese.

According to the extensive research and analysis of the data, *The Movement for the Restoration of the Ten Commandments of God* was, according to the laws *(in jure)* of the Republic of Uganda, a Non-Governmental Organization, or a moral civic association (*Ekigombe)* with many stated secular objectives and benefits, such as providing free public moral education, economic farm production of goods and demonstration of better farming techniques in rural areas. But in reality *(de facto),* the MRTCG was a "holiness Catholic Marian Movement" that could have been better and more correctly named the "Lay Order of the Holy Association of the Blessed Virgin Mary." As a religious association, the MRTCG had some of its stated main objectives being to do or promote:

- personal moral holiness and perfection
- collective prayer and worship
- silent contemplation
- meditation and listening to Mary and God for new visions or revelations
- foster holiness based on preaching repentance of sins

- live a holy life of daily penance
- promote obedience to God's Ten Commandments
- live a life of simplicity
- humility and vow of poverty
- total obedience to the leaders
- nonviolence
- practice monasticism

- discipline the body through a life of fasting
- tame sexual desires and live a life of celibacy

- observation of the code of holy silence (*kusirika*)
- live in complete obedience to Mary and God's will as a living saint.

Nevertheless, the MRTCG leaders emphasized that strict observance of the Ten Commandments of God, contemplative prayer in total silence; holy obedience and nonviolence were to be taught, as the practical moral codes of daily life, holiness and the holy path to moral perfection and salvation. But then, the Marian Movement could not have appealed to a wider audience both within and outside the Roman Catholic Church.

The Marian Movement could not have been registered, as an independent NGO (Non Governmental Organization), outside the Catholic Church, which negatively viewed and condemned the teachings of the Marian Movement, as unacceptable and dangerous heresies. That is, the Catholic Church hierarchy, especially Bishop John Baptist Kakubi, of Mbarara Diocese, most negatively assessed, and theologically judged, and rejected the religious claims of the Marian Movement leaders. He dismissed their claims of heavenly visions, and to have talked with God, in heaven and received his special urgent messages and apocalyptic revelations, to be communicated to the world, through the mediation of the Blessed Virgin Mary, saying that they were both false and dangerous doctrines, to be rejected, by all faithful and obedient Catholics.[11]

2. The Centrality of Mary's Apparitions and Visions

Accordingly, the religious claims of special visions of God and the Blessed Virgin Mary, and ultimately, the *"Messages from Heaven,"* were condemned as misleading and wrong doctrines, as judged by the traditional dogmas, or the standard doctrines of the Catholic Church. These traditional Catholic dogmas included the teaching that God's revelation and saving grace are both fully manifested and experienced within the Roman Catholic Church. Correlatively, there was the traditional Catholic dogma that affirmed and taught the Catholics that both God's essential redemptive revelation and saving grace are, adequately, both safeguarded and mediated to God's world, by the holy Catholic Church.

Before Vatican II (1963-65), wisely negated it under the holy guidance of God's redemptive grace, and the inspiration of the Holy Spirit, the religiously bigoted and exclusive traditional Catholic dogma of Christian salvation, had been used to discriminate and exclude non-Catholics from the benefits of God's true revelation, saving grace, and divine salvation. It had limited the holy work of Christ and God's power of redemptive grace to baptized, obedient, loyal or true members of the Catholic Church.

The non-Catholics and those excommunicated from the Catholic Church were supposed to be excluded from God's work of free redemptive grace in the world and salvation. Bishop Kakubi seemed to have strongly believed in this Pre-Vatican doctrine of the Roman Catholic Church and salvation, as he assessed the Marian Movement leaders' new and unorthodox claims concerning heavenly visions, God's new revelations and teachings of *The Movement of the Restoration of the Ten Commandments of God.*

It is self-evident that Bishop Kakubi thought that, based on the teachings and canons of the Catholic Church, he was the more appropriate local religious vehicle to speak to God, and serve as the Church's agent for God's true revelations, communications and moral teachings, rather than these leaders of the MRTCG, most of whom he considered to be merely ignorant and sinful lay people. This is the nature of the dogma of the *Extra Ecclesiam Nulla Salus* (Outside the [Roman Catholic] Church there is no salvation), which had traditionally been affirmed, by the Roman Catholic Church. The Catholic Church had effectively taught that the supernatural redemptive work of God was exclusively, carried out, by God, through Christ, the Blessed Virgin Mary, and the Catholic Church.

In turn, Jesus Christ also carried out his special divine mission of salvation and redemption of the world through the holy Roman Catholic Church, and its hierarchy, holy activities, sacraments and rituals. The Catholic Church, explicitly, taught that it faithfully carried out God's work and mission of salvation, through the preaching of God's Word, and diligence in the celebration and administration of the holy sacraments. The Church also did holy charitable work, healed the sick and taught the ignorant. It observed the holy religious traditions and Apostolic authority, including the normative principle and tradition of "Church's Apostolic Succession," as mediated to the Church and the world, by the Roman Church's traditional sacerdotal hierarchy, in which the bishops, especially the Popes in Rome, are the chief agents and mediators of God's redemptive grace.

These Catholic Popes, bishops, and priests believed, behaved and served God and the world, in the deep faith that they were God's actual elect, consecrated, holy agents of God's supernatural redemptive grace, and forgiveness of sins. They were God's special and holy mediators of both redemption and divine salvation, in both the Church and the world. They also simultaneously served, as God's main agents and channels of divine revelation, and divine instruments of holy communication, to the world. They were also considered God's instruments for moral and spiritual guidance, teaching and enlightenment. In addition, they served, as God's empowered and authorized agents of religious and moral instruction, correct interpretation of the Holy Scriptures, and formulation of new authoritative moral principles, and religious teachings.

The Popes also claimed that their divine activities were inerrant, or infallible, because they were based on God's revelation, and the Holy Spirit's holy guidance, saving grace and continuing divine revelation and correction, even when errors occurred within the Church, either through ignorance, or sinful revolt against God's will. For Christian Catholic thinkers and theologians, like St. Augustine, Thomas Aquinas, Karl Rahner, Pope John Paul II and Pope Benedict XVI, divine revelation and guidance are effectively mediated to the world and the Church, by the Transcendent Holy God through many divine channels and God's chosen agents. These divine agents include:

- the inspiration of God's Holy Spirit
- the prophets
- the Holy Scriptures
- heavenly visions
- reason or intellect (Mind)
- the Natural Law

Natural Law is God's universal book of God's activities and creative processes. This form of divine revelation is universally accessible through science, intellectual analysis of data attained from empirical investigations of the cosmos and its divinely imposed laws (Natural Law). For religious believers, Natural Law is God's chosen method created to regulate and guide its processes of creativity, creation and evolution of new beings. To this end, archeological data serves as a historical record of divine evolutionary processes of creation, preservation of the world and future events that can be intellectually accessed and reflected upon, by science, reason, a well-formed moral conscience, good education; and the acquisition of correct information, or sound knowledge, leading to sound moral judgment, good loving deeds, altruism, nonviolence, the promotion of knowledge, and the celebration of the Truth.

However, the leaders of the Marian Movement were convinced that their divine mission to save the world came from God, the Father through the direct mediation of the Blessed Virgin Mary. They claimed that their divine or messianic redemptive commission, included saving the very Roman Catholic Church and its hierarchy, which the Marian Movement leaders negatively viewed, as having become corrupted, materialistic and "fallen from grace."

Therefore, in serious need of some obedient moral preachers from God, like the leaders of the MRTCG to exhort them to repent, renounce evil, especially greed for wealth, corruption, sexual immorality, violence and indulgence in alcoholic drinks. Sinners were told that God warned and commanded them repent all their sins and live a holy life of true religious true piety.

All obedient believers were required to have unquestioning faith in the holy Creator God of the universe, the compassionate Blessed Virgin Mary as the Mediator of God's love, mercy, revelation and salvation of sinners in the world. They were also required to practice true godliness, as externally expressed in a holy life that is completely rooted in true holiness, daily worship, holy silence, contemplative prayer, simplicity and humility, which are based on the strict observance of the Ten Commandments of God.

Despite the fact that *The Movement for the Restoration of the Ten Commandments of God* built a church building in Kanungu, which it called *"Obwato"* (God's Ark of Salvation),[12] and also behaved as a distinct monastic religious community and registered itself as a new organization, in 1993, it remained a religious Movement, and claimed to be fully Roman Catholic in faith, tradition and ritual. However, the Catholic Church hierarchy in the Mbarara Diocese rejected the Marian reformist Movement, which it assessed and judged to be too radical, errant and heretical to be accepted. Nevertheless, the radical moral reformist Marian Movement aspired to be eventually accepted as a Benedictine monastic community within the Roman Catholic Church.

In short, the MRTCG promoted itself as a new "Marian Association" (*Ekigombe kya Bikira Maria)*, and not a new Church. The Marian Movement did not start a new church or sect, either within, or outside the Catholic Church. Consequently, the MRTCG both legally and functionally regarded itself, and also referred to itself, as a Catholic religious association (*Ekigombe)* for moral rehabilitation of the world, based on the teaching of the Ten Commandments of God. In the Runyankole-Rukiga, the official name of the Marian Movement was *"Ekigombe ky'Okujumura Ebiragiro Ikumi bya Ruhanga."*

3. The Movement as Mary's Association for Moral Crusade

The local African term *"Ekigombe"* ("Association" or "Organization"), rather than "Church," or "School," was chosen by the Marian Movement leaders to name and to identify their Marian Movement, and its main mission. "Association" (*Ekigombe*) was the ideal neutral political, religious, and social term for the new moral reformist Marian group. The term was carefully selected and employed to describe, and name the new religious association, or organization that could function, both within and outside the Catholic Church.[13]

"Mary's Movement" as "Association of Mary" (*Ekigombe kya Bikira Maria*) was the preferred name for the MRTCG by the leaders of the Marian Movement because it was shorter, more inclusive and flexible in both meaning and membership. It was unlike the term "Church," which traditionally brings to mind certain prescribed sectarian, social, and static ecclesiastical membership and religious roles in the community, and could mislead the people to believe that the Marian Movement was an official arm of the Catholic Church, and therefore, could not serve non-Catholics.

Therefore, the terms like "Movement" and "Association" were preferred, because they conveyed the idea that the MRTCG was a Catholic moral reformist Movement or Association, and yet, avoided being an official organization of the Catholic Church. At the same time, it also avoided becoming a mere secular organization, or a political liberation movement, like Alice Lakwena's *Holy Spirit Movement* (HSM) or Joseph Kony's armed *Lord's Resistance Army* (LRA) and the LRA's political wing, which is known as the *Lord's Resistance Movement* (LRM).

In contrast to the Lakwena's HSM's armed wing, which was called the *Holy Spirit Mobile Forces* (HSMF) LRA, or Kony's militant LRA, the MRTCG was completely pacifist. As a result, the term *"Ekigombe kya Maria"* (Mary's Association) was deliberate, since it implied that it was a nonviolent Catholic Marian Movement. The Marian Movement, as an association, proceeded to convince Catholics and others that it was for all God's obedient and penitent religious people, who desired to live a holy life based on God's moral Law as revealed and codified in the Ten Commandments. The Marian Movement also claimed that it had a well-defined, broad religious reformation, and moral education with a civic agenda, which had associated secular activities, in order to promote the Marian Movement's essential religious virtues, and noble social, educational, economic, and moral reform agenda.

However, the term *"Ekigombe"* was either for political reasons or erroneously translated into English as *"Movement."* Consequently, the English name for this "pietistic," "moral reformist," and "revivalist" Catholic Marian Association in Uganda is *"The Movement for the Restoration of the Ten Commandments of God."*

The term "Movement" implies that the new religious reformist, and revivalist Catholic Marian organization, was by nature non-static and evolutionary. That is, the Marian Movement consciously engaged in continuing processes of self-discovery, growth, expansion and change, while remaining within the Catholic Church. This is as opposed to the basic essence of *"Ekigombe"* (Organization), which tends to be static and have well-defined and firmly fixed objectives. As such, *Ekigombe* or an association is usually conservative and narrower in scope, when compared to a flexible and ever-growing and changing movement. It has the common characteristics of being firmly defined, set, rigid and static in its principles, teaching, structure and operations.

Consequently, the MRTCG preferred to name and describe itself as *"Ekigombe kya Bikira Maria"* (the Association of the Blessed Virgin Mary) because it wanted to convey that it was not a new Church. In addition, the term *"Ekigombe"* or association coveys the values of being more reliable and predictable modes of operation within socioeconomic, political and religious traditionally established confines of the Church, State and for the good of the community, as a whole. The term *"Ekigombe,"* is therefore, in direct contrast to the more flexible, fluid and transitory nature of "Movement." This is because most movements are flexible and transitory, whereas most "associations" are organizations, which have the common tendencies to become permanent, rigid, inflexible in their mission, unchanging in their teachings, or methods of doing things, and bureaucratic in structure, governance and operation.

It is conceivable that the term *"Ekigombe"* could have been, deliberately translated, as *"Movement,"* mainly for some expected beneficial political reasons. The "Movement" in the early 1990s, was already a very popular, inclusive religious and political term in Uganda. This was mainly due to the fact that President Yoweri Museveni and his *National Resistance Movement* (NRM) were still very popular, at that time. Like Gen. Idi Amin and his military before him, Gen. Museveni and his NRM were also joyfully welcomed and hailed as Uganda's economic, religious, military and political *"messiahs"* (deliverers).

In the case of the NRM, the term "Movement" had been constructively employed, as the most culturally meaningful, and appropriate, inclusive term to refer to the new politically, religiously and ethnically inclusive government, which they hoped to institute. Subsequently, the NRM Government had promised that it would promote regional integration, national reconciliation, harmony and peace.

As a result, many people in Uganda, President Museveni was positively welcomed and viewed, as a "religious and political messiah." This was also because President Museveni had initially rejected Uganda's destructive traditions and practices of ethnic divisions, bitter religious sectarianism and multi-party political systems based on destructive evils of:

- Religious divisions
- Exclusiveness
- Bigotry
- Intolerance
- Mutual hatred
- Ignorance

- Rivalry
- Sectarianism
- Religious hostility

- Extreme claims
- False prophets
- Religious violence.

Part of President Museveni's initial constructive solution for Uganda's tradition and history of both religious and political sectarianism, hate and intolerance was to establish a mass party Movement called the NRM (*National Resistance Movement*). In reality, the NRM was President Museveni's UPM (*Uganda People's Movement*), of 1980, which had failed to attract followers and supporters during the national elections. After five years of guerrilla warfare, Yoweri Museveni managed to overthrow President Milton Obote, whom he accused of having both wrongfully and illegally rigged the national elections that led to his terrible defeat at the ballot box, in 1980.

Ironically, the *Democratic Party* (DP) was the aggrieved party. But the DP politically cheated and wronged leaders were exemplary Christians, who were both law-abiding and peace-loving citizens. As a result, they did not resort to violence and war, like Yoweri Museveni, who's UPM, was largely unknown. As a result Museveni's UPM had attracted little political support among the politicians and the rural masses, in the country.

Nevertheless, the ambitious Museveni wanted to come into political power through the power of the "bullet," or the gun, since he could not do so, through the peaceful process of democracy and the "ballot" box, or national elections. Finally, in 1986, the Museveni's NRM, through force of arms, rather than national elections, won the right to rule Uganda. Yet, it had decried Presidents Amin and Obote's use of military force, and through intimidation, and military might, to rule Uganda, during the 1960s and 1970s. The NRM's military supremacy and political power were attained, by virtue of war, and the NRM's military victory, over its military rivals and political enemies. In a country, where violence, and military coups, had become common, most people accepted the rule of the person, who had the military support behind him.

However, in order to win true political legitimacy, the NRM wanted to co-opt every Ugandan citizen into its ranks. In this respect, NRM was a new code word, for Uganda's one inclusive mass political party, like Joseph Stalin's *Communist Party* in the former Soviet Union, that of Mao Tse Tung's mass communist movement in China, and President Julius Nyerere's *Chama Cha Mapinduzi* (Party of Change), which was another nationalist single mass socialist Party in Tanzania.

All these twentieth century's radical, political and cultural nationalist movements were either atheistic or antireligious sectarianism, as was the clear case for Nyerere's *Chama Cha Mapinduzi*. President Julius Nyerere did, such an outstanding, and excellent job, for both his party and country. As a whole, President Nyerere was highly esteemed and revered for being benevolent, upright, successful politician and great African intellectual and political theorist. He was both lovingly and reverently referred to, as *"Mwalimu"* (*"Rabbi,"* "Teacher" or "Professor), by his own people."

*Mwalimu (*Teacher or *Rabbi)* is a local *Swahili* title for a wise, knowledgeable, expert communicator, or professor/teacher. In this case, "Professor" may be a better translation of the title in the case of President Julius Nyerere, who was one of the best educated, articulate and most original African political, moral, social, and a philosophical thinker of the twentieth century. President Nyerere, along with President Kwame Nkrumah of Ghana had excellent and powerful articulation of Pan-Africanism, in their political writings and philosophies, which have guided much of Africa's pan-Africanist political philosophy. Milton Obote and his articulation of both African nationalism and protection of the poor were also well-articulated and formulated in his "Common Man's Charter."

Leopold Senghor is well-known for his articulation of philosophy in his concept of *Negritude*, which the African American scholars, Molefi Asante modified into "Afrocentrism." Nelson Mandela very effectively articulated his political views in his nationalist resistance movement to white-supremacy and apartheid, along with his political defense of the Africans' racial identity and human rights. Steve Biko, the South African political activist, thinker and political martyr had, also effectively, formulated the concept of Black consciousness, which the radical Black American Stockley Carmichael reformulated into *"Black Power."*

Radical Black Liberation theologians, like James Cone modified "Black Consciousness," and "Black Power" into the radical "Black Liberation Theology." These radical Black philosophies, theologies and ideologies were a further development, and expansion of WEB DuBois' original philosophy of Pan-Africanism, and concepts of the African American, as a person of "double consciousness," especially as articulated in the Souls of Black Folks.

During the period of White-supremacy, and apartheid in South Africa, 1948-1992, Nelson Mandela inspired the oppressed and degraded Black Africans in South Africa to believe that they were created, as true equals of Whites. Later, President Yoweri Museveni, of Uganda, another modern Pan-Africanist effectively formulated, and articulated, the need for a united Africa, beginning with East Africa.

President Museveni also implemented an effective grassroots mass and direct participatory democracy, as the real exercise of a constitutional people's direct mass political power, and the effective political participation in the processes of mass democratic governance. President Museveni's NRM Government of Uganda was based on a direct mass political participation, unhindered, by alliances and restrictions of sectarian political multi-parties.

To his credit, President Museveni modernized Uganda's economy. He accomplished this difficult task by formulating and implementing new economic policies for the liberalization of the currency, and economy, so as to attract the badly needed foreign investments and businesses. These progressive African presidents and thinkers are some excellent examples of the African political, social, philosophical and moral thinkers.

Nevertheless, Julius Nyerere towered over these African moral, philosophical and political thinkers. He was unequaled as an original political thinker, social and political activist for peace, and leader of Pan-Africanism and unity.

To this end, President Nyerere championed the liberation of South Africa and Uganda, from tyrannical governments, which had grossly abused human rights, and oppressed the majority of the citizens. He also lived a simple exemplary life that was devoid of greed, materialism and corruption, as those that have characterized the lives of most African political leaders and their subordinates, such as the former heads of states, like Mobutu of Zaire, Gen. Babangida of Nigeria, Idi Amin of Uganda, Arap Moi of Kenya and Charles Taylor of Liberia.

As a direct result of these mass political parties, and patriotic national political movements, these diverse nations and empires were forged into meaningful nations that more effectively tackled the serious problems of poverty, centralized national economic strategic planning, industrialization, policy formulation and coordination for both urban and rural area development.

Consequently, the former Soviet Union, China and Tanzania, were forged into great patriotic empires, and politically viable nations, despite their inherent regional divisive factors, and sectarian problems arising out of the great ethnic diversity of the various respective regional constituent ethnic groups. This is in addition to the inherent disintegrating factors of both cultural nationalism and religious pluralism. As such, they are positive forces of true and mature political nationalism. Nationalism can lead to the development of a true national identity, which can be used to forge national unity that transcends the local problems of parochialism and divisiveness, such as "tribalism," "ethnic or cultural sub-nationalism," religious and political sectarianism.

President Yoweri Museveni's NRM, as a new inclusive movement, and similar movements, or any religiously and ethnically inclusive political parties are positive, and national unitive forces to be both commended and nurtured, by mature politicians and well-informed citizens, who value mass democracy and national unity.

Therefore, the more inclusive national political movements and parties are great political assets for the empire-builders, and autocratic rulers, such as: the ancient Roman emperors, divine kings and dictators, like Idi Amin and Adolf Hitler, who terrorized Europe in the twentieth century, with his notorious German nationalistic, intolerant, and violent white-supremacist movement, in the form of the Nazi Party.

Characteristically and ominously, the radical kinds of political and religious movements, some of which are cited above, were responsible for the tragic deaths of millions of people, who were considered hostile outsiders, traitors or enemies of the movement. Enemies of the movement could, include some dissatisfied insiders and members of the movement, who may prefer a radical revolution, instead of a slowly changing movement, or an evolutionary one.

Just like the French Revolution in the nineteenth century, French revolutionaries found many of its perceived enemies both within the aristocratic ruling class, and within the movement, or the revolution's own ranks. They arrested these perceived enemies, summarily tried and sent them to a humiliating public execution, by means of the guillotine. Likewise, the modern African religious and political movement leaders often became paranoid and suspected that many people both within and inside their respective movements and organizations, were trying to do them harm or depose them.

Therefore, many political, military, religious and movement leaders also tended to find both imaginary and real enemies, or spies and traitors both outside and inside their respective movements, or their religious, military, or political party systems. After all, was it not Judas, as an insider, who actually monitored, sold and betrayed Jesus, his own master, teacher and friend? Or wasn't it Peter, one of Jesus' own inner circle of friends and disciples that denied knowing him three times?

Maybe, the paranoid leaders of new or radical movements have real reasons to be suspicious of some people, both within and outside their own movements. Many of them may have acceptable reasons to take measures to protect themselves from possibilities of political assassination, betrayal by their close associates due to envy, and even possibilities of malicious misrepresentation, in the public media by jealous rivals, or blackmail by jilted lovers and greedy opportunists.

4. Movements and Temptations of Power

Messianic or liberationist leaders and their liberation movements, often start off as noble, benevolent, moral purists, and idealistic political liberationists, or utopian religious reformers. But eventually, most of them become corrupted by temptations of power, pride, fame and wealth, once they succeed in coming to power. In some extreme cases, the liberators tragically become the new evil and hated oppressors of the very people they had come to liberate. This phenomenon was observed by Lord Acton (1834-1902), who correctly observed that every class of people is imperfect and unfit to rule since people are tempted and corrupted, by greed for profit and power. As a result, he warned us that "power corrupts, and absolute power corrupts absolutely."[14]

President Yoweri Museveni's *National Resistance Movement*, and both Kibwetere and Mwerinde's *Movement for the Restoration of the Ten Commandments of God,* were not going to become major exceptions to this tendency for the compulsive leaders of political and cultural mass movements, to become paranoid, isolationist, corrupt and repressive. They were also resentful of change and outside criticisms. Both of them became violent to those considered dangerous traitors, enemies of the movement, and the people, who dared to question the movement's validity or legitimacy. Therefore, in this manner, the critics were negatively perceived, as dangerous people to be either resisted or "neutralized." They were considered to be a threat to the Movement's fundamental identity, mission and the Movement's continued normal activities and survival.

Consequently, like the ruthless and murderous President Idi Amin of Uganda, Stalin, Mao and Hitler were completely ruthless in dealing with both their real and perceived opponents and enemies. They had them arrested, tortured and executed, or assassinated. George Orwell's *Animal Farm,* as a political satire, very successfully captured the essence of this moral and political degeneration that most political, cultural, religious and economic revolutions go through. The liberators turn into the new oppressors to be liberated from and likewise, reformations turn into new rigid establishments, in which the reformers become like the leaders of the past whom they had denounced. This process of establishment and corruption of most revolutionary leaders and their initial redemptive mission, and messages of liberation, may indiscriminately apply both to political and religious messianic figures and liberators or reformers.

General Napoleon Bonaparte (1769-1821) had crowned himself the emperor of France in 1804, at the *National Convention*. The governing body of the *French Revolution* (1789-1815), had abolished the monarchy on

September 21, 1792. Many of the *French Revolution*'s ideals rooted within the new important humanistic ideals and principles of *"Fraternity," "Liberty"* and *"Equality"* also fell, by the wayside as the French Republic became the French Empire. The *French Revolution*'s three initial fundamental political and moral principles are antithetical to the very political and moral ideals for the original establishment and functioning of France, as an empire. Empires and kingdoms were traditionally non-democratic. They were autocratic by nature and are political and military operational structures, and efficient functioning.

Similarly, most of the former Soviet Union leaders, especially Joseph Stalin, and other African self-proclaimed national liberators, such as Idi Amin and Yoweri Museveni, are good examples of this scenario of corruption, and betrayal of their original revolutionary ideals. They serve as examples of the leaders, who betrayed the people that had previously enthusiastically welcomed them, as God-sent liberators and messiahs.

This is especially true if these leaders had been either invited, or welcomed because of their own initial declarations of noble moral, economic and political principles for the liberation of the Nation and its citizens from the supposed evil dictators that had oppressed them; abused human rights and killed thousands of helpless, unarmed and innocent people. For instance, Gen. Idi Amin overthrew President Milton Obote and promised fair national elections, democracy and respect for human rights. Instead, he broke all these promises and established one of the most repressive and murderous regimes in modern world history.

However, instead of holding the promised national elections to elect a president, General Idi Amin, promoted himself to the rank of Field Marshall; and then, he declared himself both the Conqueror of the British Empire and the Life-President of the Republic of Uganda.

Likewise, Yoweri Museveni came into power, as "a social democrat." But instead of establishing socialism, he established the most capitalist liberal economy in Africa. President Museveni's NRM *(National Resistance Movement)* Government sold off the state factories and privatized public banks, communication and transportation systems. The rich became even richer, by buying state owned companies below cost and extremely cheaply, whereas the poor became even poorer.

Similarly, therefore, if one extends the above analysis to apply to both Joseph and Keledonia Mwerinde, as the charismatic and messianic leaders of *The Movement for the Restoration of the Ten Commandments of God*, the same process of corruption of the leadership and their message should apply. The religious acceptance of this reality means that Joseph Kibwetere and Keledonia Mwerinde would become the MRTCG's equivalent of bishops and infallible popes, whose declarations were to be accepted, by their followers, as God's revealed truth, without any questioning or hesitation.

This inherent corrupting universal process of movements to strive for public recognition, legitimacy, legalization, self-institutionalization and establishment leads to the characteristic universal correlative moderation and corruption of movements, revolutions, and reformations, as they become established and conservative institutions.

Inevitably, all idealistic political, economic, moral and religious reformist movements, or revolutions eventually get corrupted. They also lose their own original vision, inner driving moral force (energy) and spiritual power. In this eventual process, they compromise their original radical political, economic mission, vision or agenda, as the high price paid, in order to become a recognized and legally accepted organization in the community. The Marian Movement originally consciously decided to resist this corrupting process. This was also a result of the Mbarara bishops' hard-line and condemnation of their claims of their cherished Marian visions, special revelations and monastic teachings.

Instead of being co-opted, reintegrated and corrupted by the traditional Catholic Church, the Movement leaders deliberately chose, both administratively and ecclesiastically, to remain on the fringes of the Catholic Church. This decision was carried out by the Marian Movement leaders in order to safeguard the Movement's religious freedom, radical, and the reformist, moral and religious teachings, to heal diseases, live freely in a holy monastic community and worship in a Pre-Vatican II liturgical manner.

The Marian Movement leaders realized that the MRTCG's full institutionalization process would have included the rejection of the Marian Movement's central religious dogmatic declaration that Mary was God and the Co-Redeemer of the world with God, the Father, and the Son. It would have also meant the rejection of the Marian Movement's new definitive revelation from God, through the Blessed Virgin Mary, as mediated to them, that the world would tragically end at the clothing of 1999, or the beginning of the year 2000.[15]

The apocalypse and timing for the end of the world in God's punitive and cleansing heavenly fire and by other horrible disasters that would be unleashed by God as punishment for sin, disobedience and breaking God's moral Law and the Ten Commandments. The MRTCG's official publications indicated that the actual time of God's own choosing (*Kairos*). This divine decision to end the world was supposed to be based on God's holiness and justice as they operated in relation to human evil and sins. At the beginning, the MRTCG leaders were tentative on the actual date for the end of the world by God since it seemed to depend on how the people responded to God's message of warning, pleas for repentance of their sins of rebellion which were made through God's agents or Mary's Apostles, and their decisions to observe the Ten Commandments of God.[16]

5. George Orwell's Animal Farm Scenario

George Orwell's observations and satire in *Animal Farm*, when the animals led by the pigs overthrew Mr. Jones the farm owner, and took-over the running of the farm for animals' welfare and economic benefits, eventually became the "pigs' farm," were filled with great political satire and insight into future political affairs of many nations.

Orwell's descriptions the pigs dynamics and dictatorship and how they cleverly manipulated the other animals to support their autocratic rule and ownership of the farm, were accurate prophecies for what happened in the former Soviet Union and Uganda under the autocratic power and dictatorships of President Milton Obote in the 1960s, President Idi Amin in the 1970 and President Yoweri Museveni since 1986. For instance, like President Idi Amin, President Museveni would, finally, become oppressive, like President Obote and Idi Amin, and like them.

Furthermore, like President Amin sought to remain in office for life and autocratically declared himself the Life-President of Uganda, President Museveni has also sought to remain in the office beyond the constitutional term of office, as was clearly stated in the 1995 Constitution of Uganda. That strategy may be achieved more politically by unlimited successive five year terms that are ratified by the people, through regular national presidential elections, each five years.

In this manner, President Museveni's political strategy for life presidency is a more democratic and politically acceptable method for most Ugandan rural masses. This is as opposed to the President Idi Amin's crude method, when he asked his military supporters and friends to propose that he should be declared the "Life-President of Uganda."

Subsequently, speaking on behalf of the Uganda's military, Lt. Col. Sule declared, to the disbelieving people of Uganda, on June 25, 1975, that Uganda's Army had decided to elevate and appoint Field Marshal President Idi Amin Dada of Uganda, to the new permanent status of "The Life President of the Republic of Uganda."

The Government of Uganda, being a military government at the time, and President Amin, being the military appointee as Military President of Uganda, was in itself unconstitutional and made a mockery of democracy and the constitution. As a result, he suspended the constitution and ruled the country by his own devised military decrees. It demonstrated that in Uganda, a military general can become the Nation's president by virtue of being the popular military leader of the Ugandan military. This new undemocratic politics rooted in the military culture and use of military coercion to implement political unilateral decisions by the president, rendered powerless and irrelevant all the deeply cherished democratic institutions, multiparty politics, human rights, elections, the Constitution and due process.

Many Ugandans were terribly disillusioned and felt betrayed by President Idi Amin, who had come to power in Uganda by means of a military coup, on January 25, 1971, which toppled President Dr. Milton Obote with high-sounding promises of freedom, prosperity, democracy, justice and peace had actually failed to provide them. Instead, he had transformed Uganda into an Islamic military dictatorship, and persecuted Christians. President General Idi Amin's political promises included the establishment of true democracy and new national elections for the new President and members of the national Parliament.

Many Ugandan people, especially the politically marginalized Catholics and most disgruntled Baganda nationalists, who hated President Obote for having abolished the monarchies and their most prized Kingdom of Buganda in 1967, had most enthusiastically welcomed Gen. Idi Amin's military coup, and had naively believed all his political promises, until they realized that they had been fooled and that President Idi Amin had no intention of restoring their ancient kingdom, or opening the Ugandan political process for multiparty politics and elections of Uganda's President and members of the Parliament.

The Catholics, who were numerically the majority in Uganda, and yet, had been politically marginalized because they had lost the religio-political war in 1892 to the Anglicans, had truly hoped to gain political power through a national democratic process, and to reverse their political fate and economic fortunes. They had most eagerly hoped to revive the *Democratic Party* (DP) and win the national elections for both President and the majority of the members of Uganda Parliament.

Interestingly, President Museveni had to some major and considerable satisfactory degree fulfilled many of these Ugandan expectations. But to the dissatisfaction of many enthusiastic political federalists, especially the extreme cultural ethnocentric Baganda, President Museveni had restored the monarchies and kingdoms, as mere politically powerless cultural institutions.

This political process of the restoration of monarchies as mere cultural institutions in Uganda was not acceptable to all special interest groups in Uganda. Some people, especially the Catholics in Ankole Kingdom, wanted the kingdoms and monarchies permanently banished, from Uganda's political and cultural life, because they were traditionally dominated by the

Anglican kings, chiefs and their political supporters. This royalist Anglican political hegemony was non-democratic. But African hereditary monarchical institutions, were by tradition divinely instituted and therefore, traditional kings, only answered to God.

Therefore, the traditional kings in Uganda reluctantly accepted the power and control of the Central Government. This was especially true for Edward King Mutesa II of Buganda Kingdom. As a result he was twice deposed or exiled from his kingdom, first in 1953 and again, on May 24, 1966. In 1966, King Mutesa fled into exile in England following a failed political and military secession attempt by the Kingdom of Buganda.

It was this second secession attempt that led the enraged Dr. Milton Obote, the Executive Prime Minister and Head of State to abolish the kingdoms in Uganda. He declared Uganda to be a republic, transformed the position of the executive Prime Minister into a new position of an executive President and Head of State.

Subsequently, President Yoweri Museveni restored Uganda's traditional kingdoms, on July 14, 1993. But, since Uganda remained a republic, President Museveni restored the ancient monarchies as mere cultural institutions. The kings were returned to their thrones without real political, military and taxation powers, which they had exercised in the past era. The Baganda were happy to have their beloved institution of the monarchy restored.

At the same time, the Baganda were still not satisfied with their monarchy, as a mere cultural institution. They wanted the *Kabaka* (or the King of Buganda), the monarch of the most powerful and wealthy kingdom in Uganda, to be accorded the former glory and political power of the past British colonial era, in which the Kingdom of Buganda had a true political federal status in Uganda. They also remained opposed to the proposed East African federation because they realized that they would lose their own ethnic political dominance and quest for their own political self-determination, as a federal monarchy in Uganda, rather than, in East Africa.

The newly restored cultural monarchies were impoverished and powerless institutions. They existed negatively in contrast and opposition to the pre-1967 status of monarchies and kingdoms in Uganda, as powerful Anglican political institutions with real power and taxation privileges. President Museveni also restored democracy as a mass participation process where people would be nominated, stand for office and be voted for without the benefit of traditional political parties, such as DP and UPC that had become religious and almost synonymous to divisive sectarian religious denominations, namely, Roman Catholicism and British Anglicanism, respectively.

However, although the NRM is another military Government of Uganda, it is unlike former President Idi Amin's military government and reign of terror, in Uganda, 1971-1979. Unlike the semi-illiterate Gen. Idi Amin, a Muslim extremist, who wanted to transform Uganda into a Muslim country, through Christian persecution and mass murders of political enemies, especially the Anglican Christian politicians, since they were associated with the traditional Anglican political hegemony in the country.

President Amin also persecuted educators and religious leaders, President Yoweri Museveni is better educated, Christian and humane. He is a university graduate with a degree in economic and political science from the University of Dar-Salaam. To some significant degree, President Museveni respects the Constitution,[17] the rule of law and the democratic processes. For instance, he was one of the first African presidents to allow a free press and to liberalize the economy, including the unlimited access and possession of foreign currency.

Nevertheless, these freedoms of speech, the press and freedoms of religion, as well as the correlative democratic political processes, liberal economic and human rights, were honored by President Museveni, as long as he liked them. Like the deposed former Presidents Idi Amin (1979) and Milton Obote (1985), President Museveni, too had little tolerance for political opposition. As a result, President Museveni became like other African political dictators, who did not care for the constitutional processes, when they put a limit to their presidential power, or limited their term in office.

Characteristic of most African tyrant and autocratic "life-presidents," like President Mobutu, Emperor Bokassa, Idi Amin, and Robert Mugabe, President Museveni resisted the 1995 Constitution, which limited his terms of office to only two consecutive terms. In this respect, President Museveni was like President Obote, who abolished the multi-party system in order to remain in political power. Ironically, because of his love for power and its associated economic benefits, President Yoweri Museveni also became like President Idi Amin, who was a Military Head of State of Uganda, who declared himself the Life-President of Uganda, because he also wanted to remain in political power, and unopposed.

Amid great political and religious leaders' protests and accusations of corruption, dictatorship, hubris and unconstitutional desire for life-presidency, like Gen. Idi Amin before him, President Museveni initiated the legal and political processes to amend the Constitution of 1995, which mandated limitations of the presidential terms of office to two elected terms of five years each, when these terms in office were consecutive. But he cherished the Constitution, as long as it did not promote religious and tribal sectarianism, division, intolerance and lead to the kind of religious and political violence that prevailed in the Kingdom of Buganda, in 1885-1892 and the rest of Uganda 1958-1966. The 1995 Constitution was carefully designed, to serve as a political antidote to both religious and ethnic sectarian-based multiparty politics, and their correlated destructive forms of bigotry, intolerance, hate, division, or sectarianism and violence.

However, instead of the promised new government of ethnic, political and religious inclusiveness, and national reconciliation, President Museveni has presided over a nation torn by those evils. His government has been characterized by serious ethnic conflicts and religious strife. These tensions have erupted in prolonged destructive ethnic wars and religious tensions, especially in Northern and Western Uganda. Joseph Kony's *Lord's Resistance Army* (LRA), was initially an ethnic *Luo* Catholic-based rural political resistance of the *Acholi* to the Southern *Bantu* dominated NRM Government.

Like Alice Lakwena's HSM, Kony's LRA originally attracted the religiously and economically marginalized rural Catholic peasants and the unemployed former soldiers in Northern Uganda. They were the disenfranchised religio-political ethnic groups and poorly educated Catholics fighting for more political power, religious self-actualization and economic inclusion. At first, the HSMF and LRA sought political inclusion and later, having despaired about the success of a meaningful power sharing, decided the NRM Government was the embodiment of the Devil and oppression.

Therefore, the Devil had to be completely fought overcome in order to get ride of his evil incarnations and manifestations in the world, beginning with Uganda. In order to overthrow of President Museveni, as the LRA's main perceived evil incarnation and agent of the Devil, Kony believed that he had to attack and destroy him along with his supposed evil UPDF (*Uganda People's Defense Forces*) troops and repressive military NRM Government. The Luo people, especially the Catholic members of the HSFM and LRA, accused President Museveni and his NRM Government of being:

- Religiously and ethnically sectarian
- Illegitimate, being originally self-imposed on the Ugandan people for having come into power, through war, in 1986
- Completely corrupt in all its ranks and operations
- Immoral and stealing from the public funds and individuals
- Paranoid and suspicious of Catholics and non-Bantu people, especially in the military
- Evil as the manifestation of the Devil and incarnations of evil spirits to be both exorcized and destroyed in the name of God to cleanse the land
- Repressive, especially to the non-Bantu people of Northern and Eastern Uganda

- Tyrannical
- Completely brutal; murderous of both real and imaginary enemies.[18]

President Museveni has sought to accomplish his own political agenda, including that of an apparent "Life President" through a more enlightened political and legal procedure with tactful political pressure on the Uganda Parliament and his Cabinet to amend the Constitution of 1995, in order to remove the limitation of the President's term of office from two consecutive terms of five years to infinity. That is, a real Life-President, in as much as he, or she is continually reelected to the presidential office. This is possible, as long as the NRM is in control of Uganda, and President Museveni remains its President, and the UPDF's real military Commander in Chief.

Theoretically, the NRM was, also an inclusive national political party, which included all the citizens of Uganda, regardless of political party, religious affiliation and ethnicity. As such, the term "Movement" already carried this heavy political and religious baggage. It was chosen because it would make it easier for the Ugandan Government to view the new organization, as a benign, inclusive, religio-social organization. Faced with corruption, vices of theft and robbery, such an organization dedicated to preaching respect and observation of the Ten Commandments of God was bound to be warmly welcomed.

6. Keledonia Mwerinde's Conversion And Transformed Mode of Life

The notorious sinner's religious conversion, or repentance and subsequent complete transformation of life are not unique to Keledonia Mwerinde. Mary Magdalene was converted from a life of prostitution to that of a Christian saint, and Saul was converted from a life of Christian persecutor to that of Christian Apostle and missionary. These are some examples chosen from the New Testament to illustrate how true religious conversions may lead to a complete new mode of life and a new set of moral values. These biblical stories clearly show how a notorious sinner, or an evil person, can actually repent of evil ways of life, or his or her sins and become God's new, reformed and obedient saint and servant in the world.

However, the main problem remains how to devise an effective strategy for missionary activities, in order to convert the sinners in the world, and reform them into God's saints. Yet, to accomplish this noble task without scaring them with God's unquenchable and catastrophic apocalyptic hellfire, like the MRTCG leaders did.

Unlike in Islam, and some fundamentalist forms of Christianity, scare tactics are not considered by some well-informed Christian thinkers as appropriate Christian tools and missionary strategies, or evangelistic methods to be employed by God's truly loving and compassionate, Christian missionaries and servants, in order to accomplish God's work. Nevertheless, many Catholics, Evangelicals and Muslims employ scare tactics as part of preaching to sinners in order to frighten them into repentance, due to fear and dread of hellfire.

Some varying versions of Dante's *Inferno* are verbally reproduced or illustrated as part of the sermon so as to frighten people into repentance and thereby accomplish their religious divine mission for the redemption of sinners in the world. This is because for true Christianity, as originally proclaimed by Jesus as the Christ, God is essentially a Loving, Compassionate, and Forgiving heavenly Parent, who should be loved and worshipped because of his unconditional love, unmerited redemptive grace, free forgiveness of sins, and goodness, rather than to be feared as a merciless heavenly Judge, or to be merely worshipped out of fear (Matt. 5-7).

Once fear is gone, then, the people who believed in God, or did good works, primarily due to the fear of God, or to avoid present and future, or the apocalyptic divine retribution and punishment, eventually become godless skeptics, humanistic and scornful atheists.

Therefore, the traditional Evangelicals, or the American Southern Baptist-like, who preach God's "fire and brimstone," or threatening people with hellfire, like the MRTCG did, in order to convert the rebellious and corrupt sinners in the world, or to scare them into repentance, is a counterproductive and bad missionary strategy. This missionary or preaching method relies on ignorance, inducing guilt, and religious emotion, especially the fear for fire in hell or anxiety concerning divine judgment and eternal damnation.

Subsequently, most results of this negative Christian missionary approach, theology and preaching are negative. In most cases, the positive results, such as the joys of emotional religious conversions, do not last long. In some cases, these religious emotional feelings are transitory or temporary experiences, which need regular reinforcements. This is the one of the reasons why the Evangelical preachers and Catholic priests continually reinforced by calls to repent or undergo regular confessions. In extreme cases the preachers resort to God's threats of torture in hellfire, excommunication and damnation of sinners, who fail to repent and observe the Commandments of God.

As such, the MRTCG failed to devise more loving missionary strategies for effectively preaching God's messages of salvation, and converting evil people, in the world, and leading them to a positive divine transformation of life, like that which was experienced by Mary Magdalene, Paul, Constantine,

Augustine and Mwerinde, among others. They all testified that their own lives were positively transformed because of their experience of the encounter with the loving God, in Christ, rather than being threatened with divine justice, judgment and torture in hellfire. The fear of God does not produce a true love of God and peace in the sinner or worshippers of God. This was one of the major weaknesses in the teaching of the Marian Movement and life within its holy, silent and contemplative monastic community.

Despite some religious skeptics, Mwerinde's religious experience of conversion was real and transforming. Ursula Komuhangi, her sister, was one of the first people to realize that Keledonia Mwerinde was really spiritually and morally transformed, and indeed, a new person. Subsequently, Komuhangi became Mwerinde's first convert and member of the MRTCG. This occurred, when Mwerinde repented and obeyed the Marian apparitions and Mary's directives to become her messenger (Messiah and Voice of revelation and instruction) and the new apocalyptic divine instrument of God's salvation through the Blessed Virgin Mary in the world. In obedience, Mwerinde began her new life and divine ministry of preaching and calling other sinners like her to repent, come back to God and live a new holy life of moral and spiritual reformation based on the strict observation of the Ten Commandments of God.

In order to demonstrate her transformed life and piety to her fellow Roman Catholics, Mwerinde tried to display and communicate to them of her own inner, deep religious and moral conversion, by borrowing the religious language and symbols of the *Balokole* with which they were familiar. But being Catholic and speaking to Catholics, Mwerinde also had to speak and testify to them in the familiar Catholic language of devotion to the Blessed Virgin Mary and sacramental prayer.

Accordingly, Mwerinde had to use the most familiar and effective Catholic symbols, in order to accomplish this religious task most effectively, meaningfully and relevant within the Catholic context. Subsequently, she had both tried to formulate her spiritual experience in understandable concrete images and to express her conversion in those concrete religious Marian images and metaphors of her visions of the Blessed Virgin Mary to the rural Catholic masses.

Mwerinde also wanted to publicly prove the validity of her new and supernaturally transformed religious life to her fellow Roman Catholics, especially those in Kanungu in the Makiro Parish and the neighboring areas of Rugyeyo, Kambuga and Nyakishenyi. This was important because some of these local people had known her before her life-transforming religious conversion as another beer-seller and prostitute in Kanungu.

Consequently, Mwerinde's conversion and correlative transformed life, were miracles for the people with faith to see, believe and accept by faith. It was only through faith that these Marian events and claims could be accepted as God's redemptive works and revelations in the world. But for skeptics, they were regarded as clever forms of deception, in order to access wealth, or positions in the community that would lead to some religious benefits, or appointment to leadership positions that would lead to possibilities of future economic gain, or prestige, such as a pastor, in the cases of the *Balokole*.

Being dissatisfied with Gauda Kamushwa's Nyabugoto Marian Prayer Group, in Nyakishenyi, and desiring to found their own more global Marian Movement in August 1988, Keledonia Mwerinde and Ursula Komuhangi, her sister and loyal convert, went to Mbarara, in order to testify and preach their new revelations and messages to the Church and the world. Mbarara, rather than nearby Kabale, was the chosen destination and focus of their missionary task to convert Catholics to the veneration of the Blessed Virgin Mary, who required, a new strict moral, holiness, religious and political code based on the strict obedience of the Ten Commandments of God.

Mbarara was considered ideal for this task since it was the main center of Roman Catholicism in Southern and Western Uganda. However, since Mwerinde did not know the people in Mbarara, she looked for Joseph Kibwetere to assist her with accommodation, finances, transportation, preaching her Marian message and communication of her visions of the Blessed Virgin Mary to the traditional and conservative patriarchal Catholic Church and its hierarchy, in Mbarara. Kibwetere knew the bishops and the influential priests in Mbarara and Mwerinde did not. Therefore, Keledonia Mwerinde, as the Blessed Virgin's prophetess and servant, converted and appointed Joseph Kibwetere co-prophet and co-leader to her Marian Movement. She outlined to him her own religious ideas, visions of the Blessed Virgin Mary, and her being commissioned by the Blessed Virgin Mary, to preach her messages of salvation, repentance, and moral reformation to the male dominated Church, patriarchal society and world.

NOTES

1. The women, including Keledonia Mwerinde, were impressed by Joseph Kibwetere's devotion to the Blessed Virgin Mary, great knowledge, innovative ideas, wisdom, and personal wealth. Kibwetere advised these pious Catholic women and devotees of the Blessed Virgin Mary to form a formal association of Mary, and more effectively promote the

Nyabugoto Holy Mountain site and attract both pilgrims and tourists. Later, Mwerinde went to look for him to form a partnership in forming and running these women's Marian organization. Ultimately, Mwerinde converted Kibwetere to her Marian Movement and moral crusade. Eventually, Mwerinde transformed Kibwetere into her puppet, as well as her economic and administrative resource to fund and run her Marian Movement. Mrs. Theresa Kibwetere believed that Mwerinde "bewitched him." This was disclosed in an interview on August 3, 2003. Also see: Henri E. Cauvin, "Fateful Meeting Led to the Founding of the Cult [MRTCG] in Uganda," *The New York Times*, March, 2000; Matthias Mugisha, "Visions of Mary Started Cult: Joseph Kibwetere came with two trembling nuns and converted the Nyabugoto cult to his sect," Weekend Vision, *The New Vision,* Friday, March 24, 2000.

2. Keledonia Mwerinde and Ursala Komuhangi found Joseph Kibwetere at Nyamitanga Cathedral, where he had come to see Mwerinde. Kibwetere came to Mbarara, having heard the news that she was looking for him at the command of the vision of the Blessed Virgin Mary, and told him that he had been chosen and anointed by God through the Blessed Virgin Mary to help her to spread the revelations of God and the Virgin Mary concerning repentance, prayer, piety, good works and keeping the Ten Commandments of God.

Kibwetere welcomed Mwerinde and Komuhangi, and took them to his home in Kabumba, which became the first center of the Movement's activities until Mrs. Theresa Kibwetere and her sons got too distressed and fed up with the Marian Movement, and their unwelcome guests. Subsequently, Mrs. Theresa Kibwetere physically evicted them, and drove out the hundreds of Marian Movement members, along with her husband, in 1992.

See: James Mujuni, "Who is Joseph Kibwetere?" *The New Vision*, Wednesday, March 22, 2000; Henri E. Cauvin, "Fateful Meeting Led to Founding of the Cult [MRTCG] in Uganda," *New York Times*, March, 2000; Matthias Mugisha, "Visions of Mary Started Cult: Joseph Kibwetere Came with Two Trembling Nuns and Converted the Nyabugoto Cult to his Sect," Weekend Vision, *The New Vision,* Friday, March 24, 2000.

It is significant to note that Matthias Mugisha wrongly assumed that it was Joseph Kibwetere, rather than Keledonia Mwerinde, who founded the Marian Movement, which became known as: *The Movement for the Restoration of the Ten Commandments of God.* Mugisha's article is both inaccurate and prejudiced since he refers to the Nyabugoto Marian Prayer Group as the "Nyabugoto Cult" and refers to the MRTCG, which was not yet founded as a religious "sect." The poorly informed outsiders treated these kinds of erroneous and prejudiced misrepresentations of the Marian Movement as "a cult" and the MRTCG, as a Catholic sect, as true facts.

3. *See: A Timely Message from Heaven*, 72-99; Matthias Mugisha and James Mujuni, "Kataribabo with his Doctorate in Theology, was the Brain behind the Cult's Liturgy: The Priest Who Became a Killer," People: *The New Vision*, Monday, April 3, 2000. Fr. Ikazire points out that the Catholic Church in Mbarara was corrupt and they joined the Movement in order to renew and reform it. They failed in their mission because the Catholic Church hierarchy in Mbarara was ready to use its power to persecute, silence and squash dissent.

4. *A Timely Message from Heaven*, 1-21, 67-98.

5. Mrs. Annet Karooro in interview, on May 30, 2001. The Marian Movement leaders called their Kanungu headquarters: *"Ishayuriro rya Maria"* (Mary's Centre of Salvation). See *A Timely Message from Heaven*, inside the cover page.

6. These Marian devotees deified the Blessed Virgin Mary as God and really worshiped her, as God, in the same way some Christians worship Jesus, her son, as both their Christ (Messiah) and God.

7. The testimony of Fr. Chris Busingye, Makiro Parish priest, Kanungu. An Interview, on July 30, 2003. However, Bishop John Wilson Ntegyereize preached against the Movement's

apocalyptic theology, collective living, in celibate monastic communities, vow of poverty and economic ethic of self-sacrifice by selling personal possessions. Ultimately, Bishop Ntegyereize did not want the Anglican *Balokole* to be attracted to the pietistic, moral reform, Catholic Marian Movement.

8. Fr. Betungura's strong anti-Movement of Mary declaration took place, in the course of an interview, and research for this book. It was a typical example of the Catholic Church's official hostility that was directed to the MRTCG leaders and their followers. *Interviewed: June 16, 03, in Buziga, Kampala, Uganda*. Archbishop Paul Bakyenga almost felt the same way. But, he was more diplomatic than Fr. Bentungura.

9. See *A Timely Message from Heaven*, 1-3, 21, 67-98, 157-163.

10. Loyola University at Marymount in California awarded Fr. Kataribabo a Masters Degree in Religious Studies and Education, in 1987. However, there were no more records of another award of an earned doctoral degree.

11. Statements made during an interview with Bishop Kakubi, at his retirement home, in Kagongo, on August 17, 2004. Bishop Kakubi had also communicated similar information to the members of his diocese, 1991-1995.

12. See *A Timely Message from Heaven*, 65.

13. *A Timely Message from Heaven*, 1-21, 67-98. The Movement was not a new sect, new religion or new church. It was a Reform Marian Movement within a hostile Roman Catholic Church that sought to drive it out.

14. That warning has been especially true for Napoleon, Adolf Hitler, Joseph Stalin, Gen. Idi Amin, Gen. Mobutu Sese Seko, Robert Mugabe, and President Yoweri Museveni and his NRM Government in Uganda.

15. *A timely Message from Heaven*, # 57: 54; #71: 61.

16. *A Timely Message from Heaven*, # 71:61.

17. President Idi Amin abolished the Constitution of 1967, which abolished traditional kingdoms in Uganda. But he did not restore the kingdoms. Instead, he ruled by military decree. President Museveni had the Constitution of 1995 formulated. The new Constitution effectively restored the former kingdoms of Uganda with the monarchs serving as mere cultural leaders. The Baganda monarchists resented the loss of their original political power.

The 1995 Constitution also limited the president's term of office to two terms of five years each if elected in a national election both times. But in 2004, President Museveni had the Constitution amended to allow him unlimited terms in office. Gen. Idi Amin had declared himself Life-President of Uganda, President Museveni appeared to be doing the same. There was great protest by both the Church leaders and the leaders of opposition parties, like Dr. Kizza Besigye of the Uganda Reform Party, who gained international attention, for being unjustly arrested and jailed, in 2004 and 2005 by President Museveni.

18. A record based on my interviews of many people chosen at random. However, these interviews included some selected leading Catholic Church bishops and priests. These views include those of the Archbishop Cardinal Emmanuel Wamala, interviewed several times, over a period of seven years, beginning in December 1999.

Chapter Seven

MARY'S MORAL REFORM MOVEMENT AND CATHOLIC CHURCH HOSTILITY

The Roman Catholic Church is traditionally conservative and cautious in both politics and the acceptance of new cultural and religious changes. This is more the case in Africa, where the cultures are more traditionalist and the bishops are more conservative than their Western counterparts. Bishops John Baptist Kakubi and Bakyenga of Mbarara Catholic Diocese were typical examples of this case.

1. The Local Catholic Bishops' Skepticism and Hostility

The main problem for *The Movement for the Restoration of the Ten Commandments of God* was public skepticism and rejection by the Catholic bishops in Mbarara Catholic Diocese. This ecclesiastical or Episcopal pastoral and spiritual problem led to Joseph Kibwetere and Fr. Dominic Kataribabo's rebellion. They became defiant and rebellious against the wishes and directives of the Mbarara Catholic Diocese. They also accused the bishops of corruption, immorality and administrative incompetence. They cited these as real reasons for their moral indignation and subsequent moral crusade, inside the Roman Catholic Church.

Subsequently, the Marian Movement leaders appealed directly to the Pope John Paul II, in Rome for his jurisdiction, intervention, mediation and for canonical pastoral oversight. Thus, the Marian Movement leaders bypassed the local Catholic Church hierarchy, and by their direct appeal to Rome for both intervention and Episcopal and Papal jurisdiction, they effectively suspended the canonical requirements to obey their local bishops' disputed directives, until they heard from the Pope.

For the Marian Movement leaders, this included the suspension of obedience to Bishop John Baptist Kakubi's Episcopal letters of interdiction of May 7, 1991, although the Mbarara Catholic bishops believed that until they heard from the Pope, to the contrary, their evaluations of the Marian Movement as a dangerous and heretical Movement were sound. As such, according to the Mbarara Catholic bishops, there was no need to either change their views, or after their administrative actions to censure and interdict the religious leaders, whom they perceived to be errant religious teachers, religious fundamentalists, moral extremists, trouble-makers, and doomsday Catholic heretics.

The leaders of the Movement clearly viewed themselves as true Catholics, who were persecuted by the local Catholic Church hierarchy for personal, political and theological reasons. For instance, it was common knowledge among many Catholic priests in Mbarara Diocese that Fr. Dominic Kataribabo perceived himself to be a better candidate for the original position of Coadjutor Bishop of Mbarara Catholic Diocese.

Accordingly, Fr. Kataribabo regarded himself as the better qualified and more suitable successor for Bishop Kakubi, on his retirement, as the diocesan bishop. He truly believed that he was professionally and academically better qualified than Paul Bakyenga, who was selected by Bishop Kakubi, for the job of serving as the bishop, who would succeed him. As a result, Fr. Dominic Kataribabo bore a serious personal grudge against Bishop Kakubi. Their personal, professional and ecclesiastical relationships became severely strained and reached a breaking point, in May 1992.

Subsequently, Fr. Kataribabo did not trust Bishop Kakubi, anymore, even as his diocesan bishop, administrator, superior and professional supervisor. In addition, Fr. Kataribabo also wrongly perceived Bishop Paul Bakyenga, as a rival that would not accept him and promote him. Fr. Kataribabo thought that Bishop Bakyenga was still hostile to him. As a result, he both persistently and negatively viewed him, as a dangerous rival not to be trusted, or with whom to negotiate terms of truce or surrender.[1]

The mutual suspicions, personal ambitions and uneasy relationship between Fr. Dominic Kataribabo and the Catholic bishops in Mbarara set the stage for the rejection of *The Movement for the Restoration of the Ten Commandments of God* and quest for canonical interdiction, and thereby legally silencing the Catholic priests and lay leaders of the Movement with the canonical threat to excommunicate them from membership and fellowship of the Catholic Church, and theologically, the exclusion from heaven and salvation as fellowship with God and the saints, in heaven.

Therefore, Bishop Kakubi's letters of interdiction and threat of excommunication that were written to the leaders of the Movement on May 7, 1991, drove the Movement leaders out of his diocese in order to escape from his appeals to the Catholic Church's canons and injunctions. The bishops' letters were disproportionately canonical in tone and less caring or pastoral in nature and results.

The Episcopal letters carried heavy threats for the Movement leaders' interdiction and excommunication. As a result, these harsh Episcopal letters led to ecclesiastical, moral, cultural and social distress. They also led to conflict and serious mental, psychological, spiritual, religious, moral and social states of stress that threatened well-being or even led to dread due to the veiled sentence to perdition and eternal damnation, by virtue of a formal Catholic Church's excommunication.

Nevertheless, the Marian Movement leaders had four main options available to them. Instead of ritual deaths and martyrdom, as a path to escape from the world and go to heaven, the Marian Movement leaders could have chosen one of the following alternative options as a solution for their dilemma and implemented it carefully. These were some of the possible alternatives:

1. The MRTCG leaders could have become scared and fearful for their mortal souls before God and the religious community, if they were to be ostracized and excommunicated by the Catholic Church hierarchy, and alienated from its obedient congregation members. Subsequently, the Marian Movement's leaders could have acted out of dread and holy fear of excommunication, and renounced God's revelations they had taught, and the correlative claims of visions of the Blessed Virgin Mary.

The Catholic Church hierarchy could have repudiated the Movement's teachings as falsehoods, erroneous doctrines or heresies and ceremoniously returned to the traditional teachings of the Catholic Church and canonical obedience to the Diocesan bishop in Mbarara, as the embodiment and representative of Christ, the Pope and the true Catholic Church.[2] This was the option which Fr. Paul Ikazire and his congregation in Bushenyi chose to follow, in 1993. They were welcomed back, and joyfully rehabilitated by the Mbarara Catholic bishops.

OR

2. The MRTCG leaders could have chosen to become rebellious and defiant against the bishop's letter of interdiction and face excommunication. They could continue teaching the same doctrines concerning the revelations of God and the visions of the Blessed Virgin whose messages were that God was angry at human sins, including those of corrupt Church leaders, and that God was going to punish unrepentant sinners with destructive fire and other disasters that would consume them and end the world on December 31, 1999, or early, in the year 2000.[3]

OR

3. The MRTCG leaders could have chosen to ignore the Catholic hierarchy in Mbarara and Bishop Kakubi's canonical letters of warning to cease and desist from preaching and teaching unacceptable heretical doctrines concerning the visions of the Blessed Virgin Mary and urgent revelations from God concerning the supposed imminent end of the world, and willingly face interdiction. But the cantankerous moral reformist Marian Movement could have disrespectfully chosen to publicly discredit, and ceremonially burn Bishop Kakubi's letters of interdiction in a public ceremony of defiance and protest, like the Rev. Fr. Martin Luther did with Pope Leo X's Bull of Excommunication, on December 12, 1520, in Wittenberg.[4]

However, with this kind of defiant ecclesiastical action, the MRTCG would have also, thereby transformed itself, into a new "separatist," or "Reformed Catholic Church" probably called the "Mary's Church for the Restoration of the Ten Commandments of God." Therefore, by this action, the Marian Movement leaders would have publicly, effectively and ceremoniously declared themselves, to have actually, become both canonically independent from the Roman Catholic hierarchy in Mbarara and along with its jurisdiction, interdictions, and canons.

Accordingly, the Marian Movement would have existed, and operated outside the Mbarara diocesan councils, and the correlative ecclesiastical regulations, and procedures, or resolutions of those councils. As such, the resolutions, or ecclesiastical actions of the Catholic Church's officers, including the bishops, or their representatives and their legal, ecclesiastical jurisdiction, or canonical instruments and obligations, would not have applied to the Marian Movement leaders, or their followers.[5] This would be akin to the relationship between the Anglican Church and the Catholic Church's hierarchies. Their respective jurisdictions and laws do not apply to each other's followers. For instance, a Catholic bishop has no canonical authority to interdict or excommunicate an Anglican priest. Nevertheless, they have chosen to be mutually respectful to each other's teachings and traditions.

OR

4. The MRTCG leaders could have protested and appealed their interdiction, restriction of sacramental priestly functions and threat of excommunication from the Roman Catholic Church, to the Holy Father, Pope John Paul II in Rome, as the Head of the Catholic Church and Vicar of Christ on Earth to intervene on their behalf by nullifying the letters of interdiction and threats for excommunication.[6]

According to the Catholic Church's canons or ecclesiastical governing laws, only the Pope had the ultimate jurisdiction over the Catholic priest. As such, the Marian Movement Catholic priests could not be canonically excommunicated unless Pope John Paul officially sanctioned it, as the extreme and ultimate punishment for those belligerent and moral reformist priests.

Meanwhile, in good faith and holy obedience to God's calling and the commissioning of the Blessed Virgin Mary, these Marian priests could legitimately continue to do their work, in another diocese where they were not prohibited, under interdiction. Fr. Kataribabo and other Marian priests continued to carry out their priestly functions, with Fr. Kataribabo serving as their emergency supervisor or bishop. They both lived in hope, faith and in positive anticipation that Pope John Paul II would, finally, rule in their favor, or wait and see if their prophecies came true before acting on their case.

The Marian Movement priests had much hope that most of their teachings and practices would be found to be in conformity with Catholic Church's traditions, monasticism and mysticism, especially within their Medieval Catholic Church expressions.

As a theologian Fr. Kataribabo believed that what these moral reformist Marian Movement Catholic priests were teaching and practicing, prior to the end of the year 1999, were part of traditional Catholic Church's accepted both Marian and monastic teachings and practices. These practices and teachings included radical doctrines of Mariology expanding on the Marian dogmas taught by Popes Pius IX's Church constitution: *Ineffabilis Deus* and Pope Pius XII's Apostolic constitution: *Munififcentissmus Deus*; the Marian visions, divine special revelation, holy scriptures, fasting, contemplative prayer, silent meditation (*kusirika/okuhunama*)[7] and self-purgative and austere monastic practices.[8]

It was through the Rev. Fr. Dominic Kataribabo's theological advice and spiritual guidance that the lay leaders for *The Movement for the Restoration of the Ten Commandments of God* chose the fourth option. This was a wise.

2. The Marian Movement Leaders' Despair

However, due to the prolonged time of waiting for papal response, the Marian Movement leaders became impatient and failed to give the process enough time to work out. In essence, the Movement leaders' choice and action to appeal to the Pope, in Rome, for the intervention, impartial investigation of the visions of the Blessed Virgin Mary and the apocalyptic revelations from God was tactful.

The verification and validation of God's apocalyptic revelations, as they were communicated through these Marian apparitions, especially to Keledonia Mwerinde and Joseph Kibwetere, were important. The Marian Movement leaders believed that the appeal to the Pope meant that it both canonically and legally suspended Bishop John Baptist Kakubi's letters of interdiction, until the Pope had reviewed their appeal, conducted the requested ecclesiastical investigations concerning the reported apparitions of the Blessed Virgin Mary, and subsequently, duly acted, to either reaffirm the bishop's canonical action of discipline, or nullify it.[9]

This being the Marian Movement leaders' canonical understanding of the matter, they continued to celebrate mass, hear confessions and celebrate the other sacraments, as if the letters of interdiction had not been issued. Until they had heard from the Pope himself, the Marian Movement leaders and their loyal followers strongly both believed and knew that they were Catholics in good standing. Therefore, they prudently decided to relocate their headquarters from Bushenyi, and Ntungamo districts, in Mbarara Catholic Diocese, to Kanungu, in the Kabale Catholic Diocese.[10]

The Marian Movement's leaders were forced to appeal to Pope John Paul II for a direct ecclesiastical intervention,[11] oversight, and investigation of the validity of their visions of the Blessed Virgin Mary, which the Mbarara Catholic Diocese refused to do. But that was mainly due to prejudice against the belligerent leaders of the apocalyptic Marian Movement's visions that demanded moral reforms within the Catholic Church. The conservative Mbarara Catholic bishops were unaccommodating and rejected the visions, revelations and religious claims of the lay Marian Movements' leaders.

The Mbarara bishops were hostile to the Marian Movement and they condescendingly heard the testimonies of the Kibwetere and Mwerinde. They also judged the two main prophets of the Marian Movement to be unsuitable vehicles for God's special revelations to the Church and the world. Subsequently, the Catholic bishops treated the Marian Movement leaders as mere liars, false prophets, economic opportunists and religious frauds, who sought to use religion for self-promotion, national political visibility and personal economic gain.[12]   Thus, the Marian preachers of repentance and moral reformation were accused of being promoters of falsehood and economic fraud, in the guise of a new religious movement.

Joseph Kibwetere and Fr. Dominic Kataribabo appealed for the Pope's direct intervention on their behalf because they viewed themselves as good, and faithful Roman Catholics, who did not wish to leave the Church, in order to practice their true Catholic spirituality, as centered on Marian devotion, God's continuing revelations, repentance of sins, an austere life of strict celibacy and personal moral holiness. This holy life was to be lived in silence, contemplative prayer, and monastic simplicity, which were based on the strict obedience of God, as measured by the fulfillment of the Ten Commandments of God that were revealed to the world through the Prophet Moses.[13]

Without any doubt, the claims of the Movement's leaders to have seen the Blessed Virgin Mary and to have been chosen by God, like Moses, to become the new agents of God's revelation and deliverance, must have sounded strange, excessive and incredible to the conservative leaders of the Catholic Church in Uganda, especially in Mbarara.[14] As Jesus correctly realized, prophets have no acceptance or honor in their own home and towns. He was also rejected in his own hometown and by his own people who knew him well as their own local carpenter rather than a learned great Rabbi or prophet. Joseph Kibwetere and Keledonia Mwerinde were faced with similar social, ecclesiastical and spiritual hurdles, like those which Jesus encountered, during his innovative and moral reformist ministry, about two thousand years, ago.

Both Jesus and the leaders of *The Movement for the Restoration of the Ten Commandments of God* were ridiculed, rejected and persecuted by the religious establishment and its traditional authorities, who negatively viewed them, as religious upstarts and blasphemers because of their apparent excessive claims of God's new revelations through them. God's new revelations, prophecies, and warnings to repent and shun evil, or be punished, are rarely warmly received and embraced by sinners, to whom they are addressed.

This hostility is because they are too threatening, and discomforting to sinners, or the people to whom the prophets are sent by God, to save. That is one of the main reasons, why the Hebrew prophets, like Nathan, Elijah, Ezekiel, Amos, John the Baptist and Jesus, were often rejected, persecuted and sometimes killed, by the corrupt or repressive and unjust rulers, who felt threatened or condemned by their prophetic ministry. The prophets were also often either rejected or killed by the corrupt and sinful people, because they brought unbearable messages of the impending doom as God's punishment for evil, whereas the false prophets, who proclaimed God's prosperity and peace, were welcomed as the good prophets.[15]

Jesus was himself rejected, along with his new radical moral reformist and apocalyptic teachings. He taught that nonviolence, free forgiveness of all offenses and peace were the foundations and moral principles of God's reign and God's Kingdom, which had already dawned in the world. But they rejected him and his teachings were mocked, as unrealistic, crazy and utopian dreams. He was also vilified by the religious establishment and arrested as a radical teacher of new doctrines that might cause moral, religious and political rebellion in the name of God as their ultimate king, rather than King Herod in Jerusalem, or Caesar in Rome.

Like Jesus, the leaders of the apocalyptic and moral Marian Movement believed that God had also appeared to them and entrusted them with a new message of moral reformation and repentance in order to enter God's Kingdom. This claim was part of the Judeo-Christian mystic, visionary and prophetic tradition. It was also unique to the Catholic Church hierarchy, in as much as the lay Marian Movement founders, prophets and main leaders claimed that God commissioned them to start a new *Movement for the Restoration of the Ten Commandments of God,* which would be the new "Ark of God's Salvation in the world."

The Marian moral reformist Movement was also unique in that it was a radical monastic movement which renounced sex and possessions, as agencies of temptations, evil and sin. The Marian Movement leaders also alarmed many people, when they claimed that the revelations and messages from God were true and immutable, since they were conveyed to them, by the Blessed Virgin Mary, and that she had revealed to them that God hated homosexuality and the homosexuals.

The Marian Movement leaders also declared that they were directed by the Blessed Virgin Mary to preach that HIV/AIDS was God's incurable plague. And that God had sent it into the world, as a punishment for corrupt people and especially for the sexually promiscuous people. They preached that adultery, fornication and homosexuality was very offensive to God and led to divine punishment and that punishment was HIV/AIDS. God also was punishing other sinful people, who indulged in alcoholic drinks and illegal drugs. The Marian Movement sounded very unique, when Kibwetere preached that the new apocalyptic revelation and message from God was to declare that people must repent urgently because this evil, sinful and corrupt world would be destroyed by God's fire, and come to an end, at the closing of the era, or the Second Millennium. The supposed end of the corrupt era, was supposed to occur at midnight, on December 31, 1999.

3. Problems of God's Infinite Time and Human Chronological Time

In part, many of the popular and anxiety-inducing Marian teachings and apocalyptic prophecies for the imminent end of the world and the doom of sinners were rooted in the serious misunderstanding of God's time. Finally, this problem led to tragedy and martyrdoms, in early 2000.

The Marian Movement leaders' problematic dating of the millennium was based on Western calendars and did not take into account the fact the Chinese were going into their fifth millennium. In contrast, the Muslim calendar still needed more than seven hundred years, in order to complete its own Second Millennium.[16]

The above being the case, the millenarian teachings and predictions for the apocalyptic end of the world will always be unfulfilled because the dating of these events confuses God's time as *"Kairos"* with human linear and historical time, or *"Chronos."* Many prophets and speculators often forget the reality that *Chronos* exists in *Kairos*, and therefore, God's Kingdom is already here in the world, and does not need to arrive in the apocalyptic future (Matt. 16: 19-21).

Nevertheless, the Marian Movement's leaders had themselves claimed that their revelations and urgent prophetic message for the imminent end of the world were directly from God. They also demonstrated that these heavenly visions, divine revelations and directives were communicated by God the Father, the King of Heaven and Earth, through the Blessed Virgin Mary, as the Queen of Heaven and Mother of God, and all the saints of God, as God's redeemed and adopted children.

4. The Marian Visions and the Catholic Tradition and History

The leaders of the Marian Movement also theologically positively affirmed that these divine revelations, commissions and messages were part of the Christian religious tradition and continuity with the Judeo-Christian prophetic tradition. They were within the accepted sequences of the messages from God already revealed through the Holy Scriptures through the prophets, saints and apostles like Paul, Peter and John.[17] The visions of the Blessed Virgin Mary were also positively affirmed as being consistent with the previously Catholic Church investigated and approved apparitions of the Blessed Virgin Mary to other people and in other numerous sites in various countries. Accordingly, the Marian Movement leaders the following sites and visionaries were cited affirmed strongly affirmed as their predecessors and religious role models:

Jesus and the Blessed Virgin Mary have told us to write down for you also a few words of various people from various countries, who received revelations and visions of the chastisements that are coming. A lot has been revealed, and to so many people; we cannot enumerate them all. We shall only present the following few names:

1. Blessed Anna Maria Taiga in Rome.
2. Padre Pio, a Capuchin priest in Italy.
3. Sister Rose Colomba Asdente in Italy.
4. Elizabeth Canori Mora in Rome.
5. Father Nectou, a Jesuit priest in Belgium.
6. Sister Palma D'Oria in Italy.
7. Sister Marie Baourdi, a Calmelite nun from France.
8. Hildegard from Germany.
9. Marie Mantel (Normandy, a stigmatized nun in Italy).
10. The little Pebble from Australia.

These seers are reliable, and there are many more others like them.[18]

It is clearly self-evident that the African Marian apocalyptic leaders of *The Movement for the Restoration of the Ten Commandments of God* saw themselves as a vital component of other true Roman Catholic Marian movements and groups in the world. They saw themselves to be part of the universal Marian Movement within the Catholic Church. This is part of the reason why they tried to place their visions and messages of God and the Blessed Virgin Mary in a proper and more credible European Catholic Marian tradition.

The Marian Movement leaders were aware of the Africans and Latin Americans who had received the visions of the Blessed Virgin Mary. But they wanted to claim authenticity and credibility of their own visions and revelations from God by connecting them to the more credible and acceptable Western Marian tradition.

The Movement leaders were aware that their claims to have received divine revelations from God and to have seen apparitions of the Blessed Virgin Mary would be subjected to Church investigation for authentication. That is why they preferred to connect themselves to the better known and accepted European Marian traditions[19] than appealing to the new and less well-known visions of Gauda Kamushwa and her Prayer Group, in the caves of Nyabugoto, in Nyakishenyi, and the visions of the Blessed Virgin Mary, by the three shepherd boys of Kibeho Rwanda, and Uzebie in Masinde village, Kayanza Province, Burundi. Only the spiritually pure and worthy were supposed to see the Marian apparitions on the 11th day of each month.

The Marian Movement is closely associated with the Marian traditions of Rwanda, especially the visions of the Virgin Mary that Specioza Mukantabona both claimed to have received and proclaimed to the world, as

God's new apocalyptic revelations through the Blessed Virgin Mary.[20] She came to Uganda and gained fame among the rural Catholics because she was a young and beautiful woman, who claimed to be receiving as she lived in Kabale and Rakai districts of Uganda, during the early 1980s.[21]

Mukantabona returned to Mbuye, Rakai, Masaka, in November 2006, still claiming that the Blessed Virgin Mary would also publicly appear to her faithful devotees, on November 29, 2006.[22] The Uganda Police officers came both to witness and monitor the event in order to prevent a new wave of an apocalyptic ritual self-sacrifices, and martyrdoms or mass suicides. The crowds were disappointed because they did not see the expected apparitions of the Blessed Virgin Mary, but believed they heard Specioza Mukantabona talking to her. The people claimed that they heard Mukantabona speaking to the Blessed Virgin Mary, whom they could not see. But they reported that they heard the following conversation:

> Yes, you told me you were going to come! So many people have come and have been waiting to see you at Mbuye. Some of them have come to pray. Some have come to see miracles.
>
> What should I tell them? Some of them have told me to inform you that they have problems of infertility, poverty, unemployment, sickness and some want to become rich. Please help them![23]

It is also self-evident that *The Movement for the Restoration of the Ten Commandments of God* sought credibility by seeking to obtain approval and association with more traditional and credible Marian groups in Europe and Australia.[24]

This religious and mystical association with other well-known and respected international Marian groups was considered important by the MRTCG leaders. It was considered necessary in order to gain more international appeal and the Catholic Church's credibility both at home and abroad.[25] This connection was also considered essential for people to accept them and believe the validity of their own visions, and apocalyptic preaching of frightening apocalyptic messages and sermons concerning the impending catastrophic and fiery end of the world.

Furthermore, the Marian Movement leaders also promoted strange apocalyptic beliefs, which were exaggerated apocalyptic events as recorded in the books of Daniel and the Books of Revelations, especially the dramatization of the Four Horses of the Apocalypse. These apocalyptic moral purists and reformists of the Catholic leaders of the MRTCG also both taught and practiced extreme ascetic monastic practices, including the rules of permanent silence, constant fasting, celibacy, obedience, hard work, constant prayer, and a simple holy life of abject poverty as part of the traditional Marian, Catholic monastic and ascetic tradition.[26] Nevertheless, the conservative Catholic Church hierarchy in Mbarara, feeling challenged and threatened by the moral reformist Marian Movement persecuted it, in order to eradicate it from both the Catholic Church and the country.

NOTES

1. See Matthias Mugisha and James Mujuni, "Kataribabo with his Doctorate in Theology, was the Brain behind the Cult's Liturgy: The Priest Who Became a Killer," People: *The New Vision*, Monday, April 3, 2000.

2. This is what Bishop Kakubi's letter of May 6, 1991 to Kibwetere and associates or leaders of the MRTCG demanded. The letter points out that the Marian visions are causing confusions and divisions in the diocese. Therefore, for him, they were not credible or valid sources of the sound moral and religious information, revelation, teaching and spiritual or moral nurture for Christians. These were the main tests of the validity of the Marian apparitions, and revelations, according to the interview, on August 17, 2004. He said that the main test was given to him by the Vatican. He said the true visions of the Blessed Virgin Mary had to bring: 1. Unity, 2. Healing and 3. Peace within the Church Community.

3. *A Timely Message from Heaven*, 43-54. Fire, floods and monsters were part of the apocalyptic revelations to cause disasters that would end the present era. Darkness for three days was supposed to be part of the doomsday. It was clear that the saints would not be killed in this divine purgation and transformation of the world into God's Kingdom on the Earth.

4. Pope Leo X gave the Rev. Prof. Martin Luther more time and opportunities to debate and defend his dissenting Ninety-Five Theses and the associated teachings than Bishops John Baptist Kakubi and Paul Bakyenga gave to Fr. Dominic Kataribabo and his associates.

5. This is one of the main reasons why the Rev. Fr. Martin Luther and his followers in 1520 chose to form their own new independent Protestant Church over which the Pope had no canonical jurisdiction or power to excommunicate the rebels.

6. This is the unexpected courageous moral and religious option, which the Marian Movement leaders chose. They fled to Kanungu in Kabale Catholic Diocese, where they were given shelter. However, Bishop Bakyenga, the Marian Movement "Grand Inquisitor" was appointed the new Archbishop of the Western Province, in 1999. Kabale Catholic Diocese was now under Archbishop Bakyenga's jurisdiction. The MRTCG leaders became desperate, fled from the Church and the world, in which they felt rejected, persecuted and helpless.

7. *Kusirika/Okuhunama* is a traditional Catholic form of formal or informal "Silent Retreat." Holy silence and retreat became the main spiritual media of the Marian Movement. Contemplative prayer in holy silence became part of the code for their Benedictine monastic Marian Movement. Communication had to be written. Documents were burned and destroyed, prior to the church fire of Friday, March 17, 2000.

8. *The Documents of Vatican II: The Decree on Priestly Formation* (*Optatam Totius*).

9. *A Timely Message from Heaven*, 67-98, 158-163.

10. Bishop Kakubi's letter of May 6, 1991, to Kibwetere and Mwerinde and their associates were expelled from Mbarara Catholic Diocese. The letter stated: "*Murugye omu Itware ryangye rya Mbarara*" (Go away from my Mbarara Diocese). The associates listed in the letter were: Mrs. Sicola Kamagara, Mrs. Angelina Mugisha, Miss Keledonia Mwerinde and Miss Ursula Komuhangi. This letter makes it self-evidently clear the Marian Movement was

led by devout Catholic women, who were headed by Keledonia Mwerinde.

11. This is a canonically valid action. However, Archbishop Bakyenga said that the Movement's appeal was not forwarded, by the Papal Nuncio in Uganda, to Rome. He said that the Papal Nuncio threw it in the trash-can as "rubbish." This was disclosed by the Archbishop Bakyenga during an interview with the author, on August 5, 2003.

12. Bishop Kakubi's impression of the MRTCG leaders and their religious claims. See: Matthias Mugisha and James Mujuni, "Kataribabo with his Doctorate in Theology, was the Brain behind the Cult's Liturgy: The Priest Who Became a Killer," People: *The New Vision*, Monday, April 3, 2000.

13. *A Timely Message from Heaven*, 1-3, 21-33

14. This was confirmed in my interview with Bishop Kakubi.

15. False prophets are popular because they tell people, what they want to hear, and not the truth. But God is on the side of truth and not popularity. This is why Jesus was crucified. He told the truth. See Matt. 5-7.

16. According to the Islamic calendar, Prophet Muhammad's *Hijra* to Medina marks the year 1AH, which is equivalent to 622 C.E. (AD).

17. Like the apocalyptic expectations of the prophets, including Isaiah, Amos, Daniel, the Essenes and Jesus, their apocalyptic prophecies, visions and revelations did not materialize.

18. *A Timely Message from Heaven*, 44.

19. See *A Timely Message from Heaven*, 1-2, 21, 43-47.

20. See: Matthias Mugisha, "Visions of Mary Started Cult: Joseph Kibwetere came with two trembling nuns and converted the Nyabugoto cult to his sect," Weekend Vision, *The New Vision,* Friday, March 24, 2000: 22. Specioza Mukantabona was 18, when she saw the vision of the Blessed Virgin Mary and became her medium and "Apostle" (*Entumwa*).

21. Speciosa Mary Mukantabana was accepted in Kabale Catholic Diocese as a visionary. Later, she moved to Rakai and stayed at Mbuye Catholic Parish. See: Dismus Buregyeya and Chris Kiwawulo, "Police Monitoring Sect," *The New Vision*, Saturday, December 2, 2006. However, her followers were ordinary Catholic devotees of Mary.

22. Dismus Buregyeya and Chris Kiwawulo, "Police Monitoring Sect," *The New Vision*, Saturday, December 2, 2006. This Marian gathering was a continuation of the original women's benevolent Marian Movement within the Catholic Church, before Mwerinde recruited male co-leaders, who corrupted it. The men, finally tragically destroyed Mwerinde's Marian Movement, in March 2000. Mary Daly's exclusion of men from women's liberation movements was vindicated. See Mary Daly, *God Beyond the Father.*

23. Dismus Buregyeya and Chris Kiwawulo, "Police Monitoring Sect," *The New Vision*, Saturday, December 2, 2006. Speciosa Mukantabana claimed that she had an apparition of the Virgin Mary, while she was at the Mbuye Catholic Parish Church, on November 29, 1988. This was also the same time, when the Catholic women of Nyakishenyi were also most active, in their Marian devotion, at the Nyabugoto Holy Mountain, in South-Western Uganda.

24. *A Timely Message from Heaven*, 1-2, 43-47.

25. In many of these African cultural, moral, economic and political revolutions, the scenarios have been akin to the George Well's famous political satire: *Animal Farm.* Oppression and failed expectations have led to the emergence of radical messianic liberation movements, like the NRM, HSM, LRA, and MRTCG in Uganda.

26. *A Timely Message from Heaven*, 43-45.

Chapter Eight

GOD'S HOLY SERVANTS
AND MARY'S SAINTS

Africa is a vast continent with great complexities of human diversity. This includes: pluralisms of races, ethnicity, cultures, religions, and economic ideologies and political systems. Within the African traditional world-view, these coalesce into interrelated factors and inseparably interwoven societal systems were considered to be part of God's work, holy mysteries and divine providence. They were intended by God t to form a well-ordered, socioeconomic and meaningful human life. As such they are to be respected and preserved. Many of the radical reformist and liberation religio-political movements, such as the ones discussed in this book, are examples of concrete forms of historical, cultural, religious and political attempts to preserve them or even reconcile them with perceived pure forms of Christianity or Islam.

1. History and Tradition as Foundations for Change
And Protest Movements

Africa has some of the ancient world's civilizations and political systems, such as the ancient empires and kingdoms along the River Nile Basin, including Egypt, Nubia, Ethiopia, and other African kingdoms both in East and West Africa. These include the Ashanti, Benin, and the Babito-Bunyoro-Kitara Empire, and the satellite kingdoms of Buganda, Buganda, Ankle, Igara, Toro, Mpororo, Rwanda, Burundi, Karagwe, Kayonza and the like. Some of these ancient political entities still exist and have cultural and religious traditions, which have adopted some elements of foreign or missionary Asian and Western religions, including Christianity and Islam.

However, since Africa is also a continent of political and economic crises and hardships, messianic or libertarian movements, led by prophets or messiahs, like Muhumuza, Yoweri Museveni, Alice Lakwena, and Joseph Kony or apocalyptic movement, like Keledonia Mwerinde and Joseph Kibwetere, have arisen to liberate the oppressed people. Nevertheless, they carry out their liberation mission within the African world-view, cultural symbols and the African traditional religious paradigms. However, the Christian or Islamic based movements, like Lakwena's HSM or Mwerinde's

Marian Movement have heavily borrowed from their Catholic moral teachings, sacramental rituals and apocalyptic expectations.

2. God's Servants and Saints within an African Traditional Cultural World-View & Theocracy

Most of the major African traditional cultures are essentially both religious and theocratic. They are also correlatively autocratic, patriarchal and conservative. Being theocratic, the African traditional systems were akin to traditional Judaism and Islam. Like the ancient Egyptians, during the time of Prince Moses, they did not separate religion from politics, medicine, education and other components of life. Kings, chiefs, priests, prophets, healers (*Waganga/Bafumu*), mediums, teachers, wise elders, good counselors, good parents and other important leaders were esteemed as God's holy embodiments and servants in the community and the world.

The ancestors were regularly venerated and invoked and requested to intercede for them to God. Offers of livestock or meat, beer, money and other sacrifices were brought to their temples or shrines to honor them and secure their supernatural services, including healing or requests for protection, good health, and success in a particular venture such as trade, exams, agriculture and prosperity. The good ancestors were highly esteemed and venerated as God's holy saints and effective mediators between God and the living members of the community, especially their relatives and friends. The Ugandan Christian Martyrdoms have become part of these venerated African holy ancestors and saints.

However, high-priests, kings, prophets and holy people or the saints could also perform this intermediary role. The leaders of messianic movements like the *Nyabingi,* Alice Lakwena's HSM, Joseph Kony's LRA, Mwerinde and Kibwetere's MRTCG were also traditionally expected to possess these divine attributes to communicate with God and foresee the future events. The reported apocalyptic visions and prophecies were deeply rooted in this African world-view as well as Western Christianity, in its medieval monastic traditions and practices.

When Western Christianity arrived in Sub-Saharan Africa, especially Roman Catholicism linked up with the existing religious traditions, such as the concepts of sin a moral violation of God's moral law which needed repentance and atonement or self-sacrifice in order to be forgiven, and removed or expiated. Christ's Passion and self-sacrificial death on the cross was the central teaching that connected with many Africans, since many of them performed ritual sacrifices to remove sins or offenses committed again God, the ancestors or the members of the community. Some cultures of

Rwanda, Burundi, Eastern Republic of the Congo, Central and Western Uganda also had customs of human sacrifice, especially young virgins, both male and females, in order to atone for serious crimes. In some cases, the death of kings was followed by human sacrifices. Therefore, it was dangerous for some commoners to be near the palace, when the king died. In Uganda, the ancient customs of human sacrifices have been revived by unscrupulous traditional healers and business people, who wished to succeed in their economic ventures.

The Blessed Virgin Mary remains the highest popular and venerated of all the Christian saints and mediators to God, the Father and Christ, her son. Within the African cultural spiritual context, the Blessed Virgin Mary is treated as the "Ultimate Ancestor" or the "Mother of God" and the "Queen of Heaven," who can still speak and reveal herself to some chosen people, in any age, culture and nationality. As a result, the oppressed and marginalized people, like Nantabona and Mwerinde, are the women chosen and privileged with Mary's apparitions, especially in Africa, Europe and Latin America.

Fr. Dominic Kataribabo believed that the Uganda Martyrs, who died in fire, at Namugongo, were the role model for African Christians, and others who wanted to become God's true saints, who live in a hostile or corrupt world. Subsequently, he ritually martyred the repentant members of the Catholic Marian members, who sought to ascend to heaven. Fr. Kataribabo ritually sacrificed them to God as holy atonements and living sacrifices, for the removal of sins and moral guilt. He believed that they participated in the passion and self-sacrifice of the Christ. It was in this faith and hope of eternal life and salvation that Fr. Kataribabo martyred the Marian devotees in order to liberate them from the bondage of the physical body, and to free their souls so that they could be dispatched to God for salvation and eternal in heaven.

3. Depicting Marian Devotees and the HSM Victims As Christian Martyrs and Saints

Protestant Christians have no process for the canonization of Christian martyrs as saints. Therefore, for the Kanungu Balokole leaders, like the late Yokana Bakebwa, Bulasio Kalenzi, Rev. Gershom Tumuhairwe, Mrs. Annet Karooro, Jenninah Tugumanawe, and Chief John Karooro, who personally knew many of the Marian devotees, in Katojo and Kanungu Marian Centers, believe that the Marian members were saints. They provided witness that these Marian Movement members were living saints, who were akin to Mother Theresa. They affirmed that these were self-sacrificial men and women, who repented of their sins, gave up attachments to the world and its possessions. They chose to live a simple holy life and sacrificed their lives for the sake of their faith and in hope of the attainment of eternal life in heaven, qualify to be called God's holy saints. God's holy and obedient servants can be esteemed as God's religious or moral saint.

For the *Balokole* and many Christians, holy people do not have to be approved and canonized by the Catholic Church hierarchy in order to be considered God's or Christ and Mary's true saint. Similarly Marian visions and apparitions are true for many African Catholics depending on the credibility of the testimonies of the witnesses or miracles locally performed by Mary's devotees, irrespective of the investigation and official judgment of the local Catholic Church bishops. This was true for Marian visionaries in Burundi, Rwanda and Uganda, including those of the MRTCG. Alice Lakwena's visions and revelations from God through the Holy Spirit follow into this category.

The Christian martyrs, including those of Uganda, are ordinary Christian men and women who courageously choose to die for their extraordinary deep Christian faith in Christ as God, and moral principles in hope of God's vindication and reward of salvation in heaven. These Christian martyrs may include baptized people, or Christian believers who are not yet baptized. This religious scenario is clearly illustrated by the case of some Ugandan Christian Martyrs, who died at Namugongo and other locations during the Christian persecution under King Mwanga's "reign of terror," 1884-1888 in the Kingdom of Buganda. Some of these holy saints already were baptized Christians and others were still catechumen, or adult candidates for the sacrament of Holy Baptism, but who were still undergoing Christian instruction, including reading and writing, in the cases of the Anglicans.

The Anglican missionaries taught their converts reading to make sure that their baptized Christians could read the Holy Bible for their families. However, the literal reading of the Bible as God's historical book and accurate record of future events in the world, as revealed in the apocalyptic prophecies, as God's predictions of the events to be actualized in the future, led to Christian fundamentalism and heresies. The examples include the apocalyptic movement in the form of the *East African Revival (Balokole) Movement*. Christian fundamentalism and the *Balokole* apocalyptic movement influenced the MRTCG's teachings and ethical practices. The examples include Mwerinde and Kibwetere's literal reading of the Bible, and the tragic apocalyptic understanding of God's metaphorical references or symbols of: "final divine judgment," "the Kingdom of God," "sin and atonement," "living self-sacrifices," "martyrdom" and "ascension into heaven," by the saints.

Therefore, the fact that most of the Marian members and victims of the fire were predominantly pious Catholics, who were devotees of the Blessed Virgin Mary that they came to Kanungu in a strong faith in God, and hope to ascend into heaven, is a significant fact in the evaluation of their ritual deaths as holy self-sacrificial martyrdoms. These apocalyptic Catholics also strongly believed that they were going discard their bodies and ascend into heaven, assisted by the Blessed Virgin Mary, along with the angels.

Moreover, according to traditional Christian standard teachings, as found in most mainline Christian churches, God's saving grace is free and steadfast. It is neither defiled nor negated, or diminished by the sinners' evil and criminal acts of human beings, including those of persecution and martyrdom. In the case of the Marian Movement, their religious leaders' bad theology of penance and atonement for sins in terms of self-sacrifice and martyrdom, or even a criminal conspiracy to defraud them of their money and property, and then kill them, would not make a difference in God's saving grace, for these martyrs.

The above religious or theological observation also remains true for the Marian Movement and its victims or martyrs. That is the affirmation of God's unmerited saving grace was not nullified, when the clinically depressed and desperate Marian Movement leaders martyred their innocent followers, in March 2000, in order to transform them into saints, like the Martyrs of Uganda and send them out of the world, which persecuted them. Their motivations were faith, atonement and the attainment of eternal salvation and peace in heaven.

Therefore, Fr. Kataribabo as the instrument for martyring these apocalyptic Marian devotees, who practiced their deep faith in God's salvation, regardless of their ignorance or even naivety, should not nullify their religious faith and the redemptive benefits of martyrdom. In this respect, Fr. Kataribabo played the redemptive role of Judas, who betrayed Jesus. But, it was by so doing that Jesus died for sinners.

Most of these Marian Catholics died as Christian martyrs by virtue of dying for their unwavering hope for salvation and deep Christian religious faith in God the Father, Christ and the Blessed Virgin Mary. They had come and died for their Christian faith, in hope of God's unmerited redemptive grace. However, these Marian Movement members had hoped that by their own penance and accumulation of indulgences through the merits of their own holy obedience and good works of self-sacrifice, or the *Opus Dei*, and martyrdoms, as holy sacrifices and atonements to God, would save them.

The Movement members truly believed that by their own holy obedience and these self-sacrificial acts, they had fulfilled all God's requirements for moral holiness, spiritual perfection and therefore, had merited the full attainment of God's salvation, as both moral and holy Christian saints. Ultimately, the Marian or the MRTCG members were fundamentalist and apocalyptic Catholic Marian devotees. They died, along with their children for their religious faith in God, Mary and Jesus, in hope of salvation and eternal life in heaven. Since God is merciful redeemer, they did not die in vain. Furthermore, the Marian Movement leaders had appealed to Pope John Paul II for intervention and arbitration. Their appeal was still pending, when they died, in March 2000. For most of these less well-informed rural Catholic Marian devotees, Fr. Dominic Kataribabo was revered as a nationally well-known, well-educated and an outstanding Catholic priest. His moral integrity and religious teachings were received, as the credible and authoritative teachings and practices of the Catholic Church.

Therefore, both Fr. Kataribabo's presence and ministry among them were the tangible evidence needed to convince them that they were true Catholic members of an authentic, new Catholic Order, or a new Catholic monastic Marian Movement. They believed that they were also the true Catholics and morally pure Marian devotees, who were living a new apocalyptic or end of time form of Benedictine-like rule of monastic Catholic life, which was rooted in contemplative prayer in holy silence and practical holiness of daily life, in a monastic cloister and self-seclusion from the noise, temptations and constant distractions of the world.

The code and rule of silence effectively made it easy for the Movement leaders to control and finally, secretly kill the loyal members of the Movement. The observation of the strict "code of silence" kept the members of the Movement ignorant of the fact that Joseph Kibwetere and his Movement were not positively viewed by the Catholic Church as good Catholics since they had rebelled against the directives of the Mbarara Catholic Church hierarchy to stop preaching and spreading their deviant religious doctrines, and false apocalyptic prophecies for an imminent end of the world, and to disband the apocalyptic and doomsday Marian Movement.

Furthermore, most of the Marian Movement Catholic members were unaware of the fact that the Marian Movement's Catholic priests, who were their esteemed pastors and the revered religious leaders of their beloved Marian Movement, had been interdicted by the bishops in Mbarara Catholic Diocese. Therefore, these Marian Catholics were unaware that they were not considered Catholics in "good standing," by the vindictive bishops of Mbarara Catholic Diocese. Nevertheless, this would have been technically the case according to Bishop Kakubi's decrees of interdiction of Joseph Kibwetere and the other leaders of the MRTCG, in May 1992.[1] However, Bishop Kakubi's religious sanction and interdiction of the priests would not apply to them as members of Kabale Catholic Diocese. This is why they fled to from the Mbarara Diocese to Kanungu, which is within Kabale Diocese.

In any case, most lay Catholics were not knowledgeable in the Catholic Church's vast doctrines and canon law. They believed that their local religious leaders, particularly the priests, nuns and monks, were God's holy people. They were locally venerated for being God's holy agents of God's saving truths, love, compassion, sacraments, healing and salvation in the community and the world. They cared more for good deeds, as mediated by God, and the Church, to the world through them. In reality, these Marian devotees cared little for the intricate formulations of Catholic dogmas about the Blessed Virgin Mary, Episcopal powers and canon laws.

However, as devout Catholics, these Marian devotees had been taught to fear God and to observe God's commandments because of the dread of eternal punishment in God's painful hellfire. They were taught that "hell" was "a real physical place. It was like *Dante's Inferno*. Hell was a dreadful place of pain and suffering in God's fire."[2] As a result, most Catholics were like the fundamentalist Evangelicals, who constantly live in some dreadful existential anxiety and fear of God's hell-fire. This existential dread, which is a form of unhealthy religious neurosis or obsession with God's holiness, justice, divine judgment and retribution for sins, or other moral infractions, is both religiously induced and it is religiously dangerous to the believers' health and well-being. This doctrine is both erroneous and dangerous due to a lack of balance and idolatrous presumption to possess God's new infallible or absolute and definitive apocalyptic revelation and understanding of God.

Ultimately, the extreme fundamentalist Evangelical and the MRTCG's extremist religious teachings and austere monastic practices were Medieval and antiquated. As such, they were not representative of mainline modern Christianity and its central moral practices. They were based on Moses ignored Jesus' basic and essential teachings on God's free redemptive grace and Agape. They also portrayed as Moses revealed him to the world as a vengeful holy God, as opposed to God's revelation through Jesus, as a merciful and loving Father (*Abba*), who forgives human sins without condition. God as Agape (1 John 4) does not demand sacrifices for atonement, as Moses taught. God's demands his moral saints to practice virtues of: holy obedience, unconditional love, free forgiveness of offenses, prayer, charity, self-control, nonviolence, humility, a life of simplicity and peace with all God's people and creatures.

Nevertheless, that loving God still demands justice as holy action that is essentially rooted within the praxis of unconditional love and unconditional forgiveness for other people, who offend them. This is as opposed to the violent Mosaic Law of retaliation (Matt. 5-7). This is in contrast to the

Marian Movement's call to live a life of holy obedience and holiness, which are deeply rooted within the fear of God and his hell-fire, instead of being positively rooted in the praise and love of God, as the benevolent and loving heavenly "Mother" and "Father."

Accordingly, the prevailing existential conditions of angst that prevailed in East Africa, during the 1980s and the 1990s, as well as the apocalyptic and religious existential fears and anxiety relating to the doomsday prophecies and apocalyptic predications for God's imminent judgment and the end of the world in God's punitive and cleansing holy fire, were the main foundations of the MRTCG's emergence. It also, partly explains the Marian Movement's subsequent strange behaviors, extreme monastic practices and compulsive moral obsessions. These quests for moral and spiritual perfection included their compulsive ascetic forms of life and practices of extreme monastic religious practices of piety, such as:

- austere monasticism
- self-sacrificial forms of penance
- constant concern about moral and spiritual perfection
- extreme fasting
- preoccupation with holy silence
- contemplative prayer in silence

- constant silent recitations of the Rosary, "Hail Mary" and the Lord's Prayer
- fear of sinning through speech
- vows of absolute poverty
- simplicity of life
- vows of celibacy
- and vows of obedience.[3]

They did all these acts as "*Opus Dei,*" or good works of piety and salvation, not so much because of their love for God, but rather, because of their fear and dread of God and his associated hell-fire, as torture and punishment for all disobedient and unrepentant sinners, who violated the Ten Commandments. Eventually, this fear of God and disdain for the world as the realm of the Devil led to real tragedy, when the Marian devotees ritually killed and martyred themselves in order to escape from it and go to heaven.

Dante's *Inferno* provided an effective visual imagery for the horrors of hell-fire, scary savage beasts, pain and suffering as God's torment (torture) and punishment for disobedient sinners. For the Rev. Fr. Kataribabo, it also confirmed his theology that the Catholic Church and its hierarchy were corrupt, and that unless they repented and reformed the Church, they too would go to hell, in the same manner in which Dante had described it in his radical book: *The Inferno.* Dante had symbolically placed some of his unsupportive Catholic Church leaders, including the Pope, as well as his political enemies, into the depths of hell.

Dante's *Inferno* also became popular with the Protestants, who followed the teachings of Martin Luther, and subsequently, erroneously vilified and negatively viewed the Pope as the "Beast" that persecuted the true Church.

They erroneously associated the Pope, instead of the Emperor Nero, with the "Beast," as was perceived by St. John, the writer of the apocalyptic and enigmatic Book of Revelation.[4]

"Hell" was presented vividly in sermons and the Catholic Church's traditional religious art in order to scare the rural people into the Catholic Church and to seek to salvation. This quest for salvation was also treated as the sacramental holy path and spiritual method for the deliverance and therefore, holy escape from the possibility of eternal damnation, as both sinners and nonbelievers.

Subsequently, some of these people converted to the Catholic Church for mere fear of being judged by God and being sent to burn in the unquenchable hell-fire. In these kinds of John the Baptist-like sermons of "fire and brimstone," hell-fire was dramatically and effectively portrayed, like in Dante's *Inferno*. It was depicted as a real fiery and hot, or volcano-like place that was a form of God's apocalyptic punishment for all rebellious, corrupt and unrepentant sinners in the world.

Hell was depicted as the very opposite of the fellowship with God in heaven, and the attainment of a life of eternal happiness, joy and peace. In contrast to beatitude and happiness in heaven, hell, as a real place, was negatively depicted as a really horrible, painful and hot place, which was full of different hideous and frightening monsters, endless horrors, "God's unquenchable fire," intense pain, and eternal suffering.[5] In short, it was conceived as God's place of infinite torture,[6] and retaliation[7] for human rejection of his commandments, love, mercies, redemptive grace and invitations to repent and live a holy life based on the guidance of his commandments and moral law.

Due to crude forms of religious and theological anthropomorphism, many religious fundamentalists have misunderstood the true essence of religious myths, symbols and the religious functions of myths and God. This misunderstanding has led to idolatry. Ignorant or poorly educated people have thought that God is a human-like being, who is a more powerful as a cosmic monarch, or a mighty emperor. These unsophisticated scriptural literalists and religious fundamentalists are also "physicalists," who both unconsciously create the images of God within their minds or in their temples, and then, idolatrously worship them, as the true, eternal, infallible and the holy Transcendent God.

However, with the few exceptions of some skeptics and intellectuals, such as open-minded scientists, liberal theologians, philosophers and atheists, most religious people, especially, the religious fundamentalists and scriptural literalists, remain in ignorance, and worship false gods that are made by human beings in their own human images. Consequently, the less educated children, the poorly informed or ignorant people in the rural areas, as well as the religious fundamentalists, including the Evangelicals and the Muslims, who are scriptural or Qur'anic literalists and Islamic extremists, are in many cases, blinded by their unquestioning religious faith and beliefs.

As a result, many religious people have become completely unaware that their finite conceptions, comprehensible, and attractively appealing religious slogans, car-bumper stickers, or simplistic formulations of the doctrines of the infinite, essentially incomprehensible and transcendent holy God, within the finite human language and symbols, is a form of religious idolatry. It amounts to human creation of the transcendent God in their own image based on their finite language and limited cultural religious symbols.

Paul Tillich, Karl Rahner and other theologians have correctly denounced this as common cultural and religious process as idolatrous anthropomorphism that leads to the worship of images and idols as God.[8] This is especially true in cases of the reduction of the divine mysteries, into mere finite, culturally and mentally tangible and limited imageries of the transcendent God. Through these kinds of religious processes, and bad theologies, many innocent religious believers, especially the religious fundamentalists have been, effectively and idolatrously, misled to create finite and false formulations of God, which they have, then both ignorantly and idolatrously worshipped as the true God.

This is the true essence of the appealing temptations of religious idolatry and the breach of God's second commandment, which prohibits the creation of images to represent God. This is a broad and comprehensive commandment that prohibits both the creation and worship of all forms any images. That commandment prohibits the worship of God's imageries the formulated, or created within the human beings' finite and limited mental, physical, military, artistic, cultural, political capacities, expressions and dimensions of life. These kinds of human made gods are mere idols, and human creations, which are not akin to the Transcendent God, as the infinite, cosmic creative "Holy Mystery," "Spirit" and "Mind." Therefore, the religious fundamentalists are guilty of idolatry, since they insist that they know what God is truly like and claim to know God's definitive will and revelations for the world, based on the literal reading and study of their Holy Scriptures, especially the Torah, Bible and the Qur'an.

Tragically, the religious fundamentalists, invariably both consciously and unconsciously project their own cultural values, ideals and vices into their image of God, including vices, like vindictiveness and torture of enemies in hell-fire. In this process, especially in the case of the MRTCG's compulsive moral perfectionists and moral reformers, God was inadvertently misrepresented as a great sadist, unforgiving and vindictive heavenly King and Judge of the world.

As a result of the HSM and the Marian leaders' compulsive moral perfectionism and obsessions with holiness in life, and within the Church and the world, God was portrayed as holy Moral Law Giver, cosmic "Judge," the "Avenger," who punishes sinners for breaking God's Ten Commandments. In this moral theory and religious perspective, the Marian Movement was grounded in the Mosaic Law, like the ancient Hebrews. The Marian Movement members were in many ways both religiously and morally similar to the Pharisees and the apocalyptic Essenes, during the time of Jesus, in the first century.

4. Obedient Disciples of God, Christ and Mary's Saints

Like the *Balokole*, the Marian devotees were devout Christians. The Marian Movement leaders also preached that God was the Father of Jesus Christ. Yet, in contrast to Jesus' moral teaching about God, as being *Agape* (Unconditional Love) and ever forgiving (Matt. 5-7), the Marian Movement leaders preached that God was holy, righteous, and as an incorruptible Judge, God would be unmerciful and unforgiving to the disobedient and the unrepentant sinners. They believed that the holy God was justifiably revengeful against the corrupt sinners and violators of the Ten Commandments of the Omnipotent Creator, Heavenly Sovereign and impartial Judge of the world and its sinners.

The MRTCG's portrait of God the Father was more of an image of strict "Moral Enforcer," unforgiving, and "revengeful Almighty God." This understanding of God was opposed to that of an ever-loving "Father," that is also variously referred to, especially by the Muslims, as "the Benevolent," "the Compassionate," "the Merciful" and "the Forgiving" and "Redemptive God,"[9] whom Jesus preached (Matt. 5-7; 25:31-46). Jesus' teachings on God, as Unconditional Love, create a new moral and religious portrait of God that completely negates the teachings of Prophet Moses, on God, and the MRTCG leader's moral and religious teachings, and sermons.

In contrast, the primary essence of Jesus' teachings is that God is a caring heavenly "Father" (*Abba*), who is a relational, compassionate, loving and caring God. As a result, Jesus loved God and fondly referred to God as: "*Abba*" (Matt. 5-7). It is from this experience and perspective of a positive and love-relationship with God, that Jesus taught his followers to pray to God, as "Our Father, who is in Heaven." This is also the kind of compassionate and loving God that St. John defined as "*Agape*" or "Unconditional Love" (cf. 1 Jn. 4:7-8). That "*Agape*" as God as well as the ultimate moral perfection and holiness, consisted of the highest moral goodness, what St. Aquinas called the *"Summum Bonum"* (Maximum Goodness), as the concrete expression and practice of unconditional love for each other, in the same way God unconditionally loves all his or her creatures in the universe (cf. 1 Jn. 4:1-21).

False prophets and false religious teachings are those that fail to condemn the Seven Deadly Sins (*hubris, avarice, lust, anger, envy, coveting,* and *gluttony*), and also fail to teach the Cardinal Virtues (*Prudence, Justice, Temperance* or *Restraint* and *Courage*) and the Heavenly Virtues (*Chastity, Temperance, Charity, Diligence, Patience, Kindness* and *Humility*), and Christ's normative moral principles of unconditional love, nonviolence and free forgiveness of sins in the power of God's redemptive love. Jesus preached and taught these moral, spiritual, religious and social virtues as perfection (Matt. 5-7).

These cardinal and heavenly virtues are the true essence of any true religion, piety and godliness. They are the main practical divine principles for the establishment of God's Kingdom and Reign on Earth. They are externally and morally manifested by all obedient saints by:

> Feeding the hungry (especially the poor, the unemployed and refugees)
> - Clothing the naked (the poor and the refugees)
> - Giving clean water to the thirsty (in dry places, cities and rural areas)
> - Healing the sick (provision of free universal healthcare or medical insurance)
> - Providing shelter to the homeless (the poor, the unemployed and the refugees)
> - Visiting the lonely (the elderly, strangers, foreign students and the like)
> - Welcoming strangers (greeting and helping strangers to feel at home)
> - Prison ministry (advocacy for justice, counsel, mediation and rehabilitation)
> - Preaching unconditional love and forgiveness to a violent and retaliatory world
> - Serving as God's instruments of grace, redemption and free divine forgiveness of sins and all offenses without any prior conditions
> - Making peace and preaching reconciliation and harmony, where there are vices of strife, violence, retaliation and wars.[10]

The above moral principles and heavenly virtues were considered by Jesus Christ as the true and universal manifestations of true religious faith, obedience, goodness and true godliness. Jesus invited all his followers to transcend these evil forms of hate and violence and thereby to become good, benevolent and morally perfect, like God, their heavenly Father (Matt. 5-7; John 4:1-21).[11] The moral purist and perfectionist Christians, such as the *Balokole* and the Marian Catholics, especially the MRTCG members, strongly believe that God was incarnate in Jesus as the Christ, as his Son. Therefore, they seek to follow Jesus and Mary, his mother, as their ultimate role models. This includes matters of faith, prayers, humility, self-sacrificial moral perfection and holy obedience to God the Father. Jesus and Mary provide the best historical and perfect human moral examples for the obedient Christians and the saints to imitate. Nevertheless, *Lakwena*'s HSM and Kony's LRA were culturally and theologically eclectic and paradoxical.

The HSM invoked God's Holy Spirit to "possess them," "sanctify them," and fill them with divine power. This supernatural power was believed to be like "God's magical energy" that would supernaturally protect them and make them invincible to their enemies. God would bullet-proof them and also enable them to overcome all adversities of life, including political and military ones. These religious people obeyed God and carried out a moral and religious crusade to exorcise the demonic forces in the community and the world. The HSM wanted cleanse and heal the world, and thereby, restore it to its supposed original purity and God's harmonious theocracy or Kingdom, which Jesus as the Christ, taught his followers to pray for its full establishment in the world as it is heaven (Matt. 6:9-13).

As such, Alice Lakwena's HSMF and Kony's LRA messianic liberation movements and wars were intended to establish God's apocalyptic or expected messianic or perfect Kingdom on the Earth as God's temporal kingdom in the form of a theocracy based on God's Moral Law as revealed to Prophet Moses and were written down as God's Ten Commandments (Exod. 20). In contrast, Keledonia Mwerinde, Joseph Kibwetere and Fr. Dominic Kataribabo, believed that God's Kingdom was perfectly realized in Heaven. Consequently, they ritually sacrificed and martyred their loyal followers in order to transform them into Christian martyrs and to liberate their souls from the bondage of the sinful bodies, and send them to God in Heaven. Martyrdom was considered as the ultimate holy and self-sacrificial death performed in order to liberate their souls and enable them to ascend to God and the Blessed Virgin Mary in Heaven, where they hoped to attain eternal perfection, peace, happiness, divine ecstasy of the beatific vision, and eternal salvation.

Ultimately, the Marian devotees impatiently craved the apocalyptic ecstasy of the heavenly experience of the beatific union and fellowship with all the saints of God, especially the revered Ugandan Martyrs, who were persecuted and executed in June 1886, at the orders of King Mwanga. The Catholic Marian Movement members sought to become like the Ugandan Martyrs both in their courageous faith and martyrdom, as they died in the inferno, while courageously singing hymns of faith and hope for eternal salvation.[12]

Following the paradigm of the Ugandan Christian Martyrs, about 1,000 Marian Movement members sacramentally sacrificed their own lives to God the Father and the Blessed Virgin Mary. Many of them died in a church-fire, on Friday, March 17, 2000, during the penitential season of Lent. They died in a sacramental and self-sacrificial death, as voluntary living atonements to God for the forgiveness of sins of the world, and as a holy path to ascend to heaven to attain eternal life and salvation. Likewise, Mary's devotees, died in the inferno, while singing and chanting: *"Hail Mary. . . Mother of God. . . Pray for us now, at the hour of our death!"*[13] Some Christians, especially devout Catholics, who knew the Marian victims, believe and hope that these Marian devotees, who both faithfully and piously lived as God's true moral crusaders and Mary's saints, and finally, by their deep faith, died penitently, in an apocalyptic hope of God's supernatural immediate deliverance and salvation, did not live and sacrifice their lives to God in vain, when they died as God's servants and Mary's saints in 2000.[14]

NOTES

1. *A Timely Message from Heaven*, 145-163.
2. For instance, see *A Timely Message from Heaven*, 3, 20.
3. *Ibid,* 1-65.
4. The Book of Revelation is an apocalyptic book. It was written to encourage the Christians who were persecuted by the pagan Roman emperors. Christians dreaded the Roman emperors as "Beasts." Coded messages of "666" specifically referred to the Emperor Nero. Some Ugandan Christian fundamentalists rejected identity cards claiming that the numbers were "the mark the Beast" or the Devil. See *New Vision*, Wed.11, 2009.
5. *Ibid.*
6. These preachers of hell, being like Dante's *Inferno* as God's retaliation and torture of unrepentant sinners transform God into an evil and the unforgiving Judge of the world.
7. Retaliation is evil; and the perfect God cannot do what is evil. See Thomas Aquinas, *Summa Theologic, II; 3-10.*
8. See Paul Tillich, *The Dynamics of Faith; The Courage to Be; Systematic Theology (3 Vols.)*; Karl Rahner, *Theological Investigations* (25 Vols); *The Church and Sacraments; and The Foundations of Christian Faith.*
9. The Muslims have Ninety-Nine names for God. But the Muslims also state that God, as the Transcendent Holy Mystery, cannot be confined to these finite 99 names of God.
10. See Twesigye, *Religion & Ethics for a New Age*, 215-285.
11. *Ibid.* 255-270.
12. See: S. Kiwanuka, *A History of Buganda*, 32-112; *Mutesa;* R. Reid, *Political Power in Pre-Colonial Buganda,* 188-240; Jozef Muwanga, *On the Kabaka's Road for Uganda*, 17-50; Faupel, *African Holocaust*, 5-79.
13. According to the testimonies of some Kanungu residents, who came to aid the Marian fire victims. They heard the singing and the cries of pain when the fire burned the Marian Movement members. They found the church doors locked and windows nailed down.
14. It is self-evident that the Marian Movement Martyrs wanted to die in fire and become venerated like their venerated Uganda Martyrs, and Kanungu to become a holy pilgrimage site, like Namugongo.

GLOSSARY

Aba Nyabugoto: This was the local term for the members of the Marian Movement. The term originated from the Nyabugoto Holy Mountain, which the Marian Movement regarded as a sacred place of God's apocalyptic revelations and holy worship of the Blessed Virgin Mary. Some Catholics believe that the rock in the sacred cave on the Nyabugoto Mountain is the likeness and statue of the Blessed Virgin Mary. For these people, Nyabugoto Mountain is the equivalent of Mount Sinai.

Abagabe: The traditional kings of Ankole Kingdom. Their subjects believed that they were God's local embodiments. They represented God's power, wealth, prosperity, order, and well-being.

Abbot: The head of a monastic Order. He was regarded as the final administrative authority, within the respective monastery. The abbot operated under the jurisdiction of the Pope and bishops. Joseph Kibwetere and Keledonia Mwerinde were co-abbots of the Marian Movement. Mwerinde took-care of the Movement's internal affairs and Kibwetere took care of the Movement's external affairs. As a result, to the Marian Movement members, Mwerinde was perceived to be the supreme head of the Marian Movement, whereas to the outsiders, Kibwetere was perceived to be the supreme head.

Agape: Unconditional Love for the self, the neighbor and God. It was the central message and teaching of Jesus as the Christ of God. The Sermon the Mount (Matt. 5-7; 25) is the embodiment of this moral and religious teaching. Mwerinde and Kibwetere practiced these heavenly virtues.

Amagara: Life; good health, vitality, spirit, and "being alive." The term refers to the consciousness of being alive. The term is anthropocentric. It places emphasis on intelligent beings as the human beings.

Bafaransa: The French Catholic missionaries established the Roman Catholic Church in Uganda. Their followers were called *Bafransa* (the French). The local Anglicans as the followers of the British missionaries were called *"Bangereza"* or the English.

Bafumu: Traditional priests, doctors and healers. See the *"Waganga."* In Uganda, some of them are today persecuted for sacrificing virgins and children in order to attain wealth and atonement.

Bahima: The aristocratic ruling class of Ankole, Bunyoro, Toro and the Tutsi of Rwanda and Burundi. They were a privileged class. Most of them converted to the Anglican Church.

Bairu: The agriculturalist class of Ankole. They were oppressed by the Anglican ruling aristocratic class. As a result, they converted to the Roman Catholic Church in political and religious protest. Later, they advocated for the abolition of the oppressive monarchy.

Balokole: Members of the *East African Revival Movement*. They claim to "be born again." *The Balokole Movement* was founded in the early 1930s. They promoted the moral integrity of African Christianity in East until the late 1990s when materialism and secular values corrupted the Church.

Bangereza: The followers of the English Anglican missionaries were called *"Bangereza"* or the English. They became the collaborators of the British colonial agents in Uganda and were rewarded with political hegemony. This is the main root cause of political instability in Uganda.

Bantu: *"Bantu"* are a collection of different African ethnic groups that inhabit the area stretching from East Africa to South Africa. They speak a common language that is characterized by the root word *"ntu."* Alice Lakwena and Joseph Kony and their followers were non-*Bantu*.

Chama Cha Mapinduzi: The ruling party of Tanzania. Tanzania was a one party state under President Julius Nyerere. Nyerere forged diverse peoples of Tanzania into a viable political entity.

Chronos: Time linear measurements based on the successive passage of time. This kind of time has a beginning and an end. Both Mwerinde and Kibwetere made a serious error of confusing God's endless time (eternity) with the human finite and limited chronological time. Their apocalyptic prophecies for the imminent end of the world were based on linear time (*Chronos*), which does not have any application to God's time or *Kairos*.

Edini: Religions which were imported to Uganda, including Christianity and Islam. There is no word for the African Traditional Religion. It is taken for granted to be part of the African cultural and moral way of life, which was instituted by God at creation of the people as his special children. The local people erroneously believe that Roman Catholicism and Anglicanism are different religions.

Edini y'obuhabe: A false religion, heresy (*obuhabe*) or religion that misleads its followers. The Catholics used the term for the Anglicans and the Anglicans did the same for the Catholic Church. Bishop Kakubi accused of Mwerinde and Kibwetere of promoting heresy or false teachings in the Catholic Church and threatened to excommunicate them, if they did not recant of their errant moral and apocalyptic teachings,

Ekigombe: This is the local Runyankole-Rukiga term for association. The Marian Movement incorporated itself as an association for the promotion of moral education, development and religious moral reformation. The MTRCG also had objective to promote the devotion to the Blessed Virgin Mary and receive her apocalyptic revelations.

Ekigombe Ky'Okujumura Ebiragiro Ikumi Bya Ruhanga. This is the local term for *the Movement for the Restoration of the Ten Commandments of God.*

Ekyombeko Kya Bikira Maria: This was Keledonia Mwerinde's self-definition and title. By this title, Mwerinde described herself as the incarnation, or temple of the Blessed Virgin Mary.

Empabe: A heretic is a person who has become a religious deviant.

Enganzi: A Prime Minister of the Ankole Kingdom. He did not have to come from the royal family. It was an administrative position. The *Bairu* people should demand this position as a condition to revive the Ankole Kingdom.

Engisha: Fetishes. Sacred objects kept as protections against misfortune, and evil spirits.

Ensi egi: This physical cosmos or world as opposed to the heavenly one.
Entumwa: Apostle or the person sent to convey a message by God or a person with authority.

Entumwa za Bikira Maria na Yezu: The Apostles of the Blessed virgin Mary and Christ.

Glossary

Extra Ecclesiam Nulla Salus: Pre-Vatican dogma meaning that "Outside the Church, t . . no salvation." It was formulated by Bishop Cyprian of North Africa.

Gitum: Luo term for sacrifice to remove sin offenses.

Gityer: Luo term meaning the sacrificial object offered for atonement.

Imago Dei: "Image of God" in which the human being is created and exists.

Iraka: Voice or Word. Jesus as the Christ was the Voice of God or the *Logos.* The term also refers to the divine as well as the human voice or sound.

Ishayuriro Rya Maria: Mary's place of deliverance and salvation of sinners.

Itwe nitushomaEdini ya Ruhara: "We are the readers/followers of Ruhara's religion." They referred to Catholicism and Anglicanism as two different religions. Ruhara was a Catholic convert. This religious sectarianism was similar to Northern Ireland and led to religious wars between Catholics and Anglicans in Buganda in 1892. Anglicans were supported by the British and they won the war, established an Anglican hegemony and ruled the country since then. That is the main source of political instability in Uganda, especially in both Ankole and Kigezi.

Itwe nitushoma eky'Ediini y'Omugabe: "We are readers/followers of the King's religion." The king was an Anglican convert.

Jihad: Holy war. It means a struggle against evil within the self and outside the believer.

Jok: Luo term for Spirit. The Luo did not have the term for "God."

Kabaka: The King of the Kingdom of Buganda. Buganda is the largest kingdom in Uganda.

Kabaka Yekka: "King of Buganda Alone" was Baganda sectarian political party in Uganda during the 1960s. It did not promote Buganda's secession from Uganda.

Kairos: God's time for action or intervention in human time or history (*Chronos).*

Kareebi: Visionary, such as a prophet. A person who claims to foresee future events.

Kazooba: The Sun as God; *Amen-Ra.*

Kazooba Nyamuhanga: "Sun the Creator-God." This is similar to the Egyptian *Amen-Ra.*

Kihimba: The Deputy Prime Minister for Ankole Kingdom. The hold of this position can be from a non-royal family. He or she can be appointed or elected from the *Bahima* and *Bairu* groups.

Kuroga: To bewitch, poison, practice sorcery, or put a hex on an opponent.

Kubandwa: Worship the traditional God or gods in the traditional manner, including sacrifices as atonements to God or the ancestral spirits (*Emizimu*) and gods (*Emandwa*).

Kulokoka: To repent of sins; "to be born again." Those who are "born again" are called "*Balokole*." Their movement is also called "*The East African Revival Movement.*"

a diviner and to disclose divine, future or hidden mysteries of life.

at. The Marian Movement made it a mandatory way for the life of its f silence was designed to enforce it.

for "Messiah" or the "Deliverer." In 1985, Alice Auma declared that God had app~~ lessiah (*Lakwena*) for the oppressed *Acholi* people in Northern Uganda.

Lex Talionis: Moses Law of revenge by "equal retaliation." It perpetuates cycles of violence.

Maji: Water. There are several religio political liberation movements in Africa, which relied on sacred water as God's bullet-proofing for the believers and holy warriors, who fight in holy wars against God's enemies or their evil oppressors. Moses and the Red Sea miracle, is a classic example. Waters of Baptism and exorcisms are Christian examples.

Mat Oput: The Luo ritual ceremony for atonement and reconciliation of offenders.

Moya: Oil used for healing and other ritual ceremonies in Northern Uganda.

Muhima: Pastoralist and aristocratic member in Uganda.

Mukama: The title for the traditional divine King (*Omukama*) of the kingdoms of Bunyoro or Toro Kingdom. It is also the reference for "Lord," "Master" and God, in these kingdoms.

Mulokole: The "born again" member of the *Balokole Movement*.

Mwalimu: Swahili term for "Teacher" or "Rabbi." It was used as a title for President Julius Nyerere. He was accepted the Plato's African "Philosopher King." Tanzania is one of the most ethnically and religious diverse, and ye, very peaceful African countries. This is part of his legacies. He also helped oppressed people to liberate themselves from their political oppressors in South Africa and Uganda, during the President Idi Amin's "Reign of Terror," 1971-1979.

Mwiru: Member of a despised agricultural group in the Kingdom of Ankole. They resented their cattle-keeping aristocratic (*Bahima)* rulers. The *Bairu* revolted and demanded the abolition of the kingdom.

Ngai: *Masai* term for the Creator God. God is supposed to live on Kilimanjaro and Mount Kenya as God's holy Mountains, akin to the Mt. Sinai. Fire, smoke, snow and sky as well as red and black colors are the sacred symbols for God. As result, the *Masai* very beautifully decorate their items and impressively paint themselves accordingly.

Nyamuhanga: God the Creator of the cosmos. God is also variously known as "*Ruhanga*," "*Kazooba*" and "*Katonda*". The *Swahili* term of these names is "*Mungu*."

Obuhabe: Heresy; straying from the path of truth; teaching errant religious or harmful religious or moral doctrines and promoting harmful conduct as godliness or virtue. The Catholic Church excommunicates Catholics, who persist in teaching these errors.

Obusingye: Peace, shalom, and salaam as heavenly virtues and conditions of life in God's Kingdom on the Earth, "as it is in heaven" (Matt. 5-7).

Obusingye obu; The metaphor for a current peaceful era or simply, "this era" or "this mode of life." That was what was predicted to end, rather than "***Ensi egyi***" (this actual world). The Marian Movement leaders lived and taught material which was paradoxical. They built new permanent buildings and yet, preached an imminent end of the world, as we know it (***Ensi egyi***) and this era (***obunaku obu***). Some people believed that they referred to the physical end of the world. But the terms the Marina Movement leaders used literally refer to a change in era or time, and new transformed modes of life, rather than the end of the world.

Obwato bwa Ruhanga bw'okujunwa: God's Ark of Salvation. It is a reference to Noah's Ark. The Marian Movement proclaimed as God's new apocalyptic Noah's Ark of Salvation.

Okubonekyerwa: To receive God's revelation. It was mediated to the Marian Movement leaders by the Blessed Virgin Mary, instead of angels, as in the cases of Judaism and Islam.

Okuhunama (okusirika): To keep holy silence, especially in the context of religious retreat. It is the medium of contemplative prayer. The Marian Movement imposed it on all its members. Okujunwa: To be saved from evil; to be born again (***kulokoka***) and divine salvation.

Okuranga: Same as "***kuroga***;" to poison and harm people. The practitioners of witchcraft and sorcery are called "***Barogi.***" Anti-social women are sometimes accused of witchcraft.

Okushururirwa: To receive a divine revelation or disclosure of hidden mysteries. The recipient is a passive receive of the divine messages or revelations. Prophets and prophetesses are some of these examples.

Omugabe: The King of Ankole Kingdom. According to the creation myths of Ankole, the king was affirmed to be "God's Son" and temporal finite embodiment in the world.

Omunsi egyi; It refers to life within this temporal world. It does not refer to life in heaven.

Omwitsyo: Life; breath; spirit.

Opus Dei: Good deeds done to attain God's salvation; a Catholic movement that was founded to promote and perform good deeds as "*summum bonum*" (greatest good), as a holy path to God.

Orugisha: A magical object worn to wade off evil from the person wearing it. It is made and worn as a supernal armor that protects the believer from witchcraft, sorcery and misfortune.

Papal Nuncio: The Pope's ambassador in any country.

Parusia: The Christian apocalyptic doctrine that Jesus will come to take up the faithful believers and judge the world. It is part of Millenarianism.

Qur'an: Koran. The God's directly revealed infallible Holy Scriptures of Islam.

Ruhanga: *Bantu* word for God. It is the same as ***Nyamuhanga*** and ***Katonda***.

Rwot. *Luo* people's main tribal chief. They do not have kings.

Shango: A god of fire, lightning and thunder, in Nigeria. It is like Zeus with his thunderbolts.

Shari'a: Islamic religio-political codification of laws in the name of God.

Summum Bonum: The highest or greatest good that obedient or saintly human beings are able to do in God's name. It redeems the doer and the world.

Teyer: Luo term for sacrificial animal meant for atonement for sins and offenses.

Theotokos: "Mother of God." This is the traditional Catholic title for the Blessed Virgin Mary as the holy Mother of Jesus, the Christ. The African Marian devotees worshipped Mary as Goddess, the "Queen of Heaven," and "Mother of the Church" and main Mediator of God's unmerited supernatural redemptive grace, love, compassion, forgiveness and salvation in the world.

Theophany: The vision of the divine through humanity or another object, such as fire, the *Sun* and the "burning bush," which Moses saw.

Torah: Holy Scripture and Moral Law for Judaism; the "Five Books of Moses."

Tum: *Luo* word for sacrifice. *Gitum* refers to the sacrificial animal for atonement. Jesus was *gitum* according to this philosophy, and so were the members of *The Movement for the Restoration of the Ten Commandments,* who ritually martyred themselves and gave their lives as a atonement (*gitum)* and sacrifices to God

Waganga: *Swahili* term for traditional healers and priests. The *Waganga* are supposed to have access to the supernatural force or energy and can utilize it to do good or evil. They are supposed to possess the divine powers to heal clients or to do harm to their enemies. According to this African traditional world-view, Jesus' power to heal, make him one of the "*Waganga*."

*Waringa***:** Refers to an illusion, hallucination or delusion. It is an equivalent of *Maya* in oriental philosophies and religious traditions. But some people confuse it with reality even when it is false perception. Some skeptics claim that what Mwerinde and Kibwetere claimed to be Marian apparitions were actually false perceptions of reality and mental illusions. However these illusions and delusions were proclaimed to be God's new apocalyptic revelations through the Blessed Virgin Mary.

A SELECTED BIBLIOGRAPHY

Abbott, M. Walter and Gallagher, Joseph (Editors). *The Documents of Vatican II.* Piscataway: AP/New Century, 1966.

Abraham, W. E. *The Mind of Africa.* Chicago: University of Chicago Press, 1962. Aquinas, Thomas. *Providence and Predestination.* Indiana: Regnery, 1961.

———. *Summa Theologica: 4 vols.* Rome: Vatican Press, 1948.

———. *Summa contra Gentiles.* Rome: Vatican Press, 1934.

Arnold, S. and Nitecki, A. *Culture and Development in Africa.* Trenton: Africa WP, 1990.

Atterbury, A. P. *Islam in Africa.* New York and London: G. Putnam's Sons, 1899.

Baeta, Christian G. *Christianity in Tropical Africa.* London: Oxford UP, 1968.

Bamunoba, Y. K. "The Confrontation between Christianity and Ankole Traditional Religion since 1899." Occasional Research Paper No. 13, Department of Religious Studies, MUK, 1973.

———. "Diviners for the Abagabe," Uganda Journal 29: 1 (1965), 5-97.

Bamunoba, Y. K., "Emandwa Initiation in Ankole," *Uganda Journal* 29: 1 (1965), 13-25.

Banks, John G. *Healing Everywhere.* Richmond: St. Luke's Press, 1980.

Barnette, D. and Njama, Karari. *Mau Mau from Within.* London: MacGibben and Kee, 1966

Barr, James. *Fundamentalism.* Philadelphia: The Westminster Press, 1978.

Barrett, D. B. *African Initiatives in Religion.* Kenya, Nairobi: EAPH, 1971.

———. *Schism and Renewal in Africa: An Analysis.* Nairobi: Oxford University Press, 1968.

Barrett, W. *Irrational Man: A Study in Existential Philosophy.* New York: Doubleday, 1962.

Barth, Karl. *Church Dogmatics: A Selection.* New York: Harper & Row, 1961.

———. *Church Dogmatics.* Vol. 3. New York: Scribner's Sons, 1960.

———. *The Humanity of God.* Richmond, Va.: John Knox Press, 1960.

———. *Evangelical Theology: An Introduction.* New York: Holt, 1963.

Bascom, William. *Ifa Divination: Communion between Gods and Men in West Africa.* Bloomington: Indiana University Press, 1968.

Baxter, P. T. W. "The Kiga," *East African Chiefs.* New York: Praeger, 1959.

Beattie, John, and Middleton, eds. *The Banyoro.* New York: African Publishing, 1964.

———. ed. *Spirit Mediumship and Society in Africa.* New York: AP, 1969.

Beetham, T. A. *Christianity and the New Africa.* New York: Praeger, 1967.

Booth, Newell S. *African Religions: A Symposium.* New York: NOK Publishers, 1977.

Brother-Andrew. *Battle for Africa.* London: Marshall Morgan and Scott, 1977.

Brunner, Emil. *Man in Revolt.* Philadelphia: Westminster Press, 1948.

———. *Moral Man and Immoral Society*. New York: Scribner's Sons, 1960.

Bultmann, Rudolf K. *Jesus and the Word*. New York: Charles Scribner's Sons, 1934. .

———. *Kerygma and Myth*. New York: Harper & Row, 1961.

———. *Theology of the New Testament*. New York: Charles Scribner's Sons, 1955.

Buscaglia, Leo. *Love*. New York: Fawcett Crest, 1972.

Chadwick, O. *The Victorian Church: An Ecclesiastical History of the Church*. London: Oxford University Press, 1950.

Church, J. E. *Awake Uganda*. Kampala: Uganda Bookshop Press, 1954.

Cobb, John. *Christ in a Pluralistic Age*. Philadelphia: The Westminster Press, 1975.

———. *God and the World*. Philadelphia: Westminster Press, 1969.

———. *The Structure of Christian Existence*. Philadelphia: Westminster Press, 1967.

Cousins, Ewert H., ed. *Hope and the Future of Man*. Philadelphia: Fortress Press, 1972.

Desai, R. Ed. *Christianity in Africa as Seen by Africans*. Denver: Allan Swallow, 1962.

Dickson, Kwensi, *Biblical Revelation and African Beliefs*. London: Lutterworth Press, 1969.

Durkheim, Emile. *The Elementary Forms of the Religious Life*. New York: Free Press, 1965.

Edel, M. M. *The Chigga of Western Uganda*. London: Oxford University Press, 1957.

Evans-Pritchard, R. *Nuer Religion*. Oxford: Oxford University Press, 1956.

———. *Theories of Primitive Religion*. Oxford: Clarendon Press, 1965.

Fagg, W. B. *African Tribal Images*. Cleveland: Cleveland Museum of Art, 1968.

Fallers, Llyod A., ed. *The King's Men: Leadership and Status in Uganda on the Eve of Independence*. London: Oxford University Press, 1964.

Farley, E. *Ecclesial Man: A Social Phenomenology of Faith & Reality*. Phila: Fortress, 1975.

Feuerbach, L. *The Essence of Religion*. New York: Harper & Row, 1967.

Finney, G. *Revivals of Religion*. London: SCM Press, 1954.

Forde, Daryll, ed. *African World: Studies in the Cosmological Ideas and Social Values of African Peoples*. New York: Oxford University Press, 1968.

Fortes, M. and Dieterlen, G. eds. *African Systems of Thought*. New York: Oxford UP, 1965.

Fuller, R. H. *The Mission and Achievement of Christ*. London: SCM Press, 1959.

———. *Foundations of New Testament Christology*. New York: Scribner's Sons, 1965.

Gaba, Christian. *Scriptures of an African People: The Sacred Utterances of the Anlo*. New York: NOK Publishers, 1973.

Gilkey, L. *Catholicism Confronts Modernity: A Protestant View. New York*: Seabury, 1975.

Gonzales, Justo L. A History of Christian Thought (3 Vols.). Nashville: Abingdon, 1970.

Graham, B. *World Aflame*. New York: The Worlds Word, Ltd., 1966.

Green, M., ed. *The Truth of God Incarnate*. London: Hodder and Stoughton, 1977.

Guilleband, L. *A Grain of Mustard Seed*. London: C.M.S. Press, 1959.

Gutierrez, G. *A Theology of Liberation: History, Politics and Salvation*. New York: Orbis, 1973.

Hardy, Edward R. *Christology of the Later Fathers*. Phila: Westminster Press, 1954.

Harold, B. *Twice-Born Men: A Clinic of Regeneration*. New York: Revelle , 1909.

Harrelson, Walter. *The Ten Commandments and Human Rights*. Philadelphia: Fortress, 1973.

Hartshorne, C. *The Divine Relativity: A Social Conception of God*. New Haven: Yale UP, 1978.

Hastings, Adrian. *African Christianity*. New York: Seabury Press, 1976.

———. *Christian Marriage in Africa*. London: S.P.C.K., 1959.

———. *Church and Mission in Modern Africa*. London: Burns and Bates, 1967.

———. *The Faces of God*. London: Geoffrey and Chapman, 1975.

Hatch, Edwin. *The Influence of Greek Ideas on Christianity*. Gloucester, Mass, 1970.

Hayward, V. E. W., ed. *African Independent Church Movements*. London: Edinburgh P, 1963.

Hegel F. *Phenomenology of Spirit*. New York: Oxford University Press, 1977.

Heidegger, Martin. *Being and Time*. New York: Harper & Row, 1962.

Hewitt, G. *The Problems of Success: A History of the Church Missionary Society 1910-1942*. London: C.M.S. Press, 1960.

Hick, John. *Evil and the God of Love*. New York: Harper & Row, 1978.

Hillman, E. *Polygamy Reconsidered*. London: Orbis, 1975.

Hobley, Charles W. *Bantu Beliefs and Magic*. London: Franklin Cass, 1967.

Hodgson, P. C. *Jesus, Word and Presence: An Essay in Christology*. Phila: Fortress, 1971.

———. *New Birth of Freedom: A Theology of Bondage and Liberation*. Phila: Fortress, 1976.

Holger, H. & Twaddle, M. (eds). *Religion & Politics in East Africa*. Athens: Ohio UP, 1995.

Holmes, Urban T. *To Speak of God*. New York: Seabury Press, 1974.

———. *What is Anglicanism?* Wilton, Conn.: Morehouse-Barlow Co. Inc., 1982.

Horton, R. "African Traditional Thought and Western Science," *Africa* 37 (1967), 50-71, 155-187.

———. "Destiny and the Unconscious in West Africa," *Africa* 31 (1961), 110-116.

———. "Ritual Man in Africa," *Africa* 34 (1964), 85-105.

Idowu, E. Bolaji. *African Traditional Religion: A Definition*. Maryknoll: Orbis, 1973.

———. *Towards an Indigenous Church*. London: Oxford University Press, 1965.

Ignatius of Loyola, St. *The Spiritual Exercises of St. Ignatius*. Chicago: Loyola U P, 1951.

Ilogu, Edmund. *Christianity and Igbo Culture*. New York: NOK Publishers, 1973.

Jahn, Jahnheinz. *Muntu: An Outline of the New African Culture*. New York: Grove Press, 1961.

James, William. *The Varieties of Religious Experience: A Study in Human Nature.* Introduction by Reinhold Niebuhr. New York: Collier MacMillan, 1974.

Janzen, John and MacGaffey, Wyatt. *An Anthology of Kongo Religion.* Lawrence, Kansas: University of Kansas Press, 1974.

John of the Cross, St. *The Collected Works of St. John of the Cross.* Translated by Kieran Kavanaugh and Otilo R. Washington: Institute of Carmelite Studies, 1960.

Johnston, W. *The Inner Eye of Love: Mysticism and Religion.* New York: Harper, 1978.

Jones, R. B. *Rent Heavens.* London: S.C.M. Press, 1955.

Kagame, Alexis. *La Philosophie Bantu-Rwandaise de l'Etre.* Brussels: Academie Royale des Sciences Coloniales, 1956.

Kaggwa, Apolo. *The Kings of Buganda.* Translated with an introduction by S. Kiwanuka. East African Publishing House, 1971.

Kant, Immanuel. *Groundwork of the Metaphysic of Morals.* New York: Harper, 1956.

———. *Prolegomena to Any Future Metaphysics.* Indianapolis: Bobbs-Merrill, 1979.

Kanyankole, Kenneth. "A History of the Movement for the Restoration of the Ten Commandments of God," Dip.Th. Thesis, Uganda Christian University: Mukono, 2001.

Kasemann, E. *New Testament Questions for Today.* Philadelphia: Fortress Press, 1969.

Kaufman, W. *Systematic Theology: A Historical Perspective.* New York: Scribner's Sons, 1968.

Kenyatta, Jomo. *Facing Mount Kenya.* New York: Random House, 1962.

King, Noel Q. *Religions of Africa: A Pilgrimage into Traditional Religions.* New York: Harper & Row, 1970.

Kivengere, Festo. *When God Moves.* Accra: Asempa, 1970.

Kiwanuka, S. M. *A History of Buganda from Early Times to 1900.* Nairobi: Longmans, 1972.

———. *Mutesa.* Nairobi: East African Literature Bureau, 1968.

———. *Bunyoro-Kitara Empire: Myth or Reality?.* Kampala: MUK, 1971.

———. *A History of Buganda: From the Foundation of the Kingdom to 1900.* London: Longman Group Ltd., 1971.

Kung, Hans. *The Church.* New York: Image Books, Doubleday & Company, Inc, 1976.

———. *On Being a Christian.* Translated by E. Quinn. New York: Pocket Books, 1966.

Lanternari, Vittorio. *The Religions of the Oppressed: A Study of Modern Messianic Cults.* New York: Knopf, 1963.

Latourette, S. K. *The Expansion of Christianity.* Vols. 6 and 7. London: Zondervan, 1970.

———. *A History of Christianity.* London: Eyre and Scottiwoode, 1954.

Leakey, Louis S. B. *Mau Mau and the Kikuyu.* New York: John Day and Co., 1952.

Leaver, Robin A. *Luther on Justification.* St. Louis: Concordia Publishing, 1975.

Levy-Bruhl, Lucien. *Primitive Mentality*. Boston: Beacon Press, 1923.

Lewis, I. M., ed. *Islam in Tropical Africa*. London: Oxford University Press, 1966.

Lienhardt, G. *Divinity and Experience; the Religion of the Dinka*. Oxford: Oxford UP, 1961.

Lonergan, Bernad. *Method in Theology*. Darton: Longman and Todd, 1972.

Low, A.D. *Buganda in Modern History*. London: World University Press, 1970.

Maari, E. "The Balokole Movement in Nyabushozi County of Ankole," in Vol. 22, *Occasional Research Papers*, Department of Religious Studies, Makerere, August, 1974.

Macquarrie, John. *Principles of Christian Theology*. New York: Charles Scribner's Sons, 1977.

———. *Twentieth Century Religious Thought*. London: SCM Press, 1976.

———. Macquet, J. *Africanity: The Cultural Unity of Black Africa*. London: Oxford, 1972.

Mair, Lucy P. *An African People in the Twentieth Century*. New York: Russell and Russell, 1965.

———. *Witchcraft*. London: World University Press, 1969.

Martin, Marie-Louise. *Kibangu*. London: Blackwell, 1975.

Marty, I. *African Theology: Inculturation and Liberation*. Maryknoll: Orbis, 1993.

Matthews, R. *English Messiahs*. London: Methuen, 1936.

Mbiti, John. S. *African Religions and Philosophy*. London: Heinemann, 1969.

———. *Akamba Stories*. Oxford: Clarendon Press,1966.

———. *Concepts of God in Africa*. New York: Praeger, 1970.

———. *New Testament Eschatology in African Background*. London: Oxford, 1971.

———. *The Prayers of African Religion*. New York: Maryknoll, Orbis Books, 1976.

———. *Introduction to African Religion*. Nairobi: EAP, Second Revised Edition, 1991.

McGavran, A. D. *Understanding Church Growth*. Grand Rapids, Michigan: Eerdams, 1970.

McVeigh, Malcolm J. *God in Africa: Concepts of God in African Traditional Religion and Christianity*. Cape Cod, Mass.: Claude Stark, 1974.

Melland, Frank H. *In Witch-Bound Africa*. London: Seeley, 1967.

Mendelson, Jack. *God, Allah, and Juju: Religion in Africa Today*. NewYork: Nelson, 1962.

Merriam, Alan P. *An African World*. Bloomington: Indiana University Press, 1974.

Metz, J. *Theology of the World*. New York: Herder and Herder, 1969.

Middleton, J. and Winter, E. H., eds. *Gods and Rituals*. Garden City: Natural History P, 1967.

———. *Magic, Witchcraft and Curing*. Garden City: The Natural History Press, 1967.

———. *Myth and Cosmos*. Garden City, N.Y.: The Natural History Press, 1969.

———. *Witchcraft and Sorcery in East Africa*. London: Rowledge and K. Paul, 1963.

Moltmann, J. *Man: Christian Anthropology in the Conflicts of The Present*. Phila: Fortress, 1979.

Montagu, Ashley, ed. *Culture and Human Development.* Englewood Cliffs: Prentice-Hall, 1974.

MRTCG. *A Timely Message from Heaven: The End of the Present Times* (The Marian Movement's Handbook). Kampala: The Marian Movement, 1998.).

Mutebi, B. Wilson. *Towards an Indigenous Understanding and Practice of Baptism Amongst the Baganda, Uganda.* Kampala: Wavah Books, 2002.

Neill, S. C. *Christian Missions.* London: Pelican, 1966.

———. *Colonialism and Christian Missions.* London: Lutterworth Press, 1966.

———. *Twentieth Century Christianity.* London: Collins, 1962.

Neill, S. *The Christian Society: Theology and Philosophy.* London: Lutterworth, 1972.

Neuner, J. and R. Heinrich. *The Teaching of the Catholic Church as Contained in Her Documents.* Edited by Karl Rahner. New York: Alba House, 1965.

Newlands, George M. *The Theology of the Love of God.* Atlanta: John Knox, 1980. *New Vision* articles (March 18, 2000 -March 15, 2009).

Ngologoza, Paul. *Kigezi and its People.* Kampala: Fountain Publishers edition, 1998.

Niebuhr, R. H. *Christ and Culture.* New York: Harper & Row, 1951.

———. *The Purpose of the Church and Its Ministry.* New York: Harper & Row, 1956.

———. *The Social Sources of Denominationalism.* Cleveland: Meridian, 1965.

———. *The Nature and Destiny of Man.* 2 vols. New York: Charles Scribner's Sons, 1964.

Nkuruziza, D. R. K. (*et al*). *Kanungu Cult Saga: Suicide, Murder or Salvation?* Kampala: Makerere University, 2000.

Norris, Richard, ed. *The Christological Controversy.* Philadelphia: Fortress, 1980.

Northcott, Cecil. *Christianity in Africa.* London: S.C.M. Press, 1963.

O'Grady, John F. *Christian Anthropology: A Meaning for Human Life.* New York: Paulist, 1976.

Oliver, Roland. *The Missionary Factor in East Africa.* London: Longman, 1952.

Olupona, J. K. *African Traditional Religions in Contemporary Society.* New York: Paragon, 1991.

Osthuizen, G. C. *Post Christianity in Africa: A Theological and Anthropological Study.* Grand Rapids: William E. Eerdmans,1992.

P'Bitek, Okot. *African Religions in Western Scholarship.* Kampala: EALB, 1970.

———. *Religion of Central Luo.* Nairobi: EALB, 1975.

———. *The Song of Lawino.* Nairobi: EALB, 1960.

Pannenberg, W. et al. *Spirit, Faith and Church.* Philadelphia: Westminster Press, 1970.

Parrinder, Edward Geoffrey. *African Mythology.* London: Paul Hamly, 1967.

———. *African Traditional Religion.* Westport, Conn.: Greenwood Press, 1970.

———. *Religion in an African City.* London: Oxford University Press, 1953.

————. *West African Religion*. London: Epworth Press, 1961.

————. *Witchcraft: European and African*. New York: Barnes and Noble, 1963.

Patricia, St. John. *The Breath of Life*. London: Norfolk Press, 1971.

Pelikan, Jaroslav. *The Christian Tradition: A History of the Development of Doctrine, Vol. 1: The Emergence of the Catholic Tradition (100-600)*. Chicago: The University of Chicago, 1971.

Pratt, John. *A Reader in African Theology*. London: SPCK, 1987.

Rahner, Karl. *The Church and Sacraments*. London: Burns and Oates, 1978.

————. *Christianity at the Crossroads*. New York: Seabury, 1975.

————. *Grace in Freedom*. New Yorker: Herder and Herder, 1969.

————. *Foundations of Christian Faith*, New York: Herder and Herder, 1978.

————. *Theological Investigations*, 1-25. London: Longman, 1961-1985.

Ranger, T. and Kimambo, I. N., eds. *Christian Independence in Tanzania*. Dar Salaam: Historical Association of Tanzania, 1970.

————. *The Historical Study of African Religion*. Berkeley: University of California Press, 1972.

Ranger, T., and Weller, J. *The African Churches of Tanzania*. Dar Salaam: HA, Tanzania, 1969.

————. *Themes in the Christian History of Central Africa*. London: Heinemann, 1975.

Ray, Benjamin C. *African Religions*. Englewood Cliffs: Prentice Hall, 1976.

Richardson, C. C., ed. *Early Christian Fathers*. New York: MacMillan Publishing Co., 1970.

Robertson, E. H. *Man's Estimate of Man*. Richmond, Virginia: John Knox Press, 1958.

Robins, C. A. "'Tukutendereza': A Study of Social Change and Sectarian Withdrawal in the 'Balokole' Revival of Uganda." Ph.D. Dissertation, Columbia University, 1975.

Rogers, Carl. *On Becoming a Person*. Boston: Houghton Mifflin Co., 1961. Roscoe, J. *The Baganda*. London: Frank Cass, 1965.

————. *The Bagesu and Other Tribes*. Cambridge: Cambridge University Press, 1924.

————. *The Bakitara or Banyoro*. Cambridge: Cambridge University Press, 1923.

————. *The Banyankole*. Cambridge: Cambridge University Press, 1925.

————. *The Northern Bantu*. Cambridge: Cambridge University Press, 1915.

Russell, Bertrand. *Has Man a Future?* Baltimore: Penguin Books, 1961.

Russell, J. K. *Men Without God*. London: The Highway Press, 1966.

Sabatier, A. *The Religions of Authority and the Religions of the Spirit*. New York: Williams, 1904.

Sangree, Walter H. *Age, Prayer and Politics in Tikiri, Kenya*. New York: Oxford, 1966.

Sawyer, Harry. *God: Ancestor or Creator*. London: Longman, 1970.

Schaff, Philip. *History of the Christian Church*. Vol.1. Grand Rapids: Eerdmans, 1980.

Shepherd, W. C. *Man's Condition: God and the World Process*. New York: Herder, 1969.

Shorter, Aylward. *African Christian Theology*. London: Geoffrey and Chapman, 1975.

———. *African Culture and the Christian Church*. London: Geoffrey and Chapman, 1973.

———. *Prayer in the Religious Traditions of Africa*. London: Oxford University Press, 1975.

Sithole, N. *Obed Mutezo, the Mudzimi Christian Nationalist*. London: Oxford U Press, 1970.

Smith, Edwin, ed. *African Ideas of God, A Symposium*. London: Edinburgh House Press, 1961.

Smith, Huston. *The Religions of Man*. New York: Harper & Row, 1965.

Snow, Robert L. *Deadly Cults: The Crimes of True Believers*. Westport: Praeger, 2003.

Stock, E. *A History of the Church Missionary Society*. London: C.M.S. Press, 1899.

Stott, J. *Men Made New*. London: Inter Varsity Press, 1966.

Sundkler, Bengt. *Bantu Prophets in South Africa*. London: Lutterworth Press, 1948.

———. *The Christian Ministry in Africa*. London: S.C.M. Press, 1960.

———. *Zulu Zion*. London: Oxford University Press, 1976.

Tanner, Ralph E. S. *Transition in African Beliefs*. Maryknoll, N.Y.: Maryknoll P, 1967.

Taylor, J. V. *Christianity and Politics in Africa*. London: Harmondsworth, 1957.

———. *The Christians of the Copperbelt*. London: S.C.M. Press, 1963.

———. *The Church Growth in Buganda*. London: C.M.S. Press, 1958.

———. *The Cross of Christ*. London: MacMillan and Co., Ltd., 1956.

———. *The Primal Vision*. London: S.C.M. Press, 1963.

Teilhard de Chardin, Pierre. *The Phenomenon of Man*. New York: Harper & Row, 1975.

———. *The Prayer of the Universe*. New York: Harper & Row, 1973.

Tempels, P. *Bantu Philosophy*. Paris: Presence Africaine, 1959.

Temple, William. *Nature, Man and God*. London: MacMillan, 1934.

Temu, A. J. *British Protestant Missions*. London: Longman Group Limited, 1972.

TeSelle, Eugene. *Christ in Context: Divine Purpose and Human Possibility*. Phila: Fortress, 1975.

Tillich, Paul. *The Courage to Be*. New Haven: Yale University Press, 1969.

———. *Dynamics of Faith*. New York: Harper & Row, 1957.

———. *The New Being*. New York: The Scribner's Sons, 1955.

———. *Systematic Theology*: 3 Vols. Chicago: Chicago University Press, 1960.

Tracy, D. *Blessed Race for Order: The New Pluralism in Theology*. New York: Seabury, 1978.

Tucker, A. R. *My Eighteen Years in East Africa*. London: Edward Arnold, 1908.

Tuma, T. and Mutibwa, P. *A Century of Christianity in Uganda*. Nairobi: Uzima Press, 1978.

Twesigye, Emmanuel K. *Religion & Ethics for A New Age*. Lanham: AUP, 2001.

Twesigye, Emmanuel K. *African Religion, Philosophy and Christianity in Logos Christ.* New York: Peter Lang, 1996.

———. "AIDS and the Movement for the Restoration of the Ten Commandments of God," *The American Academy of Religion* Annual Meeting's Papers, November, 2001

———. "The Marian Movement for the Restoration of the Ten Commandments: The Challenge of HIV/AIDS to Christian Theology." *Scriptura: International Journal for Bible, Religion and Theology,* 89: 2005:2.

———. "The Ethics of HIV/AIDS the Movement for the Restoration of the Ten Commandments," *The American Academy of Religion* Annual Papers, November, 2004.

———. "Death Among the Bakiga of Western Uganda," *Occasional Research Paper.* Kampala: MUK, 1971.

———. *African Religion, Philosophy and Christianity.* New York: Peter Lang, 1987.

———. *The Global Human Problem.* New York: Peter Lang Press, 1988.

———. "HIV/AIDS Pandemic, Religion & Politics in Africa." A paper presented at Ohio Wesleyan University, March 5, 2005.

———. *The Global Human Problem: Ignorance, Injustice and Violence.* New York: Lang, 1988.

———. ed. *In Quest for Knowledge and Truth: Fisk University Faculty Lecture Series,* Vols. 1-2. Nashville: Fisk University Press, 1989.

———. *God, Race, Myth and Power.* New York: Peter Lang, 1991.

———. "Anonymous Christianity and Human Existence in African Perspective: A Study Based on Karl Rahner's Philosophical Theology." Ph.D. Dissertation, Vanderbilt U, 1983.

———. "Christians and Social Change," *The Franciscan,* November, 1970.

———. "The Concept of Atonement among the 'Balokole' of Uganda." S.T.M. thesis, University of the South, 1979.

———. "The Context for Theology in the Third World." Paper presented to the International Clericus Conference, New York, 16 June 1981.

———. "Death among the Bakiga of Western Uganda." *Occasional Research Papers.* Department of Religious Studies and Philosophy, Makerere University, 1971.

———. "The Evangelical Revival Movement in England and Church Planting in Uganda." M.A. Project, Wheaton Graduate School, 1978.

———. "The Role of Christians in Politics." *Occasional Research Papers,* Department of Religious Studies and Philosophy, Makerere University, 1970.

———. "African Religion as the Foundation for Societal and Religious Ethics in Africa." Paper presented to the *American Academy of Religion* in Washington, DC, November, 20, 1993.

Uganda Human Rights Commission. *Restoration of the Ten Commandments of God. A Periodical Report.* Kampala: Government of Uganda Publications, 2002..

Uganda Human Rights Commission. *The Kanungu Massacre: The Movement for the Uganda Monitor* news articles (March 18, 2000-March 15, 2009). *Uganda New Vision* news articles (March 18, 2000-March 15, 2009).

Vidler, A. R. *The Church in an Age of Revolution.* London: Penguin, 1961.

Warren, A. M. *Revival: An Inquiry.* London: C.M.S. Press, 1954.

————. *Social History and Christian Mission.* London: S.C.M. Press, 1967.

Weber, M. *The Sociology of Religion.* Boston: Beacon Press, 1964.

Webster, J. B. *West Africa Since 1800.* Ibadan: Longmans, 1968.

Weger, Karl-Heinz. *Karl Rahner: An Introduction to His Theology.* New York: Seabury, 1980.

Welbourn, F. B. *East African Christianity.* Nairobi: Oxford Press, 1967.

————. *East African Rebels: A Study of Some Independent Churches.* London: S.C.M, 1961.

————. *Religion and Politics in Uganda, 1952-1962.* Nairobi: Oxford Press, 1965.

Welbourn, F. B. and Ogot, B. A. *A Place to Feel at Home.* London: Oxford , 1965.

Werner, A. *Myths and Legends of Bantu.* London: Oxford University Press, 1933.

Whitehead, Alfred North. *Process and Reality.* New York: MacMillan, 1978.

————. *Religion in the Making.* New York: MacMillan, 1926.

Willis, J. J. *An African Church in Building.* London: C.M.S. Press, 1925.

Willoughby, William Charles. *The Soul of the Bantu.* Garden City: Doubleday, 1928.

Wilson, Bryan R., ed. *Magic and the Millennium: A Sociological Study of Religious Movements of Protest among Tribal and World Peoples.* New York: Humanities Press, 1975.

————. *Patterns of Sectarianism: Organization and Ideology in Social and Religious Movements.* London: Heinemann, 1967.

————. *Religious Sects.* London: Weidenfield and Nicholson, 1970.

Wilson, C. J. *Uganda in the Days of Bishop Tucker.* London: MacMillan & Co., Ltd., 1955.

Wilson, Monica. *Communal Rites of the Nyakyusa.* London: Oxford University Press, 1949.

————. *Religion and the Transformation of Society.* Cambridge: The University Press, 1971.

Wiredu, Kwasi. *Philosophy and African Culture.* London/New York: Cambridge, 1980.

INDEX

Bible & Theology in Africa

The twentieth century made sub-Saharan Africa a Christian continent. This formidable church growth is reflected in a wide range of attempts at contextualizing Christian theology and biblical interpretation in Africa. At a grassroots level ordinary Christians express their faith and read the bible in ways reflecting their daily situation; at an academic level, theologians and biblical scholars relate the historical traditions and sources of Christianity to the socio- and religio-cultural context of Africa. In response to this, the Bible and Theology in Africa series aims at making African theology and biblical interpretation its subject as well as object, as the concerns of African theologians and biblical interpreters will be voiced and critically analyzed. Both Africans and Western authors are encouraged to consider this series.

Inquiries and manuscripts should be directed to:

> Professor Knut Holter
> MHS School of Mission and Theology
> Misjonsmarka 12
> N-4024 Stavanger, Norway
> knut.holter@mhs.no

To order other books in this series, please contact our Customer Service Department:

> (800) 770-LANG (within the U.S.)
> (212) 647-7706 (outside the U.S.)
> (212) 647-7707 FAX

Or browse online by series:

> www.peterlang.com